SELBORNE CHURCH, FROM THE NORTH.

THE

NATURAL HISTORY

OF

SELBORNE,

WITH

OBSERVATIONS ON VARIOUS PARTS OF NATURE,

AND

THE NATURALIST'S CALENDAR.

BY THE LATE

REV. GILBERT WHITE, A.M.

FELLOW OF ORIEL COLLEGE, OXFORD.

WITH NOTES,

BY CAPTAIN THOMAS BROWN, F.L.S. &c.

A NEW EDITION.

LONDON:

PUBLISHED BY ALLAN BELL & CO. AND
SIMPKIN & MARSHALL; FRASER & CO. EDINBURGH;
AND W. CURRY, JUN. & CO. DUBLIN.

1834.

PREFACE.

GILBERT WHITE was the eldest son of John White, of Selborne, Esq. and of Anna, the daughter of the Rev. Thomas Holt, rector of Streatham in Surrey. He was born at Selborne, on July 18, 1720, and received his school education at Basingstoke, under the Rev. Thomas Warton, vicar of that place, and father of those two distinguished literary characters, Dr Joseph Warton, master of Winchester school, and Mr Thomas Warton, poetry professor at Oxford. He was admitted at Oriel College, Oxford, in December, 1739, and took his degree of Bachelor of Arts in June, 1743. In March, 1744, he was elected Fellow of his College. He became Master of Arts in October, 1746, and was admitted one of the senior Proctors of the University in April, 1752. Being of an unambitious temper, and strongly attached to the charms of rural scenery, he early fixed his residence in his native village, where he spent the greater part of his life in literary occupations, and especially in the study of Nature. This he followed with patient assiduity, and a mind ever open to the lessons of piety and benevolence, which such a study is so well calculated to afford. Though several occasions offered of settling upon a college living, he could never persuade himself to quit the beloved spot, which was indeed a peculiarly happy situation for an observer. Thus his days passed tranquil and serene, with scarcely any other vicissitudes than those of the seasons, till they closed at a mature age, on June 26, 1793.

The above short sketch was prefixed to the edition of Mr White's work published after his death, by his friend Dr Aiken of Warrington. It is abundantly meagre, but except the many pleasing allusions to himself throughout his letters, it contains all that the public have ever known of our author's personal history. An enthusiastic admirer of his, who lately visited the village of Selborne, thus sums up his account : — " Of Gilbert White himself, I could collect few personal reminiscences ; and all that an old dame, who had nursed several of the family, could tell me of the philosophical old bachelor was, that ' he was a still, quiet body,' and that ' there wasn't a bit of harm in him, I'll assure ye, sir : there was'nt indeed.' "

Mr White is principally known to the world by his *Natural History of Selborne,* which, although purporting to be but the description of the natural objects of a single parish, is, nevertheless, a book of general interest, embracing, in its details, varied and extensive inquiries into the phenomena of Nature. It originated in a series of letters, written to Thomas Pennant, Esq. and the Honourable Daines Barrington,—gentlemen of high literary and scientific acquirements in their day,— the former, the well-known author of the *British Zoology, History of Quadrupeds, Tour in Scotland,* and many other esteemed works.

The *Natural History of Selborne* was first published in quarto, in 1789, along with what Mr White considered as essential in parochial history, namely, its Antiquities. This last, however, although of sufficient local interest, can offer few attractions to the general reader.

The originality and instructive details of his chief work soon commanded general attention, and attracted even continental notice ; and, we believe, it was translated into more than one foreign language. We know that a translation of it was printed in Germany, so early as 1792, and published at Berlin in that year.

This work is written in an unconnected form, without any attempt at scientific arrangement, with which, however, Mr White shews himself well acquainted ; and the minute exactness of his facts — the good taste displayed in their selection — and the elegance and liveliness with which they are described, — render this one of the most amusing books of the kind ever published, and it has gained for the author a high and just reputation.

Mr White's long series of observations were skilfully and attentively repeated, and have tended greatly to enlarge and correct our knowledge of those departments of natural history of which he has treated. He may be esteemed a worthy successor to Ray and Derham; while his remarks, being almost exclusively original, are, in some measure, even better entitled to our attention than the writings of these celebrated naturalists.

It has been thought proper to insert in the present edition the author's Poems, partly on account of their intrinsic merit, which is not inconsiderable, but principally because they are upon local subjects, and therefore naturally connected with the present work. They are also valuable and appropriate, as illustrating the author's strong attachment to the study of Nature.

EDINBURGH, *January* 25, 1833.

POEMS.

THE INVITATION TO SELBORNE.

See, Selborne spreads her boldest beauties round
The varied valley, and the mountain ground,
Wildly majestic! What is all the pride
Of flats, with loads of ornament supplied ?—
Unpleasing, tasteless, impotent expense,
Compared with Nature's rude magnificence.
 Arise, my stranger, to these wild scenes haste ;
The unfinish'd farm awaits your forming taste :
Plan the pavilion, airy, light, and true ;
Through the high arch call in the length'ning view ;
Expand the forest sloping up the hill ;
Swell to a lake the scant, penurious rill ;
Extend the vista ; raise the castle mound
In antique taste, with turrets ivy-crown'd ;
O'er the gay lawn the flow'ry shrub dispread,
Or with the blending garden mix the mead ;
Bid China's pale, fantastic fence delight ;
Or with the mimic statue trap the sight.
 Oft on some evening, sunny, soft, and still,
The Muse shall lead thee to the beech-grown hill,
To spend in tea the cool, refreshing hour,
Where nods in air the pensile, nest-like bower : *
Or where the hermit hangs the straw-clad cell, †
Emerging gently from the leafy dell,
By Fancy plann'd ; as once th' inventive maid
Met the hoar sage amid the secret shade :

* A kind of arbour on the side of a hill.
 † A grotesque building, contrived by a young gentleman, who
used on occasion to appear in the character of a hermit.

Romantic spot! from whence in prospect lies
Whate'er of landscape charms our feasting eyes,—
The pointed spire, the hall, the pasture plain,
The russet fallow, or the golden grain,
The breezy lake that sheds a gleaming light,
Till all the fading picture fail the sight.
   Each to his task; all different ways retire:
Cull the dry stick; call forth the seeds of fire;
Deep fix the kettle's props, a forky row,
Or give with fanning hat the breeze to blow.
   Whence is this taste, the furnish'd hall forgot,
To feast in gardens, or th' unhandy grot?
Or novelty with some new charms surprises,
Or from our very shifts some joy arises.
Hark, while below the village bells ring round,
Echo, sweet nymph, returns the soften'd sound;
But if gusts rise, the rushing forests roar,
Like the tide tumbling on the pebbly shore.
   Adown the vale, in lone, sequester'd nook,
Where skirting woods imbrown the dimpling brook,
The ruin'd convent lies: here wont to dwell
The lazy canon midst his cloister'd cell,*
While Papal darkness brooded o'er the land,
Ere Reformation made her glorious stand:
Still oft at eve belated shepherd swains
See the cowl'd spectre skim the folded plains.
   To the high Temple† would my stranger go
The mountain-brow commands the woods below:
In Jewry first this order found a name,
When madding Croisades set the world in flame;
When western climes, urged on by pope and priest,
Pour'd forth their millions o'er the deluged East:
Luxurious knights, ill-suited to defy
To mortal fight Turcéstan chivalry.
   Nor be the parsonage by the Muse forgot—
The partial bard admires his native spot;
Smit with its beauties, loved, as yet a child,
Unconscious why, its capes, grotesque and wild.

  * The ruins of a Priory, founded by Peter de Rupibus, Bishop of Winchester.
  † The remains of a Preceptory of the Knights Templars; at least it was a farm dependent upon some preceptory of that order. I find it was a preceptory, called the *Preceptory of Suddington;* now called Southington.

High on a mound th' exalted gardens stand,
Beneath, deep valleys, scoop'd by Nature's hand.
A Cobham here, exulting in his art,
Might blend the general's with the gardener's part ;
Might fortify with all the martial trade
Of rampart, bastion, fosse, and palisade ;
Might plant the mortar with wide threat'ning bore,
Or bid the mimic cannon seem to roar.

   Now climb the steep, drop now your eye below
Where round the blooming village orchards grow ;
There, like a picture, lies my lowly seat,
A rural, shelter'd, unobserved retreat.

   Me far above the rest Selbornian scenes,
The pendent forests, and the mountain greens,
Strike with delight : there spreads the distant view,
That gradual fades till sunk in misty blue :
Here Nature hangs her slopy woods to sight,
Rills purl between and dart a quivering light.

SELBORNE HANGER.

A WINTER PIECE. — TO THE MISS B ✳✳✳✳✳ S.

THE bard, who sang so late in blithest strain
Selbornian prospects, and the rural reign,
Now suits his plaintive pipe to sadden'd tone,
While the blank swains the changeful year bemoan.

   How fallen the glories of these fading scenes!
The dusky beach resigns his vernal greens ;
The yellow maple mourns in sickly hue,
And russet woodlands crowd the dark'ning view.

   Dim, clust'ring fogs involve the country round,
The valley and the blended mountain ground
Sink in confusion ; but with tempest-wing
Should Boreas from his northern barrier spring,
The rushing woods with deaf'ning clamour roar,
Like the sea tumbling on the pebbly shore.
When spouting rains descend in torrent tides,
See the torn zigzag weep its channel'd sides :
Winter exerts its rage ; heavy and slow,
From the keen east rolls on the treasured snow ;
Sunk with its weight the bending boughs are seen,
And one bright deluge whelms the works of men.

Amidst this savage landscape, bleak and bare,
Hangs the chill hermitage in middle air ;
Its haunts forsaken, and its feasts forgot,
A leaf-strown, lonely, desolated cot !
    Is this the scene that late with rapture rang,
Where Delphy danced, and gentle Anna sang ?
With fairy step where Harriet tripp'd so late,
And, on her stump reclined, the musing Kitty sate ?
    Return, dear nymphs ; prevent the purple spring,
Ere the soft nightingale essays to sing ;
Ere the first swallow sweeps the fresh'ning plain,
Ere love-sick turtles breathe their amorous pain ;
Let festive glee th' enliven'd village raise,
Pan's blameless reign, and patriarchal days ;
With pastoral dance the smitten swain surprise,
And bring all Arcady before our eyes.
    Return, blithe maidens ; with you bring along
Free, native humour ; all the charms of song ;
The feeling heart, and unaffected ease ;
Each nameless grace, and ev'ry power to please.

    November 1, 1763.

ON THE RAINBOW.

Look upon the Rainbow, and praise him that made it : very beautiful is it in the brightness thereof.—Eccles. xliii. 11.

On morning or on evening cloud impress'd,
Bent in vast curve, the watery meteor shines
Delightfully, to th' level'd sun opposed :
Lovely refraction ! while the vivid brede
In listed colours glows, th' unconscious swain,
With vacant eye, gazes on the divine
Phenomenon, gleaming o'er the illumined fields,
Or runs to catch the treasures which it sheds.
    Not so the sage : inspired with pious awe,
He hails the federal arch ;* and, looking up,
Adores that God, whose fingers form'd this bow
Magnificent, compassing heaven about
With a resplendent verge : " Thou mad'st the cloud
Maker omnipotent, and thou the bow ;
And by that covenant graciously hast sworn

        * Genesis, ix. 12—17.

Never to drown the world again : * henceforth,
Till time shall be no more, in ceaseless round,
Season shall follow season : day to night,
Summer to winter, harvest to seed-time,
Heat shall to cold in regular array
Succeed."— Heav'n-taught, so sang the Hebrew bard.†

A HARVEST SCENE.

WAKED by the gentle gleamings of the morn
Soon clad, the reaper, provident of want,
Hies cheerful-hearted to the ripen'd field ;
Nor hastes alone : attendant by his side
His faithful wife, sole partner of his cares,
Bears on her breast the sleeping babe ; behind,
With steps unequal, trips her infant train :
Thrice happy pair, in love and labour join'd !
   All day they ply their task ; with mutual chat,
Beguiling each the sultry, tedious hours.
Around them falls in rows the sever'd corn,
Or the shocks rise in regular array:
   But when high noon invites to short repast,
Beneath the shade of sheltering thorn they sit,
Divide the simple meal, and drain the cask :
The swinging cradle lulls the whimpering babe
Meantime ; while growling round, if at the tread
Of hasty passenger alarm'd, as of their store
Protective, stalks the cur with bristling back,
To guard the scanty scrip and russet frock.

ON THE DARK, STILL, DRY, WARM WEATHER,

Occasionally happening in the Winter Months.

TH' imprison'd winds slumber within their caves,
Fast bound : the fickle vane, emblem of change,
Wavers no more, long settling to a point.
   All Nature nodding seems composed : thick steams,
From land, from flood up-drawn, dimming the day,
" Like a dark ceiling stand :" slow through the air

Gen. viii. 22.   † Moses.

Gossamer floats, or stretch'd from blade to blade,
The wavy network whitens all the field.
Push'd by the weightier atmosphere, up springs
The ponderous mercury, from scale to scale
Mounting, amidst the Torricellian tube. *
While high in air, and poised upon his wings,
Unseen, the soft, enamour'd wood-lark runs
Through all his maze of melody ; the brake,
Loud with the blackbird's bolder note, resounds.
Sooth'd by the genial warmth, the cawing rook
Anticipates the spring, selects her mate,
Haunts her tall nest-trees, and with sedulous care
Repairs her wicker eyrie, tempest-torn.
The ploughman inly smiles to see upturn
His mellow glebe, best pledge of future crop :
With glee the gardener eyes his smoking beds :
E'en pining sickness feels a short relief.
The happy schoolboy brings transported forth
His long-forgotten scourge, and giddy gig :
O'er the white paths he whirls the rolling hoop,
Or triumphs in the dusty fields of taw.
Not so the museful sage : abroad he walks
Contemplative, if haply he may find
What cause controls the tempest's rage, or whence,
Amidst the savage season, Winter smiles.
For days, for weeks, prevails the placid calm.
At length some drops prelude a change : the sun,
With ray refracted, bursts the parting gloom,
When all the chequer'd sky is one bright glare.
Mutters the wind at eve ; th' horizon round
With angry aspect scowls : down rush the showers,
And float the deluged paths, and miry fields.

* The barometer.

NATURAL HISTORY

SELBORNE.

LETTER I.

TO THOMAS PENNANT, ESQ.

THE parish of Selborne lies in the extreme eastern corner of the county of Hampshire, bordering on the county of Sussex, and not far from the county of Surrey; is about fifty miles south-west of London, in latitude 51, and near midway between the towns of Alton and Petersfield. Being very large and extensive, it abuts on twelve parishes, two of which are in Sussex, viz. Trotton and Rogate. If you begin from the south, and proceed westward, the adjacent parishes are Emshot, Newton, Valence, Faringdon, Harteley, Mauduit, Great Ward-le-ham, Kingsley, Hedleigh, Bramshot, Trotton, Rogate, Lysse, and Greatham. The soils of this district are almost as various and diversified as the views and aspects. The high part to the south-west consists of a vast hill of chalk, rising three hundred feet above the village; and is divided into a sheep down, the high wood, and a long hanging wood called the Hanger. The covert of this eminence is altogether beech, the most lovely of all forest trees, whether we consider its smooth rind, or bark, its glossy foliage, or graceful pendulous boughs.* The down, or sheep-walk, is a

---

* While the beech is admitted to be one of the most beautiful trees of the forest, it must yield in grandeur, dignity, and picturesque beauty, to the oak, which, in these respects, stands pre-eminent in the British sylva: like the lion amongst animals, it is the unquestionable king of the forest. Beauty of a sublime kind, united with strength, is characteristic of the oak. — ÉD.

A

pleasing park-like spot, of about one mile by half that space, jutting out on the verge of the hill country, where it begins to break down into the plains, and commanding a very engaging view, being an assemblage of hill, dale, woodlands, heath, and water. The prospect is bounded to the south-east and east by the vast range of mountains called the Sussex Downs, by Guild-down near Guildford, and by the Downs round Dorking, and Ryegate in Surrey, to the north-east, which altogether, with the country beyond Alton and Farnham, form a noble and extensive outline.

At the foot of this hill, one stage, or step, from the uplands, lies the village, which consists of one single straggling street, three quarters of a mile in length, in a sheltered vale, and running parallel with the Hanger. The houses are divided from the hill by a vein of stiff clay, (good wheat land,) yet stand on a rock of white stone, little in appearance removed from chalk; but seems so far from being calcareous, that it endures extreme heat. Yet that the freestone still preserves somewhat that is analogous to chalk, is plain from the beeches, which descend as low as those rocks extend, and no farther, and thrive as well on them, where the ground is steep, as on the chalks.

The cart-way of the village divides, in a remarkable manner, two very incongruous soils. To the south-west is a rank clay, that requires the labour of years to render it mellow; while the gardens to the north-east, and small enclosures behind, consist of a warm, forward, crumbling mould, called black malm, which seems highly saturated with vegetable and animal manure; and these may perhaps have been the original site of the town; while the woods and coverts might extend down to the opposite bank.

At each end of the village, which runs from south-east to north-west, arises a small rivulet; that at the north-west end frequently fails; but the other is a fine perennial spring, little influenced by drought or wet seasons, called Wellhead.* This breaks out of some high grounds adjoining to Nore Hill, a noble chalk promontory, remarkable for sending forth two streams into two different seas. The one to the south becomes

* This spring produced, September 14, 1781, after a severe hot summer, and a preceding dry spring and winter, nine gallons of water in a minute, which is five hundred and forty in an hour, and twelve thousand nine hundred and sixty, or two hundred and sixteen hogsheads, in twenty-four hours, or one natural day. At this time many of the wells failed, and all the ponds in the vales were dry.

a branch of the Arun, running to Arundel, and so falling into the British Channel; the other to the north. The Selborne stream makes one branch of the Wey; and, meeting the Black-down stream at Hedleigh, and the Alton and Farnham stream at Tilfordbridge, swells into a considerable river, navigable at Godalming; from whence it passes to Guildford, and so into the Thames at Weybridge; and thus at the Nore into the German Ocean.

Our wells, at an average, run to about sixty-three feet, and when sunk to that depth, seldom fail; but produce a fine limpid water, soft to the taste, and much commended by those who drink the pure element, but which does not lather well with soap.*

To the north-west, north and east of the village, is a range of fair enclosures, consisting of what is called a white malm, a sort of rotten or rubble stone, which, when turned up to the frost and rain, moulders to pieces, and becomes manure to itself.†

Still on to the north-east, and a step lower, is a kind of white land, neither chalk nor clay, neither fit for pasture nor for the plough, yet kindly for hops, which root deep into the freestone, and have their poles and wood for charcoal growing just at hand. This white soil produces the brightest hops.

As the parish still inclines down towards Wolmer Forest, at the juncture of the clays and sand, the soil becomes a wet sandy loam, remarkable for timber, and infamous for roads. The oaks of Temple and Blackmoor stand high in the estimation of purveyors, and have furnished much naval timber; while the trees on the freestone grow large, but are what workmen call *shakey*, and so brittle as often to fall to pieces in sawing.‡ Beyond the sandy loam the soil becomes an hungry lean sand, till it mingles with the forest; and will produce little without the assistance of lime and turnips.

---

* This hardness of the water is occasioned by the great proportion of earthy salts which it holds in solution, the most common of which is sulphate of lime. These salts have the property of decomposing common soap. Their acids unite with the alkali of the soap, while the earthy basis forms with the oil of the soap a substance not soluble in water, which envelopes the soap and gives it a greasy feel. These waters may in general be cured by dropping into them an alkaline carbonate. — ED.

† This soil produces good wheat and clover.

‡ The larch does not thrive on land with a substratum of sandstone. When the roots get deep, and approach the sandstone, the tree makes no progress, and grows crooked. This is probably from the porous nature of the sandstone absorbing the moisture. — ED.

LETTER II.

TO THOMAS PENNANT, ESQ.

I<small>N</small> the court of Norton farm-house, a manor farm to the north-west of the village, on the white malms, stood, within these twenty years, a broad-leaved elm, or wych hazel, *ulmus folio latissimo scabro* of Ray, which, though it had lost a considerable leading bough in the great storm in the year 1703, equal to a moderate tree, yet, when felled, contained eight loads of timber ; and being too bulky for a carriage, was sawn off at seven feet above the but, where it measured near eight feet in the diameter. * This elm I mention, to shew to what a bulk planted elms may attain ; as this tree must certainly have been such from its situation. † In the centre of the village, and near the church, is a square piece of ground, surrounded by houses, and vulgarly called the Plestor. ‡ In the midst of this spot stood, in old times, a vast oak, with a short squat body, and huge horizontal arms, extending almost to the extremity of the area. This venerable tree, surrounded with stone steps, and seats above them, was the delight of old and young, and a place of much resort in summer evenings ; where the former sat in grave debate, while the latter frolicked and danced before them. Long might it have stood, had not

---

* In Evelyn's *Sylva*, vol. ii. p. 189, we are informed of a witch elm that grew in the park of Sir Walter Baggot, Staffordshire, which was seventeen feet diameter at the base, and extended, when felled, one hundred and twenty feet. Its timber was estimated at the amazing quantity of ninety-seven tons. — E<small>D</small>.

† It is a well established fact, that planted trees do not in general attain the size of natural wood. — E<small>D</small>.

‡ The *Plestor* was left by Sir Adam Gordon, a gentleman of Scottish extraction, who was leader of the Mountfort faction during the reign of Henry III, and is thus described by Mr White in the Antiquities of Selborne, — " As Sir Adam began to advance in years, he found his mind influenced by the prevailing opinion of the reasonableness and efficacy of prayers for the dead ; and, therefore, in conjunction with his wife Constantia, in the year 1271, granted to the prior and convent of Selborne all his right and claim to a certain place, *placea*, called *La Pleystow*, in the village aforesaid, ' in *liberam, puram, et perpetuam elemosinam.*' This *pleystow — locus ludorum*, or play-place — is in a level area near the church, of about forty-four yards by thirty-six, and is known now by the name of the *Plestor*. It continues still, as it was in old times, to be the scene of recreation for the youths and children of the neighbourhood ; and impresses an idea on the mind, that this village, even in Saxon times, could not be the most abject of places, when the inhabitants thought proper to assign so spacious a spot for the sports and amusements of its young people."— E<small>D</small>.

COWTHORPE OAK, AT WETHERBY.

the amazing tempest in 1703 overturned it at once, to the infinite regret of the inhabitants, and the vicar, who bestowed several pounds in setting it in its place again ; but all his care could not avail ; the tree sprouted for a time, then withered and died. * This oak I mention, to shew to what a bulk planted oaks also may arrive ; and planted this tree must certainly have been, as appears from what is known concerning the antiquities of the village.†

On the Blackmoor estate there is a small wood, called Losel's, of a few acres, that was lately furnished with a set of oaks of a peculiar growth and great value : they were tall and taper like firs, but, standing near together, had very small heads — only

* It is very probable that this great oak was planted, in the year 1271, by the prior mentioned in the preceding note ; so that it must have been four hundred and thirty-two years old when blown down. — ED.

† The Shire Oak, so named from its peculiar local situation, standing on a spot where the counties of Derby, Nottingham, and York join, is one of the largest in the kingdom. The area which it covers is seven hundred and seven square yards. In February, 1828, an ash tree was felled in Blackburn Hollows, near Shires Green, Yorkshire, containing seven hundred and fifty feet of solid timber: it was ten feet six inches across the stool. An oak was also felled in Shining Cliff, near Crich, Derbyshire, containing nine hundred and sixty-five feet, and was thirteen feet four inches across the stool. One of the most gigantic and venerable trees of this species is the celebrated Cowthorpe Oak, which stands on the extremity of the village of that name, near Wetherby, county of York. The late Dr Hunter, while describing an oak of extraordinary size, which decorates Sheffield Park, notices this majestic production of nature, in his edition of Evelyn's *Sylva*, in the following terms : — " Neither this, nor any of the oaks mentioned by Mr Evelyn, bears any proportion to one now growing at Cowthorpe. The dimensions are almost incredible. Within three feet of the ground it measures sixteen yards, and close to the ground twenty-six yards. Its height, in its present ruinous state, (1776,) is almost eighty-five feet, and its principal limb extends sixteen yards from the bole. Throughout the whole tree the foliage is extremely thin ; so that the anatomy of the ancient branches may be distinctly seen in the height of summer. When compared to this, all other trees are but children of the forest."—Book iii. p. 500.

The description here given answers as nearly as possible to the present condition of the tree, as may be seen by comparing it with the accompanying cut. The common oak is the *quercus robur* of botanists.

The girth of our largest forest trees sinks into comparative insignificance, when contrasted with that of some which are to be met with in the equinoctial regions of America. Mr Exter, in 1827, measured a cypress tree in the churchyard of Santa Maria de Tesla, two leagues and a half west of Oaxaca, whose trunk was one hundred and twenty-seven English feet in circumference, and one hundred and twenty feet in height. It appeared in the prime of its growth, and had not a single dead branch. — ED.

a little brush, without any large limbs. About twenty years ago the bridge at the Toy, near Hampton Court, being much decayed, some trees were wanted for the repairs that were fifty feet long without bough, and would measure twelve inches diameter at the little end.   Twenty such trees did a purveyor find in this little wood, with this advantage, that many of them answered the description at sixty feet. These trees were sold for twenty pounds a-piece.*

In the centre of this grove there stood an oak, which, though shapely and tall on the whole, bulged out into a large excrescence about the middle of the stem.   On this a pair of ravens had fixed their residence for such a series of years, that the oak was distinguished by the title of the Raven Tree. Many were the attempts of the neighbouring youths to get at this eyry: the difficulty whetted their inclinations, and each was ambitious of surmounting the arduous task.   But when they arrived at the swelling, it jutted out so in their way, and was so far beyond their grasp, that the most daring lads were awed, and acknowledged the undertaking to be too hazardous. So the ravens built on, nest upon nest, in perfect security, till the fatal day arrived in which the wood was to be levelled. It was in the month of February, when those birds usually sit. The saw was applied to the but, the wedges were inserted into the opening, the woods echoed to the heavy blows of the beetle, or mallet, the tree nodded to its fall ; but still the dam sat on. At last, when it gave way, the bird was flung from her nest ; and, though her parental affection deserved a better fate, was whipped down by the twigs, which brought her dead to the ground.†

* In the hall of Dudly Castle there is an oak table, seventy-five feet long, and three feet broad, which grew in the park of that estate.—ED.

† During the time of incubation, the natural timidity of birds is greatly lessened ; and, in many instances, the females will allow themselves to be taken rather than desert their nests. The following instance, recorded by William Henry Hill, Esq. of Newland, Gloucestershire, in 1828, finely illustrates this : — He says, " Some time since, a pair of blue titmice (parus cæruleus) built their nest in the upper part of an old pump, fixing on the pin on which the handle worked. It happened that, during the time of building, and laying the eggs, the pump had not been in use; when again set going, the female was sitting, and it was naturally expected the motion of the pump-handle would drive her away.   The young brood were hatched safely, however, without any other misfortune than the loss of part of the tail of the sitting bird, which was rubbed off by the friction of the pump-handle ; nor did they appear disturbed by the visitors who were frequently looking at her."—Magazine of Natural History, ii. p. 64.

LETTER III.

TO THOMAS PENNANT, ESQ.

THE fossil shells of this district, and sorts of stone, such as have fallen within my observation, must not be passed over in silence. And first, I must mention, as a great curiosity, a specimen that was ploughed up in the chalky fields, near the side of the Down, and given to me for the singularity of its appearance, which, to an incurious eye, seems like a petrified fish, of about four inches long, the cardo passing for a head and mouth. It is in reality a bivalve of the Linnæan genus of *mytilus* and the species of *crista galli;* called by Lister, *rastellum;* by Rumphius, *ostreum plicatum minus;* by D'Argenville, *auris porci, crista galli;* and by those who make collections, cock's comb.* Though I applied to several such in London, I never could meet with an entire specimen ; nor could I ever find in books any engraving from a perfect one. In the superb museum at Leicester House, permission was given me to examine for this article ; and, though I was disappointed as to the fossil, I was highly gratified with the sight of several of the shells themselves, in high preservation. This bivalve is only known to inhabit the Indian Ocean, where it fixes itself to a zoophyte, known by the name *gorgonia*.

Cornua ammonis are very common about this village. As we were cutting an inclining path up the Hanger, the labourers found them frequently on that steep, just under the soil, in the chalk, and of a considerable size. In the lane above Well-head, in the way to Emshot, they abound in the bank in a darkish sort of marl ; and are usually very small and soft ; but in Clay's Pond, a little farther on, at the end of the pit, where the soil is dug out for manure, I have occasionally observed them of large dimensions, perhaps fourteen or sixteen inches

---

* *Ostrea carinata*, or keeled oyster, of Lamark. It is met with in the department of Sarthe, and other places of France. The author is mistaken in supposing that this species is found in a recent state. It has been satisfactorily proved, that there are no living species of those fossil shells discovered in the old limestone formations, although there are some existing individuals nearly allied to them.

Petrifactions occur in three states ; sometimes they are a little altered, sometimes they are converted into stone, and at other times the impressions only of them, or the moulds in which they have been enclosed, remain. — ED.

in diameter. But as these did not consist of firm stone, but were formed of a kind of *terra lapidosa*, or hardened clay, as soon as they were exposed to the rains and frost, they mouldered away. These seemed as if they were a very recent production. In the chalk-pit, at the north-west end of the Hanger, large *nautili* are sometimes observed.*

In the very thickest strata of our freestone, and at considerable depths, well-diggers often find large scallops, or pectines, having both shells deeply striated, and ridged and furrowed alternately. They are highly impregnated with, if not wholly composed of, the stone of the quarry.†

LETTER IV.

TO THOMAS PENNANT, ESQ.

As, in last letter, the freestone of this place has been only mentioned incidentally, I shall here become more particular.

This stone is in great request for hearth-stones, and the beds of ovens; and in lining of lime-kilns it turns to good account; for the workmen use sandy loam instead of mortar, the sand

---

* Modern naturalists have constituted twenty genera of those fossil shells, known by the general appellation of *cornu ammonis*. The conclusions which geologists have come to regarding them, are these: — 1st, That they are first found in the formation called the lias, and appear in most of the succeeding strata, but seem to have become extinct in the ocean which deposited the *hard chalk*. The division here alluded to, is what has been named the *ammonacea* by Lamark, which are shells with a sinuous septa, lobed and cut at the margin, meeting together upon the inner wall of the shell, and articulated by jagged sutures. 2d, The *orthocerata* appear in the early strata, and are continued upwards to the *soft chalk* stratum, after which they are not seen. These shells are straight, or nearly so, and not spiral. 3d, The oval *ammonitæ* are not known in the early strata, but in the *hard chalk* only, and are not seen afterwards, as if they had been created at a comparatively late period, and had been soon suffered to become extinct. The shells alluded to by our author, which mouldered away, had been the impressions only of these *cornua ammonis*. — ED.

† In Corncockle Moor, Dumfries-shire, there is a sandstone quarry, on the slabs of which are distinctly imprinted the tracks of the foot marks of animals. These were discovered in the year 1812. They differ in size from that of a hare's paw to the hoof of a pony. On a slab, which forms part of the wall of a summer-house, in Dr Duncan's garden, at the Manse of Ruthwell, there are twenty-four impressions, twelve of the right, and as many of the left foot. Professor Buckland considers that the animals must have been crocodiles or tortoises.—ED.

of which fluxes,* and runs, by the intense heat, and so cases
over the whole face of the kiln with a strong vitrified coat like
glass, that it is well preserved from injuries of weather, and
endures thirty or forty years. When chiselled smooth, it
makes elegant fronts for houses, equal in colour and grain to
the Bath stone, and superior in one respect, that, when sea-
soned, it does not scale. Decent chimneypieces are worked
from it, of much closer and finer grain than Portland ; and rooms
are floored with it ; but it proves rather too soft for this purpose.
It is a freestone, cutting in all directions ; yet has something
of a grain parallel with the horizon, and therefore should not
be surbedded, but laid in the same position that it grows in
the quarry.† On the ground abroad this firestone will not
succeed for pavements, because, probably some degree of salt-
ness prevailing within it, the rain tears the slabs to pieces.‡
Though this stone is too hard to be acted on by vinegar, yet
both the white part, and even the blue rag, ferment strongly
in mineral acids. Though the white stone will not bear wet,
yet in every quarry, at intervals, there are thin strata of blue
rag, which resist rain and frost, and are excellent for pitching
of stables, paths, and courts, and for building of dry walls
against banks, a valuable species of fencing, much in use in
this village, and for mending of roads. This rag is rugged
and stubborn, and will not hew to a smooth face, but is very
durable ; yet, as these strata are shallow, and lie deep, large
quantities cannot be procured but at considerable expense.
Among the blue rags turn up some blocks, tinged with a stain
of yellow, or rust colour, which seem to be nearly as lasting as
the blue ; and every now and then balls of a friable substance,
like rust of iron, called rust balls.

In Wolmer Forest I see but one sort of stone, called by the
workmen sand, or forest stone. This is generally of the colour
of rusty iron, and might probably be worked as iron ore ; is

---

* May not the fact here noticed shew the possibility of what are called
vitrified forts being produced by fires lighted for signals, or some other
purpose, as an instance is here given of heat causing sand to flux. — ED.
There may probably be also in the chalk itself that is burnt for lime a
proportion of sand; for few chalks are so pure as to have none.

† To *surbed* stone is to set it edgewise, contrary to the posture it had
in the quarry, says Dr Plot, *Oxfordshire*, p. 77. But surbedding does
not succeed in our dry walls; neither do we use it so in ovens, though
he says it is best for Teynton stone.

‡ " Firestone is full of salts, and has no sulphur ; must be close-grained,
and have no interstices. Nothing supports fire like salts ; saltstone perishes
exposed to wet and frost."— Plot's *Staff.* p. 152.

very hard and heavy, and of a firm, compact texture, and composed of a small roundish crystalline grit, cemented together by a brown, terrene, ferruginous matter; will not cut without difficulty, nor easily strike fire with steel. Being often found in broad flat pieces, it makes good pavement for paths about houses, never becoming slippery in frost or rain; is excellent for dry walls, and is sometimes used in buildings. In many parts of that waste it lies scattered on the surface of the ground; but is dug on Weaver's Down, a vast hill on the eastern verge of that forest, where the pits are shallow, and the stratum thin. This stone is imperishable.

From a notion of rendering their work the more elegant, and giving it a finish, masons chip this stone into small fragments about the size of the head of a large nail; and then stick the pieces into the wet mortar along the joints of their freestone walls. This embellishment carries an odd appearance, and has occasioned strangers sometimes to ask us pleasantly, "Whether we fastened our walls together with tenpenny nails?"

LETTER V.

TO THOMAS PENNANT, ESQ.

AMONG the singularities of this place, the two rocky hollow lanes, the one to Alton, and the other to the forest, deserve our attention. These roads, running through the malm lands, are, by the traffic of ages, and the fretting of water, worn down through the first stratum of our freestone, and partly through the second; so that they look more like watercourses than roads, and are bedded with naked rag for furlongs together. In many places they are reduced sixteen or eighteen feet beneath the level of the fields; and after floods, and in frosts, exhibit very grotesque and wild appearances, from the tangled roots that are twisted among the strata, and from the torrents rushing down their broken sides; and especially when those cascades are frozen into icicles, hanging in all the fanciful shapes of frostwork. These rugged gloomy scenes affright the ladies when they peep down into them from the paths above, and make timid horsemen shudder while they ride along them; but delight the naturalist with their various botany, and particularly with their curious filices, with which they abound.

The manor of Selborne, were it strictly looked after, with all its kindly aspects, and all its sloping coverts, would swarm

with game; even now, hares, partridges, and pheasants abound;
and in old days woodcocks were as plentiful. There are few
quails, because they more affect open fields than enclosures.
After harvest, some few land-rails are seen.

The parish of Selborne, by taking in so much of the forest,
is a vast district. Those who tread the bounds are employed
part of three days in the business, and are of opinion that the
outline, in all its curves and indentings, does not comprise
less than thirty miles.

The village stands in a sheltered spot, secured by the Hanger
from the strong westerly winds. The air is soft, but rather
moist, from the effluvia of so many trees; yet perfectly healthy
and free from agues.

The quantity of rain that falls on it is very considerable, as
may be supposed in so woody and mountainous a district. As
my experience in measuring the water is but of short date, I
am not qualified to give the mean quantity.* I only know
that,

	Inch.	Hund.
From May 1, 1779, to the end of the year, there fell . .	28	37!
From January 1, 1780, to January 1, 1781 . . .	27	32
From January 1, 1781, to January 1, 1782 . . .	30	71
From January 1, 1782, to January 1, 1783 . . .	50	26!
From January 1, 1783, to January 1, 1784 . . .	33	71
From January 1, 1784, to January 1, 1785 . . .	33	80
From January 1, 1785, to January 1, 1786 . . .	31	55
From January 1, 1786, to January 1, 1787 . . .	39	57

The village of Selborne, and large hamlet of Oakhanger,
with the single farms, and many scattered houses along the
verge of the forest, contain upwards of six hundred and seventy
inhabitants.

We abound with poor, many of whom are sober and
industrious, and live comfortably, in good stone or brick
cottages, which are glazed, and have chambers above stairs:
mud buildings we have none. Besides the employment from
husbandry, the men work in hop gardens, of which we have
many, and fell and bark timber. In the spring and summer

* A very intelligent gentleman assures me, (and he speaks from
upwards of forty years' experience,) that the mean rain of any place
cannot be ascertained till a person has measured it for a very long period.
"If I had only measured the rain," says he, "for the four first years,
from 1740 to 1743, I should have said the mean rain at Lyndon was
16¾ inches for the year; if from 1740 to 1750, 1½ inches. The mean
rain before 1763, was 20¾; from 1763 and since, 25½; from 1770 to
1780, 26. If only 1773, 1774, and 1775, had been measured, Lyndon
mean rain would have been called 32 inches, increasing from 16.6 to 32."

the women weed the corn, and enjoy a second harvest in
September by hop-picking. Formerly, in the dead months,
they availed themselves greatly by spinning wool, for making
of barragons, a genteel corded stuff, much in vogue at that
time for summer wear, and chiefly manufactured at Alton,
a neighbouring town, by some of the people called Quakers.
The inhabitants enjoy a good share of health and longevity,
and the parish swarms with children

LETTER VI.

TO THOMAS PENNANT, ESQ.

SHOULD I omit to describe with some exactness the Forest
of Wolmer, of which three-fifths perhaps lie in this parish, my
account of Selborne would be very imperfect, as it is a district
abounding with many curious productions, both animal and
vegetable ; and has often afforded me much entertainment
both as a sportsman and as a naturalist.

The royal Forest of Wolmer is a tract of land of about seven
miles in length, by two and a half in breadth, running nearly
from north to south, and is abutted on, to begin to the south,
and so to proceed eastward, by the parishes of Greatham,
Lysse, Rogate, and Trotton, in the county of Sussex ; by
Bramshot, Hedleigh, and Kingsley.   This royalty consists
entirely of sand, covered with heath and fern ; but is somewhat
diversified with hills and dales, without having one standing
tree in the whole extent.   In the bottoms, where the waters
stagnate, are many bogs, which formerly abounded with
subterraneous trees ; though Dr Plot says positively,* that
" there never were any fallen trees hidden in the mosses of
the southern counties."   But he was mistaken ; for I myself
have seen cottages on the verge of this wild district, whose
timbers consisted of a black hard wood, looking like oak,
which the owners assured me they procured from the bogs
by probing the soil with spits, or some such instruments, but
the peat is so much cut out, and the moors have been so well
examined, that none has been found of late.†   Besides the

---

* See his *History of Staffordshire.*
† Old people have assured me, that on a winter's morning they have
discovered these trees, in the bogs, by the hoar frost, which lay longer
over the space where they were concealed, than on the surrounding
morass.   Nor does this seem to be a fanciful notion, but consistent with
true philosophy.   Dr Hales saith, " That the warmth of the earth, at

oak, I have also been shewn pieces of fossil wood, of a paler colour, and softer nature, which the inhabitants called fir ; but, upon a nice examination, and trial by fire, I could discover nothing resinous in them ; and therefore rather suppose that they were parts of a willow, or alder, or some such aquatic tree.*

This lonely domain is a very agreeable haunt for many sorts of wild fowls, which not only frequent it in the winter, but breed there in the summer ; such as lapwings, snipes, wild-ducks, and, as I have discovered within these few years, teals.   Partridges in vast plenty are bred in good seasons on the verge of this Forest, into which they love to make excursions ; and in particular, in the dry summer of 1740 and 1741, and some years after, they swarmed to such a degree, that parties of unreasonable sportsmen killed twenty and sometimes thirty, brace in a day.

But there was a nobler species of game in this forest, now extinct, which I have heard old people say abounded much before shooting flying became so common, and that was the heath-cock, or black game.   When I was a little boy, I recollect one coming now and then to my father's table.   The last pack remembered was killed about thirty-five years ago ; and within these ten years, one solitary gray-hen was sprung by some beagles in beating for a hare.   The sportsman cried out, " A hen pheasant !" but a gentleman present, who had often seen black game in the north of England, assured me that it was a gray-hen.†

some depth under ground, has an influence in promoting a thaw, as well as the change of the weather from a freezing to a thawing state, is manifest from this observation ; viz. November 29, 1731, a little snow having fallen in the night, it was, by eleven the next morning, mostly melted away on the surface of the earth, except in several places in Bushy Park, where there were drains dug and covered with earth, on which the snow continued to lie, whether those drains were full of water or dry ; as also where elm-pipes lay under ground : a plain proof this, that those drains intercepted the warmth of the earth from ascending from greater depths below them ; for the snow lay where the drain had more than four feet depth of earth over it.   It continued also to lie on thatch, tiles, and the tops of walls."   See Hales's *Hæmastatics*, p. 360.   Quere, Might not such observations be reduced to domestic use, by promoting the discovery of old obliterated drains and wells about houses ; and in Roman stations and camps, lead to the finding of pavements, baths, and graves, and other hidden relics of curious antiquity ?

* Fossils of this kind, including oaks and pines, are common in most marshes and bogs of Europe. — ED.

† It is very doubtful whether the black grouse ever was plentiful in the less mountainous counties of England.   At present they are very

Nor does the loss of our black game prove the only gap in the *Fauna Selborniensis;* for another beautiful link in the chain of beings is wanting,—I mean the red deer, which toward the beginning of this century amounted to about five hundred head, and made a stately appearance. There is an old keeper, now alive, named Adams, whose great-grandfather (mentioned in a perambulation taken in 1635), grandfather, father, and self, enjoyed the head keepership of Wolmer Forest in succession far more than an hundred years. This person assures me, that his father has often told him that Queen Anne, as she was journeying on the Portsmouth road, did not think the Forest of Wolmer beneath her royal regard ; for she came out of the great road at Lippock, which is just by, and, reposing herself on a bank smoothed for that purpose, lying about half a mile to the east of Wolmer Pond, and still called Queen's Bank, saw, with great complacency and satisfaction, the whole herd of red deer brought by the keepers along the vale before her, consisting then of about five hundred head. A sight this, worthy the attention of the greatest sovereign ! But he farther adds, that, by means of the Waltham Blacks, or, to use his own expression, as soon as they began blacking, they were reduced to about fifty head, and so continued decreasing, till the time of the late Duke of Cumberland. It is now more than thirty years ago, that his Highness sent down an huntsman, and six yeomen prickers, in scarlet jackets laced with gold, attended by the stag-hounds ; ordering them to take every deer in this forest alive, and to convey them in carts to Windsor. In the course of the summer, they caught every stag, some of which shewed extraordinary diversion ; but in the following winter, when the hinds were also carried off, such fine chases were

scarce in the southern counties ; a few are to be met with in the New Forest, Hampshire, Dartmore, and Sedgemore, in Devonshire, and in some of the heathy hills of Somersetshire, which lie contiguous to Devonshire ; and in Staffordshire and North Wales. They abound in the south and north of Scotland. The Earl of Fife has procured a breed of that splendid bird the capercalzie, or cock of the woods, which promises to increase. It is his Lordship's intention to turn them out at Marr Lodge, and endeavour to naturalize them ; in which project there can be little doubt of his succeeding, as they were formerly plentiful in Scotland. The Virginian partridge has been successfully introduced into Staffordshire, and has become abundant, and spread over part of the adjoining counties. The red-legged partridge, a native of France, has lately been introduced into preserves in England with great success. Wherever it obtains ground, it drives the common species out of the preserves, and threatens in time, like the Norway rat, to exterminate the aboriginal race.—Ed.

exhibited, as served the country people for matter of talk and
wonder for years afterwards. I saw myself one of the yeomen
prickers single out a stag from the herd, and must confess that
it was the most curious feat of activity I ever beheld, superior
to any thing in Mr Astley's riding-school. The exertions
made by the horse and deer much exceeded all my expecta-
tions, though the former greatly excelled the latter in speed.
When the devoted deer was separated from his companions,
they gave him, by their watches, law, as they called it, for
twenty minutes ; when, sounding their horns, the stop-dogs
were permitted to pursue, and a most gallant scene ensued.

LETTER VII.

TO THOMAS PENNANT, ESQ.

Though large herds of deer do much harm to the neighbourhood, yet the injury to the morals of the people is of more
moment than the loss of their crops. The temptation is
irresistible ; for most men are sportsmen by constitution, and
there is such an inherent spirit for hunting in human nature,
as scarce any inhibitions can restrain. Hence, towards the
beginning of this century, all this country was wild about deer-
stealing. Unless he was a hunter, as they affected to call
themselves, no young person was allowed to be possessed of
manhood or gallantry. The Waltham Blacks at length com-
mitted such enormities, that government was forced to interfere
with that severe and sanguinary act called the Black Act, *
which now comprehends more felonies than any law that ever
was framed before. And, therefore, a late bishop of Winchester, when urged to re-stock Waltham Chase, refused, from
a motive worthy of a prelate, replying, that "It had done
mischief enough already." †

Our old race of deer-stealers are hardly extinct yet. It was
but a little while ago that, over their ale, they used to recount
the exploits of their youth ; such as watching the pregnant hind
to her lair, and, when the calf was dropped, paring its feet,
with a penknife, to the quick, to prevent its escape, till it was
large and fat enough to be killed ; the shooting at one of their
neighbours with a bullet, in a turnip field by moonshine,
mistaking him for a deer ; and the losing a dog in the following

---

* Statute 9 Geo. I, c. 22.
† This Chase remains unstocked to this day : the bishop was Dr
Hoadley.

extraordinary manner :—Some fellows, suspecting that a calf new fallen was deposited in a certain spot of thick fern, went with a lurcher to surprise it ; when the parent hind rushed out of the brake, and, taking a vast spring, with all her feet close together, pitched upon the neck of the dog, and broke it short in two.*

Another temptation to idleness and sporting, was a number of rabbits, which possessed all the hillocks and dry places ; but these being inconvenient to the huntsmen, on account of their burrows, when they came to take away the deer, they permitted the country people to destroy them all.

Such forests and wastes, when their allurements to irregularities are removed, are of considerable service to neighbourhoods that verge upon them, by furnishing them with peat and turf for their firing; with fuel for the burning their lime ; and with ashes for their grasses ; and by maintaining their geese and their stock of young cattle at little or no expense.

The manor farm of the parish of Greatham has an admitted claim, I see, (by an old record taken from the Tower of London,) of turning all live stock on the forest, at proper seasons, *bidentibus exceptis.*† The reason, I presume, why sheep‡ are excluded is, because, being such close grazers, they would pick out all the finest grasses, and hinder the deer from thriving.

Though (by statute 4th and 5th William and Mary, c. 23) " to burn on any waste, between Candlemas and Midsummer, any grig, ling, heath, and furze, goss or fern, is punishable with whipping, and confinement in the house of correction ; " yet, in this forest, about March or April, according to the dryness of the season, such vast heath-fires are lighted up, that they often get to a masterless head, and, catching the hedges, have sometimes been communicated to the underwoods, woods, and coppices, where great damage has ensued.

---

* The hind will expose herself to the fury of the hounds, and suffer all the terrors of the chase, in order to draw off the dogs from the hiding-place of the calf. She is exceedingly bold in the protection of her offspring, defends herself with great courage, and frequently obliges the dog and wolf to give way upon these occasions. William Duke of Cumberland caused a stag and tiger to be enclosed in the same area, to see the result ; and the stag made so bold a defence, that the tiger was obliged to give up the contest. — ED.

† For this privilege, the owner of that estate used to pay to the king annually seven bushels of oats.

‡ In the Holt, where a full stock of fallow deer has been kept up till lately, no sheep are admitted to this day.

The plea for these burnings is, that, when the old coat of heath, &c. is consumed, young will sprout up, and afford much tender browse for cattle ; but, where there is large old furze, the fire, following the roots, consumes the very ground ; so that, for hundreds of acres, nothing is to be seen but smother and desolation, the whole circuit round looking like the cinders of a volcano ; and the soil being quite exhausted, no traces of vegetation are to be found for years. These conflagrations, as they take place usually with a north-east or east wind, much annoy this village with their smoke, and often alarm the country ; and once, in particular, I remember that a gentleman, who lives beyond Andover, coming to my house, when he got on the downs between that town and Winchester, at twenty-five miles distance, was surprised much with smoke, and a hot smell of fire, and concluded that Alresford was in flames ; but, when he came to that town, he then had apprehensions for the next village, and so on to the end of his journey.

On two of the most conspicuous eminences of this forest, stand two arbours, or bowers, made of the boughs of oaks ; the one called Waldon Lodge, the other Brimstone Lodge : these the keepers renew annually, on the feast of St Barnabas, taking the old materials for a perquisite. The farm called Blackmoor, in this parish, is obliged to find the posts and brushwood for the former ; while the farms at Greatham, in rotation, furnish for the latter ; and are all enjoined to cut and deliver the materials at the spot. This custom I mention, because I look upon it to be of very remote antiquity.

LETTER VIII.

TO THOMAS PENNANT, ESQ.

On the verge of the forest, as it is now circumscribed, are three considerable lakes,—two in Oakhanger, of which I have nothing particular to say ; and one called Bin's, or Bean's Pond, which is worthy the attention of a naturalist or a sportsman : for, being crowded at the upper end with willows, and with the *carex cespitosa*,* it affords such a safe and pleasant shelter to wild ducks, teals, snipes, &c. that they breed there. In the winter, this covert is also frequented by foxes, and

---

* I mean that sort which, rising into tall hassocks, is called by the foresters *torrets ;* a corruption, I suppose, of turrets.

Note.—In the beginning of the summer 1787, the royal forests of Wolmer and Holt were measured by persons sent down by government.

B

sometimes by pheasants ; and the bogs produce many curious plants.*

By a perambulation of Wolmer Forest and the Holt, made in 1635, and in the eleventh year of Charles the First, (which now lies before me,) it appears that the limits of the former are much circumscribed.   For, to say nothing of the farther side, with which I am not so well acquainted, the bounds on this side, in old times, came into Binswood, and extended to the ditch of Ward-le-ham Park, in which stands the curious mount called King John's Hill and Lodge Hill, and to the verge of Hartley Mauduit, called Mauduit-hatch ; comprehending also Shortheath, Oakhanger, and Oakwoods, — a large district, now private property, though once belonging to the royal domain.

It is remarkable, that the term *purlieu* is never once mentioned in this long roll of parchment.   It contains, besides the perambulation, a rough estimate of the value of the timbers, which were considerable, growing at that time in the district of the Holt ; and enumerates the officers, superior and inferior, of those joint forests, for the time being, and their ostensible fees and perquisites.   In those days, as at present, there were hardly any trees in Wolmer Forest.

Within the present limits of the forest are three considerable lakes, — Hogmer, Cranmer, and Wolmer ; all of which are stocked with carp, tench, eels, and perch : but the fish do not thrive well, because the water is hungry, and the bottoms are a naked sand.

A circumstance respecting these ponds, though by no means peculiar to them, I cannot pass over in silence ; and that is, that instinct by which, in summer, all the kine, whether oxen, cows, calves, or heifers, retire constantly to the water during the hotter hours ; where, being more exempt from flies, and inhaling the coolness of that element, some belly deep, and some only to mid-leg, they ruminate and solace themselves from about ten in the morning till four in the afternoon, and then return to their feeding.   During this great proportion of the day, they drop much dung, in which insects nestle ; and so supply food for the fish, which would be poorly subsisted but for this contingency.   Thus Nature, who is a great economist, converts the recreation of one animal to the support of another !   Thomson, who was a nice observer of natural

* For which consult Letter LXXXIV. to Mr Barrington.

occurrence*, did not let this pleasing circumstance escape him. He says, in his Summer,—

> A various group the herds and flocks compose:
> ———————— on the grassy bank
> Some, ruminating, lie; while others stand
> Half in the flood, and, often bending, sip
> The circling surface.

Wolmer Pond—so called, I suppose, for eminence sake—is a vast lake for this part of the world, containing, in its whole circumference, two thousand six hundred and forty-six yards, or very near a mile and a half. The length of the north-west and opposite side is about seven hundred and four yards, and the breadth of the south-west end, about four hundred and fifty-six yards. This measurement, which I caused to be made with good exactness, gives an area of about sixty-six acres, exclusive of a large irregular arm at the north-east corner, which we did not take into the reckoning.

On the face of this expanse of waters, and perfectly secure from fowlers, lie all day long, in the winter season, vast flocks of ducks, teals, and widgeons, of various denominations: where they preen, and solace, and rest themselves, till towards sunset, when they issue forth in little parties (for, in their natural state, they are all birds of the night) to feed in the brooks and meadows; returning again with the dawn of the morning. Had this lake an arm or two more, and were it planted round with thick covert, (for now it is perfectly naked,) it might make a valuable decoy.

Yet neither its extent, nor the clearness of its water, nor the resort of various and curious fowls, nor its picturesque groups of cattle, can render this *meer* so remarkable, as the great quantity of coins that were found in its bed about forty years ago.*

LETTER IX.

TO THOMAS PENNANT, ESQ.

By way of supplement, I shall trouble you once more on this subject, to inform you that Wolmer, with her sister forest,

---

* These coins were all copper, as were also some medallions which were found at the same time, all of the lower Empire of Rome; some dozens of which fell to the share of Mr White. Part of these were of Marcus Aurelius, and his empress, Faustina. — ED.

Ayles Holt, *alias* Alice Holt,* as it is called in old records, is held by grant from the crown for a term of years.

The grantees that the author remembers are, Brigadier-General Emanuel Scroope Howe, and his lady, Ruperta, who was a natural daughter of Prince Rupert, by Margaret Hughs; a Mr Mordaunt, of the Peterborough family, who married a dowager Lady Pembroke; Henry Bilson Legge, and lady; and now Lord Stawel, their son.

The lady of General Howe lived to an advanced age, long surviving her husband; and, at her death, left behind her many curious pieces of mechanism of her father's constructing, who was a distinguished mechanic and artist,† as well as warrior; and, among the rest, a very complicated clock, lately in possession of Mr Elmer, the celebrated game painter, at Farnham, in the county of Surrey.

Though these two forests are only parted by a narrow range of enclosures, yet no two soils can be more different; for the Holt consists of a strong loam, of a miry nature, carrying a good turf, and abounding with oaks, that grow to be large timber, while Wolmer is nothing but a hungry, sandy, barren waste.

The former, being all in the parish of Binsted, is about two miles in extent from north to south, and near as much from east to west, and contains within it many woodlands and lawns, and the Great Lodge where the grantees reside, and a smaller lodge called Goose Green; and is abutted on by the parishes of Kingsley, Frinsham, Farnham, and Bentley, all of which have right of common.

One thing is remarkable, that, though the Holt has been of old well stocked with fallow-deer, unrestrained by any pales or fences more than a common hedge, yet they are never seen within the limits of Wolmer; nor were the red deer of

---

* " In Rot. Inquisit. de statu forest. in Scaccar. 36 Ed. III, it is called Aisholt." In the same, " Tit. Woolmer and Aisholt Hantisc. Dominus Rex habet unam capellam in *haia suâ* de Kingesle." " *Haia, sepes, sepimentum, parcus:* a Gall. *haie* and *hàye*." — SPELMAN's *Glossary*.

† This prince was the inventor of mezzotinto.‡

‡ The invention of mezzotinto engraving is generally ascribed to Prince Rupert; but, in Elme's Life of Sir Christopher Wren, it is given to that eminent architect. The journals of the Royal Society, for October 1, 1662, record that Dr Wren presented some cuts, done by himself, in a new way; whereby he could almost as soon do a subject on a plate of brass or copper, as another could draw it with a crayon on paper. On this subject, the editor of *Parentalia* speaks with decision, that " he was the first inventor of the art of engraving in mezzotinto; which was afterwards prosecuted and improved by his Royal Highness Prince Rupert, in a manner somewhat different, upon the suggestion, as it is said, of the learned John Evelyn, Esq."—ED.

Wolmer ever known to haunt the thickets or glades of the Holt.*

At present the deer of the Holt are much thinned and reduced by the night-hunters, who perpetually harass them in spite of the efforts of numerous keepers, and the severe penalties that have been put in force against them as often as they have been detected, and rendered liable to the lash of the law. Neither fines nor imprisonments can deter them; so impossible is it to extinguish the spirit of sporting, which seems to be inherent in human nature.

General Howe turned out some German wild boars and sows in his forests, to the great terror of the neighbourhood; and, at one time, a wild bull or buffalo: but the country rose upon them, and destroyed them.

A very large fall of timber, consisting of about one thousand oaks, has been cut this spring (viz. 1784) in the Holt Forest; one-fifth of which, it is said, belongs to the grantee, Lord Stawel. He lays claim also to the lop and top; but the poor of the parishes of Binsted and Frinsham, Bentley and Kingsley, assert that it belongs to them; and, assembling in a riotous manner, have actually taken it all away. One man, who keeps a team, has carried home, for his share, forty stacks of wood. Forty-five of these people his lordship has served with actions. These trees, which were very sound, and in high perfection, were winter-cut, viz. in February and March, before the bark would run.† In old times, the Holt was estimated to be eighteen miles, computed measure, from water carriage, viz. from the town of Chertsey, on the Thames; but now it is not half that distance, since the Wey is made navigable up to the town of Godalming, in the county of Surrey.

---

* There is a curious fact, not generally known, which is, that at one period the horns of stags grew into a much greater number of ramifications than at the present day. Some have supposed this to have arisen from the greater abundance of food, and from the animal having more repose, before population became so dense. In some individuals these multiplied to an extraordinary extent. There is one in the museum of Hesse Cassel with twenty-eight antlers. Baron Cuvier mentions one with sixty-six, or thirty-three on each horn. — ED.

† The superiority of wood cut in winter arises from its being divested of sap at that season of the year. Timber felled in summer is liable to crack, and is very subject to the dry-rot; both of which are caused by the sap not having properly escaped in the process of drying. The sap rises only in the spring, and descends at the fall of the year. — ED.

LETTER X.

TO THOMAS PENNANT, ESQ.

August 4, 1767.

IT has been my misfortune never to have had any neighbours whose studies have led them towards the pursuit of natural knowledge ; so that, for want of a companion to quicken my industry and sharpen my attention, I have made but slender progress in a kind of information to which I have been attached from my childhood.

As to swallows (*hirundines rusticæ*) being found in a torpid state during the winter in the Isle of Wight, or any part of this country, I never heard any such account worth attending to. But a clergyman, of an inquisitive turn, assures me that, when he was a great boy, some workmen, in pulling down the battlements of a church tower early in the spring, found two or three swifts (*hirundines apodes*) among the rubbish, which were, at first appearance, dead ; but, on being carried towards the fire, revived. He told me that, out of his great care to preserve them, he put them in a paper bag, and hung them by the kitchen fire, where they were suffocated.

Another intelligent person has informed me that, while he was a schoolboy at Brighthelmstone, in Sussex, a great fragment of the chalk cliff fell down one stormy winter on the beach, and that many people found swallows among the rubbish ; but, on my questioning him whether he saw any of those birds himself, to my no small disappointment he answered me in the negative, but that others assured him they did.*

Young broods of swallows began to appear this year on July the 11th, and young martens (*hirundines urbicæ*) were

---

* That a few solitary instances of swallows remaining in this country, in a state of torpidity, have occurred, there can be little doubt ; but that they generally hybernate is out of the question. Charles Lucian Bonaparte, in a letter to the Secretary of the Linnæan Society, dated from on board the Delaware, near Gibraltar, March 20, 1828, says,—" A few days ago, being five hundred miles from the coasts of Portugal, four hundred from those of Africa, we were agreeably surprised by the appearance of a few swallows, (*hirundo urbica* and *rustica.*) This, however extraordinary, might have been explained by an easterly gale, which might have cut off the swallows migrating from the main to Madeira, only two hundred miles distant from us ; but what was my surprise in observing several small warblers popping about the deck and rigging. These poor little strangers were soon caught and brought to me." These warblers were the *sylvia trochilus*, or hay bird, &c. —ED.

then fledged in their nests. Both species will breed again once; for I see by my *fauna* of last year, that young broods came forth so late as September the 18th. Are not these late hatchings more in favour of hiding than migration? Nay, some young martens remained in their nests last year so late as September the 29th; and yet they totally disappeared with us by the 5th of October.

How strange it is, that the swift, which seems to live exactly the same life with the swallow and house-marten, should leave us before the middle of August invariably! while the latter stay often till the middle of October; and once I saw numbers of house-martens on the 7th of November. * The martens and red-wing fieldfares were flying in sight together,—an uncommon assemblage of summer and winter birds!

A little yellow bird (it is either a species of the *alauda trivialis*, † or rather, perhaps, of the *motacilla trochilus* ‡) still continues to make a sibilous shivering noise in the tops of tall woods. The *stoparola* of Ray (for which we have as yet no name in these parts) is called, in your *Zoology*, the fly-catcher. There is one circumstance characteristic of this bird, which seems to have escaped observation; and that is, it takes its stand on the top of some stake or post, from whence it springs forth on its prey, catching a fly in the air, and hardly ever touching the ground, but returning still to the same stand for many times together.·

---

* The latest time which the swift has been known to remain in this country was till September 15, in the year 1817. Two or three were seen sporting about with the large assemblies of swallows and martens, by the sea side, near Penzance, to the eastward. These birds, there can be little doubt, were on their passage from this country to a more southern climate. The swallow (*H. rustica*) was seen, by the Rev. W. T. Bree, in the year 1806, so late as November 20; and Mr Sweet mentions having seen one pass over his garden, near London, November 23, 1828. The day was fine, and flies plentiful; but, he asks, how did it subsist during the severe frosty days that were past? The earliest period noticed by that keen observer of nature is on the 3d April, 1803; while he records having seen the sand-marten (*H. riparia*) on the 31st March, in the years 1818 and 1822, the former at Penzance, and adds, "I have been informed by an intelligent friend, that a house-swallow once took up its residence late in the autumn within St Mary's Church at Warwick, and was regularly observed there by the congregation until Christmas eve, after which it disappeared, and was seen no more." These birds arrive in the following order:—The sand-marten, the house-swallow, house-marten, swift.—ED.

† The grasshopper lark.—ED.
‡ The yellow willow-wren.—ED. .

I perceive there are more than one species of the *motacilla trochilus*; Mr Derham supposes, in Ray's *Philosophical Letters*, that he has discovered three. In these, there is again an instance of some very common birds that have as yet no English name.*

Mr Stillingfleet makes a question whether the black-cap (*motacilla atricapilla*) be a bird of passage or not. I think there is no doubt of it; for, in April, in the first fine weather, they come trooping in all at once into these parts, but are never seen in the winter.† They are delicate songsters.

Numbers of snipes breed every summer in some moory ground on the verge of this parish. It is very amusing to see the cock bird on wing at that time, and to hear his piping and humming notes.

I have had no opportunity yet of procuring any of those mice which I mentioned to you in town. The person that brought me the last says they are plenty in harvest, at which time I will take care to get more; and will endeavour to put the matter out of doubt whether it be a nondescript species or not.

I suspect much there may be two species of water-rats. Ray says, and Linnæus after him, that the water-rat is web-footed behind. Now, I have discovered a rat on the banks of our little stream that is not web-footed, and yet is an excellent swimmer and diver: it answers exactly to the *mus amphibius* of Linnæus, (see *Syst. Nat.*) which, he says, " *natat in fossis et urinatur.*" I should be glad to procure one " *plantis palmatis.*" Linnæus seems to be in a puzzle about his *mus amphibius*, and to doubt whether it differs from his *mus terrestris*; which, if it be, as he allows, the " *mus agrestis capite grandi brachyuros*" of Ray, is widely different from the water-rat, both in size, make, and manner of life.

As to the *falco*, which I mentioned in town, I shall take the liberty to send it down to you into Wales; presuming on your candour, that you will excuse me if it should appear as familiar to you as it is strange to me. Though mutilated, " *qualem dices . . . antehac fuisse, tales cum sint reliquiæ!*"

It haunted a marshy piece of ground in quest of wild ducks and snipes; but, when it was shot, had just knocked down a rook, which it was tearing in pieces. I cannot make it

---

* The three species are, the one mentioned in the text, the common willow-wren, and the least willow-wren, or chiff-chaff. — ED.

† The black-cap is unquestionably migratory; it appears about the middle of April and retires in September. — ED.

answer to any of our English hawks; neither could I find any like it at the curious exhibition of stuffed birds in Spring Gardens. I found it nailed up at the end of a barn, which is the countryman's museum.

The parish I live in is a very abrupt uneven country, full of hills and woods, and therefore full of birds.

LETTER XI.

TO THOMAS PENNANT, ESQ.

SELBORNE, *September* 9, 1767.

IT will not be without impatience that I shall wait for your thoughts with regard to the *falco*. As to its weight, breadth, &c. I wish I had set them down at the time; but, to the best of my remembrance, it weighed two pounds and eight ounces, and measured, from wing to wing, thirty-eight inches. Its cere and feet were yellow, and the circle of its eyelids a bright yellow. As it had been killed some days, and the eyes were sunk, I could make no good observation on the colour of the pupils and the irides.

The most unusual birds I ever observed in these parts were a pair of hoopoes, (*upupa*,) which came, several years ago, in the summer, and frequented an ornamented piece of ground, which joins to my garden, for some weeks. They used to march about in a stately manner, feeding in the walks, many times in the day, and seemed disposed to breed in my outlet; but were frighted and persecuted by idle boys, who never let them be at rest.*

* In Latham's *General Synopsis*, there is an account of a young hoopoe having been shot in May. These birds have been seen in many parts of Great Britain, from Devonshire to the north of Scotland. Some years ago, one was shot near Banff; and it has been killed in Devonshire and South Wales. Mr Selby says, " the specimen in my possession, and from which the figure in my illustrations is taken, was caught, after some severe weather, and overcome by fatigue, upon the sea coast of Northumberland, near Bamburgh Castle." The Rev. Percival Hunter says, they were frequently seen, during the brumal months, in various parts of Kent, in 1829. The *upupa epops* can only be reckoned an occasional visitant, its chief residence, during the summer months, being the south of Europe, from whence it migrates to Africa. Colonel Williamson, late of the 92d regiment, informed us, that it is to be met with, in vast numbers, near Ceuta, in Africa, opposite to Gibraltar, during the whole year. The nest is formed of bents, and lined with soft materials; it is built in the hollow of a tree, and is said to be extremely fetid. The eggs are four in number, bluish white, spotted with pale brown. — ED.

Three grossbeaks (*loxia coccothraustes*) appeared, some years ago, in my fields, in the winter; one of which I shot. Since that, now and then one is occasionally seen in the same dead season. *

A crossbill (*loxia curvirostra*) was killed last year in this neighbourhood. †

Our streams, which are small, and rise only at the end of the village, yield nothing but the bull's-head, or miller's-thumb, (*gobius fluviatilis capitatus,*) the trout, (*trutta fluviatilis,*) the eel, (*anguilla,*) the lampern, (*lampætra parva et fluviatilis,*) and the stickleback, (*pisciculus aculeatus.*‡)

* This is the hawfinch of British naturalists; the *fringilla coccothraustes* of Temminck; and is only an occasional autumnal visitant, continuing with us till the month of April. It seldom visits the northern counties. There is, however, one instance recorded by T. F. of London, in the first volume of the *Magazine of Natural History*, p. 374. He says, — " On the 14th May, 1828, the nest of a hawfinch was taken in an orchard belonging to Mr Waring, at Chelsfield, Kent. The old female was shot on the nest, which was of a slovenly, loose form, and shallow, not being so deep as those of the greenfinch or linnet, and was placed against the large bough of an apple tree, about ten feet from the ground. It was composed externally of dead twigs and a few roots, mixed with coarse white moss, or lichen, and lined with horse hair and a little fine, dried grass. The eggs were five in number, about the size of a skylark's, but shorter and rounder, and spotted with bluish ash and olive brown, some of the spots inclining to dusky, or blackish brown. The markings were variously distributed on the different eggs." It is a native of Italy, Germany, Sweden, and South of France. — ED.

† The crossbill is only an occasional visitant in Britain, and generally appear in large flocks. Mr Selby mentions that, in June, 1821, a vast number visited Britain, and spread themselves through the country in all places where fir trees were abundant, the cones of which being their principal food. These consisted chiefly of females. A pretty large flock made its appearance in the neighbourhood of Ambleside, Westmoreland, in November, 1828. Their favourite haunt was a plantation of young larches. The crossbill is a native of Northern Europe. — ED.

‡ There are five species of sticklebacks inhabiting the British streams, three of which were discovered by Mr Yarrell. In the *Magazine of Natural History*, we have a curious account of the pugnacious propensities of these little animals. " Having, at various times," says a correspondent, " kept these little fish during the spring, and part of the summer months, and paid close attention to their habits, I am enabled, from my own experience, to vouch for the facts I am about to relate. I have generally kept them in a deal tub, about three feet two inches wide, and about two feet deep. When they are put in, for some time, probably a day or two, they swim about in a shoal, apparently exploring their new habitation. Suddenly one will take possession of the tub, or, as it will sometimes happen, the bottom, and will instantly commence an attack upon his companions; and, if any of them venture to oppose his sway, a regular and most furious battle ensues. They swim round and round,

We are twenty miles from the sea, and almost as many from a great river; and, therefore, see but little of sea birds. As to wild fowls, we have a few teams of ducks, bred in the moors where the snipes breed; and multitudes of widgeons and teals, in hard weather, frequent our lakes in the forest.

Having some acquaintance with a tame brown owl, I find that it casts up the fur of mice, and the feathers of birds, in pellets, after the manner of hawks; when full, like a dog, it hides what it cannot eat.

The young of the barn owl are not easily raised, as they want a constant supply of fresh mice; whereas the young of the brown owl will eat indiscriminately all that is brought snails, rats, kittens, puppies, magpies, and any kind of carrion or offal.

The house-martens have eggs still, and squab young. The last swift I observed was about the 21st of August; it was a straggler.

Redstarts, flycatchers, white-throats, and *reguli non cristati*, still appear; but I have seen no black-caps lately.

I forgot to mention, that I once saw, in Christ Church College quadrangle, in Oxford, on a very sunny, warm morning, a house-marten flying about, and settling on the parapet, so late as the 20th of November.

At present, I know only two species of bats, the common *vespertilio murinus* and the *vespertilio auribus*.*

each with the greatest rapidity; biting, (their mouths being well furnished with teeth,) and endeavouring to pierce each other with their lateral spines, which, on these occasions, are projected. I have witnessed a battle of this sort, which lasted several minutes before either would give way; and, when one does submit, imagination can hardly conceive the vindictive fury of the conqueror, who, in the most persevering and unrelenting way, chases his rival from one part of the tub to another, until fairly exhausted with fatigue. From this period an interesting change takes place in the conqueror, who, from being a speckled and greenish looking fish, assumes the most beautiful colours; the belly and lower jaws becoming a deep crimson, and the back sometimes a cream colour, but generally a fine green; and the whole appearance full of animation and spirit. I have occasionally known three or four parts of the tub taken possession of by these little tyrants, who guard their territories with the strictest vigilance, and the slightest invasion brings on invariably a battle. A strange altera-tion immediately takes place in the defeated party: his gallant bearing forsakes him; his gay colours fade away; he becomes again speckled and ugly; and he hides his disgrace among his peaceable companions." It is the male fish only which are so pugnacious. — ED.

* Seven species of bats have now been ascertained; namely, the horse-shoe bat, (*rhinolophus ferrum-equinum* of Geoffroy,) discovered by Colonel Montagu, in caverns, at Torquay, Devonshire; the lesser

I was much entertained last summer with a tame bat, which would take flies out of a person's hand. If you gave it any thing to eat, it brought its wings round before the mouth, hovering and hiding its head in the manner of birds of prey when they feed. The adroitness it shewed in shearing off the wings of the flies, which were always rejected, was worthy of observation, and pleased me much. Insects seemed to be most acceptable, though it did not refuse raw flesh when offered ; so that the notion, that bats go down chimneys and gnaw men's bacon, seems no improbable story. While I amused myself with this wonderful quadruped, I saw it several times confute the vulgar opinion, that bats, when down on a flat surface, cannot get on the wing again, by rising with great ease from the floor. It ran, I observed, with more despatch than I was aware of ; but in a most ridiculous and grotesque manner.

Bats drink on the wing, like swallows, by sipping the surface, as they play over pools and streams. They love to frequent waters, not only for the sake of drinking, but on account of insects, which are found over them in the greatest plenty. As I was going some years ago, pretty late, in a boat from Richmond to Sunbury, on a warm summer's evening, I think I saw myriads of bats between the two places ; the air swarmed with them all along the Thames, so that hundreds were in sight at a time.

LETTER XII.

TO THOMAS PENNANT, ESQ.

November 4, 1767.

It gave me no small satisfaction to hear that the *falco* * turned out an uncommon one. I must confess I should have been better pleased to have heard that I had sent you a bird that you had never seen before ; but that, I find, would be a difficult task.

horse-shoe bat, (*r. hipposideros,*) discovered by the same gentleman in Wiltshire and Devonshire; the common bat, the emarginated bat, (*vespertilio emarginatus,*) discovered by Dr Fleming in Fife; the great bat, (*v. noctula,*) of our author; the eared bat, (*plecotus auritus,*) of Pennant; and the barbed bat, (*p. burbastellus,*) found in Devonshire by Colonel Montagu, and at Dartford, in Kent, by Mr Peel. — Ed.

Mr John Greig, author of the *Heavens Displayed,* &c. saw a bat flying about in February, in England, during a very hard frost and deep snow. — Ed.

* This hawk proved to be the *falco peregrinus* — a variety.

THE BOHEMIAN WAXWING.

I have procured some of the mice mentioned in my former letters,—a young one, and a female with young, both of which I have preserved in brandy. From the colour, shape, size, and manner of nesting, I make no doubt but that the species is nondescript. They are much smaller, and more slender, than the *mus domesticus medius* of Ray, and have more of the squirrel or dormouse colour. Their belly is white; a straight line along their sides divides the shades of their back and belly. They never enter into houses; are carried into ricks and barns with the sheaves; abound in harvest; and build their nests amidst the straws of the corn above the ground, and sometimes in thistles. They breed as many as eight at a litter, in a little round nest composed of the blades of grass or wheat.

One of these nests I procured this autumn, most artificially platted, and composed of the blades of wheat; perfectly round, and about the size of a cricket-ball; with the aperture so ingeniously closed, that there was no discovering to what part it belonged. It was so compact and well filled, that it would roll across the table without being discomposed, though it contained eight little mice that were naked and blind. As this nest was perfectly full, how could the dam come at her litter respectively, so as to administer a teat to each? Perhaps she opens different places for that purpose, adjusting them again when the business is over; but she could not possibly be contained herself in the ball with her young, which, moreover, would be daily increasing in bulk. This wonderful procreant cradle, an elegant instance of the efforts of instinct, was found in a wheat field suspended in the head of a thistle.

A gentleman, curious in birds, wrote me word that his servant had shot one last January, in that severe weather, which he believed would puzzle me. I called to see it this summer, not knowing what to expect; but, the moment I took it in hand, I pronounced it the male *garrulus bohemicus*, or German silk-tail, from the five peculiar crimson tags, or points, which it carries at the ends of five of the short remiges. It cannot, I suppose, with any propriety, be called an English bird; and yet I see, by Ray's *Philosophical Letters*, that great flocks of them, feeding on haws, appeared in this kingdom in the winter of 1685.*

* This beautiful bird (the *ampelis garrula* of Temminck) is a frequent visitor of Britain, and always appears in flocks. The Rev. Perceval Hunter mentions a flock of them having been seen in Kent in 1828. Bewick remarks that great numbers were taken in Northumberland in the years 1789 and 1790. In 1810, large flocks were dispersed through

The mention of haws puts me in mind that there is a total failure of that wild fruit, so conducive to the support of many of the winged nation. For the same severe weather, late in the spring, which cut off all the produce of the more tender and curious trees, destroyed also that of the more hardy and common.

Some birds, haunting with the missel-thrushes, and feeding on the berries of the yew-tree, which answered to the description of the *merula torquata*, or ringousel, were lately seen in this neighbourhood. I employed some people to procure me a specimen, but without success.

Query—Might not Canary birds be naturalized to this climate, provided their eggs were put, in the spring, into the nests of some of their congeners, as gold-finches, green-finches, &c.? Before winter, perhaps, they might be hardened, and able to shift for themselves.*

About ten years ago, I used to spend some weeks yearly at Sunbury, which is one of those pleasant villages lying on the Thames, near Hampton Court. In the autumn I could not help being much amused with those myriads of the swallow kind which assemble in those parts. But what struck me most was, that, from the time they began to congregate, forsaking the chimneys and houses, they roosted every night in the osierbeds of the aits of that river. Now this resorting towards that element, at that season of the year, seems to give some countenance to the northern opinion (strange as it is) of their retiring under water. A Swedish naturalist is so much persuaded of that fact, that he talks, in his Calendar of Flora, as familiarly of the swallow's going under water in the beginning of September, as he would of his poultry going to roost a little before sunset.†

various districts of Britain. Mr Selby mentions some having been observed in 1822; and one was shot at Edinburgh, in December 1830; another was shot at Coventry; and, during the years 1829, 1830, and 1831, there have been recorded no fewer than twenty specimens, killed in the counties of Suffolk and Norfolk. — ED.

* Various experiments have been tried to naturalize Canary birds in Britain, but they have all proved abortive. — ED.

† Our author seems strongly inclined to the doctrine of the submersion of the swallow tribe during winter; but the temperature of places situated at great depths below the surface of the land and water, is sufficient objection to the circumstance of birds remaining in a torpid state, during the winter, in solitary caverns, or at the bottom of deep lakes, as many authors have affirmed.

It is an established fact, that all places situated eighty feet below the surface of the earth are constantly of the same temperature. In these

An observing gentleman in London writes me word, that he saw a house-marten, on the 23d of last October, flying in and out of its nest in the Borough; and I myself, on the 29th of last October, (as I was travelling through Oxford,) saw four or five swallows hovering round and settling on the roof of the County Hospital.

Now, is it likely that these poor little birds (which, perhaps, had not been hatched but a few weeks) should, at that late season of the year, and from so midland a county, attempt a voyage to Goree or Senegal, almost as far as the equator?*

I acquiesce entirely in your opinion, that, though most of the swallow kind may migrate, yet some do stay behind and hide with us during the winter.

As to the short-winged soft-billed birds, which come trooping in such numbers in the spring, I am at a loss even what to suspect about them. I watched them narrowly this year, and saw them abound till about Michaelmas, when they appeared no longer. Subsist they cannot openly among us, and yet elude the eyes of the inquisitive; and as to their hiding, no man pretends to have found any of them in a torpid state in the winter. But with regard to their migration, what difficulties attend that supposition! that such feeble bad fliers (who the summer long never flit but from hedge to hedge) should be able to traverse vast seas and continents, in order to enjoy milder seasons amidst the regions of Africa!

LETTER XIII.

TO THOMAS PENNANT, ESQ.

SELBORNE, *January* 22, 1768.

As, in one of your former letters, you expressed the more satisfaction from my correspondence on account of my living in the most southerly county; so now I may return the compliment, and expect to have my curiosity gratified by your living much more to the north.

For many years past I have observed that, towards Christmas, vast flocks of chaffinches have appeared in the fields—many more, I used to think, than could be hatched in any one

situations, therefore, the sun can have no influence; and what else would call forth the dormant organs of these birds into action? It is but reasonable to conclude that cold, which kept them benumbed by its sleepy torpor, would evidently perpetuate their slumbers. — ED.

* See Adanson's *Voyage to Senegal.*

neighbourhood. But, when I came to observe them much more narrowly, I was amazed to find that they seemed to me to be almost all hens. I communicated my suspicions to some intelligent neighbours, who, after taking pains about the matter, declared that they also thought them all mostly females; at least fifty to one. This extraordinary occurrence brought to my mind the remark of Linnæus, that, " before winter, all their hen chaffinches migrate through Holland into Italy." Now, I want to know, from some curious person in the north, whether there are any large flocks of these finches with them in the winter, and of which sex they mostly consist ? For, from such intelligence, one might be able to judge whether our female flocks migrate from the other end of the island, or whether they come over to us from the Continent.*

We have, in the winter, vast flocks of the common linnets, more, I think, than can be bred in any one district. These, I observe, when the spring advances, assemble on some tree in the sunshine, and join all in a gentle sort of chirping, as if they were about to break up their winter quarters, and betake themselves to their proper summer homes. It is well known, at least, that the swallows and the fieldfares do congregate with a gentle twittering before they make their respective departures.†

You may depend on it, that the bunting, *emberiza miliaria*, does not leave this country in the winter. In January, 1767, I saw several dozens of them, in the midst of a severe frost, among the bushes on the downs near Andover; in our woodland enclosed districts it is a rare bird. ‡

---

* Mr Selby says, that " in Northumberland and Scotland, this separating takes place about the month of November; and from that period till the return of spring, few females are to be seen, and these few in distinct societies." To this, however, there are exceptions, as we have met them of both sexes during the depths of winter. We can say confidently, that during several years' residence in the county of Fife, the females in our shrubbery and garden were as plentiful as the males; and that the sexes were not separated into distinct societies. — ED.

† Linnets in a state of captivity do not acquire the fine colours with which they are adorned during the summer months while at freedom; the fine red tinge of the nuptial season never appearing.

" At once brilliant and soft," says Bechstein, " the song of the linnet consists of many irregular notes, tastefully put together, in a clear and sonorous tone, which continues the whole year, except in the moulting season."—ED.

‡ The common buntings congregate during winter, but do not migrate. We, however, receive accessions of them at the fall, from more

Wagtails, both white and yellow, are with us all the winter. Quails crowd to our southern coast, and are often killed in numbers by people that go on purpose.*

Mr Stillingfleet, in his *Tracts*, says, that, " if the wheatear (*œnanthe*) does not quit England, it certainly shifts places ; for, about harvest, they are not to be found where there was before great plenty of them." This well accounts for the vast quantities that are caught about that time on the south downs near Lewes, where they are esteemed a delicacy. There have been shepherds, I have been credibly informed, that have made many pounds in a season by catching them in traps. And though such multitudes are taken, I never saw (and I am well acquainted with those parts) above two or three at a time ; for they are never gregarious.† They may perhaps migrate in general ; and, for that purpose, draw towards the coast of Sussex in autumn ; but that they do not all withdraw I am sure, because I see a few stragglers in many counties, at all times of the year, especially about warrens and stone quarries.

I have no acquaintance at present among the gentlemen of the navy, but have written to a friend, who was a sea chaplain in the late war, desiring him to look into his minutes, with respect to birds that settled on their rigging during their voyage up or down the Channel. What Hasselquist says on

northerly climates, which probably leave us again in the spring. In winter they become familiar, and often visit farm-yards in large flocks. Mr Knapp says, " I witnessed this morning a rick of barley entirely stripped of its thatching, which the buntings had effected, by seizing the end of the straw, and deliberately drawing it out, to search for any grain that might yet remain. The sparrow and other birds will burrow in the stack, and pilfer the corn ; and the deliberate operations of unroofing the edifice appears to be peculiar to the bunting."

There is considerable difficulty in conceiving how short-winged birds, which must be bad flyers, should be able to cross extensive tracts of water. St Pierre says, " Towards the end of September, the quails avail themselves of a northerly wind to take their departure from Europe, and flapping one wing, while they present the other to the gale, half sail, half oar, they graze the billows of the Mediterranean with their feathered rumps, and bring themselves to the sands of Africa, that they may serve as food to the famished inhabitants of Zara."— Ed.

* The spring wag-tail is migratory ; it visits us in May, and departs in September. It is said to be found in Siberia and Russia in summer. It continues in France the whole year.

† Our author is wrong in stating that this species is *never* gregarious ; for we are informed by Montagu, that on the 24th of March, 1804, a vast flock of these birds, consisting entirely of males, made their appearance on the south Devon coast, near Kingsbridge, and continued in flocks during the day, busied in search of food. — Ed.

that subject is remarkable : there were little short-winged birds frequently coming on board the ship all the way from our Channel quite up to the Levant, especially before squally weather.

What you suggest with regard to Spain is highly probable. The winters of Andalusia are so mild, that, in all likelihood, the soft-billed birds that leave us at that season may find insects sufficient to support them there.

Some young man, possessed of fortune, health, and leisure, should make an autumnal voyage into that kingdom, and should spend a year there, investigating the natural history of that vast country. Mr Willughby passed through that kingdom on such an errand; but he seems to have skirted along in a superficial manner, and an ill humour, being much disgusted at the rude, dissolute manners of the people.

I have no friend left now at Sunbury to apply to about the swallows roosting on the aits of the Thames ; nor can I hear any more about those birds which I suspected were *merulæ torquatæ*.

As to the small mice,* I have farther to remark, that though they hang their nests for breeding up amidst the straws of the standing corn, above the ground, yet I find that, in the winter, they burrow deep in the earth, and make warm beds of grass; but their grand rendezvous seems to be in corn ricks, into which they are carried at harvest. A neighbour housed an oat rick lately, under the thatch of which were assembled near a hundred, most of which were taken ; and some I saw. I measured them, and found that, from nose to tail, they were just two inches and a quarter, and their tails just two inches long. Two of them, in a scale, weighed down just one copper halfpenny, which is about the third of an ounce avoirdupois ; so that I suppose they are the smallest quadrupeds in this island. A full grown *mus medius domesticus* weighs, I find, one ounce lumping weight, which is more than six times as much as the mouse above, and measures, from nose to rump, four inches and a quarter, and the same in its tail. We have had a very severe frost and deep snow this month. My thermometer was one day fourteen degrees and a half below the freezing point, within doors. The tender evergreens were injured pretty much. It was very providential that the air was still, and the ground well covered with snow, else

---

* This is the harvest mouse, or *mus messorius*, of Shaw's *Zoology*, and first discovered by White. — ED.

vegetation in general must have suffered prodigiously. There is reason to believe that some days were more severe than any since the year 1739-40.

LETTER XIV.

TO THOMAS PENNANT, ESQ.

SELBORNE, *March* 12, 1768.

DEAR SIR,—If some curious gentleman would procure the head of a fallow deer, and have it dissected, he would find it furnished with two spiracula, or breathing places, besides the nostrils ; probably analogous to the *puncta lachrymalia* in the human head.* When deer are thirsty, they plunge their noses, like some horses, very deep under water, while in the act of drinking, and continue them in that situation for a considerable time ; but, to obviate any inconveniency, they can open two vents, one at the inner corner of each eye, having a communication with the nose. Here seems to be an extraordinary provision of nature worthy our attention, and which has not, that I know of, been noticed by any naturalist : for it looks as if these creatures would not be suffocated, though both their mouths and nostrils were stopped. This curious formation of the head may be of singular service to beasts of chase, by affording them free respiration ; and no doubt these additional nostrils are thrown open when they are hard run.† Mr Ray observed, that at Malta the owners slit up the nostrils of such asses as were hard worked ; for they, being naturally strait or small, did not admit air sufficient to serve them when they travelled or laboured in that hot climate. And we know that grooms and gentlemen of the turf, think large nostrils necessary, and a perfection, in hunters and running horses.

Oppian, the Greek poet, by the following line, seems to have had some notion that stags have four spiracula : —

---

* This is termed the lachrymal sinus, is common to the whole of the genus *cervus*, and exists in many of the antelopes.—ED.

† In answer to this account, Mr Pennant sent me the following curious and pertinent reply : — " I was much surprised to find in the antelope something analogous to what you mention as so remarkable in deer. This animal also has a long slit beneath each eye, which can be opened and shut at pleasure. On holding an orange to one, the creature made as much use of those orifices as of his nostrils, applying them to the fruit, and seeming to smell it through them."

Τετραδυμοι ρ᾿ ινες, πισυρες πνοιησι διαυλοι.
Quadrifidæ nares, quadruplices ad respirationem canales.
Opp. *Cyn.* Lib. ii. l. 181.

Writers, copying from one another, make Aristotle say, that goats breathe at their ears, whereas he asserts just the contrary : — Αλχμαιων γαρ ουχ αληθη λεγει, φαμενος αναπνειν τας αιγας χατα τα ωτα.—" Alcmæon does not advance what is true, when he avers that goats breathe through their ears."— *History of Animals,* Book i. chap. xi.

LETTER XV.

TO THOMAS PENNANT, ESQ.

SELBORNE, *March* 30, 1768.

DEAR SIR,— Some intelligent country people have a notion that we have, in these parts, a species of the genus *mustelinum,* besides the weasel, stoat, ferret, and polecat ; a little reddish beast, not much bigger than a field mouse, but much longer, which they call a *cane.* This piece of intelligence can be little depended on ; but farther inquiry may be made.*

A gentleman in this neighbourhood had two milk-white rooks in one nest. A booby of a carter, finding them before they were able to fly, threw them down, and destroyed them, to the regret of the owner, who would have been glad to have preserved such a curiosity in his rookery. I saw the birds myself nailed against the end of a barn, and was surprised to find that their bills, legs, feet, and claws, were milk-white.

A shepherd saw, as he thought, some white larks on a down above my house this winter : were not these the *emberiza nivalis,* the snow-flake of the *British Zoology?* No doubt they were.†

---

* The cane has been satisfactorily proved to be the common weasel. It is called in Suffolk the mouse-hunt.—ED.

† We can see no reason why the bird referred to may not have been a white lark, as well as a snow-bunting. We have seen white birds of many British species. There was a white lark shot in the neighbourhood of Kingston Rectory, near Canterbury, in October, 1828. In the Natural History Magazine there is a notice of a blackbird's nest found at St Anstell, Cornwall, containing two birds, one of them perfectly white. In the summer of 1831, a blackbird's nest was found at Newbottle, near Edinburgh, containing four young ; two of which were of the ordinary colour, and two perfectly white. The former turned out females, and the latter were both male birds. On the grounds of Drumsheugh, the property of our friend Sir Patrick Walker, there was, some years ago, a beautifully mottled blackbird, which became so tame that it fed along

A few years ago, I saw a cock bullfinch in a cage, which had been caught in the fields after it was come to its full colours. In about a year, it began to look dingy, and, blackening every succeeding year, it became coal-black at the end of four. Its chief food was hempseed. Such influence has food on the colour of animals! The pied and mottled colours of domesticated animals are supposed to be owing to high, various, and unusual food. *

I had remarked, for years, that the root of the cuckoo-pint (*arum*) was frequently scratched out of the dry banks of hedges, and in severe snowy weather. After observing, with some exactness, myself, and getting others to do the same, we found it was the thrush kind that searched it out. The root of the *arum* is remarkably warm and pungent.

Our flocks of female chaffinches have not yet forsaken us. The blackbirds and thrushes are very much thinned down by that fierce weather in January.

In the middle of February, I discovered, in my tall hedges, a little bird that raised my curiosity : it was of that yellow-green colour that belongs to the *salicaria* kind, and, I think, was soft-billed. It was no *parus*, and was too long and too big for the golden-crowned wren, appearing most like the largest willow-wren. It hung sometimes with its back downwards, but never continuing one moment in the same place. I shot at it, but it was so desultory that I missed my aim.†

---

with the domestic fowls. It continued at Drumsheugh for some years, and was shot by a gentleman from a back window in Melville Street, who had not heard of it, and supposed it a bird of some very uncommon species. It is now in the museum of Sir Patrick. Another mottled blackbird was some years ago kept in a cage by Mr Veitch, the distinguished optician, at Inchbonny, near Jedburgh. We have seen white crows very often ; a white robin, with red eyes ; a white sparrow, and a white jack-daw. These accidental varieties, we believe, have existed in almost every species of birds. Sir William Jardine mentions a pair of magpies of a cream colour, which were hatched at a farm-steading in Eskdale, Dumfriesshire. In the *Natural History Magazine* it is stated, that a greenfinch was shot in the neighbourhood of Ross, Herefordshire, the prevailing colour of which was a rich yellow, mottled with green, yellow, and dirty white.—ED.

* Food, climate, and domestication, have a great influence in changing the colour of animals. Hence the varied plumage of almost all our domestic birds. In a wild state, the dark colour of most birds is a great safeguard to them against their enemies. Naturalists suppose that this is the reason why birds, which have a very varied plumage, seldom assume their gay attire till the second or third year, when they have acquired cunning and strength to avoid their enemies.—ED.

† In all probability the bearded titmouse.—ED.

I wonder that the stone curlew, *charadrius oedicnemus*, should be mentioned by the writers as a rare bird: it abounds in all the champaign parts of Hampshire and Sussex, and breeds, I think, all the summer, having young ones, I know, very late in the autumn. Already they begin clamouring in the evening. They cannot, I think, with any propriety, be called, as they are by Mr Ray, "*circa aquas versantes;*" for with us (by day at least) they haunt only the most dry, open, upland fields and sheep-walks, far removed from water: what they may do in the night I cannot say. Worms are their usual food, but they also eat toads and frogs.

I can shew you some good specimens of my new mice. Linnæus, perhaps, would call the species *mus minimus.*

LETTER XVL

TO THOMAS PENNANT, ESQ.

SELBORNE, *April* 18, 1768.

DEAR SIR,— The history of the stone curlew, *charadrius oedicnemus*, is as follows:— It lays its eggs, usually two, never more than three, on the bare ground, without any nest, in the field, so that the countryman, in stirring his fallows, often destroys them. The young run immediately from the egg like partridges, &c. and are withdrawn to some flinty field by the dam, where they skulk among the stones, which are their best security; for their feathers are so exactly of the colour of our grey spotted flints, that the most exact observer, unless he catches the eye of the young bird, may be eluded. The eggs are short and round, of a dirty white, spotted with dark bloody blotches. Though I might not be able, just when I pleased, to procure you a bird, yet I could shew you them almost any day; and any evening you may hear them round the village; for they make a clamour which may be heard a mile. *Oedicnemus* is a most apt and expressive name for them, since their legs seem swollen like those of a gouty man. After harvest, I have shot them before the pointers in turnip fields.

I make no doubt but there are three species of the willow-wrens;[*] two I know perfectly, but have not been able yet to

* These are the wood-wren, *s. sibilatrix*, the hay bird, *s. trochilus*, and the chiff-chaff, *s. hippolais*, the latter of which generally appears in this country in the end of April. Mr Sweet says, the chiff-chaff soon becomes familiar in confinement; so much so, that one he captured took a fly out of his hand in three or four days, and "learnt to drink milk out

procure the third. No two birds can differ more in their notes, and that constantly, than those two that I am acquainted with ; for the one has a joyous, easy, laughing note, the other a harsh loud chirp. The former is every way larger, and three quarters of an inch longer, and weighs two drachms and a half, while the 'latter weighs but two; so that the songster is one-fifth heavier than the chirper. The chirper (being the first summer bird of passage that is heard, the wryneck sometimes excepted) begins his two notes in the middle of March, and continues them through the spring and summer, till the end of August, as appears by my journals. The legs of the larger of these two are flesh-coloured ; of the less, black.

The grasshopper lark began his sibilous note in my fields last Saturday.* Nothing can be more amusing than the whisper of this little bird, which seems to be close by, though at an hundred yards' distance ; and, when close at your ear, is scarcely any louder than when a great way off. Had I not been a little acquainted with insects, and known that the grasshopper kind is not yet hatched, I should have hardly believed but that it had been a *locusta* whispering in the bushes. The country people laugh when you tell them that it is the note of a bird. It is a most artful creature, skulking in the thickest part of a bush, and will sing at a yard distance, provided it be concealed. I was obliged to get a person to go on the other side of the hedge where it haunted ; and then it would run, creeping like a mouse before us for an hundred yards together, through the bottom of the thorns ; yet it would not come into fair sight ; but in a morning early, and when undisturbed, it sings on the top of a twig, gaping, and shivering with its wings. Mr Ray himself had no knowledge of this bird, but received his account from Mr Johnston, who apparently confounds it with the *reguli non cristati*, from which it is very distinct. See Ray's *Philosophical Letters*, p. 108.

The fly-catcher (*stoparola*) has not yet appeared : it usually breeds in my vine. The redstart begins to sing : its note is

---

of a tea-spoon, of which it was so fond, that it would fly after it all round the room, and perch on the hand that held it, without shewing the least symptoms of fear ; it would fly up to the ceiling, and bring down a fly in its mouth every time. At last it got so tame, that it would sit on my knee at the fire, and sleep."—ED.

* The grasshopper warbler, *sylvia locustella* of Latham. It is quite distinct in habits and character from the lark genus; it is destitute of the long claw behind ; it resides in thickets, and is incapable of running on the ground like a lark ; its progressive movement consists of hopping. It frequents low and damp situations.—ED.

short and imperfect, but is continued till about the middle of June.*   The willow-wrens (the smaller sort) are horrid pests in a garden, destroying the pease, cherries, currants, &c. and are so tame that a gun will not scare them.

A List of the Summer Birds of Passage discovered in this neighbourhood, ranged somewhat in the order in which they appear.

	LINNÆI NOMINA.
Smallest willow-wren,	*Motacilla trochilus.*
Wry-neck,	*Yunx torquilla.*
House-swallow,	*Hirundo rustica.*
Marten,	*Hirundo urbica.*
Sand-marten,	*Hirundo riparia.*
Cuckoo,	*Cuculus canorus,*
Nightingale,	*Motacilla luscinia.*
Black-cap,	*Motacilla atricapilla.*
White-throat,	*Motacilla sylvia.*
Middle willow-wren,	*Motacilla trochilus.*
Swift,	*Hirundo apus.*
Stone-curlew?	*Charadrius oedicnemus?*
Turtle-dove?	*Turtur aldrovandi?†*
Grasshopper lark,	*Alauda trivialis.*
Landrail,	*Rallus crex.*
Largest willow-wren,	*Motacilla trochilus.*
Redstart,	*Motacilla phœnicurus.*
Goat-sucker, or fern-owl,	*Caprimulgus europæus.*
Fly-catcher,	*Muscicapa grisola.*

My countrymen talk much of a bird that makes a clatter with its bill against a dead bough, or some old pales, calling it a jar-bird. I procured one to be shot in the very fact; it proved to be the *sitta europæa* (the nuthatch.) Mr Ray says,

---

* Bechstein says the song of the redstart, *sylvia phœnicurus*, is lively and agreeable. " One which had built its nest under my house," says he, " imitated very exactly the note of a chaffinch I had in a cage in the window; and my neighbour had another in his garden, which repeated all the notes of the fauvette."

It arrives in this country early in April, and quits us again in the end of September; an instance is, however, recorded, in LOUDON's *Magazine,* of a female having been seen on the cliff called Dumpton Stairs, in the Isle of Thanet, on Christmas day, 1830. — ED.

† Our author, in placing a note of interrogation after this species, seems to doubt its being one of our migratory birds. The turtle dove, *Columba turtur,* of Linnæus, is common enough in the southern counties of England; arriving in the end of April or beginning of May, and departing in September. It has lately been met with as far north as Newcastle-upon-Tyne. Bewick mentions a flock of them which visited

that the less spotted woodpecker does the same. This noise
may be heard a furlong or more. *

Now is the only time to ascertain the short-winged summer
birds ; for, when the leaf is out, there is no making any remarks
on such a restless tribe ; and, when once the young begin to
appear, it is all confusion ; there is no distinction of genus,
species, or sex.

In breeding time, snipes play over the moors, piping and
humming ; they always hum as they are descending. Is not
their hum ventriloquous, like that of the turkey ? Some suspect
that it is made by their wings. †

This morning, I saw the golden-crowned wren, whose crown

Prestwick Car, near Newcastle, in 1794 ; and Selby has one, which was
shot at North Sunderland, in 1818.

Under the craw of the turtle dove, are placed glands, which secrete a
lacteal fluid, probably common to all the genus. — ED.

* A nuthatch, which had been accidentally winged by a sportsman,
was kept in a small cage of plain oak wood and wire. During a night
and a day in which he was in captivity, his tapping labour was incessant ;
and after occupying his prison for that short time, he left the wood-work
pierced and worn like worm-eaten timber. He manifested extreme
impatience at his situation ; he was unremitting in his endeavours to
effect his escape, and in these efforts exhibited much intelligence and
cunning. He was fierce, fearlessly bold, and eat voraciously of food
which was placed before him. At the close of the third day, he sank
under the combined effects of vexation, assiduous labour, and voracious
appetite. This nuthatch was peculiarly laborious under his confinement,
and pecked in a manner different from all other birds ; " grasping hard
with his immense feet, he turned upon them as upon a pivot, and struck
with the whole weight of his body." §

Mr Bree informs us, that having caught a nuthatch in the common
brick trap used by boys, he was struck with the singular appearance of
its bill. It was so obliquely obtuse at the point, that it had the appearance
of being cut off, which he had no doubt was produced by its efforts to
escape. No persecution will force this bold little bird from its nest
during incubation. It defends it with determined courage ; strikes the
intruder with its bill and wings, making all the while a loud hissing noise,
and will allow itself to be taken in the hand rather than yield. — ED.

† The sound proceeds from the throat, and not the wings. Montagu
says, " in the breeding season the snipe changes its note entirely from
that it makes in winter. The male will keep on the wing for an hour
together, mounting like a lark, uttering a shrill piping noise ; it then
descends with great velocity, making a bleating sound, not unlike an old
goat, which is repeated alternately round the spot possessed by the female,
especially while she is sitting on her nest."—ED.

§ *Mag. of Nat. Hist.* i. p. 328 ; II. 242

glitters like burnished gold.   It often hangs, like a titmouse, with its back downwards. *

LETTER XVII.

TO THOMAS PENNANT, ESQ.

SELBORNE, *June* 18, 1768.

DEAR SIR,—On Wednesday last, arrived your agreeable letter of June the 10th.   It gives me great satisfaction to find that you pursue these studies still with such vigour, and are in such forwardness with regard to reptiles and fishes.

The reptiles, few as they are, I am not acquainted with, so well as I could wish, with regard to their natural history. There is a degree of dubiousness and obscurity attending the propagation of this class of animals something analogous to that of the *cryptogamia* in the sexual system of plants; and the case is the same with regard to some of the fishes,—as the eel, &c.†

* This elegant little species is the smallest of British birds; its weight seldom exceeds eighty grains.   This minute bird braves the severest winter of our climates.   Two remarkable instances of its being migratory are recorded by Selby.   He says, on the 24th and 25th October, 1822, "after a very heavy gale and thick fog from the north-west, thousands of these birds were seen to arrive upon the sea shore and sandbanks of the Northumbrian coast."

"A more extraordinary circumstance in the economy of this bird took place during the same winter, viz. the total disappearance of the whole tribe, *natives* as well as strangers, throughout Scotland and the north of England.   This happened towards the conclusion of the month of January, 1823, and a few days previous to the long continued snow-storm, so severely felt through the northern counties of England, and along the eastern parts of Scotland.   The range and point of this migration are unascertained, but it must probably have been a distant one, from the fact, that not a single pair returned to breed or pair the succeeding summer, in the situations they had been known always to frequent : nor was one of the species to be seen till the following October." * —ED.

† Many absurd opinions have prevailed regarding the propagation of eels, such as their originating from the hairs of the mane and tail of horses thrown into rivers, with various other theories equally unfounded. These have arisen from the circumstance that the roe of the eel does not present the same appearance as that of other fishes.   On this intricate subject Mr Couch makes the following observations :— "The generation of eels has been involved in extraordinary obscurity, notwithstanding the attention which eminent naturalists have paid to the subject.   I have no doubt that the pearly substance which lies along the course of the spine

* *Wernerian Memoirs*, v. p. 397.

The method in which toads procreate and bring forth, seems to be very much in the dark. Some authors say that they are viviparous; and yet Ray classes them among his oviparous animals, and is silent with regard to the manner of their bringing forth. Perhaps they may be ἴσω μὲν ὠοτόκοι, ἔξω δὲ ζωοτόκοι, as is known to be the case with the viper.*

The copulation of frogs (or at least the appearance of it— for Swammerdam proves that the male has no *penis intrans*) is notorious to every body; because we see them sticking upon each other's backs, for a month together, in the spring; and

of this fish (the situation of the roe in most fishes) is the roe. Contrary to what is found in most species of fish, this roe contains a large quantity of fine oil, so free from fishy flavour, as to be commonly employed (at least that found in the conger) in crust and other culinary uses in Cornwall. In the fish, its use seems to be to protect the delicate sexual organs from cold. The whole constitution of the eel is remarkably susceptible of cold; it feels every change of temperature. There are no eels in the Danube, nor in any of its tributary streams. The rivers of Siberia, though large and numerous, are destitute of them."

It appears pretty evident that eels are not viviparous, although this opinion has long prevailed amongst naturalists.

That snakes are oviparous there can be little doubt. A correspondent in the *Magazine of Natural History*, iv. p. 268, having killed an adder in Essex, opened it, and "discovered a string of eggs, fourteen in number, in each of which was a young adder, perfectly formed, and enveloped in a glutinous fluid. These little creatures, although they had never seen the light, were lively, and, I thought, even evinced an inclination to bite. I took some of them out of the eggs, and they soon died; but those which were laid on a piece of paper, with their envelope unbroken, were alive and active many hours afterwards. As may be supposed, the present animal was now in nearly an empty state; but, on examining its heart, I perceived that it was still strongly convulsed. I removed it with a penknife; and, laying it on a piece of white paper, was much interested in watching its motions. It continued to beat, with little abatement of force, for an hour, when its palpitations, though strong, became less rapid; and ceased in half an hour more."—ED.

* Toads procreate exactly in the same manner as frogs, and are also oviparous. The eggs are imbued by the spermatic fluid of the male, at the time of their extrusion. The eggs of frogs are deposited in water, in irregular congeries, while those of the toad are extruded in catinated strings. Schneider, a zealous observer of nature, affirms, that toads eat the skin which they cast periodically. This fact has been confirmed by Mr Bell, in a paper in the *Zoological Journal*.

The manner in which a frog takes his prey is very curious. When he first notices a worm or fly, he makes a point at it, like a pointer dog setting game. After a pause of some seconds, the frog makes a dart at the worm, endeavouring to seize it with his mouth; in which attempt he frequently fails more than once, and generally waits for a short interval before he renews the attack.—ED.

yet I never saw, or read of toads being observed in the same situation. It is strange that the matter with regard to the venom of toads has not been yet settled. That they are not noxious to some animals is plain ; for ducks, buzzards, owls, stone-curlews, and snakes, eat them, to my knowledge, with impunity. And I well remember the time, but was not eye-witness to the fact, (though numbers of persons were,) when a quack, at this village, ate a toad to make the country people stare : afterwards he drank oil.

I have been informed also, from undoubted authority, that some ladies (ladies, you will say, of peculiar taste) took a fancy to a toad, which they nourished, summer after summer, for many years, till he grew to a monstrous size, with the maggots which turn to flesh flies. The reptile used to come forth, every evening, from a hole under the garden steps ; and was taken up, after supper, on the table to be fed. But at last a tame raven, kenning him as he put forth his head, gave him such a severe stroke with his horny beak, as put out one eye. After this accident, the creature languished for some time, and died.

I need not remind a gentleman of your extensive reading, of the excellent account there is from Mr Derham, in Ray's *Wisdom of God in the Creation*, p. 365, concerning the migration of frogs from their breeding ponds. In this account, he at once subverts that foolish opinion, of their dropping from the clouds in rain ; shewing, that it is from the grateful coolness and moisture of those showers that they are tempted to set out on their travels, which they defer till those fall.* Frogs

---

* The following paragraph is extracted from a late number of the Belfast Chronicle :— " As two gentlemen were sitting conversing on a causey pillar, near Bushmills, they were very much surprised by an unusually heavy shower of frogs, half formed, *falling* in all directions ; some of which are preserved in spirits of wine, and are now exhibited to the curious by the two resident apothecaries in Bushmills."

Mr Loudon says,— " When at Rouen, in September, 1828, I was assured by an English family, resident there, that, during a very heavy thunder shower, accompanied by violent wind, and almost midnight darkness, an innumerable multitude of young frogs fell on and around the house. The roof, the window-sills, and the gravel walks, were covered with them ; they were very small, but perfectly formed ; all dead ; and the next day being excessively hot, they were dried up to so many points, or pills, about the size of the heads of pins. The most obvious way of accounting for this phenomenon, is by supposing the water and frogs of some adjacent ponds to have been taken up by wind in a sort of whirl, or tornado."—*Mag. of Nat. Hist.* ii. p. 103.

We have records of this kind, in all ages ; and I have selected the above

are as yet in their tadpole state; but, in a few weeks, our lanes, paths, fields, will swarm, for a few days, with myriads of those emigrants, no larger than my little finger nail. Swammerdam gives a most accurate account of the method and situation in which the male impregnates the spawn of the female. How wonderful is the economy of Providence with regard to the limbs of so vile a reptile! While it is an *aquatic*, it has a fish-like tail, and no legs; as soon as the legs sprout, the tail drops off as useless, and the animal betakes itself to the land!

Merret, I trust, is widely mistaken when he advances that the *rana arborea* is an English reptile; it abounds in Germany and Switzerland.*

It is to be remembered that the *salamandra aquatica* of Ray, (the water newt, or eft,) will frequently bite at the angler's bait, and is often caught on his hook. I used to take it for granted, that the *salamandra aquatica* was hatched, lived, and died, in the water. But John Ellis, Esq. F. R. S. (the Coralline Ellis) asserts, in a letter to the Royal Society, dated June the 5th, 1766, in his account of the *mud inguana*, an amphibious *bipes* from South Carolina, that the water eft, or newt, is only the larva of the land eft, as tadpoles are of frogs. Lest I should be suspected to misunderstand his meaning, I shall give it in his own words. Speaking of the *opercula*, or coverings to the gills of the *mud inguana*, he proceeds to say, that " the form of these pennated coverings approaches very near to what I have some time ago observed in the *larva*, or *aquatic* state, of our English *lacerta*, known by the name of eft, or newt, which serve them for coverings to their gills, and for fins to swim with while in this state; and which they lose, as well as the fins of their tails, when they change their state, and

two recent instances, to prove that our author is wrong. A shower of young herrings fell in Kinross-shire, about ten years ago, many of which were picked up, in the fields around Loch Leven, by persons with whom I am acquainted. The reason why frogs go abroad during showers, is thus accounted for by Dr Townson, founded on certain experiments which he instituted regarding them. He says, " That frogs take in their supply of liquid through the *skin* alone, all the aqueous fluids which they imbibe being absorbed by the skin, and all they reject being transpired through it. One frog, in an hour and a half, absorbed nearly its own weight of water."—ED.

* It has never been verified that the tree-frog is a native of Britain. But Mr Don discovered the edible frog, *rana esculenta*, in the neighbourhood of lakes in Forfarshire. This species is principally distinguished from the common one, by its larger size, and having three longitudinal yellow lines on its back.—ED.

become land animals, as I have observed, by keeping them alive for some time, myself." *

Linnæus, in his *Systema Naturæ*, hints at what Mr Ellis advances more than once.

Providence has been so indulgent to us as to allow of but one venomous reptile of the serpent kind in these kingdoms, and that is the viper. As you propose the good of mankind to be an object of your publications, you will not omit to mention common salad oil as a sovereign remedy against the bite of the viper. As to the blind worm, (*anguis fragilis,* so called because it snaps in sunder with a small blow,) I have found, on examination, that it is perfectly innocuous. A neighbouring yeoman (to whom I am indebted for some good hints) killed and opened a female viper about the 27th of May : he found her filled with a chain of eleven eggs, about the size of those of a blackbird ; but none of them were advanced so far towards a state of maturity as to contain any rudiments of young. Though they are oviparous, yet they are viviparous also, hatching their young within their bellies, and then bringing them forth. Whereas snakes lay chains of eggs every summer in my melon beds, in spite of all that my people can do to prevent them ; which eggs do not hatch till the spring following, as I have often experienced. Several intelligent folks assure me, that they have seen the viper open her mouth and admit her helpless young down her throat on sudden surprises, just as the female opossum does her brood into the pouch under her belly, upon the like emergencies ; and yet the London viper catchers insist on it, to Mr Barrington, that no such thing ever happens. The serpent kind eat, I believe, but once in a year ; or, rather, but only just at one season of the year.† Country people talk much of a water snake, but, I am pretty sure, without any reason ; for the common snake (*coluber natrix*) delights much

---

* In an excellent paper on this subject, in the seventeenth numoer of the *Edinburgh Philosophical Journal*, the metamorphoses of these animals are well described ; from which it would appear, that the aquatic salamander is three years of being capable of reproducing ; that its first change from the egg is to the tadpole state, and that it undergoes several changes in progressing to maturity. — ED.

† All the snake tribe eat only periodically, but it is a mistake to suppose they feed but once a year, or at a particular time of the year. After having gorged their prey, they are overcome by a sleepy torpor, and remain for days, and sometimes even weeks, in this state, when they again become lively, and crawl abroad in quest of prey. Most of the tribe, like nearly the whole amphibia, cast their skins periodically. — ED.

to sport in the water, perhaps with a view to procure frogs, and other food. *

I cannot well guess how you are to make out your twelve species of reptiles, unless it be by the various species, or rather varieties, of our *lacerti*, of which Ray enumerates five. † I have not had opportunity of ascertaining these, but remember well to have seen, formerly, several beautiful green *lacerti* on the sunny sandbanks near Farnham, in Surrey ; and Ray admits there are such in Ireland.

.

LETTER XVIII.

TO THOMAS PENNANT, ESQ.

Selborne, *July* 27, 1768.

Dear Sir,—I received your obliging and communicative letter of June the 28th, while I was on a visit at a gentleman's house, where I had neither books to turn to, nor leisure to sit down, to return you an answer to many queries, which I wanted to resolve in the best manner that I am able.

A person, by my order, has searched our brooks, but could find no such fish as the *gasterosteus pungitius ;* he found the *gasterosteus aculeatus* in plenty.‡ This morning, in a basket, I packed a little earthen pot full of wet moss, and in it some sticklebacks, male and female, the females big with spawn ; some lamperns ; some bull-heads ; but I could procure no minnows. This basket will be in Fleet Street by eight this evening ; so I hope Mazel will have them fresh and fair

---

* The whole of the snake tribe take the water: we have numerous records of this fact. They swim with much ease, and in America frequently cross the great rivers. The natives say they catch fish. Mr Murray mentions a curious instance of an adder having seized the artificial fly of an individual fishing in one of the lakes of Scotland, on the verge of the estuary of a river. It was finally drowned by dragging it into the current against the stream.

On the 2d August, 1828, a fisherman caught a specimen of the ringed-snake, (*coluber natrix* of Linnæus,) while fishing in Haslar Lake, one of the branches of Portsmouth Harbour; and, on the following morning, a seaman caught another at the same place, both of which were brought to Mr Slight, surgeon, Portsmouth.—Ed.

† There have been just twelve species of reptiles discovered in Britain up to the present time.—Ed.

‡ The *gasterosteus pungitius*, or ten-spined stickleback, is very common in our rivers and in estuaries ; few British species have been ascertained. Besides the above two, there are the *g. trachurus, g. semiarmatus,* and *g. leiurus.* See note at page 26.—Ed.

to-morrow morning. I gave some directions, in a letter, to what particulars the engraver should be attentive.

Finding, while I was on a visit, that I was within a reasonable distance of Ambresbury, I sent a servant over to that town, and procured several living specimens of loaches, which he brought, safe and brisk, in a glass decanter. They were taken in the gulleys that were cut for watering the meadows. From these fishes (which measured from two to four inches in length) I took the following description :— The loach, in its general aspect, has a pellucid appearance; its back is mottled with irregular collections of small black dots, not reaching much below the *linea lateralis*, as are the back and tail fins ; a black line runs from each eye down to the nose; its belly is of a silvery white ; ·the upper jaw projects beyond the lower, and is surrounded with six feelers, three on each side; its pectoral fins are large, its ventral much smaller ; the fin behind its anus small; its dorsal fin large, containing eight spines ; its tail, where it joins to the tail fin, remarkably broad, without any taperness, so as to ·be characteristic of this genus; the tail fin is broad, and square at the end. From the breadth and muscular strength of the tail, it appears to be an active nimble fish. *

In my visit I was not very far from Hungerford, and did not forget to make some inquiries concerning the wonderful method of curing cancers by means of toads. Several intelligent persons, both gentry and clergy, do, I find, give a great deal of credit to what was asserted in the papers ; and I myself dined with a clergyman who seemed to be persuaded that what is related is matter of fact; but, when I came to attend to his account, I thought I discerned circumstances which did not a little invalidate the woman's story of the manner in which she came by her skill. She says of herself, that, " labouring under a virulent cancer, she went to some church where there was a vast crowd ; on going into a pew, she was accosted by a strange clergyman, who, after expressing compassion for her situation, told her, that if she would make such an application of living toads as is mentioned, she would be well." Now, is it likely that this unknown gentleman should express so much tenderness for this single sufferer, and not feel any for the many thousands that daily languish under this terrible disorder ? Would he not have made use of

---

* The species above described is the *cobitis barbatula*, or bearded loach : there is another species found in most of the streams of Britain, *c. tænia*.—ED.

this invaluable nostrum for his own emolument; or, at least, by some means of publication or other, have found a method of making it public for the good of mankind? In short, this woman, as it appears to me, having set up for a cancer doctress, finds it expedient to amuse the country with this dark and mysterious relation.

The water-eft has not, that I can discern, the least appearance of any gills; for want of which it is continually rising to the surface of the water to take in fresh air. I opened a big-bellied one, indeed, and found it full of spawn. Not that this circumstance at all invalidates the assertion that they are *larvæ*; for the *larvæ* of insects are full of eggs, which they exclude the instant they enter their last state. The water-eft is continually climbing over the brim of the vessel, within which we keep it in water, and wandering away; and people every summer see numbers crawling out of the pools where they are hatched, upon the dry banks. There are varieties of them, differing in colour; and some have fins up their tail and back, and some have not. *

LETTER XIX.

TO THOMAS PENNANT, ESQ.

SELBORNE, *August* 17, 1768.

DEAR SIR, — I have now, past dispute, made out three distinct species of the willow-wrens, *motacillæ trochili*, which constantly and invariably use distinct notes. But, at the same time, I am obliged to confess that I know nothing of your willow-lark.† In my letter of April the 18th, I had told you peremptorily that I knew your willow-lark, but had not seen it then; but, when I came to procure it, it proved, in all respects, a very *motacilla trochilus*; only that it is a size larger than the two other, and the yellow green of the whole upper part of the body is more vivid, and the belly of a clearer white. I have specimens of the three sorts now lying before me, and can discern that there are three gradations of sizes, and that the least has black legs, and the other two flesh-coloured ones. The yellowest bird is considerably the largest, and has its quill feathers and secondary feathers tipped with white,

---

* The eft is liable to a change in the size of its fins during the season of love; at which time the membranes of the tail and back increase considerably.—ED.

† *Brit. Zool.* edit. 1776, octavo, p. 381.

which the others have not. This last haunts only the tops of trees in high beechen woods, and makes a sibilous grasshopper-like noise now and then, at short intervals, shivering a little with its wings when it sings; and is, I make no doubt now, the *regulus non cristatus* of Ray ; which he says, " *cantat voce stridulā locustæ.*" Yet this great ornithologist never suspected that there were three species. *

LETTER XX.

TO THOMAS PENNANT, ESQ.

SELBORNE, *October* 8, 1768.

IT is, I find, in zoology as it is in botany : all nature is so full, that that district produces the greatest variety which is the most examined. Several birds, which are said to belong to the north only, are, it seems, often in the south. I have discovered this summer three species of birds with us, which writers mention as only to be seen in the northern counties. The first that was brought me, on the 14th of May, was the sandpiper, *tringa hypoleucus:* it was a cock bird, and haunted the banks of some ponds near the village ; and, as it had a companion, doubtless intended to have bred near that water. Besides, the owner has told me since, that, on recollection, he has seen some of the same birds round his ponds in former summers. †

The next bird that I procured, on the 21st of May, was a male red backed butcher-bird, *lanius collurio.* My neighbour, who shot it, says that it might easily have escaped his notice, had not the outcries and chattering of the white-throats and other small birds drawn his attention to the bush where it was : its craw was filled with the legs and wings of beetles. ‡

---

* See our note at page 24. —ED.

† This bird is the *totanus hypoleucus* of Temminck. It visits Britain in the spring, and chiefly frequents our lakes and rivers ; on the borders of which it makes a nest composed of moss and dried leaves. Great numbers breed in Scotland. This bird is found in most parts of Europe, even as far north as Siberia. It migrates in October to the shores of Asia and Africa. — ED.

‡ This is rather a local species, although not uncommon in Gloucester-shire and Somersetshire. It visits us in May, and departs in September. The species is very voracious, preying on small birds, and transfixing them to a thorn to feed on. Montagu mentions having found young ones, " which lived in amity for about two months, when violent battles ensued, and two out of the four were killed. The other two were chained

The next rare birds (which were procured for me last week) were some ringousels, *turdi torquati.*

This week twelvemonths a gentleman from London, being with us, was amusing himself with a gun, and found, he told us, on an old yew hedge, where there were berries, some birds like blackbirds, with rings of white round their necks ; a neighbouring farmer also at the same time observed the same ; but, as no specimens were procured, little notice was taken. I mentioned this circumstance to you in my letter of November the 4th, 1767 ; you, however, paid but small regard to what I said, as I had not seen these birds myself : but last week the aforesaid farmer, seeing a large flock, twenty or thirty of these birds, shot two cocks and two hens ; and says, on recollection, that he remembers to have observed these birds again last spring, about Ladyday, as it were, on their return to the north. Now, perhaps these ousels are not the ousels of the north of England, but belong to the more northern parts of Europe ; and may retire before the excessive rigour of the frosts in those parts ; and return to breed in spring, when the cold abates. If this be the case, here is discovered a new bird of winter passage, concerning whose migrations the writers are silent ; but if these birds should prove the ousels of the north of England, then here is a migration disclosed within our own kingdom never before remarked. It does not yet appear whether they retire beyond the bounds of our island to the south ; but it is most probable that they usually do, or else one cannot suppose that they would have continued so long unnoticed in the southern counties.* The ousel is larger than a blackbird, and feeds on haws ; but last autumn (when there were no haws) it fed on yew-berries ; in the spring it feeds on ivy-berries, which ripen only at that season, in March and April.

in the manner goldfinches frequently are; they were extremely docile ; would come to the call for the sake of a fly, of which they were extremely fond ; when raw meat was given them, would endeavour to fasten it to some part of their cage in order to tear it ; would eat mice and small birds cut in pieces, feathers, fur, and bones, disgorging the refuse like the hawk tribe. One was killed by swallowing too large a quantity of mouse fur, which it could not eject.— ED.

* The ring-blackbird, as Selby informs us, is a bird of passage. It arrives in this country in the spring, and immediately resorts to its breeding quarters in the mountainous districts of England and Scotland, preferring the most barren retreats. It migrates in the end of October to France and Germany, but is said to be found in Africa and Asia under different degrees of latitude.— ED.

I must not omit to tell you (as you have been so lately on the study of reptiles) that my people, every now and then, of late, draw up, with a bucket of water from my well, which is sixty-three feet deep, a large black warty lizard, with a fin tail, and yellow belly. How they first came down at that depth, and how they were ever to have got out thence without help, is more than I am able to say.*

My thanks are due to you for your trouble and care in the examination of a buck's head. As far as your discoveries reach at present, they seem much to corroborate my suspicions; and I hope Mr —— may find reason to give his decision in my favour ; and then, I think, we may advance this extraordinary provision of nature as a new instance of the wisdom of God in the creation.

As yet I have not quite done with my history of the *oedicnemus*, or stone-curlew ; for I shall desire a gentleman in Sussex, near whose house these birds congregate in vast flocks in the autumn, to observe nicely when they leave him, (if they do leave him,) and when they return again in the spring : I was with this gentleman lately, and saw several single birds.†

LETTER XXI.

TO THOMAS PENNANT, ESQ.

SELBORNE, *November* 28, 1768.

DEAR SIR,—With regard to the *oedicnemus*, or stone-curlew, I intend to write very soon to my friend near Chichester, in whose neighbourhood these birds seem most to abound ; and shall urge him to take particular notice when they begin to congregate, and afterward to watch them most narrowly, whether they do not withdraw themselves during the dead of

---

* We found a very large specimen of this animal in an old wooden conduit at Fountainbridge, Edinburgh, which had been stopped at both ends for upwards of twenty years. So that the animal must have been, at least, that age, as it was not possible that it could obtain access from the time the conduit was stopped.—ED.

† This is the *oedicnemus crepitans* of Temminck, the stone-curlew of British authors. It is a migratory species, appearing in the latter end of April, or beginning of May, and leaving Britain early in October. It makes no nest, but lays two eggs on the bare ground ; these are of a light brown colour, blotched and streaked with dusky. This bird confines its range to the southern counties, never having been noticed except in Norfolk, Hampshire, Sussex, and Dorsetshire.—ED.

the winter   When I have obtained information with respect
to this circumstance, I shall have finished my history of the
stone-curlew, which I hope will prove to your satisfaction, as
it will be, I trust, very near the truth.   This gentleman, as
he occupies a large farm of his own, and is abroad early and
late, will be a very proper spy upon the motions of these birds;
and besides, as I have prevailed on him to buy the *Naturalist's
Journal*, (with which he is much delighted,) I shall expect that
he will be very exact in his dates.   It is very extraordinary,
as you observe, that a bird so common with us should never
straggle to you.

And here will be the properest place to mention, while I
think of it, an anecdote which the above mentioned gentleman
told me when I was last at his house; which was, that in a
warren joining to his outlet, many daws, *corvi monedulæ*, build
every year in the rabbit burrows under ground.   The way he
and his brothers used to take their nests, while they were boys,
was by listening at the mouths of the holes, and if they heard
the young ones cry, they twisted the nest out with a forked
stick.   Some water fowls (viz. the puffins) breed, I know, in
this manner ; but I should never have suspected the daws of
building in holes on the flat ground. *

Another very unlikely spot is made use of by daws as a
place to breed in, and that is Stonehenge.   These birds
deposit their nests in the interstices between the upright and
the impost stones of that amazing work of antiquity ; which
circumstance alone speaks the prodigious height of the upright
stones, that they should be tall enough to secure those nests
from the annoyance of shepherd boys, who are always idling
round that place.

One of my neighbours last Saturday, (November the 26th,)

* This is a curious illustration of an animal departing from its ordinary
habits.   There is in the trans-Mississippian states of America, a bird
which is habitually a *day owl* — the burrowing owl, *strix cunicularia*
of Bonaparte.   This bird, unlike its congeners, burrows in the ground,
and the nest is always kept in the neatest repair, and frequently inhabited
by several individuals.   When alarmed, they invariably fly to their
subterranean abodes for refuge.   These birds take up their residence in
burrows dug by the marmot in the locality above referred to ; but in
other situations, they dig excavations for themselves.   Unlike the tribe
in general, they are seen only during the day, flying rapidly along, in
search of food or pleasure.   There is no direct evidence that these owls
and the marmot live habitually in one burrow, although they are well
known to fly to the same excavation, under the impulse of fear ; even
rattlesnakes and lizards have been found in the same retreat. — Ed.

saw a marten in a sheltered bottom ; the sun shone warm, and the bird was hawking briskly after flies. I am now perfectly satisfied that they do not all leave this island in the winter.

You judge very right, I think, in speaking with reserve and caution concerning the cures done by toads ; for, let people advance what they will on such subjects, yet there is such a propensity in mankind towards deceiving and being deceived, that one cannot safely relate any thing from common report, especially in print, without expressing some degree of doubt and suspicion.

Your approbation with regard to my new discovery of the migration of the ringousel, gives me satisfaction ; and I find you concur with me in suspecting that they are foreign birds which visit us. You will be sure, I hope, not to omit to make inquiry whether your ringousels leave your rocks in the autumn. What puzzles me most, is the very short stay they make with us ; for in about three weeks they are all gone. I shall be very curious to remark whether they will call on us at their return in the spring, as they did last year.*

I want to be better informed with regard to ichthyology. If fortune had settled me near the sea-side, or near some great river, my natural propensity would soon have urged me to have made myself acquainted with their productions ; but as I have lived mostly in inland parts, and in an upland district, my knowledge of fishes extends little farther than to those common sorts which our brooks and lakes produce.

LETTER XXII.

TO THOMAS PENNANT, ESQ.

SELBORNE, *January* 2, 1769.

DEAR SIR,—As to the peculiarity of jack-daws building with us under the ground, in rabbit burrows, you have, in part, hit upon the reason ; for, in reality, there are hardly any towers or steeples in all this country. And perhaps, Norfolk excepted, Hampshire and Sussex are as meanly furnished with churches as almost any counties in the kingdom. We have many livings of two or three hundred pounds a-year, whose houses of worship make little better appearance than

---

* The ring blackbirds invariably remain a week or two in the cultivated districts of the country previous to their migration, and commit great havock amongst fruits ; seemingly to make up for their more meagre repasts during incubation. — ED.

dovecots. When I first saw Northamptonshire, Cambridge-shire, and Huntingdonshire, and the Fens of Lincolnshire, I was amazed at the number of spires which presented themselves · in every point of view. As an admirer of prospects, I have reason to lament this want in my own country, for such objects are very necessary ingredients in an elegant landscape.

What you mention with respect to reclaimed toads raises my curiosity.* An ancient author, though no naturalist, has

* There have been many instances of toads being tamed. Mr Arscott mentions one which lived upwards of thirty-five years. Not the least wonderful part of the history of the toad, is the circumstance of its being frequently found alive in the heart of solid rocks, and internal cavities of trees. In 1777, Herissant undertook some experiments to ascertain the truth of what has been related on this point. He shut up three toads in sealed boxes in plaster, and they were deposited in the Academy of Sciences. At the end of eighteen months, the boxes were opened, and one of these toads was dead, but the other two were still living. Nobody could doubt the authenticity of this fact; yet the experiments were severely criticised, as well as the observations which they seemed to confirm. It was contended that the air must have come to these animals through some imperceptible hole, which escaped the notice of the observer. Some probability was given to this supposition by the researches of Dr Edwards, published in 1817. He has observed, that toads shut up totally in plaster, and absolutely deprived of air, lived for a greater number of days, and much longer than those which were forced to remain under water. This certainly is one of the most extra-ordinary phenomena which the history of the physiology of reptiles can furnish, and seems to be an exception to the rule that air is indispensable to animal life. It appears, however, that in the above instance, some air did penetrate the plaster, as Dr Edwards afterwards proved by the fact, that as soon as the plaster which enclosed them was placed under water, the toads perished. The opponents of Herissant were therefore justified to a certain extent in their scepticism. Still the facts of animals existing so long a time under such circumstances, even with a little air, is most surprising, and calculated to produce very strange reflections. If these reptiles lived in this manner longer than they would have done in the open dry air, the reason must be, that they had lost less by transpiration; and if they died much later than they would have done in water, it was because the air certainly had some access to them.

Professor Buckland has recently made some experiments, in order to throw light on this obscure subject. Two blocks of stone were taken, one of porous oolite limestone, and one of a compact silicious sand-stone; twelve cells, five inches wide, and six inches deep, were cut in the sandstone, and twelve others, five inches wide, and twelve inches deep, in the limestone. In November, 1825, one live toad was placed in each of the twenty-four cells, its weight being previously ascertained with care. A glass plate was placed over each cell as a cover, with a circular slate above to protect it; and the two blocks of stone, with the immured toads, were buried in Dr Buckland's garden under three feet of earth. They were uncovered after the lapse of a year,

well remarked, that " Every kind of beasts, and of birds, and of serpents, and things in the sea, is tamed, and hath been tamed of mankind." (St James, chap. iii. 7.)

in December, 1826. All the toads in the small cells of compact sandstone were dead, and their bodies so much decayed as to prove that they had been dead for some months. The greater number of the toads in the larger cells of porous limestone were alive; but they were all a good deal emaciated, except two, which had increased in weight, the one from one thousand one hundred and eighty-five grains to one thousand two hundred and sixty-five, the other from nine hundred and eighty-eight to one thousand one hundred and sixteen. With regard to these two, Dr Buckland thinks they had both been nourished by insects, which had got into the one cell through a crack found in the glass cover, and into the other probably by some small aperture in the luting, which was not carefully examined. No insects were found in either cell, but an assemblage of insects was found on the outside of another glass, and a number within one of the cells whose cover was cracked, and where the animal was dead. Of the emaciated toads, one had diminished in weight from nine hundred and twenty-four grains to six hundred and ninety-eight, and one from nine hundred and thirty-six to six hundred and fifty-two. " The results of the experiments," says Dr Buckland, " amount to this : — All the toads, both large and small, enclosed in the sandstone, and the small toads enclosed in the limestone also, were dead at the end of thirteen months. Before the expiration of the second year, all the large ones also were dead. These were examined several times, during the second year, through the glass covers of the cells, but without removing them to admit air. They appeared always awake, with their eyes open, and never in a state of torpor, their meagreness increasing at each interval, until at length they were found dead. Those which had gained an increase of weight at the end of the first year, and were then carefully closed up again, were emaciated and dead before the expiration of the second year." Four toads, enclosed in cavities cut in the trunk of an apple tree, and closed up by plugs so tightly as to exclude insects, and " apparently air," were found dead at the end of a year.

The phenomena, then, of live toads enclosed in rocks, he explains in this way. The young toad, as soon as it leaves its tadpole state, and emerges from the water, seeks shelter in holes and crevices of rocks and , trees. One may thus enter a small opening in a rock, and when there find food, by catching the insects which seek shelter in the same retreat; and its increase of size may prevent it from getting out again by the same opening. It is probable that there are some small apertures in all the stones in which toads are found, though they escape the notice of the workmen, who have no motive to induce them to make a narrow examination. In other cases, there may have been an opening, which had been closed up, after the animal was immured, by stalactitic incrustation. Deprived of food and air, it might fall into that state of torpor, or suspended animation, to which certain animals are subject in winter; but how long it might continue in this state is uncertain.

The Rev. George Young, in his *Geological Survey of the Yorkshire Coast*, second edition, 1828, mentions several recent instances of living toads having been found within solid blocks of sandstone. " We are the

It is a satisfaction to me to find that a green lizard has actually been procured for you in Devonshire, because it corroborates my discovery, which I made many years ago, of the same sort, on a sunny sand-bank near Farnham, in Surrey. I am well acquainted with the south hams of Devonshire, and can suppose that district, from its southerly situation, to be a proper habitation for such animals in their best colours.

Since the ringousels of your vast mountains do certainly not forsake them against winter, our suspicions that those which visit this neighbourhood about Michaelmas are not English birds, but driven from the more northern parts of Europe by the frosts, are still more reasonable ; and it will be worthy your pains to endeavour to trace from whence they come, and to inquire why they make so short a stay.

In your account of your error with regard to the two species of herons, you incidentally gave me great entertainment in your description of the heronry at Cressi-hall, which is a curiosity I never could manage to see. Fourscore nests of such a bird on one tree is a rarity which I would ride half as many miles to have a sight of. Pray be sure to tell me in your next whose seat Cressi-hall is, and near what town it lies.* I have often thought that those vast extents of fens have never been sufficiently explored. If half-a-dozen gentlemen, furnished with a good strength of water spaniels, were to beat them over for a week, they would certainly find more species.

There is no bird, I believe, whose manners I have studied more than that of the *caprimulgus*, the goat-sucker, as it is a wonderful and curious creature ; but I have always found, that though sometimes it may chatter as it flies, as I know it does, yet in general it utters its jarring note sitting on a bough ; and I have for many a half hour watched it as it sat with its under mandible quivering, and particularly this summer. It perches usually on a bare twig, with its head lower than its tail, in an attitude well expressed by your draughtsman in the folio *British Zoology*. This bird is most punctual in beginning its

more particular in recording these facts," he observes, " because some modern philosophers have attempted to explode such accounts as wholly fabulous." Mr Jesse informs us, that he knew a gentleman who put a toad into a small flower-pot, and secured it, so that no insect could penetrate it, and then buried it so deep in his garden that it was secured against the influence of frost. At the end of twenty years, he took it up, and found the toad increased in bulk, and healthy.—Ed.

* Cressi-hall is near Spalding, in Lincolnshire.

song exactly at the close of day ; so exactly, that I have known
it strike up more than once or twice just at the report of the
Portsmouth evening gun, which we can hear when the weather
is still. It appears to me past all doubt, that its notes are
formed by organic impulse, by the powers of the parts of its
windpipe formed for sound, just as cats pur. You will credit
me, I hope, when I assure you, that, as my neighbours were
assembled in an hermitage on the side of a steep hill where
we drink tea, one of these churn-owls came and settled on the
cross of that little straw edifice, and began to chatter, and
continued his note for many minutes ; and we were all struck
with wonder to find that the organs of that little animal, when
put in motion, gave a sensible vibration to the whole building!
This bird also sometimes makes a small squeak, repeated four
or five times ; and I have observed that to happen when the
cock has been pursuing the hen in a toying manner through
the boughs of a tree.

It would not be at all strange if your bat, which you have
procured, should prove a new one, since five species have been
found in a neighbouring kingdom. The great sort that I
mentioned is certainly a nondescript : I saw but one this
summer, and that I had no opportunity of taking.

Your account of the Indian grass was entertaining. I am
no angler myself ; but inquiring of those that are, what they
supposed that part of their tackle to be made of, they replied,
" of the intestines of a silk-worm."

Though I must not pretend to great skill in entomology,
yet I cannot say that I am ignorant of that kind of knowledge :
I may now and then, perhaps, be able to furnish you with a
little information.

The vast rain ceased with us much about the same time as
with you, and since, we have had delicate weather. Mr Barker,
who has measured the rain for more than thirty years, says, in
a late letter, that more rain has fallen this year than in any he
ever attended to ; though, from July, 1763, to January, 1764,
more fell than in any seven months of this year.*

* At Joyeuse, in the department of the Ardéche, during October, 1827,
thirty-six inches of rain in depth fell within eleven days ; and, on the
9th of that month, twenty-nine inches and a half fell within the space of
two hours. During this excessive fall of rain, the barometer remained
nearly stationary, at two or three lines below the mean altitude, notwithstanding the continuance of the most violent thunder and lightning during
the whole time. — ED.

LETTER XXIII.

TO THOMAS PENNANT, ESQ

SELBORNE, *February* 28, 1769.

DEAR SIR,—It is not improbable that the Guernsey lizard and our green lizards may be specifically the same ; all that I know is, that when, some years ago, many Guernsey lizards were turned loose in Pembroke college garden, in the university of Oxford, they lived a great while, and seemed to enjoy themselves very well ; but never bred. Whether this circumstance will prove any thing either way, I shall not pretend to say.

I return you thanks for your account of Cressi-hall ; but recollect, not without regret, that in June, 1746, I was visiting for a week together at Spalding, without ever being told that such a curiosity was just at hand. Pray send me word in your next what sort of tree it is that contains such a quantity of herons' nests ; and whether the heronry consists of a whole grove, or wood, or only of a few trees.

It gave me satisfaction to find we accorded so well about the *caprimulgus ;* all I contended for was, to prove that it often chatters sitting as well as flying, and therefore the noise was voluntary, and from organic impulse, and not from the resistance of the air against the hollow of its mouth and throat.*

---

* This is a common species in the United States of America, and is called by the natives whip-poor-will, from the similarity of his cry to these words. The following interesting account of their cry is given by Wilson : — " Every morning and evening his shrill and rapid repetitions are heard from the adjoining woods ; and, when two or more are calling out at the same time, as is often the case in the pairing season, and at no great distance from each other, the noise, mingling with the echoes from the mountains, is really surprising. Strangers, in parts of the country where these birds are numerous, find it almost impossible for some time to sleep ; while, to those long acquainted with them, the sound often serves as a lullaby to assist their repose.

" These notes seem pretty plainly to articulate the words which have been generally applied to them, *whip-poor-will,* the first and last syllables being uttered with great emphasis, and the whole in about a second to each repetition ; but when two or more males meet, their whip-poor-will altercations become much more rapid and incessant, as if each were straining to overpower or silence the other. When near, you often hear an introductory cluck between the notes. At these times, as well as at almost all others, they fly low, not more than a few feet from the surface, skimming about the house and before the door, alighting on the wood

If ever I saw any thing like actual migration, it was last Michaelmas-day. I was travelling, and out early in the morning . at first there was a vast fog, but, by the time that I was got seven or eight miles from home towards the coast, the sun broke out into a delicate warm day. We were then on a large heath, or common, and I could discern, as the mist began to break away, great numbers of swallows, *hirundines rusticæ*, clustering on the stunted shrubs and bushes, as if they had roosted there all night. As soon as the air became clear and pleasant, they all were on the wing at once ; and, by a placid and easy flight, proceeded on southward, towards the sea : after this I did not see any more flocks, only now and then a straggler.

I cannot agree with those persons that assert, that the swallow kind disappear some and some, gradually, as they come ; for the bulk of them seem to withdraw at once; only some stragglers stay behind a long while, and do never, there is the greatest reason to believe, leave this island. Swallows seem to lay themselves up, and to come forth in a warm day, as bats do continually of a warm evening, after they have disappeared for weeks. For a very respectable gentleman assured me, that, as he was walking with some friends, under Merton-wall, on a remarkably hot noon, either in the last week in December, or the first week in January, he espied three or four swallows huddled together on the moulding of one of the windows of that college. I have frequently remarked that swallows are seen later at Oxford than elsewhere : is it owing to the vast, massy buildings of that place, to the many waters round it, or to what else ?

When I used to rise in a morning last autumn, and see the swallows and martens clustering on the chimneys and thatch of the neighbouring cottages, I could not help being touched with a secret delight, mixed with some degree of mortification : with delight, to observe with how much ardour and punctuality those poor little birds obeyed the strong impulse towards migration, or hiding, imprinted on their minds by their great Creator ; and with some degree of mortification, when I reflected that, after all our pains and inquiries, we are yet not quite certain to what regions they do migrate ; and are still farther embarrassed to find that some actually do not migrate at all.

pile, or settling on the roof. Towards midnight, they generally become silent, unless in clear moonlight, when they are heard, with little intermission, till morning." — ED.

These reflections made so strong an impression on my imagination, that they became productive of a composition, that may perhaps amuse you for a quarter of an hour when next I have the honour of writing to you.

LETTER XXIV.

TO THOMAS PENNANT, ESQ.

SELBORNE, *May* 29, 1769.

DEAR SIR,— The *scarabæus fullo* I know very well, having seen it in collections ; but have never been able to discover one wild in its natural state. Mr Banks told me he thought it might be found on the sea-coast.

On the 13th of April, I went to the sheep-down, where the ringousels have been observed to make their appearance at spring and fall, in their way, perhaps, to the north or south ; and was much pleased to see three birds about the usual spot. We shot a cock and a hen ; they were plump and in high condition. The hen had but very small rudiments of eggs within her, which proves they are late breeders ; whereas those species of the thrush kind that remain with us the whole year have fledged young before that time. In their crops was nothing very distinguishable, but somewhat that seemed like blades of vegetables nearly digested. In autumn they feed on haws and yew-berries, and in the spring on ivy-berries. I dressed one of these birds, and found it juicy and well-flavoured. It is remarkable that they make but a few days' stay in their spring visit, but rest near a fortnight at Michaelmas. These birds, from the observations of three springs and two autumns, are most punctual in their return ; and exhibit a new migration unnoticed by the writers, who supposed they never were to be seen in any of the southern counties.

One of my neighbours lately brought me a new *salicaria,* which, at first, I suspected might have proved your willow-lark,* but on a nicer examination, it answered much better to the description of that species which you shot at Revesby, in Lincolnshire. My bird I describe thus :— It is a size less than the grasshopper-lark ; the head, back, and coverts of the wings, of a dusky brown, without the dark spots of the grasshopper-lark ; over each eye is a milk-white stroke; the chin and throat are white, and the under parts of a yellowish white;

* For this *salicaria,* see Letter XXVI.

the rump is tawny, and the feathers of the tail sharp pointed ; the bill is dusky and sharp, and the legs are dusky, the hinder claw long and crooked."*   The person that shot it says, that it sung so like a reed-sparrow, that he took it for one; and that it sings all night: but this account merits farther inquiry. For my part, I suspect it is a second sort of locustella, hinted at by Dr Derham in Ray's *Letters :* see p. 74. He also procured me a grasshopper-lark.

The question that you put with regard to those genera of animals that are peculiar to America, namely, How they came there, and whence ? is too puzzling for me to answer ; and yet so obvious as often to have struck me with wonder. If one looks into the writers on that subject, little satisfaction is to be found. Ingenious men will readily advance plausible arguments to support whatever theory they shall choose to maintain ; but then the misfortune is, every one's hypothesis is each as good as another's, since they are all founded on conjecture.   The late writers of this sort, in whom may be seen all the arguments of those that have gone before, as I remember, stock America from the western coast of Africa, and the south of Europe ; and then break down the isthmus that bridged over the Atlantic.   But this is making use of a violent piece of machinery : it is a difficulty worthy of the interposition of a god ! " *Incredulus odi.* "

TO THOMAS PENNANT, ESQUIRE.

THE NATURALIST'S SUMMER EVENING WALK.

——— equidem credo, quia sit divinitas illis
Ingenium.   VIRG. *Georg.*

WHEN day, declining, sheds a milder gleam,
What time the May-fly† haunts the pool or stream;

---

* The sedge bird, *sylvia phragmitis*, of Bechstein. Mr Sweet says,. " It is almost constantly in song, both by night and by day, and may be heard at a considerable distance, beginning with chit, chit, chiddy, chiddy, chiddy, chit, chit, chit. It is a very lively bird, and shews scarcely any symptoms of fear, approaching very near to any person who does not drive or frighten it."—ED.

† The angler's May-fly, the *ephemera vulgata*, Linn. comes forth from its aurelia state, and emerges out of the water, about six in the evening, and dies about eleven at night, determining the date of its fly state in

When the still owl skims round the grassy mead,
What time the timorous hare limps forth to feed ;
Then be the time to steal adown the vale,
And listen to the vagrant cuckoo's* tale ;
To hear the clamorous curlew† call his mate,
Or the soft quail his tender pain relate ;
To see the swallow sweep the dark'ning plain,
Belated, to support her infant train ;
To mark the swift, in rapid giddy ring,
Dash round the steeple, unsubdued of wing :
Amusive birds ! say where your hid retreat,
When the frost rages and the tempests beat ?
Whence your return, by such nice instinct led,
When Spring, soft season, lifts her bloomy head?
Such baffled searches mock man's prying pride,
The God of Nature is your secret guide!
    While deep'ning shades obscure the face of day,
To yonder bench, leaf-shelter'd, let us stray,
Till blended objects fail the swimming sight,
And all the fading landscape sinks in night ;
To hear the drowsy dorr come brushing by
With buzzing wing, or the shrill cricket‡ cry ;
To see the feeding bat glance through the wood ;
To catch the distant falling of the flood ;
While o'er the cliff th' awaken'd churn-owl hung,
Through the still gloom protracts his chattering song ;
While, high in air, and poised upon his wings,
Unseen, the soft enamour'd woodlark§ sings :
These, Nature's works, the curious mind employ,
Inspire a soothing, melancholy joy :
As fancy warms, a pleasing kind of pain
Steals o'er the cheek, and thrills the creeping vein!
    Each rural sight, each sound, each smell, combine ;
The tinkling sheep-bell, or the breath of kine ;

---

about five or six hours. They usually egin to appear about the 4th of
June, and continue in succession for near a fortnight. See Swammerdam,
Derham, Scopoli, &c.

  * Vagrant cuckoo; so called, because, being tied down by no incubation,
or attendance about the nutrition of its young, it wanders without control.

  † *Charadrius oedicnemus.*

  ‡ *Gryllus campestris.*

  § In hot summer nights, woodlarks soar to a prodigious height, and
hang singing in the air.

The new-mown hay that scents the swelling breeze,
Or cottage chimney smoking through the trees.
  The chilling night-dews fall : away, retire ;
For see, the glow-worm lights her amorous fire! *
Thus, ere night's veil had half obscured the sky,
Th' impatient damsel hung her lamp on high ;
True to the signal, by love's meteor led,
Leander hasten'd to his Hero's bed.†

LETTER XXV.

TO THE HON. DAINES BARRINGTON.

SELBORNE, *June* 30, 1769.

DEAR SIR,—When I was in town last month, I partly engaged that I would some time do myself the honour to write to you on the subject of natural history ; and I am the more ready to fulfill my promise, because I see you are a gentleman of great candour, and one that will make allowances, especially where the writer professes to be an out-door naturalist,—one that takes his observations from the subject itself, and not from the writings of others.

The following is a List of the Summer Birds of Passage which I have discovered in this neighbourhood, arranged somewhat in the order in which they appear : —

	RAII NOMINA.	USUALLY APPEARS ABOUT
1. Wryneck,	*Yunx, sive torquilla.*	The middle of March: harsh note.
2. Smallest willow-wren,	*Regulus non cristatus.*	March 23: chirps till September.
3. Swallow,	*Hirundo domestica.*	April 13.
4. Marten,	*Hirundo rustica.*	Ditto.
5. Sand-marten,	*Hirunda riparia.*	Ditto.
6. Black-cap,	*Atricapilla.*	Ditto : a sweet wild note.
7. Nightingale,	*Luscinia.*	Beginning of April.
8. Cuckoo,	*Cuculus.*	Middle of April.
9. Middle willow-wren,	*Regulus non cristatus.*	Ditto : a sweet plaintive note.
10. White-throat,	*Ficedulæ affinis.*	Ditto: mean note : sings till September.
11. Redstart,	*Ruticilla.*	Ditto : more agreeable song.

* The light of the female glow-worm (as she often crawls up the stalk of a grass to make herself more conspicuous) is a signal to the male, which is a slender, dusky *scarabæus.*
† See the story of Hero and Leander.

12. Stone-curlew,	Oedicnemus.	End of March : loud nocturnal whistle.
13. Turtle-dove,	Turtur.	
14. Grasshopper-lark,	Alauda minima locustæ voce.	Middle of April : a small sibilous note, till the end of July.
15. Swift,	Hirundo apus.	About April 27.
16. Less reed-sparrow,	Passer arundinaceus minor.	A sweet polyglot, but hurrying : it has the notes of many birds.
17. Landrail,	Ortygometra.	A loud, harsh note, crex, crex.
18. Largest willow-wren,	Regulus non cristatus.	Cantat voce stridula locustæ : end of April, on the tops of high beeches.
19. Goat-sucker, or fern-owl,	Caprimulgus.	Beginning of May : chatters by night with a singular noise.
20. Fly-catcher,	Stoparola.	May 12. A very mute bird : this is the latest summer bird of passage.

This assemblage of curious and amusing birds belongs to ten several genera of the Linnæan system ; and are all of the *ordo* of *passeres*, save the *yunx* and *cuculus*, which are *picæ*, and the *charadrius* (*oedicnemus*) and *rallus*, (*ortygometra*,) which are *grallæ*.

These birds, as they stand numerically, belong to the following Linnæan genera :—

1.	Yunx,	13, Columba.
2, 6, 7, 9, 10, 11, 16, 18,	Motacilla.	17, Rallus.
3, 4, 5, 15,	Hirundo.	19, Caprimulgus.
8,	Cuculus.	14, Alauda.
12,	Charadrius.	20, Muscicapa.

Most soft-billed birds live on insects, and not on grain and seeds, and therefore at the end of summer they retire ; but the following soft-billed birds, though insect eaters, stay with us the year round :—

RAII NOMINA.

Red-breast,	Rubecula.	These frequent houses ; and haunt out-buildings in the winter : eat spiders.
Wren,	Passer troglodytes.	
Hedge-sparrow,	Curruca.	Haunt sinks, for crumbs, and other sweepings.

E

White-wagtail,	*Motacilla alba.*	These frequent shallow rivulets, near the spring heads, where they never freeze: eat the aureliæ of *phryganea.* The smallest birds that walk.
Yellow-wagtail,	*Motacilla flava.*	
Gray-wagtail,	*Motacilla cinerea.*	
Wheatear,	*Oenanthe.*	Some of these are to be seen with us the winter through.
Whin-chat,	*Oenanthe secunda.*	
Stone-chatter,	*Oenanthe tertia.*	
Golden-crowned wren,	*Regulus cristatus.*	This is the smallest British bird: haunts the tops of tall trees; stays the winter through.

A List of the Winter Birds of Passage round this neighbourhood, ranged somewhat in the order in which they appear.

RAII NOMINA.

1. Ringousel,	*Merula torquata.*	This is a new migration, which I have lately discovered about Michaelmas week, and again about March the 14th.
2. Redwing,	*Turdus iliacus.*	About old Michaelmas.
3. Fieldfare,	*Turdus pilaris.*	Though a percher by day, roosts on the ground.
4. Royston-crow,	*Cornix cinerea.*	Most frequently on downs.
5. Woodcock,	*Scolopax.*	Appears about old Michaelmas.
6. Snipe,	*Gallinago minor.*	Some snipes constantly breed with us.
7. Jack-snipe,	*Gallinago minima.*	
8. Wood-pigeon,	*Oenas.*	Seldom appears till late; not in such plenty as formerly.
9. Wild-swan,	*Cygnus ferus.*	On some large waters.
10. Wild-goose.	*Anser ferus.*	
11. Wild-duck,	*Anas torquata minor.*	On our lakes and streams.
12. Pochard,	*Anas fera fusca.*	
13. Widgeon,	*Penelope.*	
14. Teal, breeds with us in Wolmer Forest,	*Querquedula.*	
15. Crossbeak,	*Coccothraustes.*	These are only wanderers that appear occasionally, and are not observant of any regular migration.
16. Crossbill,	*Loxia.*	
17 Silk-tail,	*Garrulus Bohemicus.*	

These birds, as they stand numerically, belong to the following Linnæan genera :—

1, 2, 3, *Turdus.*	9, 10, 11, 12, 13, 14, *Anas.*
4, *Corvus.*	15, 16, *Loxia.*
5, 6, 7, *Scolopax.*	17, *Ampelis.*
8, *Columba.*	

Birds that sing in the night are but few :—

Nightingale,	*Luscinia.*	{ "In shadiest covert hid." MILTON.
Woodlark,	*Alauda arborea.*	Suspended in mid air.
Less reed-sparrow,	} *Passer arundinaceus minor.*	{ Among reeds and willows.

I should now proceed to such birds as continue to sing after midsummer, but as they are rather numerous, they would exceed the bounds of this paper ; besides, as this is now the season for remarking on that subject, I am willing to repeat my observations on some birds, concerning the continuation of whose song I seem at present to have some doubt.

LETTER XXVI.

TO THOMAS PENNANT, ESQ.

SELBORNE, *August* 30, 1769.

DEAR SIR,— It gives me satisfaction to find that my account of the ousel migration pleases you. You put a very shrewd question, when you ask me how I know that their autumnal migration is southward ? Were not candour and openness the very life of natural history, I should pass over this query just as a sly commentator does over a crabbed passage in a classic ; but common ingenuousness obliges me to confess, not without some degree of shame, that I only reasoned in that case from analogy. For as all other autumnal birds migrate from the northward to us, to partake of our milder winters, and return to the northward again, when the rigorous cold abates, so I concluded that the ringousels did the same, as well as their congeners, the fieldfares ; and especially as ringousels are known to haunt cold mountainous countries ; but I have good reason to suspect since, that they may come to us from the westward ; because I hear, from very good authority, that they breed on Dartmoor : and that they forsake that wild district about the time that our visitors appear, and do not return till late in the spring.

I have taken a great deal of pains about your *salicaria* and mine, with a white stroke over its eye, and a tawny rump. I have surveyed it alive and dead, and have procured several specimens; and am perfectly persuaded myself (and trust you will soon be convinced of the same) that it is no more or less than the *passer arundinaceus minor* of Ray.* This bird, by some means or other, seems to be entirely omitted in the *British Zoology;* and one reason probably was, because it is so strangely classed in Ray, who ranges it among his *pici affines.* It ought, no doubt, to have gone among his *aviculæ caudâ unicolore,* and among your slender-billed small birds of the same division. Linnæus might, with great propriety, have put it into his genus of *motacilla;* and the *motacilla salicaria* of his *fauna suecica* seems to come the nearest to it. It is no uncommon bird, haunting the sides of ponds and rivers, where there is covert, and the reeds and sedges of moors. The country people in some places call it the sedge-bird. It sings incessantly, night and day, during the breeding time, imitating the note of a sparrow, a swallow, a skylark; and has a strange hurrying manner in its song. My specimens correspond most minutely to the description of your fen salicaria shot near Revesby. Mr Ray has given an excellent characteristic of it when he says, " *Rostrum et pedes in hâc aviculâ multò majores sunt quàm pro corporis ratione.*"

I have got you the egg of an *oedicnemus,* or stone-curlew, which was picked up in a fallow on the naked ground. There were two; but the finder inadvertently crushed one with his foot before he saw them.

When I wrote to you last year on reptiles, I wish I had not forgot to mention the faculty that snakes have of stinking *se defendendo.* I knew a gentleman who kept a tame snake, which was in its person as sweet as any animal, while in good humour and unalarmed; but, as soon as a stranger, or a dog or cat, came in, it fell to hissing, and filled the room with such nauseous effluvia, as rendered it hardly supportable. Thus the squnck, or stonck, of Ray's *Synop. Quadr.* is an innocuous, and sweet animal; but, when pressed hard by dogs and men, it can eject such a most pestilent and fetid smell and excrement, that nothing can be more horrible.†

---

* See Letter XXIV.

† The skunk (*Mephitis Americanis* of Desmarest) is an animal nearly allied to a weasel, and a native of South America. Professor Kalm mentions that a skunk was once perceived by a servant in a cellar. She attacked and killed it, without thinking of the effluvia which it would occasion; and the place was instantly filled with a horrid stench,

A gentleman sent me lately a fine specimen of the *lanius minor cinerascens cum maculâ in scapulis albâ, Raii;* which is a bird that, at the time of your publishing your two first volumes of *British Zoology,* I find you had not seen. You have described it well from Edward's drawing. *

LETTER XXVII.

TO THE HON. DAINES BARRINGTON.

SELBORNE, *November* 2, 1769.

DEAR SIR,—When I did myself the honour to write to you, about the end of last June, on the subject of natural history, I sent you a list of the summer birds of passage which I have observed in this neighbourhood, and also a list of the winter birds of passage : I mentioned, besides, those soft-billed birds that stay with us the winter through in the south of England, and those that are remarkable for singing in the night.

According to my proposal, I shall now proceed to such birds (singing birds, strictly so called) as continue in full song till after midsummer, and shall range them somewhat in the order in which they first begin to open as the spring advances :—

RAII NOMINA.

1. Woodlark	*Alauda arborea.*	In January, and continues to sing through all the summer and autumn.
2. Song-thrush,	*Turdus simpliciter dictus.*	In February, and on to August; resume their song in autumn.
3. Wren,	*Passer troglodytes.*	All the year, hard frost excepted.
4. Red-breast,	*Rubecula.*	Ditto.
5. Hedge-sparrow,	*Curuca.*	Early in February, to July the 10th.
6. Yellow-hammer,	*Emberiza flava.*	Early in February, and on through July to August the 21st.

which so affected the thoughtless woman, that she was taken seriously ill, in which state she continued for some considerable time. — ED.

* This is probably the wood-shrike, (*lanius rutilus* of Latham.) It is amongst the rarest of our occasional visitants, but not so much so as some imagine, being often mistaken for the common butcher-bird. Mr Hoy mentions two having been killed near Canterbury, and another at Swaffham, Norfolk, within these few years. He says it places its nest invariably on trees, preferring the oak. One lately killed is in the collection of the Rev. R. Hammond, Swaffham. — Ed.

7. Skylark,	*Alauda vulgaris.*	In February, and on to October.
8. Swallow,	*Hirundo domestica.*	From April to September.
9. Black-cap,	*Atricapilla.*	Beginning of April to July 13th.
10. Titlark,	*Alauda pratorum.*	From middle of April to July the 16th.
11. Blackbird,	*Merula vulgaris.* *	Sometimes in February and March, and so on to July the 23d; re-assumes in autumn.
12. White-throat,	*Ficedulæ affinis.*	In April, and to July 23.
13. Goldfinch,	*Carduelis.*	April, and through to September 16.
14. Greenfinch,	*Chloris.*	On to July and August 2d.
15. Less reed-sparrow,	*Passer arundinaceus minor.*	May, on to beginning of July.
16 Common linnet,	*Linaria vulgaris.*	Breeds and whistles on till August; re-assumes its note when they begin to congregate in October, and again early before the flocks separate.

* The following circumstance, as to the imitative powers of the black-bird, is a new fact in natural history, and was recorded by the Rev. Barton Bouchier, of Wold Rectory, near Northampton, in April, 1831. " Within half a mile of my residence," says he, " there is a blackbird which crows constantly, and as accurately as the common cock, and nearly as loud ; as it may, on a still day, be heard at the distance of several hundred yards. When first told of the circumstance, I conjectured that it must have been the work of a cock pheasant, concealed in a neighbouring brake ; but on the assurance that it was nothing more or less than a common blackbird, I determined to ascertain the fact with my own eyes and ears; and this day I had the gratification of getting close to it, seated on the top bough of an ash-tree, and pursuing with unceasing zeal its unusual note.   The resemblance to the crow of the domestic cock is so perfect, that more than one in the distance were answering to it, and the little fellow seemed to take delight in competing with its rivals of the dunghill.   It occasion-ally indulged in its usual song ; but only for a second or two, resuming its more favourite note ; and once or twice it commenced with crowing, and broke off in the middle to its more natural whistle.   I am not aware that the blackbird has even been included among those birds which could be taught to imitate sounds; such as the starling, jay, or magpie ; and in what way this bird has acquired its present propensity, I am unable to say, except that, as its usual haunt is near a mill where poultry are kept, it may have learnt the note from the common fowl."

Blackbirds can be taught various airs, while in a state of captivity, but we consider the circumstance of this bird, in a wild state, imitating the crowing of a cock, as very remarkable. — ED.

Birds that cease to be in full song, and are usually silent at or before midsummer :—

17. Middle willow-wren,	*Regulus non crista-tus.*	Middle of June ; begins in April.
18. Redstart,	*Ruticilla.*	Ditto ; begins in May.
19. Chaffinch,	*Fringilla.*	Beginning of June ; sings first in February.
20. Nightingale.	*Luscinia.*	Middle of June; sings first in April.

Birds that sing for a short time, and very early in the spring :—

21. Missel-bird,	*Turdus viscivorus.*	January the 2d, 1770, in January. Is called in Hampshire and Sussex the storm-cock, because its song is supposed to forebode windy wet weather ; it is the largest singing bird we have.*
22. Great titmouse, or ox-eye,	*Fringillago.*	In Feb. March, April ; re-assumes for a short time in September.

Birds that have somewhat of a note or song, and yet are hardly to be called singing birds :—

RAII NOMINA.

23. Golden-crowned wren,	*Regulus cristatus.*	Its note as minute as its person; frequents tops of high oaks and firs : the smallest British bird.

* Although our author has ranked this species amongst our singing birds, much variety of opinion prevails, up to the present day, whether or not it is a bird of song. Several articles, however, which have recently appeared in the *Magazine of Natural History*, places this beyond a doubt. The following are the facts recorded :— One writer says, vol. iii. p. 193, " The note resembles that of the blackbird more than the common thrush, and is, I believe, generally mistaken for the former, but it is much louder, and less mellow, and free from that warbling nature so peculiar to the blackbird." Another correspondent, in Ayrshire, says, " It often happens that the woods resound, far and near, with its powerful melody, on a still day, or middle of winter, or early in the spring, when no other songster is heard." Mr J. D. Marshall, of Belfast, an authority which we highly respect, says, " This bird seems to have two kinds of song, one not unlike the notes of the blackbird, the other very sweet, though in a much lower tone, and more nearly resembling those of the common thrush. I have one which I reared from the nest ; and, having been kept a year near a canary, it has, to a certain degree, acquired its song, as, in several notes, it has imitated it almost to perfection." — ED.

24. Marsh titmouse,	*Parus palustris.*	Haunts great woods; two harsh, sharp notes.
25. Small willow-wren,	*Regulus non crista-tus.*	Sings in March, and on to September.
26. Largest do.	*Do.*	*Cantat voce stridula locustæ ;* from end of April to August.
27. Grasshopper-lark,	*Alauda minima voce locustæ.*	Chirps all night, from the middle of April to the end of July.
28. Marten,	*Hirundo agrestis.*	All the breeding time; from May to September.
29. Bullfinch,	*Pyrrhula.* *	
80. Bunting,	*Emberiza alba.*	From the end of January to July.

All singing birds, and those that have any pretensions to song, not only in Britain, but perhaps the world through, come under the Linnæan *ordo* of *passeres.*

The above-mentioned birds, as they stand numerically, belong to the following Linnæan genera :—

1, 7, 10, 27,	*Alauda.*	8, 28,	*Hirundo.*
2, 11, 21,	*Turdus.*	13, 16, 19,	*Fringilla.*
3, 4, 5, 9, 12, 15, 17, 18, 20, 23, 25, 26,	*Motacilla.*	22, 24,	*Parus.*
		14, 29,	*Loxia.*
6, 30,	*Emberiza.*		

Birds that sing as they fly are but few :—

	RAII NOMINA.	
Skylark,	*Alauda vulgaris.*	Rising, suspended, and falling.
Titlark,	*Alauda pratorum.*	In its descent; also sitting on trees, and walking on the ground.
Woodlark,	*Alauda arborea.*	Suspended; in hot summer nights, all night long.
Blackbird,	*Merula.*	Sometimes from bush to bush.

* Both male and female bullfinches sing; their notes are not much varied, but possess a degree of simple wildness, which is delivered in a low, but pleasing strain. The call note is very audible, and greatly resembles the action of metallic substances against each other. In a domesticated state, these birds are capable of attaining various tunes in a high degree of perfection. We have heard them singing, with much exactness, " Braw, braw lads o' Gala Water," and other melodies. In Germany, they are taught a variety of waltzes. Our friend, William Sharp, Esq. Cononsyth, near Montrose, has one of these foreign birds, which sings several difficult waltzes and airs in a beautiful manner. — ED.

White-throat,	*Ficedula affinis.*	{ Uses, when singing on the wing, odd jerks and gesticulations.
Swallow,	*Hirundo domestica.*	In soft, sunny weather.
Wren,*	*Passer troglodytes.*	{ Sometimes from bush to bush.

Birds that breed most early in these parts : —

Raven,	*Corvus.*	{ Hatches in February and March.
Song-thrush,	*Turdus.*	In March.
Blackbird,	*Merula.*	In March.
Rook,	*Cornix frugilega.*	{ Builds in the beginning of March.
Woodlark,	*Alauda arborea.*	Hatches in April.
Ringdove,	*Palumbus torquatus.*	{ Lays in the beginning of April.

All birds that continue in full song till after midsummer, appear to me to breed more than once.

Most kinds of birds seem to me to be wild and shy, somewhat in proportion to their bulk ; I mean in this island, where they are much pursued and annoyed ; but in Ascension Island, and many other desolate places, mariners have found fowls so unacquainted with a human figure, that they would stand still to be taken, as is the case with boobies, &c. As an example of what is advanced, I remark that the golden-crested wren, (the smallest British bird,) will stand unconcerned till you come within three or four yards of it, while the bustard, (*otis,*) the largest British land fowl, does not care to admit a person within so many furlongs.

LETTER XXVIII.

TO THOMAS PENNANT, ESQ.

SELBORNE, *December* 8, 1769.

DEAR SIR, — I was much gratified by your communicative letter on your return from Scotland, where you spent, I find, some

---

* The missel-thrush occasionally sings on the wing. In Loudon's *Magazine*, we have the following statement by a correspondent : — " I have once in my life observed one to sing, whilst in the act of flying from one side of a field to the other ; " and the Rev. W. T. Bree remarks, in the above, " On the 3d of March, 1831, I was an eye and ear witness of the fact of a missel-thrush singing — and singing in good style — on the wing, flying over the Lammas Fields, between the village of Allesley and Coventry." — Ed.

considerable time, and gave yourself good room to examine the natural curiosities of that extensive kingdom, both those of the islands, as well as those of the Highlands. The usual bane of such expeditions is hurry, because men seldom allot themselves half the time they should do; but, fixing on a day for their return, post from place to place, rather as if they were on a journey that required despatch, than as philosophers investigating the works of nature.* You must have made, no doubt, many discoveries, and laid up a good fund of materials for a future edition of the *British Zoology*, and will have no reason to repent that you have bestowed so much pains on a part of Great Britain that perhaps was never so well examined before.

It has always been matter of wonder to me, that fieldfares, which are so congenerous to thrushes and blackbirds, should never choose to breed in England : but that they should not think even the Highlands cold and northerly, and sequestered enough, is a circumstance still more strange and wonderful.† The ringousel, you find, stays in Scotland the whole year round ; so that we have reason to conclude that those migrators that visit us for a short space every autumn, do not come from thence.

And here, I think, will be the proper place to mention, that those birds were most punctual again in their migration this autumn, appearing, as before, about the 30th of September ; but their flocks were larger than common, and their stay

---

* The justice of this remark will be appreciated by every person of reflection, when it is considered that the examination of the parish of Selborne was the principal business of the intelligent White for nearly a lifetime, although he paid but little attention to the insects and botany of the parish. We remember an account of the geology of the country betwixt Cork and Dublin having been read before a certain learned society, from observations made by a certain learned and Reverend Doctor, from the top of a mail coach ! — Ed.

† In the *Nat. Hist. Mag.* v. p. 276, the following remarkable circumstance is narrated : — " Last week, (19th February, 1832,) as Mr Mitcalf, keeper to Lord Lowther, in Ravenstondale, was ranging the fields with his gun, he observed a hawk hovering near him; and while preparing to give it a shot, a fieldfare flew in terror against his breast, and then perched upon his shoulder. He fired at the hawk with the first barrel, (while the fieldfare sat still,) but missed; the hawk, intent upon his prey, disregarded that shot; with the second barrel he brought the bird down. The fieldfare left his shoulder, and fluttered for a short time around its fallen and dead enemy, uttering a chirp of joy, and then winged away from its friend and unexpected protector. There is something more than instinct in such a circumstance." — Ed.

protracted somewhat beyond the usual time. If they came to spend the whole winter with us, as some of their congeners do, and then left us, as they do, in spring, I should not be so much struck with the occurrence, since it would be similar to that of the other winter birds of passage ; but when I see them for a fortnight at Michaelmas, and again for about a week in the middle of April, I am seized with wonder, and long to be informed whence these travellers come, and whither they go, since they seem to use our hills merely as an inn, or baiting place.

Your account of the greater brambling, or snow-fleck, is very amusing; and strange it is, that such a short-winged bird should delight in such perilous voyages over the northern ocean!* Some country people in the winter time have every now and then told me that they have seen two or three white larks on our downs ; but, on considering the matter, I begin to suspect that these are some stragglers of the birds we are talking of, which sometimes, perhaps, may rove so far to the southward.

It pleases me to find that white hares are so frequent on the Scottish mountains, and especially as you inform me that it is a distinct species ; for the quadrupeds of Britain are so few, that every new species is a great acquisition.†

---

* See note, page 36. The snow-fleck, *plectrophanes nivalis*, has been separated from the genus *emberiza* by Myer, on account of the length of its wings greatly exceeding those of other birds, which now form this natural genus. Hence they are fitted for more extensive excursions.—ED.

† This is the Alpine hare, *lepus variabilis*, of British naturalists. Its ears are shorter than the head, and black towards the tips ; the rest of the body, dusky in summer, and white in winter. There appears to be a correlative connection in the distribution of colour in animals as regards temperature. In tropical regions, the colour of man and animals exhibits more variety and intensity than in northern latitudes. In temperate climates, animals, in general, suffer little change from the vicissitudes of the seasons, although, in many cases, winter and summer clothing is very different in some species. In Britain, the white hare is an instance, whose fur is tawny gray in summer, but changes, in September or October, to a snowy white. This remarkable transition takes place in the following manner : — About the middle of September, the gray feet begin to get white, and, before the end of the month, all the four feet are white, and the ears and muzzle are of a brighter colour. The white generally ascends the legs and thighs, and whitish spots are osberved under the gray hairs, which continue to increase till the end of October ; but still the back remains of a gray colour, while the eyebrows and ears are nearly white. From this period, the change of colour advances very rapidly, and, by the middle of November, the whole fur, with the exception of the tips of the ears, which continue black, is of a shining white.

The eagle-owl,* could it be proved to belong to us, is so majestic a bird, that it would grace our *fauna* much. I never was informed before where wild geese are known to breed.

You admit, I find, that I have proved your fen salicaria to be the lesser reed-sparrow of Ray; and I think you may be secure that I am right; for I took very particular pains to clear up that matter, and had some fair specimens; but, as they were not well preserved, they are decayed already. You will, no doubt, insert it in its proper place in your next edition. Your additional plates will much improve your work.

De Buffon, I know, has described the water shrew-mouse;† but still I am pleased to find you have discovered it in Lincoln-

---

The back becomes white within eight days. During the whole of this remarkable change in the fur, no hair falls from the animal. Hence it appears, that the hair actually changes its colour, and that there is no renewal of it. The fur continues white till the month of March, or even later, depending on the temperature of the atmosphere, and, by the middle of May, it has again assumed its gray colour. But the spring change is different from the winter, as the hair is completely shed.

An instance of a similar change may be instanced in the ptarmigan, (*tetrao lagopus*.) Its summer plumage is ash gray, mottled with dusky spots and bars. At the approach of winter, the dark colours disappear, and its feathers are then found to be pure white. We are naturally led to inquire what benefit the animals receive from this periodical change, as we know that the All-wise does nothing in vain. Colour has a great influence on the ratio at which bodies cool. It is an established law, that surfaces which reflect heat most readily, allow it to escape very slowly by radiation. White objects reflect most readily, consequently there will be a proportionate difficulty in its radiation of heat. If a black animal and a white one were placed in a higher temperature than that of their own body, the heat will enter the black one with the greatest rapidity, and soon elevate its temperature considerably above that of the other. These differences manifest themselves in wearing black and white coloured clothing during hot weather; so that if these animals are placed in a temperature considerably lower than their own, the animal which is black will give out its heat by radiation to the surrounding objects sooner than itself, by which its temperature will speedily be reduced, while the white animal will part with its heat by radiation at a much slower rate. Hence it would appear that the clothing of animals is suited in colour to the temperature of the situations where they localise. Accidental variations, however, sometimes occur, as in some birds we have already mentioned at page 36. A black hare was shot at Combe, near Coventry, in February, 1828; and another was killed at Netley, Shropshire, by the Rev. F. W. Hope. — ED.

* The *strix bubo* has been killed in Yorkshire, Sussex, and Scotland. It is a native of Norway and other parts of Europe. — ED.

† This quadruped has been found in many parts of Great Britain: it seems to have been long overlooked in this country. In Turton's *British Fauna*, there is a second species of water shrew mentioned by the name,

shire, for the reason I have given in the article of the white hare.

As a neighbour was lately ploughing in a dry chalky field, far removed from any water, he turned out a water-rat, that was curiously laid up in an hybernaculum artificially formed of grass and leaves. At one end of the burrow lay above a gallon of potatoes, regularly stowed, on which it was to have supported itself for the winter. But the difficulty with me is, how this *amphibius mus* came to fix its winter station at such a distance from the water. Was it determined in its choice of that place by the mere accident of finding the potatoes which were planted there? or is it the constant practice of the aquatic rat to forsake the neighbourhood of the water in the colder months?

Though I delight very little in analogous reasoning, knowing how fallacious it is with respect to natural history; yet, in the following instance, I cannot help being inclined to think it may conduce towards the explanation of a difficulty that I have mentioned before, with respect to the invariable early retreat of the *hirundo apus*, or swift, so many weeks before its congeners; and that not only with us, but also in Andalusia, where they begin to retire about the beginning of August.

The great large bat* (which, by the by, is at present a nondescript in England, and what I have never been able yet to procure) retires or migrates very early in the summer: it also ranges very high for its food, feeding in a different region of the air; and that is the reason I never could procure one.†
Now, this is exactly the case with the swifts; for they take their food in a more exalted region than the other species, and are very seldom seen hawking for flies near the ground, or over the surface of the water. From hence I would conclude, that these *hirundines*, and the larger bats, are supported by some sorts of high-flying gnats, scarabs, or *phalænæ*, that are of short continuance; and that the short stay of these strangers is regulated by the defect of their food.

---

the *ciliatus*, or fringe-tailed water-shrew: he says it is entirely black, with hardly any white underneath. In Loudon's *Magazine*, there is a description of a water shrew nearly double the size of the *fodiens*, and said to be of a darker colour. — ED.

* The little bat appears almost every month in the year; but I have never seen the large ones till the end of April, nor after July. They are most common in June, but never in any plenty: are a rare species with us.

† This is the great bat, *vespertilio noctula*, of Turton's *British Fauna*, first noticed and described by our author. — ED.

By my journal it appears, that curlews clamoured on to October the thirty-first ; since which, I have not seen or heard any. Swallows were observed on to November the third.

LETTER XXIX. '

TO THE HON. DAINES BARRINGTON.

SELBORNE, *January* 15, 1770.

DEAR SIR,— It was no small matter of satisfaction to me to find that you were not displeased with my little *methodus* of birds. If there was any merit in the sketch, it must be owing to its punctuality. For many months I carried a list in my pocket of the birds that were to be remarked, and, as I rode or walked about my business, I noted each day the continuance or omission of each bird's song ; so that I am as sure of the certainty of my facts as a man can be of any transaction whatsoever.

I shall now proceed to answer the several queries which you put in your two obliging letters, in the best manner that I am able. Perhaps Eastwick, and its environs, where you heard so very few birds, is not a woodland country, and, therefore, not stocked with such songsters. If you will cast your eye on my last letter, you will find that many species continued to warble after the beginning of July.

The titlark and yellow-hammer breed late, the latter very late ; and, therefore, it is no wonder that they protract their song : for I lay it down as a maxim in ornithology, that as long as there is any incubation going on, there is music.* As

---

* While we admit the truth of our author's remarks, we are inclined to believe that birds sing frequently from buoyancy of spirits and joy, as well as from rivalry. Every one must have observed, that birds in confinement immediately commence singing whenever a noise is made in the room where they are situated.

Mr Sweet, who has devoted much time to taming the musical genus *sylvia*, has, by diligent observation, and appropriate management, actually changed most of the species from annual to perennial songsters. In the month of March, these interesting choristers may be heard, pouring forth the familiar strains of midsummer. A little room, with a fireplace, serves as an aviary ; and in this he has two large cages, which contain the nightingale, white-throat, pettychaps, white-ear, whin-chat, stone-chat, redstart, black-cap, willow-wren, siskin, and other birds.

The management of an aviary is a most interesting amusement to the lover of nature. If the apartment be sufficiently large, the little songsters feel none of the tedium of imprisonment, but sport about, with all the ardour manifested in their natural groves. The scene is greatly heightened

to the red-breast and wren, it is well known to the most
incurious observer, that they whistle the year round, hard frost
excepted; especially the latter.

It was not in my power to procure you a black-cap, or a
less reed-sparrow, or sedge-bird, alive. As the first is, undoubt-
édly, and the last, as far as I can yet see, a summer bird of
passage, they would require more nice and curious management in a cage than I should be able to give them: they were
both distinguished songsters. The note of the former has
such a wild sweetness that it always brings to my mind those
lines in a song in "As You Like It,"—

> And tune his merry note
> Unto the *wild* bird's throat.

The latter has a surprising variety of notes, resembling the
song of several other birds; but then it has also a hurrying
manner, not at all to its advantage. It is, notwithstanding, a
delicate polyglot.

It is new to me that titlarks in cages sing in the night; perhaps only caged birds do so. I once knew a tame red-breast
in a cage that always sang as long as candles were in the
room; but in their wild state no one supposes they sing in
the night.

I should be almost ready to doubt the fact, that there are to
be seen much fewer birds in July than in any former month,
notwithstanding so many young are hatched daily. Sure I
am, that it is far otherwise with respect to the swallow tribe,
which increases prodigiously as the summer advances; and I
saw, at the time mentioned, many hundreds of young wagtails
on the banks of the Cherwell, which almost covered the meadows. If the matter appears, as you say, in the other species,
may it not be owing to the dams being engaged in incubation,
while the young are concealed by the leaves?

Many times have I had the curiosity to open the stomachs of
woodcocks and snipes; but nothing ever occurred that helped
to explain to me what their subsistence might be; all that I
could ever find was a soft mucus, among which lay many
pellucid small gravels.*

by the addition of orange trees and evergreens, where they will breed, as
in a state of nature. Here they exhibit no signs of suffering captivity;
on the contrary, it is delightful to see them, in a stormy day, enjoying
the warmth of summer, while their cheerful notes prove they have no
heart-rending cares. — ED.

* The food of the woodcock and snipe has not yet been properly

LETTER XXX.

TO THE HON. DAINES BARRINGTON.

SELBORNE, *February* 19, 1770.

DEAR SIR,—Your observation, that "the cuckoo does not deposit its egg indiscriminately in the nest of the first bird that comes in its way, but probably looks out a nurse in some degree congenerous, with whom to intrust its young," is perfectly new to me; and struck me so forcibly, that I naturally fell into a train of thought that led me to consider whether the fact were so, and what reason there was for it. When I came to recollect and inquire, I could not find that any cuckoo had ever been seen in these parts, except in the nest of the wagtail, the hedge-sparrow, the titlark, the white-throat, and the red-breast, all soft-billed insectivorous birds. The excellent Mr Willughby mentions the nest of the *palumbus*, (ring-dove,) and of the *fringilla*, (chaffinch,) birds that subsist on acorns and grains, and such hard food; but then he does not mention them as of his own knowledge; but says afterwards, that he saw himself a wagtail feeding a cuckoo. It appears hardly possible that a soft-billed bird should subsist on the same food with the hard-billed; for the former have thin membranaceous stomachs suited to their soft food; while the latter, the granivorous tribe, have strong muscular gizzards, which, like mills, grind, by the help of small gravels and pebbles, what is swallowed. This proceeding of the cuckoo, of dropping its eggs as it were by chance, is such a monstrous outrage on maternal affection, one of the first great dictates of nature, and such a violence on instinct, that, had it only been related of a bird in the Brazils, or Peru, it would never have merited our belief. But yet, should it farther appear that this simple bird, when divested of that natural στοργή that seems to raise the kind in general above themselves, and inspire them with extraordinary degrees of cunning and address, may be still endued with a more enlarged faculty of discerning what species are suitable and congenerous nursing

ascertained; but we find from Montagu's *Ornithological Dictionary*, second edition, that they are very fond of worms, as stated in the following paragraph:—" A woodcock, in our menagerie, very soon discovered and drew forth every worm in the ground, which was dug up to enable it to be done; and worms put into a large garden pot, covered with earth, five or six inches deep, are always cleared by the next morning, without one being left.—ED."

mothers for its disregarded eggs and young, and may deposit them only under their care, this would be adding wonder to wonder, and instancing, in a fresh manner, that the methods of Providence are not subjected to any mode or rule, but astonish us in new lights, and in various and changeable appearances. *

* There exists much opposition of opinion among naturalists on this curious question. We give the following as the latest observations made by an attentive observer of nature, Mr Hoy, of Stoke Nayland, Suffolk, in 1831: — "A pair of wagtails (*motacilla alba*) fixed their nest, early in April, among the ivy which covers one side of my house, and reared and took off their young. A few days after the young birds had left the nest, I observed the old birds apparently collecting materials for building, and was much amused at seeing the young running after the parent birds, with imploring looks and gestures, demanding food; but the old birds, with roots or pieces of grass in their bills, seemed quite heedless of them, and intent on their new habitation. Their motions were narrowly watched by a female cuckoo, which I saw constantly near the place; but the wagtails had placed their second nest within a yard of the door, and so well concealed among some luxuriant ivy, that the cuckoo, being often frightened away, was not able to discover the nest. The intruder being thus thwarted in its design, the birds hatched their second brood, which was accidentally destroyed a few days after. In about ten days they actually commenced a third nest, within a few feet of the situation of the second, in safety. I have repeatedly taken the cuckoo's eggs from the wagtail's nest; in this locality, it has a decided preference to it. I do not recollect finding it in any other, excepting in two instances, once in the hedge-warbler's, and another time in the redstart's nest. In this vicinity, whether the wagtail selects the hole of a pollard tree, a cleft in the wall, or a projecting ledge under a bridge, it does not often escape the prying eye of the cuckoo, as, in all these situations, I have frequently found either egg or young. The cuckoo appears to possess the power of retaining its egg for some time after it is ready for extrusion. On one occasion, I had observed a cuckoo during several days anxiously watching a pair of wagtails building; I saw the cuckoo fly from the nest two or three times before it was half completed; and at last the labour of the wagtails not going on, I imagine, so rapidly as might be wished, the cuckoo deposited its egg before the lining of the nest was finished. The egg, contrary to my expectation, was not thrown out; and on the following day the wagtail commenced laying, and, as usual, the intruder was hatched at the same time as the rest, and soon had the whole nest to itself. I once observed a cuckoo enter a wagtail's nest, which I had noticed before to contain one egg; in a few minutes the cuckoo crept from the hole, and was flying away with something in its beak, which proved to be the egg of the wagtail, which it dropped on my firing a gun at it. On examining the nest, the cuckoo had only made an exchange, leaving its own egg for the one taken. In May, 1829, I found two cuckoo's eggs in the same nest, and depended on witnessing a desperate struggle between the parties, but my hopes were frustrated by some person destroying it."

This subject is still involved in great obscurity, notwithstanding the above striking facts. — Ed.

F

What was said by a very ancient and sublime writer concerning the defect of natural affection in the ostrich, may be well applied to the bird we are talking of : — "She is hardened against her young ones, as though they were not hers : Because God hath deprived her of wisdom, neither hath he imparted to her understanding."*

Query, — Does each female cuckoo lay but one egg in a season, or does she drop several in different nests, according as opportunity offers?

LETTER XXXI.

TO THOMAS PENNANT, ESQ.

SELBORNE, *February* 22, 1770.

DEAR SIR, — Hedge-hogs abound in my gardens and fields. The manner in which they eat the roots of the plantain in my grass walks is very curious : with their upper mandible, which is much longer than their lower, they bore under the plant, and so eat the root off upwards, leaving the tuft of leaves untouched. In this respect they are serviceable, as they destroy a very troublesome weed ; but they deface the walks in some measure, by digging little round holes. It appears, by the dung that they drop upon the turf, that beetles are no inconsiderable part of their food.† In June last, I procured a

---

* Job, xxxix. 16, 17.

† We are surprised to find that some naturalists of the present day deny the fact that hedge-hogs eat flesh. Buffon says, speaking of some tame ones, — "They ate caterpillars, beetles, and worms, and were also very fond of flesh, which they devoured, boiled or raw." Later observations prove them to be predatory animals. We saw one in the possession of Mr Woodcock, surgeon, Bury, Lancashire, which he got from a peasant, who caught it in the act of eating a toad, and which it pertinaciously kept hold of when taken, rolling itself up, and keeping firm hold of the toad with its mouth. We attempted to pull the toad from it, but it held its victim the firmer. It had consumed the head and one of the legs, when discovered. Hedge-hogs also feed on eggs, and do considerable mischief to game during the breeding season. They have been known to enter a hen-house, drive the hen off her nest, and devour the eggs.

In 1829, a labourer of the name of Copland, while abroad in the fields near Terraughty, Dumfriesshire, heard a sound which convinced him that a hare was at hand, and in jeopardy. The squeaking, however, soon ceased, and the man, after looking carefully round, came upon a leveret, which was lying dead by the side of a hedge-hog. The enemy had, by this time, coiled himself into a ball; but, as appearances indicated that he had both bit and smothered the leveret, Copland was so enraged at

litter of four or five young hedge-hogs, which appeared to be about five or six days old : they, I find, like puppies, are born blind, and could not see when they came to my hands. No doubt their spines are soft and flexible at the time of their birth, or else the poor dam would have but a bad time of it in the critical moment of parturition : but it is plain that they soon harden ; for these little pigs had such stiff prickles on their backs and side as would easily have fetched blood, had they not been handled with caution. Their spines are quite white at this age ; and they have little hanging ears, which I do not remember to be discernible in the old ones. They can, in part, at this age, draw their skin down over their faces ; but are not able to contract themselves into a ball, as they do, for the sake of defence, when full grown. The reason, I suppose, is, because the curious muscle that enables the creature to roll itself up in a ball was not then arrived at its full tone and firmness. Hedge-hogs make a deep and warm hybernaculum with leaves and moss, in which they conceal themselves for the winter ; but I never could find that they stored in any winter provision, as some quadrupeds certainly do.

I have discovered an anecdote with respect to the fieldfare, (*turdus pilaris*,) which I think is particular enough. This bird, though it sits on trees in the day-time, and procures the greatest part of its food from white-thorn hedges ; yea, moreover, builds on very high trees, as may be seen by the *Fauna Suecica;* yet always appears with us to roost on the ground. They are seen to come in flocks just before it is dark, and to settle and nestle among the heath on our forest. And, besides, the larkers, in dragging their nets by night, frequently catch them in the wheat stubbles ; while the bat fowlers, who take many red-wings in the hedges, never entangle any of this species. Why these birds, in the matter of roosting, should differ from all their congeners, and from themselves also with respect to their proceedings by day, is a fact for which I am by no means able to account.

his audacity, that he took the top of his axe and despatched him in an instant. Various game-keepers have frequently told us that they suspected the predatory habits of the hedge-hog, though we never knew an instance in which the fact was so satisfactorily proved as in the present.

In the year 1799, there was a hedge-hog in the possession of Mr Sample, of the Angel Inn at Felton, in Northumberland, which performed the duty of a turnspit, as well, in all respects, as the dog called the turnspit. It ran about the house with the same familiarity as any other domestic quadruped, and displayed an obedience, till then unknown in this species of animal. — ED.

I have somewhat to inform you of concerning the moose-deer; but, in general, foreign animals fall seldom in my way; my little intelligence is confined to the narrow sphere of my own observations at home.

LETTER XXXII.

TO THOMAS PENNANT, ESQ.

SELBORNE, *March*, 1770.

ON Michaelmas day, 1768, I managed to get a sight of the female moose belonging to the Duke of Richmond, at Good-wood; but was greatly disappointed, when I arrived at the spot, to find that it died, after having appeared in a languishing way for some time, on the morning before. However, under-standing that it was not stripped, I proceeded to examine this rare quadruped ; I found it in an old greenhouse, slung under the belly and chin by ropes, and in a standing posture; but, though it had been dead for so short a time, it was in so putrid a state that the stench was hardly supportable. The grand distinction between this deer and any other species that I have ever met with, consisted in the strange length of its legs; on which it was tilted up much in the manner of the birds of the *grallæ* order. I measured it, as they do a horse, and found that, from the ground to the wither, it was just five feet four inches, which height answers exactly to sixteen hands, a growth that few horses arrive at : but then, with this length of legs, its neck was remarkably short, no more than twelve inches ; so that, by straddling with one foot forward and the other backward, it grazed on the plain ground, with the greatest difficulty, between its legs : the ears were vast and lopping, and as long as the neck ; the head was about twenty inches long, and ass-like ; and had such a redundancy of upper lip as I never saw before, with huge nostrils. * This lip, travellers say, is esteemed a dainty dish in North America.

* The gigantic moose-deer is said by some travellers to attain from eleven to twelve feet ; but it is probable that the size of a large horse is more near its dimensions. The European elk reaches from seven to eight feet, and measures in length, from the muzzle to the insertion of the tail, ten feet.

The elk was at one time a native of Ireland, as its remains in a fossil state are often discovered in that country. A very large fossil skeleton was found in the Isle of Man, in 1821, while digging a marle pit. It was obtained for the Edinburgh College Museum, by that patriotic nobleman the late Duke of Atholl. — ED.

THE MOOSE-DEER, OR ELK.

It is very reasonable to suppose, that this creature supports itself chiefly by browsing of trees, and by wading after water plants, towards which way of livelihood the length of legs and great lip must contribute much. I have read somewhere, that it delights in eating the *nymphœa*, or water lily. From the fore-feet to the belly, behind the shoulder, it measured three feet and eight inches; the length of the legs before and behind consisted a great deal in the *tibia*, which was strangely long; but, in my haste to get out of the stench, I forgot to measure that joint exactly. Its scut seemed to be about an inch long; the colour was a grizzly black; the mane about four inches long; the fore-hoofs were upright and shapely, the hind flat and splayed. The spring before, it was only two years old, so that most probably it was not then come to its growth. What a vast tall beast must a full-grown stag be! I have been told some arrive at ten feet and a half! This poor creature had at first a female companion of the same species, which died the spring before. In the same garden was a young stag, or red-deer, between whom and this moose it was hoped that there might have been a breed; but their inequality of height must have always been a bar to any commerce of the amorous kind. I should have been glad to have examined the teeth, tongue, lips, hoofs, &c. minutely; but the putrefaction precluded all farther curiosity. This animal, the keeper told me, seemed to enjoy itself best in the extreme frost of the former winter. In the house, they shewed me the horn of a male moose, which had no front antlers, but only a broad palm, with some snags on the edge. The noble owner of the dead moose proposed to make a skeleton of her bones.

Please to let me hear if my female moose corresponds with that you saw; and whether you think still that the American moose and European elk are the same creature.

LETTER XXXIII.

TO THE HON. DAINES BARRINGTON.

SELBORNE, *April* 12, 1770.

DEAR SIR,—I heard many birds of several species sing last year after midsummer; enough to prove that the summer solstice is not the period that puts a stop to the music of the woods. The yellow-hammer, no doubt, persists with more steadiness than any other; but the woodlark, the wren, the red-breast, the swallow, the white-throat, the goldfinch, the common linnet, are all undoubted instances of the truth of what I advanced.

If this severe season does not interrupt the regularity of the summer migrations, the black-cap will be here in two or three days.* I wish it was in my power to procure you one of those songsters; but I am no bird catcher; and so little used to birds in a cage, that I fear, if I had one, it would soon die for want of skill in feeding.

Was your reed-sparrow, which you kept in a cage, the thick billed reed-sparrow of the *Zoology*, p. 320 ? or was it the less reed-sparrow of Ray, the sedge-bird of Mr Pennant's last publication, p. 16 ?

As to the matter of long billed birds growing fatter in moderate frosts, I have no doubt within myself what should be the reason. The thriving at those times appears to me to arise altogether from the gentle check which the cold throws upon insensible perspiration. The case is just the same with blackbirds, &c. ; and farmers and warreners observe, the first, that their hogs fat more kindly at such times, and the latter, that their rabbits are never in such good case as in a gentle frost. But, when frosts are severe, and of long continuance, the case is soon altered ; for then a want of food soon over-balances the repletion occasioned by a checked perspiration. I have observed, moreover, that some human constitutions are more inclined to plumpness in winter than in summer.

When birds come to suffer by severe frost, I find that the first that fail and die are the red-wing field-fares, and then the song-thrushes.

You wonder, with good reason, that the hedge-sparrows, &c. can be induced at all to sit on the egg of the cuckoo, without being scandalized at the vast disproportioned size of the supposititious egg ; but the brute creation, I suppose, have very little idea of size, colour, or number.† For, the

---

* Sir William Jardine supposes that the black-cap of Britain migrates to Madeira, having received specimens from that island; but Dr Heineken, who resided there, informs us that it is resident all the year round. Mr Lewin shot one in Kent, in January.—Ed.

† The egg of the cuckoo is less than that of the hedge-sparrow ; thus proving the fitness of all natural bodies to the ends for which they are intended. Were we unacquainted with the fact, that cuckoos do not, like other birds, incubate their own eggs, we would marvel at their great disproportion compared with the size of the bird. There is, no doubt, some wise end to be fulfilled in this singular economy in the habits of the cuckoo, which has yet eluded human scrutiny.—Ed.

common hen, I know, when the fury of incubation is on her, will sit on a single shapeless stone, instead of a nest full of eggs that have been withdrawn; and, moreover, a hen turkey, in the same circumstances, would sit on, in the empty nest, till she perished with hunger.

I think the matter might easily be determined whether a cuckoo lays one or two eggs, or more, in a season, by opening a female during the laying time. If more than one were come down out of the ovary, and advanced to a good size, doubtless then she would that spring lay more than one.*

I will endeavour to get a hen, and examine.

Your supposition, that there may be some natural obstruction in singing birds while they are mute, and that, when this is removed, the song recommences, is new and bold. I wish you could discover some good grounds for this suspicion.

I was glad you were pleased with my specimen of the *caprimulgus*, or fern-owl; you were, I find, acquainted with the bird before.

When we meet, I shall be glad to have some conversation with you concerning the proposal you make of my drawing up an account of the animals in this neighbourhood. Your partiality towards my small abilities persuades you, I fear, that I am able to do more than is in my power; for it is no small undertaking for a man, unsupported and alone, to begin a natural history from his own autopsia. Though there is endless room for observation in the field of nature, which is boundless, yet investigation (where a man endeavours to be sure of his facts) can make but slow progress; and all that one could collect in many years would go into a very narrow compass.

Some extracts from your ingenious " Investigations of the difference between the present temperature of the air in Italy," &c. have fallen in my way, and gave me great satisfaction. They have removed the objection that always arose in my mind whenever I came to the passages which you quote. Surely the judicious Virgil, when writing a didactic poem for the region of Italy, could never think of describing freezing rivers, unless such severity of weather pretty frequently occurred!

P.S. Swallows appear amidst snows and frost.

---

* The fact we have recorded in our note, at page 81, shews that they produce more than one egg; and, if we may reason from analogy, it may be mentioned that the yellow-billed cuckoo of America lays three or four eggs, and the black-billed cuckoo of the same country lays from four to five eggs; and these birds are very closely allied in physical structure to the common cuckoo. — ED.

LETTER XXXIV.

TO THOMAS PENNANT, ESQ.

SELBORNE, *May* 12, 1770.

DEAR SIR,—Last month we had such a series of cold tur-bulent weather, such a constant succession of frost, and snow, and hail, and tempest, that the regular migration, or appearance of the summer birds, was much interrupted. Some did not shew themselves (at least were not heard) till weeks after their usual time, as the black-cap and white-throat; and some have not been heard yet, as the grasshopper-lark and largest willow-wren. As to the fly-catcher, I have not seen it; it is indeed one of the latest, but should appear about this time; and yet, amidst all this meteorous strife and war of the elements, two swallows discovered themselves as long ago as the eleventh of April, in frost and snow; but they withdrew quickly, and were not visible again for many days. House-martens, which are always more backward than swallows, were not observed till May came in.

Among the *monogamous* birds, several are to be found, after pairing time, single, and of each sex: but whether this state of celibacy is matter of choice or necessity, is not so easily discoverable. When the house-sparrows deprive my martens of their nests, as soon as I cause one to be shot, the other, be it cock or hen, presently procures a mate, and so for several times following. *

---

* The late Mr Jamieson, of Portobello, told us a remarkable circum-stance of the swallow, which was equal to human sagacity. A pair of these birds built a nest in the corner of one of his windows at Portobello. They had scarcely finished their labour, when a pair of house-sparrows took forcible possession, and drove the rightful owners from their domicile. The swallows made several unsuccessful attempts to regain possession, being always beaten off by the sparrows, who defended the entrance with determined obstinacy. At last, finding their attempts fruitless, they departed, and, in a short time, returned with a host of their companions, who did not attempt to take the intruders by storm, but, in a very short time, by their united efforts, built up the entrance to the nest, determined seemingly to imprison, for life, the occupiers of the property which had been unlawfully acquired.

Male birds procure mates by the power of their song. Hence it has been inferred, that if a confined bird had acquired the song of another species, without retaining any notes of its own, and was set at liberty, the pro-bability is, that it would never find a mate of its own species; and, even.

I have known a dove-house infested by a pair of white owls, which made great havock among the young pigeons : one of the owls was shot as soon as possible ; but the survivor readily found a mate, and the mischief went on.   After some time the new pair were both destroyed, and the annoyance ceased. *

Another instance I remember, of a sportsman, whose zeal for the increase of his game being greater than his humanity, after pairing time, he always shot the cock-bird of every couple of partridges upon his grounds, supposing that the rivalry of many males interrupted the breed.   He used to say, that, though he had widowed the same hen several times, yet he found she was still provided with a fresh paramour, that did not take her away from her usual haunt.

Again : I knew a lover of setting, an old sportsman, who has often told me, that soon after harvest, he has frequently taken small coveys of partridges, consisting of cock birds alone : these he pleasantly used to call old bachelors.

There is a propensity belonging to common house cats that is very remarkable ; I mean their violent fondness for fish, which appears to be their most favourite food ; and yet, nature in this instance seems to have planted in them an appetite that, unassisted, they know not how to gratify : for of all quadrupeds, cats are the least disposed towards water ;

although it did, there is no reason to doubt but the young of that bird would be devoid of its native notes.

There has been much controversy among naturalists, whether the notes of birds are innate or acquired ; the greater part of which has originated amongst those who argue on general principles without experimenting. We have ourselves instituted these experiments, and have hence proved clearly, that the song of birds is innate.   We have brought up repeatedly broods of young chaffinches, and they invariably sang their native notes when they arrived at maturity ; and this without the possibility of their hearing the song of their kindred.   Nay, on the contrary, they were brought up in the same room with a gray linnet, and never acquired any of its notes ; but had their *peculiar* notes, which cannot possibly be mistaken. — Ed.

* It is a fact not generally known that owls feed on fish.   The Rev. Mr Bree took some young brown owls (*strix stridula*) from the nest, and placed them among the trees in the garden of Allesley rectory.   In that situation the parent birds repeatedly brought them live fish, such as bull-heads, and loach, which they had procured in a neighbouring brook.   Many years ago, the gold and silver fish in the fishpond in the garden of Bulstrode, the property of the Duke of Portland, were captured by the common brown owl.   This fact was discovered by men set to watch the pond. — Ed.

and will not, when they can avoid it, deign to wet a foot, much less to plunge into that element.*

Quadrupeds that prey on fish are amphibious ; such as the otter, which by nature is so well formed for diving, that it makes great havock among the inhabitants of the waters. Not supposing that we had any of those beasts in our shallow brooks, I was much pleased to see a male otter brought to me, weighing twenty-one pounds, that had been shot on the bank of our stream, below the Priory, where the rivulet divides the parish of Selborne from Harteley Wood.

LETTER XXXV.

TO THE HON. DAINES BARRINGTON.

SELBORNE, *May* 21, 1770.

DEAR SIR, — The severity and turbulence of last month so interrupted the regular process of summer migration, that some of the birds do but just begin to shew themselves, and others are apparently thinner than usual ; as the white-throat, the black-cap, the redstart, the fly-catcher. I well remember, that, after the very severe spring, in the year 1739-40, summer birds of passage were very scarce. They come probably hither with a south-east wind, or when it blows between those points ; but in that unfavourable year, the winds blew the

---

* Many instances have been recorded of cats catching fish. Mr Moody of Jesmond, near Newcastle-upon-Tyne, had a cat in 1829, which had been in his possession for some years, that caught fish with great assiduity, and frequently brought them home alive! Besides minnows and eels, she occasionally carried home pilchards, one of which, about six inches long, was found in her possession in August, 1827. She also contrived to teach a neighbour's cat to fish ; and the two have been seen together watching by the Uis for fish. At other times, they have been seen at opposite sides of the river, not far from each other, on the look out for their prey.

The following still more extraordi ry circumstance of a cat fishing in the sea, appeared in the *Plymouth Journal*, June, 1828 : —

" There is now at the battery on the Devil's Point, a cat, which is an expert catcher of the finny tribe, being in the constant habit of diving into the sea, and bringing up the fish alive in her mouth, and depositing them in the guard-room, for the use of the soldiers. She is now seven years old, and has long been a useful caterer. It is supposed that her pursuit of the water-rats first taught her to venture into the water, to which it is well known puss has a natural aversion. She is as fond of the water as a Newfoundland dog, and takes her regular peregrinations along the rocks at its edge, looking out for her prey, ready to dive for them at a moment's notice. — ED.

whole spring and summer through from the opposite quarters. And yet, amidst all these disadvantages, two swallows, as I mentioned in my last, appeared this year as early as the eleventh of April, amidst frost and snow ; but they withdrew again for a time. *

I am not pleased to find that some people seem so little satisfied with Scopoli's new publication. † There is room to expect great things from the hands of that man, who is a good naturalist ; and one would think that a history of the birds of so distant and southern a region as Carniola would be new and interesting. I could wish to see that work, and hope to get it sent down. Dr Scopoli is physician to the wretches that work in the quicksilver mines of that district.

When you talked of keeping a reed-sparrow, and giving it seeds, I could not help wondering ; because the reed-sparrow which I mentioned to you, (*passer arundinaceus minor*, Raii,) is a soft-billed bird, and most probably migrates hence before winter; whereas the bird you kept (*passer torquatus*, Raii,) abides all the year, and is a thick-billed bird. I question whether the latter be much of a songster ; but in this matter I want to be better informed. The former has a variety of hurrying notes, and sings all night. Some part of the song of the former, I suspect, is attributed to the latter. We have plenty of the soft-billed sort, which Mr Pennant had entirely left out of his *British Zoology*, till I reminded him of his omission. See *British Zoology* last published, p. 16.‡

* In 1830, the following summer birds were noticed by Mr J. D. Hoy, at Stoke Rayland, Suffolk, as appearing very early :—

Least willow-wren,	.	March 18	Sedge warbler,	.	April 22
Wry-neck,	. .	— 31	Cuckoo,	. .	— 25
Sand martens, a flock of			Lesser white-throat,		— 25
ten,	. . .	April 1	Wood-wren,	. .	— 26
Chimney swallow ; saw			Martens ; several	.	— 28
four,	. . .	— 3	Spotted flycatcher, one ;		
Yellow wagtail,	.	— 3	several seen 1st May,		— 29
Willow-wren,	. .	— 5	Turtle dove, .	. .	— 30
Redstart, . .	.	— 6	Great pettychaps,	.	— 30
Black-cap, .	. .	— 7	Reed warbler,	.	May 4
Nightingale,	. .	— 9	Hobby, .	. .	— 4
Greater white-throat ; saw			Redbacked shrike,	.	— 7
one,	. . .	— 10	Swifts ; several,	.	— 10
Field lark,	. .	— 14	Quail, .	. .	— 10
Grasshopper warbler,	.	— 14	Goatsucker,	. .	— 14
Whinchat,	. .	— 15			ED.

† This work he calls his "*Annus Primus Historico-Naturalis.*"
‡ See Letter XXVI. To Thomas Pennant, Esq.

I have somewhat to advance on the different manners in which different birds fly and walk; but as this is a subject that I have not enough considered, and is of such a nature as not to be contained in a small space, I shall say nothing farther at present.*

* See Letter LXXXIV. To the Hon. Daines Barrington.
There is much variety in the flight of birds; some fly by jerks, closing their wings every third or fourth stroke, which produces an undulatory motion, as may be observed in the flight of woodpeckers warblers, wagtails, and most other small birds; others pursue a smooth and even course; while others, again, are buoyant, without perceptible motion, as the kite, kestril, and many of the hawk tribe.   The greater number of birds fly with their legs drawn up, and their neck extended; others again, from their great length of neck, and its consequent weight, are obliged to contract, or bend it in flight, for the purpose of bringing the centre of gravity on the wings, in aid of which the legs are stretched behind, as exemplified in the heron, stork, and bittern.   Others fly with protruded necks, but are compelled to throw out their legs behind, as the goose, duck, and other aquatic birds.
Aquatic birds, and those termed waders, run in the ordinary manner, by alternately placing one foot before the other; but nearly all the smaller birds jump, or hop along, as if their legs were united.   The crow, starling, lark, and wagtail, are regular walkers. — Ed.
 "The flight of a strong falcon," says Dr Shaw, "is wonderfully swift. It is recorded that a falcon belonging to the Duke of Cleve, flew out of Westphalia into Prussia in one day; and in the county of Norfolk, a hawk has made a flight at a woodcock near thirty miles in an hour."
 "But what are these," says Professor Rennie, "compared to the actual velocity and continuance of the falcon that is recorded to have belonged to Henry IV. King of France, which escaped from Fontainbleau, and in twenty-four hours after was killed in Malta, a space computed to be not less than one thousand three hundred and fifty miles! a velocity equal to fifty-seven miles in an hour, supposing the hawk to have been on the wing the whole time.   But as such birds never fly by night, and allowing the day to be at the longest, or to be eighteen hours light, this would make seventy-five miles an hour.   It is probable, however, that he neither had so many hours of light in the twenty-four to perform the journey, nor that he was retaken the moment of his arrival, so that we may fairly conclude much less time was occupied in performing this distant flight."
We do not agree with the opinion entertained by Professor Rennie, that the falcon in question did not fly by night.   Although the birds of this tribe are diurnal, still there must be instances of their flying by night, as in the case above referred to.   We would ask, where did he rest during the night in crossing the Mediterranean? Birds which make long migrations, must fly by night as well as by day in crossing a great extent of ocean.
Audubon says, "The passenger pigeon (columba migratoria) moves with extreme rapidity, propelling itself by repeated flaps of the wings, which it brings more or less near to the body, according to the degree of velocity which is required. Like the domestic pigeon, it often flies

No doubt the reason why the sex of birds in their first plumage is so difficult to be distinguished is, as you say, " because they are not to pair and discharge their parental functions till the ensuing spring." As colours seem to be the chief external sexual distinction in many birds, these colours do not take place till sexual attachments begin to obtain. And the case is the same in quadrupeds ; among whom, in their younger days, the sexes differ but little ; but, as they advance to maturity, horns and shaggy manes, beards and brawny necks, &c. strongly discriminate the male from the female. We may instance still farther in our own species, where a beard and stronger features are usually characteristic of the male sex ; but this sexual diversity does not take place in earlier life ; for a beautiful youth shall be so like a beautiful girl, that the difference shall not be discernible :—*

> Quem si puellarum insereres choro,
> Mirè sagaces falleret hospites
> Discrimen obscurum, solutis
>   Crinibus, ambiguóque vultu. — Hor.

during the love season, in a circling manner, supporting itself with both wings angularly elevated, in which position it keeps them until it is about to alight. Now and then, during these circular flights, the tips of the primary quills of each wing are made to strike against each other, producing a sharp rap, which may be heard at a distance of thirty or forty yards. Before alighting, the passenger pigeon, like the Carolina parrot, and a few other species of birds, breaks the force of its flight by repeated flappings, as if apprehensive of receiving injury from coming too suddenly into contact with the branch, or the spot of ground, on which it intends to settle."

Mr Audubon calculates that the passenger pigeon must travel at the rate of a mile in a minute, a velocity which would enable one of these birds to visit the European continent in less than three days. —Ed.

* There is a remarkable physiological fact in the animal economy, — that of the females of many species assuming somewhat of the character of the male when they become aged. This obtains in a strong degree in many animals, and something similar takes place in the human species ; for example, that increase of hair observable in the faces of many women advanced in life, is certainly an approximation towards a beard, which is one of the most distinguishing secondary properties of man. It is also well known that old mares approach the form of the horse, in the thickening of the crest.

Dr Butter, of Plymouth, has satisfactorily proved, that our female domestic fowls have all a tendency to assume the male plumage at an advanced period of their lives, so as to make them resemble the cock of their own species. In illustration, he states, that " Mr Corham, at Compton, near Plymouth, has, for a long series of years, possessed an excellent breed of game-fowls, the cocks of which are of a beautifully dark-red colour, and the hens of a dusky brown. One hen of this

LETTER XXXVI.

TO THOMAS PENNANT, ESQ.

SELBORNE, *August* 1, 1770.

DEAR SIR,—The French, I think, in general, are strangely prolix in their natural history. What Linnæus says with

breed was allowed to live as long as possible, because her chickens became so renowned in the cock-pit. When, however, she had attained the age of fifteen years, she was observed, after moulting, to have acquired some arched cock's feathers in her tail, whilst others (old feathers) remained straight and brown, as formerly. By degrees, and during one moulting season, the whole of her dusky plumage was thrown off, and succeeded by a covering of red, and more beautiful feathers, quite like those of the cock of her own breed. In the course of the single season, the change was so fully accomplished, that, as she walked about, any stranger might have pronounced her rather to have been a cock than a hen. Spurs, likewise, sprouted out on her legs; she acquired a comb and wattles on her head; and even crowed hoarsely, not unlike a young cock. Her wattles were, however, cut off afterwards, for the purpose of making her look like a fighting cock. After the completion of this change of plumage, she discontinued to lay eggs; and lived no very considerable time to enjoy her recently acquired, but splendid costume." This bird is now in Dr Butter's collection. This gentleman adduces other evidence of a similar change, in two old hens, kept for him by a Mrs Adams, of Bowden, near Totness, on purpose to ascertain if the change was general. One of these was fifteen years old, and the other thirteen. Of these she says, " I bought them both when pullets. They were of the common domestic breed, and excellent layers, which was the reason I kept them so long. I first observed the change on them after an absence of five months; when I inquired of my dairy-maid, ' From whence come these two young cocks?' for such they appeared to me in their plumage and crowing. I was greatly surprised at being informed, that they were my two old hens."

In Tucker's *Ornithologia Danmoniensis*, there is an account of a domestic hen, which changed her feathers to those of the cock; and Aristotle, in his *Hist. Anim.* lib. ix. c. 36, makes mention of a domestic hen assuming the male plumage.

When we were in Downpatrick, our friend, William Johnstone, Esq. informed us of a circumstance which, no doubt, was referable to this cause. He had succeeded to a large fortune by the will of an uncle, and among the animals which he acquired was an old cock, a favourite of the old gentleman. It was, out of respect for his memory, permitted to live until it died a natural death. Mr Johnstone shewed me the cock, which was then alive, and which he considered as a very miraculous one, having, at short intervals, laid two small eggs, not larger than those of a blackbird, and nearly circular, with very strong shells. He was quite certain that they were extruded by this supposed cock, as no other fowl could possibly get into the place where he was kept at the time. We told him we had no doubt but it was a hen, with the male plumage from age; but he was firmly of belief that it was an old cock. From circumstances of this kind have arisen, no doubt, the fable of the cockatrice. —ED.

DOMESTIC HEN WITH MALE PLUMAGE.

respect to insects, holds good in every other branch : " *Verbo-sitas præsentis sæculi, calamitas artis*."

Pray how do you approve of Scopoli's new work ? As I admire his *Entomologia*, I long to see it.

I forgot to mention in my last letter, and had not room to insert in the former, that the male moose, in rutting time, swims from island to island, in the lakes and rivers of North America, in pursuit of the females. My friend, the chaplain, saw one killed in the water, as it was on that errand, in the river of St Lawrence : it was a monstrous beast, he told me ; but he did not take the dimensions.

When I was last in town, our friend Mr Barrington most obligingly carried me to see many curious sights. As you were then writing to him about horns, he carried me to see many strange and wonderful specimens. There is, I remember, at Lord Pembroke's, at Wilton, a horn-room furnished with more than thirty different pairs :. but I have not seen that house lately.

Mr Barrington shewed me many astonishing collections of stuffed and living birds from all quarters of the world.   After I had studied over the latter for a time, I remarked that every species almost that came from distant regions, such as South America, the coast of Guinea, &c. were thick-billed birds, of the *loxia* and *fringilla* genera ; and no *motacillæ* or *muscicapidæ*,* were to be met with. When I came to consider, the reason was obvious enough ; for the hard-billed birds subsist on seeds which are easily carried on board, while the soft-billed birds, which are supported by worms and insects, or, what is a succedaneum for them, fresh raw meat, can meet with neither in long and tedious voyages. It is from this defect of food that our collections (curious as they are) are defective, and we are deprived of some of the most delicate and lively genera.

LETTER XXXVII.

TO THOMAS PENNANT, ESQ.

SELBORNE, *September* 14, 1770.

DEAR SIR,— You saw, I find, the ringousels again among their native crags ; and are farther assured that they continue

---

* The flycatchers and warblers abound in South America, and these of many beautiful and curious species.—ED.

resident in those cold regions the whole year. From whence then do our ringousels migrate so regularly every September, and make their appearance again, as if in their return, every April? They are more early this year than common, for some were seen at the usual hill on the fourth of this month.

An observing Devonshire gentleman tells me, that they frequent some parts of Dartmoor, and breed there, but leave those haunts about the end of September, or beginning of October, and return again about the end of March.

Another intelligent person assures me, that they breed in great abundance all over the Peak of Derby, and are called there torousels, withdraw in October and November, and return in spring. This information seems to throw some light on my new migration.

Scopoli's new work * (which I have just procured) has its merits, in ascertaining many of the birds of the Tyrol and Carniola. Monographers, come from whence they may, have, I think, fair pretence to challenge some regard and approbation from the lovers of natural history; for, as no man can alone investigate all the works of nature, these partial writers may, each in his department, be more accurate in their discoveries, and freer from errors, than more general writers, and so by degrees may pave the way to an universal correct natural history. Not that Scopoli is so circumstantial and attentive to the life and conversation of his birds as I could wish: he advances some false facts; as when he says of the *hirundo urbica*, that "*pullos extra nidum non nutrit.*" This assertion I know to be wrong, from repeated observation this summer; for house-martens do feed their young flying, though, it must be acknowledged, not so commonly as the house-swallow: and the feat is done in so quick a manner as not to be perceptible to indifferent observers. He also advances some (I was going to say) improbable facts; as when he says of the woodcock that "*pullos rostro portat fugiens ab hoste.*" But candour forbids me to say absolutely that any fact is false, because I have never been witness to such a fact. I have only to remark, that the long unwieldy bill of the woodcock is perhaps the worst adapted of any among the winged creation for such a feat of natural affection.

* *Annus Primus Historico-Naturalis.*

LETTER XXXVIII.

RINGMER, near LEWES, *October* 8, 1770.

DEAR SIR,—I am glad to hear that Kuekalm is to furnish you with the birds of Jamaica. A sight of the *hirundines* ot that hot and distant island would be a great entertainment to me.

The *Anni* of Scopoli are now in my possession ; and I have read the *Annus Primus* with satisfaction ; for, though some parts of this work are exceptionable, and he may advance some mistaken observations, yet the ornithology of so distant a country as Carniola is very curious. Men that undertake only one district, are much more likely to advance natural knowledge, than those that grasp at more than they can possibly be acquainted with. Every kingdom, every province, should have its own monographer.

The reason, perhaps, why he mentions nothing of Ray's *Ornithology*, may be the extreme poverty and distance of his country, into which the works of our great naturalists may have never yet found their way. You have doubts, I know, whether this *Ornithology* is genuine, and really the work of Scopoli : as to myself, I think I discover strong tokens of authenticity; the style corresponds with that of his *Entomology;* and his characters of his Ordines and Genera are many of them new, expressive, and masterly. He has ventured to alter some of the Linnæan genera, with sufficient show of reason.

It might, perhaps, be mere accident that you saw so many swifts and no swallows at Staines ; because, in my long observation of those birds, I never could discover the least degree of rivalry or hostility between the species.

Ray remarks, that birds of the *galinæ* order, as cocks and hens, partridges and pheasants, &c. are *pulveratrices*, such as dust themselves, using that method of cleansing their feathers, and ridding themselves of their vermin. As far as I can observe, many birds that dust themselves never wash ; and I once thought that those birds that wash themselves would never dust : but here I find myself mistaken ; for common house-sparrows are great *pulveratrices*, being frequently seen grovelling and wallowing in dusty roads ; and yet they are great washers. Does not the skylark dust ?

G

Query,— Might not Mahomet and his followers take one method of purification from these *pulveratrices?* because I find, from travellers of credit, that if a strict Mussulman is journeying in a sandy desert, where no water is to be found, at stated hours he strips off his clothes, and most scrupulously rubs his body over with sand or dust.

A countryman told me he had found a young fern-owl in the nest of a small bird on the ground; and that it was fed by the little bird.   I went to see this extraordinary phenomenon, and found that it was a young cuckoo hatched in the nest of a titlark; it was become vastly too big for its nest, appearing

$$\text{————————— in tenui re}$$
$$\text{Majores pennas nido extendisse,——}$$

and was very fierce and pugnacious, pursuing my finger, as I teased it, for many feet from the nest, and sparring and buffeting with its wings like a game-cock.   The dupe of a dam appeared at a distance, hovering about, with meat in its mouth, and expressing the greatest solicitude.

In July, I saw several cuckoos skimming over a large pond; and found, after some observation, that they were feeding on the *libellulæ,* or dragon-flies, some of which they caught as they settled on the weeds, and some as they were on the wing. Notwithstanding what Linnæus says, I cannot be induced to believe that they are birds of prey.*

This district affords some birds that are hardly ever heard of at Selborne.   In the first place, considerable flocks of crossbeaks (*loxiæ curvirostræ*) have appeared this summer in the pine groves belonging to this house; † the water-ousel is

* The food of the cuckoo is insects and caterpillars, particularly those of the lepidopterous order, both smooth and rough, as also butterflies and moths themselves.   Audubon says, the yellow-billed cuckoo of America robs smaller birds of their eggs, which it sucks on all occasions, and that the black-billed cuckoo lives on fruits, fresh water shell-fish, aquatic larvæ, and very young frogs. — Ed.

\ † Three species of crossbills have been identified as occasional visitants of Britain, namely, the American crossbill, (*curvirostra Americana,*) the white-winged crossbill, (*curvirostra leucoptera,*) and parrot-billed crossbill, (*c. pytiopsittacus,*) a specimen of which was shot in Scotland, and is in the cabinet of Sir William Jardine, Bart.   In the autumn of 1821, a large flock of crossbills was discovered feeding in a grove of firs. " After watching them for some time," says a narrator, " with a gun, I procured fifteen specimens, out of which only two were in full feather, the breasts and backs of the others being nearly bare.   After this, they used to visit the same spot pretty regularly twice a day.   The males varied very much in colour, some being of a deeper red, and others inclining

said to haunt the mouth of the Lewes river, near Newhaven;✳ and the Cornish chough builds, I know, all along the chalky cliffs of the Sussex shore.

I was greatly pleased to see little parties of ringousels (my newly discovered migrators) scattered, at intervals, all along the Sussex downs from Chichester to Lewes. Let them come from whence they will, it looks very suspicious that they are cantoned along the coast in order to pass the Channel when severe weather advances. They visit us again in April, as it should seem, in their return, and are not to be found in the dead of winter. It is remarkable that they are very tame, and

rather more to yellow, particularly on the tail coverts, and being a little mottled with yellow upon the breast and back. The Weymouth pine was their particular favourite, indeed, I scarcely observed them on any other tree, except the sentinel, who regularly took his station on the top of a spruce-fir, which happened to be the highest in the immediate neighbourhood of their haunt. Their note, or call, very much resembled the chirping of a chicken. They continued their visits, though the flock certainly gradually diminished, during a great part of the winter; and one pair remained long after the rest had left, being constantly seen in February and beginning of March, 1822." This was the year in which Mr Selby mentions them as being so plentiful throughout the kingdom. See our note, page 26. — ED.

✳ This is the dipper of modern ornithologists, (*cinclus aquaticus* of Bechstein.) White does not seem to have been acquainted with the musical powers of this interesting species. The dipper begins to pour forth its strong, distinct, and varied notes in the beginning of spring, and is the earliest warbler of the remote situations where it usually localises. Montagu says, " This bird is amongst the few that sing so early in the spring as the months of January and February. In hard frost, on the 11th of the latter month, when the thermometer in the morning had been at twenty-six degrees, we heard this bird sing incessantly in a strong and elegant manner, and with much variation in notes, many of which were peculiar to itself, intermixed with a little of the piping of the woodlark. At the time it was singing, the day was bright, but freezing in the shade; the sun had considerably passed the meridian, and was obscured from the bird by the lofty surrounding hills. The dipper devours a considerable quantity of fishes' spawn, especially the large ova of the salmon."

The dipper dives with great dexterity, and can swim a considerable way under water, emerging at a distance from the spot where it disappeared. " We found a nest of this bird," says Colonel Montagu, " in a steep bank, projecting over a rivulet, clothed with moss. The nest was so well adapted to the surrounding materials, that nothing but the old bird flying in with a fish in its bill would have led to a discovery. The young were nearly full feathered, but incapable of flight; and the moment the nest was disturbed, they fluttered out, and dropped into the water, and, to our astonishment, instantly vanished; but, in a little time, made their appearance at some distance down the stream; and it was with difficulty that two out of the five were taken, as they dived on being approached."— ED.

seem to have no manner of apprehensions of danger from a person with a gun. There are bustards on the wide downs near Brighthelmstone. No doubt you are acquainted with the Sussex downs. The prospects and rides round Lewes are most lovely.

As I rode along near the coast, I kept a very sharp look-out in the lanes and woods, hoping I might, at this time of the year, have discovered some of the summer short-winged birds of passage crowding towards the coast, in order for their departure ; but it was very extraordinary that I never saw a redstart, white-throat, black-cap, uncrested wren, flycatcher, &c. ; and I remember to have made the same remark in former years, as I usually come to this place annually about this time. The birds most common along the coast, at present, are the stone-chatters, whinchats, buntings, linnets, some few wheat-ears, titlarks, &c. Swallows and house-martens abound yet, induced to prolong their stay by this soft, still, dry season.

A land tortoise, which has been kept for thirty years in a little walled court belonging to the house where I am now visiting, retires under ground about the middle of November, and comes forth again about the middle of April. When it first appears, in the spring, it discovers very little inclination towards food ; but, in the height of summer, grows voracious ; and then, as the summer declines, its appetite declines ; so that, for the last six weeks in autumn, it hardly eats at all. Milky plants, such as lettuces, dandelions, sow-thistles, are its favourite dish. In a neighbouring village, one was kept till, by tradition, it was supposed to be an hundred years old,—an instance of vast longevity in such a poor reptile! *

* In the library of Lambeth Palace, is the shell of a tortoise, brought there in 1623; it lived until 1730, and was killed by being carelessly exposed to the inclemency of the weather. Another, at the episcopal palace at Fulham, procured by Bishop Laud, in 1628, died in 1753. One at Peterborough was known to have lived to the extraordinary age of two hundred and twenty years!

During the hybernation of animals, a temporary stagnation or suspension of active life ensues: their temperature becomes diminished, and the circulation of the blood slower; respiration less frequent, and sometimes entirely suspended ; the action of their stomach and digestive organs are also suspended ; and the irritability and sensibility of the muscular and nervous powers are greatly diminished. Heat and air are the only agencies which rouse them from their death-like lethargy. Judging from the circumstance of toads, lizards, and bats, being found alive in solid rocks, and in the centre of trees, this torpidity may endure the lapse of ages, without the extinction of life. Mr Murray, in his *Researches in Natural History*, says, " a toad was found, under the coal seam, in the ironstone

LETTER XXXIX.

TO THOMAS PENNANT, ESQ.

SELBORNE, *October* 29, 1770.

DEAR SIR,—After an ineffectual search in Linnæus, Brisson, &c. I begin to suspect that I discern my brother's *hirundo hyberna* in Scopoli's newly discovered *hirundo rupestris*, p. 167 His description of " *Supra murina, subtus albida ; rectrices maculâ ovali albâ in latere interno ; pedes nudi, nigri ; rostrum nigrum ; remiges obscuriores quam plumæ dorsales ; rectrices remigibus concolores ; caudâ emarginatâ nec forcipatâ,*" agrees very well with the bird in question ; but, when he comes to advance that it is " *statura hirundinis urbicæ,*" and that " *definitio hirundinis ripariæ Linnæi huic quoque convenit,*" he, in some measure, invalidates all he has said ; at least, he shews at once that he compares them to these species merely from memory ; for I have compared the birds themselves, and find they differ widely in every circumstance of shape, size, and colour. However, as you will have a specimen, I shall be glad to hear what your judgment is in the matter.

Whether my brother is forestalled in his nondescript or not, he will have the credit of first discovering that they spend their winters under the warm and sheltery shores of Gibraltar and Barbary.

Scopoli's characters of his ordines and genera are clear, just, and expressive, and much in the spirit of Linnæus. These few remarks are the result of my first perusal of Scopoli's *Annus Primus.*

The bane of our science is the comparing one animal to the other by memory. For want of caution in this particular, Scopoli falls into errors. He is not so full with regard to the manners of his indigenous birds as might be wished, as you justly observe : his Latin is easy, elegant, and expressive, and very superior to Kramer's. *

over which it rests, in a coal mine at Auchincruive, in Ayrshire." This fact invalidates the Huttonian theory of the primitive formation of the earth, and is in favour of the Wernerian hypothesis. — ED.

* See his *Elenchus Vegetabilium et Animalium per Austriam Inferiorem, &c.*

LETTER XL.

TO THOMAS PENNANT, ESQ.

SELBORNE, *November* 26, 1770.

DEAR SIR,—I was much pleased to see, among the collection of birds from Gibraltar, some of those short-winged English summer birds of passage, concerning whose departure we have made so much inquiry. Now, if these birds are found in Andalusia to migrate to and from Barbary, it may easily be supposed that those that come to us may migrate back to the continent, and spend their winters in some of the warmer parts of Europe. This is certain, that many soft-billed birds that come to Gibraltar appear there only in spring and autumn, seeming to advance in pairs towards the northward, for the sake of breeding during the summer months, and retiring in parties and broods towards the south at the decline of the year; so that the rock of Gibraltar is the great rendezvous and place of observation, from whence they take their departure each way towards Europe or Africa. It is therefore no mean discovery, I think, to find that our small short-winged summer birds of passage are to be seen, spring and autumn, on the very skirts of Europe; it is a presumptive proof of their emigrations.

Scopoli seems to me to have found the *hirundo melba*, (the great Gibraltar swift,) in Tyrol, without knowing it. For what is his *hirundo alpina*, but the aforementioned bird in other words? Says he " *Omnia prioris*, (meaning the swift,) *sed pectus album; paulo major priore.*" I do not suppose this to be a new species. It is true also of the melba, that " *nidificat in excelsis Alpium rupibus.*" Vid. *Annum Primum,*.

My Sussex friend, a man of observation and good sense, but no naturalist, to whom I applied on account of the stone-curlew, (*oedicnemus*,) sends me the following account :—" In looking over my *Naturalist's Journal* for the month of April, I find the stone-curlews are first mentioned on the 17th and 18th, which date seems to me rather late. They live with us all the spring and summer, and at the beginning of autumn prepare to take leave, by getting together in flocks. They seem to me a bird of passage that may travel into some dry hilly country south of us, probably Spain, because of the abundance of sheep-walks in that country; for they spend their summers with us in such districts. This conjecture I hazard, as I never met with any one that has seen them in England in the winter. I believe they are not fond of going near the water, but feed on earth-worms, that are common on sheep-walks and downs. They breed on fallows and lay-fields abounding with grey mossy flints, which much resemble their young in colour, among which they skulk and conceal themselves. They make no nest, but lay their eggs on the bare ground, producing in common but two at a time. There is reason to think their young run soon after they are hatched, and that the old ones do not feed them, but only lead them about at the time of feeding, which, for the most part, is in the night." Thus far my friend.

In the manners of this bird, you see, there is something very analogous to the bustard, whom it also somewhat resembles in aspect and make, and in the structure of its feet. *

For a long time I have desired my relation to look out for these birds in Andalusia ; and now he writes me word that, for the first time, he saw one dead in the market, on the 3d of September.

When the *oedicnemus* flies, it stretches out its legs straight behind, like a heron.

LETTER XLI.

TO THE HON. DAINES BARRINGTON.

SELBORNE, *December* 20, 1770.

DEAR SIR,—The birds that I took for aberdavines were reed-sparrows (*passeres torquati*.)

* The bustard is the largest of British birds; but we fear it is now nearly, if not entirely, extinct in this country. Some years ago, a pair of these, male and female, were kept in a garden at Norwich infirmary. The male was an extremely majestic bird, and possessed of much courage, for he feared nothing, seizing any one who approached near him by the coat. The female, on the contrary, was shy and timid. It was, however, remarkable that the male bird, on discovering even a small hawk, however high in the air, squatted down on the ground, exhibiting strong marks of fear. In 1804, a fine bustard was shot, and taken to Plymouth market, where it was purchased by a publican for a shilling, its value being unknown, whereas it would have brought three or four pounds in the London market. So completely lost was this rare wanderer, that it was rejected at the second table, in consequence of the pectoral muscles differing in colour from the other parts of the breast, which is not unusual in birds of the grouse kind. Some country gentlemen arriving at the inn the following evening, and hearing of the circumstance, desired that the princely bird might be introduced, and partook of it cold at their repast. — ED.

There are, doubtless, many home internal migrations within
this kingdom that want to be better understood ; witness those
vast flocks of hen chaffinches that appear with us in the winter
without hardly any cocks among them.*   Now, were there a
due proportion of each sex, it would seem very improbable
that any one district should produce such numbers of these
little birds, and much more when only one half of the species
appears ; therefore, we may conclude, that the *fringillæ cœlebes,*
for some good purposes, have a peculiar migration of their
own, in which the sexes part.   Nor should it seem so wonderful
that the intercourse of sexes in this species of birds should be
interrupted in winter ; since, in many animals, and particularly
in bucks and does, the sexes herd separately, except at the
season when commerce is necessary for the continuance of
the breed.   For this matter of the chaffinches, see *Fauna
Suecica,* p. 85, and *Systema Naturæ,* p. 318.   I see every winter
vast flights of hen chaffinches, but none of cocks.

Your method of accounting for the periodical motions of
the British singing birds, or birds of flight, is a very probable
one, since the matter of food is a great regulator of the actions
and proceedings of the brute creation : there is but one that
can be set in competition with it, and that is love.   But I
cannot quite acquiesce with you in one circumstance, when
you advance that, " When they have thus feasted, they again
separate into small parties of five or six, and get the best fare
they can within a certain district, having no inducement to go
in quest of fresh-turned earth."   Now, if you mean that the
business of congregating is quite at an end from the conclusion
of wheat-sowing, to the season of barley and oats, it is not the
case with us ; for larks and chaffinches, and particularly linnets,
flock and congregate as much in the very dead of winter as
when the husbandman is busy with his ploughs and harrows.

Sure there can be no doubt but that woodcocks and fieldfares leave us in the spring, in order to cross the seas, and
to retire to some districts more suitable to the purpose of
breeding.†   That the former pair before they retire, and that

* We have already stated, in a note at page 32, that chaffinches do not
always separate into flocks of male and female during winter.   May not
the supposed hen chaffinches, so frequently seen, be the young birds of the
previous summer, and the males not having yet assumed the complete
plumage, are not to be distinguished from the females ? — ED.

† Fieldfares visit us in October, and leave us again about the beginning
of April.   Their principal food in this country is the fruit of the haw-
thorn, and other berries, worms, and insects.   " Perfectly gregarious as
the fieldfare is," says Knapp, " yet we observe every year, in some tall

the hens are forward with egg, I myself, when I was a sportsman, have often experienced. It cannot indeed be denied, but that now and then we hear of a woodcock's nest, or young hedgerow, or little quiet pasture, two or three of them, that have withdrawn from the main flocks, and there associate with the blackbird and the thrush."

The woodcocks arrive in Great Britain in flocks; some of them in October, but not in great numbers till November and December. They generally take advantage of the night, being seldom seen to come before sunset.

The time of their arrival depends considerably on the prevailing winds; for adverse gales always detain them, they not being able to struggle with the boisterous squalls of the Northern Ocean. The greater part of them leave this country about the latter end of February, or beginning of March, always pairing before they set out. They retire to the coast, and, if the wind be fair, set out immediately; but, if contrary, they are often detained in the neighbouring woods and thickets for some time. So well skilled are these birds in atmospherical changes, that the instant a fair wind springs up, they seize the opportunity; and where the sportsman has seen hundreds in one day, he will not find even a single bird the next.

At the Landsend, Cornwall, every fisherman and peasant can tell, from the temperature of the air, the week, if not the day, on which the woodcocks will arrive on the coast. They come in prodigious flocks, which reach the shore at the same time, and from their state of exhaustion, induced by their long flight, they are easily knocked down, or caught by dogs. A short respite soon invigorates them, so that they are enabled to pursue their inland course, but till thus recruited they are an easy prey, and produce no small profit to those who live in the neighbourhood.

Mr Warner informs us, that "We were told at Truro, as a proof of the definitive time of their arrival, that a gentleman then had sent to the Landsend for several brace, to be forwarded to him for a particular occasion. This correspondent acquainted him in answer, that no woodcocks had yet arrived; but that, on the third day from his writing, if the weather continued as it then was, there would be plenty. The state of the atmosphere remained unchanged, the visitors came as it was asserted they would, and the gentleman received the number of birds he had ordered."

It seems quite certain that the migratory birds usually return to their former haunts. The following well authenticated circumstance is related by Bewick, on the authority of Sir John Trevelyan, Bart. "In the winter of 1797," says he, "the gamekeeper of E. M. Pleydell, Esq. of Watcombe, in Dorsetshire, brought him a woodcock, alive and unhurt, which he had caught in a net set for rabbits. Mr Pleydell scratched the name upon a bit of thin brass, bent it round the woodcock's leg, and let it fly. In December, the next year, Mr Pleydell shot this bird, with the brass about its leg, in the same wood where it had been first caught." We caught a swallow, which built in the corner of a window, tied a silk thread about one of its limbs, and set it at liberty. Next year the same corner was taken possession of by a pair of swallows. We caught them, and found that one had still round its limb the piece of thread which we had tied on the preceding year. — ED.

birds, discovered in some part or other of this island; * but then they are always mentioned as rarities, and somewhat out of the common course of things ; but as to redwings and field-fares, no sportsman or naturalist has ever yet, that I could hear, pretended to have found the nest or young of those species in any part of these kingdoms.† And I the more admire at this instance as extraordinary, since, to all appearance, the same food in summer, as well as in winter, might support them here which maintains their congeners, the blackbirds and thrushes, did they choose to stay the summer through. From hence it appears, that it is not food alone which determines some species of birds with regard to their stay or departure. Fieldfares and redwings disappear sooner or later, according as the warm weather comes on earlier or later ; for I well remem-ber, after that dreadful winter, 1739-40, that cold northeast winds continued to blow on through April and May, and that these kinds of birds (what few remained of them) did not depart as usual, but were seen lingering about till the beginning of June.

The best authority that we can have for the nidification of the birds above mentioned, in any district, is the testimony of faunists that have written professedly the natural history of particular countries. Now, as to the fieldfare, Linnæus, in his *Faunâ Suecica*, says of it, that " *maximis in arboribus nidi-ficat;*" and of the redwing, he says in the same place, that " *nidificat in mediis arbusculis, sive sepibus ; ova sex cæruleo-viridia maculis nigris variis.*" Hence we may be assured that fieldfares and redwings breed in Sweden. Scopoli says, in his *Annus. Primus*, of the woodcock, that, " *nupta ad nos venit circa æquinoctium vernale,*" meaning in Tyrol, of which he is a native. And afterwards, he adds, " *nidificat in paludibus alpinis : ova ponit* 3—5." It does not appear from Kramer that wood-cocks breed at all in Austria ; but he says, " *Avis hæc septen-trionalium provinciarum æstivo tempore incola est ; ubi plerumque nidificat. Appropinquante hyeme australiores provincias petit :*

* A woodcock's nest, with four eggs in it, was found in Chicksand woods, near Sheffield, in Bedfordshire, on the 15th April, 1828. The eggs were about the size of a bantam hen's, of a bluish white ground, with irregular brown spots. — Ed.

† Mr Knapp says, " I have before me the egg of a bird, which I believe to be that of a fieldfare, taken from a nest, somewhat like that formed by the song-thrush in 1824."

Mr Bullock found the nest of a redwing at the island of Harris, one of the Hebrides. Mr Jennings says, he has been informed by a friend, on whose accuracy he can rely, that the redwing occasionally sings in this country before its departure in the spring. — Ed.

hinc circa plenilunium potissimum mensis Octobris plerumque Austriam transmigrat. Tunc rursus circa plenilunium potissimum mensis Martii per Austriam matrimonio juncta ad septentrionales provincias redit." For the whole passage (which I have abridged) see *Elenchus, &c.* p. 351. This seems to be a full proof of the emigration of woodcocks ; though little is proved concerning the place of their breeding.

P.S. — There fell in the county of Rutland, in three weeks of this present very wet weather, seven inches and a half of rain, which is more than has fallen in any three weeks for these thirty years past, in that part of the world. A mean quantity in that county for one year is twenty inches and a half. *

LETTER XLII.

TO THE HON. DAINES BARRINGTON.

FYFIELD, near ANDOVER, *February* 12, 1771.

DEAR SIR, — You are, I know, no great friend to migration ; and the well-attested accounts from various parts of the kingdom seem to justify you in your suspicions, that at least many of the swallow kind do not leave us in the winter, but lay themselves up, like insects and bats, in a torpid state, and slumber away the more uncomfortable months, till the return of the sun and fine weather awakens them.

But then we must not, I think, deny migration in general ; because migration certainly does subsist in some places, as my brother in Andalusia has fully informed me. Of the motions of these birds he has ocular demonstration, for many weeks together, both spring and fall ; during which periods, myriads of the swallow kind traverse the Straits from north to south,† and

* The average quantity of rain, which falls annually, has been calculated at between thirty-one and thirty-two inches. In Scotland, it varies, as in all other countries, with the locality. In Glasgow, it is thirty-one inches; Dumfries, thirty-six inches; and Dalkeith, twenty-five inches, making an average between thirty and thirty-one inches, or twenty-eight cubit feet of water. Countries adjacent to the coast of an extended ocean have usually more rain than inland districts. In some parts of India it is from one hundred and three to one hundred and twelve, but the average is eighty-five inches annually. — ED.

† The migration of swallows is not confined to Britain, for they appear to be influenced by a general law in every variety of climate. It has been satisfactorily proved, that swallows leave even the most extreme southern parts of Europe, as the kingdom of Naples, Sicily, the Morea, &c. and migrate to Africa and Asia. Mr Rae Wilson gives us positive

from south to north, according to the season. And these vast migrations consist not only of hirundines, but of bee-birds,*

assurance of these migrations in his travels in Egypt. He says, he had the proof, in the immense bodies of these birds which he perceived pushing their way in the direction of Egypt from Europe, during the month of November, when the winter sets in.

We are told by Wilson, that the swallows of America are also migratory, "arriving in Pennsylvania late in April, or early in May; dispersing themselves over the whole country, wherever there are vacant chimneys, in summer, sufficiently high and convenient for their accommodation. In no other situation, with us, are they observed at present to build. This circumstance naturally suggests the query, Where did these birds construct their nests before the arrival of Europeans in this country, when there were no such places for their accommodation? I would answer, Probably in the same situations in which they still continue to build in the remote regions of our western forests, where European improvements of this kind are scarcely to be found, namely, in the hollow of a tree, which, in some cases, has the nearest resemblance to their present choice, of any other. One of the first settlers in the state of Kentucky informed me, that he cut down a large hollow beech tree, which contained forty or fifty nests of the chimney swallow, most of which, by the fall of the tree, or by the weather, were lying at the bottom of the hollow; but sufficient fragments remained, adhering to the sides of the tree, to enable him to number them. They appeared, he said, to be of many years' standing."

Dr Richardson says, " In the fur countries, where the habitations of man are few and far between, the barn-swallow inhabits caves, particularly in the limestone rocks; and it frequents the out-houses of all the trading ports. When Fort Franklin was erected on the shores of the Great Bear Lake, in the autumn of 1825, we found many of the nests in the ruins of a house that had been abandoned for more than ten years." In that northern latitude they arrive about the 15th of May, and take their departure early in August. Swallows were noticed by Dr Richardson at Fort Good Hope in latitude sixty-seven and a half degrees, the most northerly post in America.— ED.

* What our author calls bee-bird, is the European bee-eater, *merops apiaster* of Linnæus. It is the only one of the genus found in Europe. It is not uncommon in the south of France, Italy, Germany, and Sweden, but abounds in the southern Russian provinces bordering on the Don and Wolga. It is gregarious and migratory, leaving its summer quarters for more southern latitudes in autumn. This bird has been frequently taken in Britain, but was not noticed till July, 1794, when one was shot at Mattishall, county of Norfolk. In the same year, a flock of about twenty was seen in June, and, in October following, a flight, much fewer in number — in all probability the same — passed over the place where they had been first seen. This bird feeds on all winged insects, which it takes on the wing like a swallow.—ED.

Sir William Jardine, in a paper on "the Birds of Madeira," in the *Edinburgh Journal of Natural and Geographical Science*, mentions that the common swift remains in that island all the year round. Notwithstanding the very respectable authority of Mr Carruthers, on whose observations he states this, we are inclined to suppose his conclusions

THE HOOPOE.

hoopoes, *oro pendolos,*⁕ or golden thrushes,† &c. and also of many of our soft-billed summer birds of passage, and moreover, of birds which never leave us, such as all the various sorts of hawks and kites.   Old Belon, two hundred years ago, gives a curious account of the incredible armies of hawks and kites which he saw in the spring time traversing the Thracian Bosphorus, from Asia to Europe. Besides the above mentioned, he remarks that the procession is swelled by whole troops of eagles and vultures.‡

must have been formed from a few solitary instances, as we firmly believe that all the species of swifts and swallows are strictly migratory over the whole globe. It has been observed, that these birds migrate under even Afric's burning sun, the equinoctial regions of America, and the more uniform temperature of all intertropical climates. It would certainly be a remarkable deviation, were the common swift of Madeira to differ from its species, which are guided by one similar law in all other parts of the world.

⁕ We have noticed the occasional appearance of the hoopoe in Britain, at page 25.   This beautiful bird is twelve inches in length, and nineteen in breadth.   The bill is about two inches long, black, slender, and somewhat curved; the eyes hazel; the tongue very short and triangular; the head is surmounted by a crest, consisting of a double row of feathers of a pale orange colour, tipped with black, the largest being about two inches in length; the neck is of a faint reddish brown; the breast and belly, white; the back, scapulars, and wings, are crossed with broad bars of black and white; the lesser coverts of the wings are light brown; the rump is white, and the tail consists of ten feathers, each marked with white, and, when closed, assumes the form of a crescent, with the horns pointing downwards; the legs are short and black.   Except when under some excitement, the crest usually falls behind on its neck.

Bechstein informs us, that, in Germany, hoopoes frequent the meadows all the summer. In the month of August, they form themselves into families in the plains; and, early in September, leave that country, returning again in the month of April. — Ed.

† The golden thrush of our author is the golden oriole, *oriolus galbula* of Linnæus. It is an occasional visitant. This very elegant species is about the size of a blackbird; the male being of a bright golden yellow, with black wings, marked here and there with yellow; the two middle tail feathers are also black, the rest yellow. The female is of a dull greenish brown in those parts where the male is black; the breast is spotted with black. A male and female were shot in the neighbourhood of the Pentland Hills, near Edinburgh, and are now in the College Museum. These birds are plentiful in France and Germany: they congregate in August, and migrate to the warmer regions of Asia, and return again in May. — Ed.

‡ The geographical range of the vultures and eagles is much extended in various species; for example, the golden eagle has been found to breed in Britain, the continent of Europe, and also in America.   That some of them have roving habits, extending their predatory excursions frequently to a great distance, is quite true; but we cannot admit the

Now, it is no wonder that birds residing in Africa should retreat before the sun as it advances, and retire to milder regions, and especially birds of prey, whose blood being heated with hot animal food, are more impatient of a sultry climate; but then I cannot help wondering why kites and hawks, and such hardy birds as are known to defy all the severity of England, and even of Sweden and all north Europe, should want to migrate from the south of Europe, and be dissatisfied with the winters of Andalusia.

It does not appear to me that much stress may be laid on the difficulty and hazard that birds must run in their migrations, by reason of vast oceans, cross winds, &c.; because, if we reflect, a bird may travel from England to the Equator without lanching out and exposing itself to boundless seas, and that by crossing the water at Dover, and again at Gibraltar. And I with the more confidence advance this obvious remark, because my bróther has always found that some of his birds, and particularly the swallow kind, are very sparing of their pains in crossing the Mediterranean; for, when arrived at Gibraltar, they do not,

> ——————— Ranged in figure, wedge their way,
> ————————————— and set forth
> Their airy caravan, high over seas
> Flying, and over lands with mutual wing
> Easing their flight;   MILTON.

but scout and hurry along in little detached parties, of six or seven in a company; and, sweeping low, just over the surface of the land and water, direct their course to the opposite continent, at the narrowest passage they can find. They usually slope across the bay to the south-west, and so pass over opposite to Tangier, which, it seems, is the narrowest space.*

In former letters, we have considered, whether it was probable that woodcocks, in moonshiny nights, cross the German Ocean from Scandinavia. As a proof that birds of less speed may pass that sea, considerable as it is, I shall relate the following incident, which, though mentioned to have happened so many years ago, was strictly matter of fact:—As

birds of these tribes to be classed among those which are migratory. It occasionally happens that these birds extend their flight from one country to another; but, then, these excursions are not marked by periodical regularity, nor influenced by atmospherical changes, but proceed from some unknown cause. — ED.

* Ceuta is the narrowest part of the Straits of Gibraltar. — ED.

some people were shooting in the parish of Trotton, in the county of Sussex, they killed a duck in that dreadful winter, 1708-9, with a silver collar about its neck, * on which were engraven the arms of the King of Denmark. This anecdote the rector of Trotton at that time has often told to a near relation of mine; and, to the best of my remembrance, the collar was in the possession of the rector.

At present, I do not know any body near the seaside that will take the trouble to remark at what time of the moon woodcocks first come: if I lived near the sea myself, I would soon tell you more of the matter. One thing I used to observe when I was a sportsman, that there were times in which woodcocks were so sluggish and sleepy, that they would drop again when flushed just before the spaniels, nay, just at the muzzle of a gun that had been fired at them: whether this strange laziness was the effect of a recent fatiguing journey, I shall not presume to say. †

Nightingales not only never reach Northumberland and Scotland, but also, as I have been always told, Devonshire and Cornwall. In those two last counties, we cannot attribute the failure of them to the want of warmth: the defect in the west is rather a presumptive argument, that these birds come over to us from the continent at the narrowest passage, and do not stroll so far westward. ‡

Let me hear from your own observation whether skylarks do not dust. I think they do: and if they do, whether they wash also.

The *alauda pratensis* of Ray was the poor dupe that was educating the booby of a cuckoo mentioned in my letter of October last. §

Your letter came too late for me to procure a ringousel for Mr Tunstal during their autumnal visit; but I will endeavour to get him one when they call on us again in April. I am glad that you and that gentleman saw my Andalusian birds;

* I have read a like anecdote of a swan.
† It is quite evident that such must be attributed to fatigue after their long excursions, as mentioned in our note at page 105. — ED.
‡ The farthest north which this bird has been known to extend in England, is the neighbourhood of Doncaster, in Yorkshire. It is certainly a strange circumstance that the nightingale has never been met with in Devonshire and Cornwall, as these counties appear peculiarly calculated for their residence, both from the mildness of the temperature and the variety of ground. The bounds prescribed to all animals and plants, is one of the most singular arrangements in the economy of nature. — ED.
§ Letter XXXVIII. To the Hon. Daines Barrington.

I hope they answered your expectation. Royston, or gray, crows, are winter birds that come much about the same time with the woodcock : they, like the fieldfare and redwing, have no apparent reason for migration ; for, as they fare in the winter like their congeners, so might they, in all appearance, in the summer.* Was not Tenant, when a boy, mistaken ? Did he not find a missel-thrush's nest, and take it for the nest of a fieldfare ?

The stock-dove, or wood-pigeon, *œnas* Raii, is the last winter bird of passage which appears with us, and is not seen till towards the end of November. About twenty years ago, they abounded in the district of Selborne, and strings of them were seen morning and evening that reached a mile or more ; but, since the beechen woods have been greatly thinned, they have much decreased in number. The ring-dove, *palumbus* Raii, stays with us the whole year, and breeds several times through the summer.†

Before I received your letter of October last, I had just remarked in my journal that the trees were unusually green. This uncommon verdure lasted on late into November, and may be accounted for from a late spring, a cool and moist summer, but more particularly from vast armies of chaffers, or tree-beetles, which, in many places, reduced whole woods to a leafless naked state. These trees shot again at midsummer, and then retained their foliage till very late in the year.

My musical friend, at whose house I am now visiting, has tried all the owls that are his near neighbours, with a pitch-

---

* The royston crow, or chough, (*pyrrhocorax graculus*, of Temminck,) is not migratory. It is well known in Scotland, and also in England, all the year round. In other countries, however, it appears to be migratory. We are told that this bird has been observed to attend the inundation of the Nile, in September and October. It is a widely diffused species, being an inhabitant of the Alps, Siberia, and Persia.
Colonel Montagu had one, which would stand quietly for hours to be caressed ; and if an affront were offered to it, would resist the injury with bill and claws. — ED.

† Considerable confusion arises respecting the stock-dove and rock-dove ; their history and individuality have been strangely confounded ; some considering them as the same bird, and others as only varieties of the same species. The stock-dove, *columba œnas*, is not migratory, as White supposes, although it is limited to certain districts of the country. It is common in Staffordshire, and some of the midland counties ; but it has never been found in the northern parts of Britain. The stock-dove is abundant in southern Europe. It occurs also in Africa, but does not extend to the southward of the tropic. Those of Germany and France are, however, migratory. — ED.

pipe set at concert pitch, and finds they all hoot in B flat. He will examine the nightingales next spring.

LETTER XLIII.

TO THOMAS PENNANT, ESQ.

SELBORNE, *March* 30, 1771.

DEAR SIR,— There is an insect with us, especially on chalky districts, which is very troublesome and teasing all the latter end of the summer, getting into people's skins, especially those of women and children, and raising tumours, which itch intolerably. This animal (which we call an harvest bug) is very minute, scarce discernible to the naked eye, of a bright scarlet colour, and of the genus of *acarus.** They are to be met with in gardens, on kidney beans, or any legumens, but prevail only in the hot months of summer. Warreners, as some have assured me, are much infested by them on chalky downs, where these insects swarm sometimes to so infinite a degree as to discolour their nets, and to give them a reddish cast; while the men are so bitten as to be thrown into fevers.

There is a small, long, shining fly, in these parts, very troublesome to the housewife, by getting into the chimneys, and laying its eggs in the bacon, while it is drying. These eggs produce maggots, called jumpers, which, harbouring in

* This is the *acarus autumnalis,* or harvest bug, which is one of the most teasing little insects in nature. Though bred to live on vegetable substances, such as French beans, currants, raspberries, and other fruits, yet it deserts these, whether by accident or design, to live on, and among, the most sensitive portions of the human race. These insects are so minute, that they are hardly visible to the naked eye, and that only when they are placed on a smooth, white surface: they are best known by their effects. Females and children are most liable to their attacks, and chiefly where any part of the dress fits closely to the skin: there they seat themselves, at the intersection of the lines, and lay such firm hold with their feet and jaw, that they cannot be displaced by rubbing, or by washing, unless a powerful spirit is used. The point of a fine needle is best calculated for removing them, while the person so employed must use a magnifying glass, to enable him to do so. They lacerate the skin in some way or other, and cause extreme itching, and considerable inflammation, which surrounds small vesicles, filled with a semi-transparent fluid. These animals have a fastidious taste, for there are some individuals whom they will not attack. Of two persons, for instance, who had been together, during a day's nutting in the woods, and who afterwards slept in the same bed-chamber, one of them was entirely covered with red blotches, from the attack of the bug, while the other was quite untouched. — ED.

H

the gammons and best parts of the hogs, eat down to the bone, and make great waste. This fly I suspect to be a variety of the *musca putris* of Linnæus. It is to be seen, in the summer, in farm kitchens, on the bacon racks, and about the mantle-pieces, and on the ceilings.

The insect that infests turnips, and many crops in the garden, (destroying often whole fields, while in their seedling leaves,) is an animal that wants to be better known. The country people here call it the turnip fly and black dolphin ; but I know it to be one of the *coleoptera*, the " *chrysomela oleracea, saltatoria, femoribus posticis crassissimis.** In very

* The *haltica nemorum* of Illiger, and the root weevil (*nedigus contractus*) of Stephens, are both formidable depredators, in turnip and other crops. The former of these is that probably meant by White. The caterpillar of another species of the genus *athalia*, is no less destructive. Marshall records an instance, in the *Philosophical Transactions*, of many thousand acres, which had to be ploughed up, in consequence of the devastations caused by these insects. The Norfolk farmers think they come from beyond the sea, and one even averred, that he saw them arrive in clouds, so as to darken the air ; while the fishermen reported, that they had repeatedly witnessed flights of them pass over their heads, when they were at a distance from the shore. So numerous were they upon the beach and cliffs, and lay in such heaps, that they might have been taken up with shovels. Three miles inland, they were found congregated like swarms of bees.

The maggots or larvæ of the blow-flies are an equally destructive race to animal matter. Linnæus says, the *musca vomitaria* will devour the carcass of a horse as quickly as a lion would do. And this is not at all improbable, when we know, that a species nearly allied to this (the *musca carnaria*) produces not fewer than twenty thousand at a time ; and that they have been proved by Redi to increase in weight two hundred fold within the short space of twenty-four hours. One of the most extraor-dinary circumstances connected with the destructive powers of maggots, and of their attacking the human frame, is recorded in Bell's *Weekly Messenger*. " On the 25th June, 1829, died at Asbornby, Lincoln-shire, John Page, a pauper, belonging to Little Willoughby, under circumstances truly singular. He being of a restless disposition, and not choosing to stay in the parish workhouse, was in the habit of strolling about the neighbouring villages, subsisting on the pittance obtained from door to door ; the support he usually received from the benevolent was bread and meat ; and after satisfying the cravings of nature, it was his custom to deposit the surplus provisions, particularly the meat, betwixt his shirt and skin. Having a considerable portion of this provision in store, so deposited, he was taken rather unwell, and laid himself down in a field, in the parish of Scredington ; when, from the heat of the season at that time, the meat speedily became putrid, and was of course struck by the flies : these not only proceeded to devour the inanimate pieces of flesh, but also literally to prey upon the living substance ; and when the wretched man was accidentally found by some of the inhabitants,

hot summers, they abound to an amazing degree; and, as you walk in a field, or in a garden, make a pattering like rain, by jumping on the leaves of the turnips or cabbages.

There is an oestrus, known in these parts to every plough-boy, which, because it is omitted by Linnæus, is also passed over by late writers; and that is the *curvicauda* of old Moufet, mentioned by Derham, in his *Physico-Theology*, p. 250: an insect worthy of remark, for depositing its eggs, as it flies, in so dexterous a manner on the single hairs of the legs and flanks of grass horses. But then, Derham is mistaken when he advances that this oestrus is the parent of that wonderful star-tailed maggot which he mentions afterwards; for more modern entomologists have discovered that singular production to be derived from the egg of the *musca chamæleon*. See *Geoffroy*, t. 17, f. 4.

A full history of noxious insects, hurtful in the field, garden, and house, suggesting all the known and likely means of destroying them, would be allowed by the public to be a most useful and important work. What knowledge there is of this sort lies scattered, and wants to be collected: great improvements would soon follow, of course. A knowledge of the properties, economy, propagation, and, in short, of the life and conversation, of these animals, is a necessary step to lead us to some method of preventing their depredations.

As far as I am a judge, nothing would recommend entomology more than some neat plates, that should well express the generic distinctions of insects according to Linnæus; for I am well assured that many people would study insects, could they set out with a more adequate notion of those distinctions than can be conveyed at first by words alone.

he was so eaten by the maggots, that his death seemed inevitable. After clearing away, as well as they were able, these shocking vermin, those who found courage conveyed him to Asbornby, and a surgeon was immediately procured, who declared that his body was in such a state, that dressing it must be little short of instantaneous death: and, in fact, the man did survive the operation but a few hours. When first found, and again when examined by the surgeon, he presented a sight loathsome in the extreme; white maggots of enormous size were crawling in and upon his body, which they had most shockingly mangled, and the removing of the external ones served only to render the sight more horrid."—ED.

LETTER XLIV.

TO THOMAS PENNANT, ESQ.

SELBORNE, 1771.

DEAR SIR,— Happening to make a visit to my neighbour's peacocks, I could not help observing, that the trains of those magnificent birds appear by no means to be their tails, those long feathers growing not from their *uropygium*, but all up their backs. A range of short, brown, stiff feathers, about six inches long, fixed in the *uropygium*, is the real tail, and serves as the *fulcrum* to prop the train, which is long and top-heavy, when set on end. When the train is up, nothing appears of the bird before, but its head and neck ; but this would not be the case, were these long feathers fixed only in the rump, as may be seen by the turkey cock, when in a strutting attitude.* By a strong muscular vibration, these birds can make the shafts of their long feathers clatter like the swords of a sword-dancer ; they then trample very quick with their feet, and run backwards towards the females.

I should tell you that I have got an uncommon *calculus ægogropila*, taken out of the stomach of a fat ox. It is perfectly round, and about the size of a large Seville orange : such are, I think, usually flat.

LETTER XLV.

TO THE HON. DAINES BARRINGTON.

SELBORNE, *August* 1, 1771.

DEAR SIR,— From what follows, it will appear that neither owls nor cuckoos keep to one note. A friend remarks that many (most) of his owls hoot in B flat ; but that one went almost half a note below A. The pipe he tried their notes

* The female peacock, like the hen of the domestic fowl and the pheasant, has sometimes been known to assume the plumage of the male. Lady Tynte had a favourite peahen, which at eight several times produced chicks. Having moulted when eleven years old, the lady and her family were astonished by her displaying the feathers peculiar to the other sex, and appearing like a pied peacock. In the process the tail, which was like that of the cock, first appeared. In the following year she moulted again and produced similar feathers ; in the third year she did the same, and then had also spurs resembling those of the cock. The hen never bred after this change of plumage. —ED.

by was a common half-crown pitch-pipe, such as masters use for tuning of harpsichords ; it was the common London pitch.,

A neighbour of mine, who is said to have a nice ear, remarks, that the owls about this village hoot in three different keys, in G flat or F sharp, in B flat, and A flat. He heard two hooting to each other, the one in A flat, and the other in B flat. Query : Do these different notes proceed from different species, or only from various individuals ? The same person finds, upon trial, that the note of the cuckoo (of which we have but one species) varies in different individuals ; for, about Selborne wood, he found they were mostly in D ; he heard two sing together, the one in D, and the other in D sharp, which made a disagreeable concert ; he afterwards heard one in D sharp, and about Wolmer Forest, some in C. As to nightingales, he says, that their notes are so short, and their transitions so rapid, that he cannot well ascertain their key. Perhaps in a cage, and in a room, their notes may be more distinguishable. This person has tried to settle the notes of a swift, and of several other small birds, but cannot bring them to any criterion.

As I have often remarked that redwings are some of the first birds that suffer with us in severe weather, it is no wonder at all that they retreat from Scandinavian winters ; and much more the *ordo* of *grallæ*, who all, to a bird, forsake the northern parts of Europe at the approach of winter.* " *Grallæ tanquam conjuratæ unanimiter in fugam se conjiciunt ; ne earum unicam quidem inter nos habitantem invenire possimus ; ut enim æstate in australibus degere nequeunt ob defectum lumbricorum, terramque siccam ; ita nec in frigidis ob eandem causam,*" says Ekmark the Swede, in his ingenious little treatise called *Migrationes Avium*, which by all means you ought to read, while your thoughts run on the subject of migration.— See *Amænitates Academicæ*, vol. iv. p. 565.

Birds may be so circumstanced as to be obliged to migrate in one country, and not in another ; but the *grallæ* (which procure their food from marshes and boggy ground) must, in winter, forsake the more northerly parts of Europe, or perish for want of food.

---

* In the very severe winter of 1799, immense flocks of redwings resorted to the west of England, where a sudden fall of snow, unusually deep in that quarter, cut off these poor birds from all supply of food ; and being reduced to too great weakness to attempt a passage over the ocean to some more congenial climate, thousands of them, as well as fieldfares, were starved to death. —ED.

I am glad you are making inquiries from Linnæus concerning the woodcock ; it is expected of him that he should be able to account for the motions and manner of life of the animals of his own *Fauna.* *

Faunists, as you observe, are too apt to acquiesce in bare descriptions, and a few synonyms : the reason is plain ; because all that may be done at home in a man's study ; but the investigation of the life and conversation of animals, is a concern of much more trouble and difficulty, and is not to be attained but by the active and inquisitive, and by those that reside much in the country.

Foreign systematists are, I observe, much too vague in their specific differences ; which are almost universally constituted by one or two particular marks, the rest of the description running in general terms.   But our countryman, the excellent Mr Ray, is the only describer that conveys some precise idea in every term or word, maintaining his superiority over his

---

* The woodcock is found in all parts of the old Continent, from north to south.   In some places, it is said to remain the whole year, only changing its haunts, in the breeding season, from the plains to the mountainous districts.   The habits of all the woodcocks hitherto discovered — only two or three in number — are alike : they are observed to make partial migrations from north to south during the breeding season.
The woodcock is among the few winter birds that occasionally breed in Britain.   Besides what we have mentioned at page 106, young birds have been killed in August, and eggs found in June.   In the year 1795, the Rev. Mr Wheatear, of Hastings, found a nest, with four eggs, in a wood near Battle, in Sussex.   In 1802, Mr Foljamb possessed a specimen of a half fledged bird, taken in Broodsworth Wood, near Doncaster ; and, in 1805, a brood of four were hatched in a wood at Shucoaks, near Worksop.   The nest from which these last were taken, consisted of moss, bent, and dry leaves.   On the 19th May, 1828, James Smith, keeper to John Chetwood, Esq. of Ansley, near Naneaton, shot two young woodcocks in a wood called Hore Park, in that neighbourhood ; and, on the following day, an old bird was shot by Smith, at the same spot.   The young ones are said to have been dry and bad when brought to table, but the old bird was excellent.   John Wigson, woodman to W. Dilke, Esq. discovered a woodcock sitting on four eggs, in Regton Wood, near Coventry, in the beginning of May, 1829.   From some cause, however, the nest was deserted, and several of the eggs destroyed.   On breaking one that remained, it was found to be nearly ready to hatch ; a fact proving that the adults must have commenced the business of nidification about the beginning of April, which is earlier than many individuals of this species leave Britain for northern climates ; thus affording pretty strong evidence in favour of woodcocks pairing previous to their departure.   On the 8th August, 1828, a woodcock was shot in Florida demesne, county of Down, Ireland, which must have remained through the summer.—ED.

followers and imitators, in spite of the advantage of fresh
discoveries and modern information.

At this distance of years, it is not in my power to recollect
at what periods woodcocks used to be sluggish or alert, when
I was a sportsman ; but, upon my mentioning this circumstance
to a friend, he thinks he has observed them to be remarkably
listless against snowy foul weather : if this should be the case,
then the inaptitude for flying arises only from an eagerness
for food, as sheep are observed to be very intent on grazing
against stormy wet evenings.

LETTER XLVI.

TO THOMAS PENNANT, ESQ.

September, 1771.

DEAR SIR,— The summer through, I have seen but two of
that large species of bat which I call *vespertilio altivolans*,
from its manner of feeding high in the air. I procured one
of them, and found it to be a male, and made no doubt, as
they accompanied together, that the other was a female ; but,
happening in an evening or two to procure the other likewise,
I was somewhat disappointed when it appeared to be also of
the same sex. This circumstance, and the great scarcity of
this sort, at least in these parts, occasions some suspicions in
my mind whether it is really a species, or whether it may not
be the male part of the more known species, one of which
may supply many females, as is known to be the case in sheep,
and some other quadrupeds. But this doubt can only be
cleared by a farther examination, and some attention to the
sex, of more specimens. All that I know at present is, that
my two were amply furnished with the parts of generation,
much resembling those of a boar.

In the extent of their wings, they measured fourteen inches
and an half, and four inches and an half from the nose to the
tip of the tail : their heads were large, their nostrils bilobated,
their shoulders broad and muscular, and their whole bodies
fleshy and plump. Nothing could be more sleek and soft
than their fur, which was of a bright chestnut colour ; their
maws were full of food, but so macerated, that the quality
could not be distinguished ; their livers, kidneys, and hearts,
were large, and their bowels covered with fat. They weighed
each, when entire, full one ounce and one drachm. Within
the ear, there was somewhat of a peculiar structure, that I did

not understand perfectly ; but refer it to the observation of the curious anatomist. These creatures send forth a very rancid and offensive smell. *

LETTER XLVII.

TO THOMAS PENNANT, ESQ.

SELBORNE, 1771.

DEAR SIR, — On the twelfth of July, I had a fair opportunity of contemplating the motions of the *caprimulgus*, or fern-owl, as it was playing round a large oak that swarmed with *scarabæi*

* Mr Jesse says, — "Bats seem to be gregarious animals. Vast numbers of them were lately found under the roof of an old building in Richmond Park. I had two sorts of them brought to me, nearly similar in shape, but one very considerably larger than the other. This latter is probably the *vespertilio altivolans*, mentioned by Mr White, in his *Natural History of Selborne*, answering to his description of it. It measured nearly fifteen inches from the tip of one wing to that of the other. These larger bats were quite as numerous as the smaller species. A great number of them were also found in an old building in Combe Wood, adjoining Richmond Park; and, subsequently, ten of them were discovered in a decayed tree in that park." This is pretty strong evidence against the migration of the bat in question. Several of these were sent by Mr Jesse to the Zoological Societies of London.

A workman employed in the repairs of Cardinal Wolsey's hall, Hampton-Court Palace, found the skeleton of a bat at the end of one of the rafters of the ceiling, which is calculated to have been nearly as large as a pigeon when alive.

Bats are possessed of a sense with which we are yet unacquainted, that of avoiding objects in the dark. Spallanzani hung up some cloths across a room, with holes cut in them at various distances, large enough to allow a bat to fly through. He deprived the poor animals of light, and stopt their hearing as much as possible. These animals on being turned loose, flew through the perforations with as much correctness as if they had had the use of their eyes.

Respecting the hybernation of the bat, the following fact is very curious: " In the beginning of November, 1821, a woodman engaged in splitting timber for rails in the woods close to the lake at Haining, a seat of Mr Pringle in Selkirkshire, discovered in the centre of a large wild cherry tree, a living bat, of a bright scarlet colour, which, as soon as it was relieved from its entombment, took to its wings and escaped. In the tree there was a recess sufficiently large to contain the animal ; but all around the wood was perfectly sound, solid, and free from any fissure through which the atmosphere could reach the animal. A man employed in the same manner at Kelsall, in December, 1826, met with a similar phenomenon, and allowed the bat to escape, under the influence of fear, protesting that it was not a ' being of this world.' "— *Blackwood's Magazine*, vol. viii. p. 467. — ED.

solstitiales, or fern-chaffers. The powers of its wing were wonderful, exceeding, if possible, the various evolutions and quick turns of the swallow genus. But the circumstance that pleased me most was, that I saw it distinctly more than once put out its short leg when on the wing, and, by a bend of the head, deliver somewhat into its mouth. If it takes any part of its prey with its foot, as I have now the greatest reason to suppose it does these chaffers, I no longer wonder at the use of its middle toe, which is curiously furnished with a serrated claw. *

Swallows and martins—the bulk of them, I mean—have forsaken us sooner this year than usual; for, on September the 22d, they rendezvoused in a neighbour's walnut tree, where, it seemed probable, they had taken up their lodgings for the night. At the dawn of the day, which was foggy, they rose altogether in infinite numbers, occasioning such a rushing, from the strokes of their wings against the hazy air, as might be heard to a considerable distance : since that, no flock has appeared, only a few stragglers.

Some swifts staid late, till the 22d of August; a rare instance! for they usually withdraw within the first week.†

On September the 24th, three or four ringousels appeared in my fields, for the first time this season. How punctual are these visitors in their autumnal and spring migrations!

LETTER XLVIII.

TO THE HON. DAINES BARRINGTON.

SELBORNE, *February* 8, 1772.

DEAR SIR,—When I ride about in winter, and see such prodigious flocks of various kinds of birds, I cannot help

---

* The use of the serrated claw of the goat-sucker has occasioned much controversy amongst naturalists within the last few years, but is satisfactorily accounted for by Wilson, in his description of the Carolina night-jar. " Their mouths," says he, " are capable of prodigious expansion, to seize their prey with more certainty, and furnished with long hairs or bristles, serving as palisades to secure what comes between them. Reposing much during the heat of day, they are greatly infested with vermin, particularly about the head, and are provided with a comb on the under edge of the middle claw, with which they are often employed in ridding themselves of these pests, at least when in a state of captivity."—ED.

† See letter XCVII. to the Hon. Daines Barrington.—In the *Magazine of Natural History,* we are informed that swifts were seen at Chipping Norton, on the 27th September, 1830.—ED.

admiring at these congregations, and wishing that it was in my power to account for those appearances, almost peculiar to the season.   The two great motives which regulate the proceedings of the brute creation, are love and hunger: the former incites animals to perpetuate their kind, the latter induces them to preserve individuals.   Whether either of these should seem to be the ruling passion, in the matter of congregating, is to be considered.   As to love, that is out of the question, at a time of the year when that soft passion is not indulged ; besides, during the amorous season, such a jealousy prevails between the male birds, that they can hardly bear to be together in the same hedge or field.   Most of the singing and elation of spirits of that time, seem to me to be the effect of rivalry and emulation ; and it is to this spirit of jealousy, that I chiefly attribute the equal dispersion of birds in the spring, over the face of the country.

Now as to the business of food.   As these animals are actuated by instinct to hunt for necessary food, they should not, one would suppose, crowd together in pursuit of sustenance, at a time when it is most likely to fail; yet such associations do take place in hard weather chiefly, and thicken as the severity increases.   As some kind of self-interest and self-defence is, no doubt, the motive for the proceeding, may it not arise from the helplessness of their state in such rigorous seasons, as men crowd together, when under great calamities, though they know not why?   Perhaps approximation may dispel some degree of cold ; and a crowd may make each individual appear safer from the ravages of birds of prey, and other dangers.

If I admire when I see how much congenerous birds love to congregate, I am the more struck when I see incongruous ones in such strict amity.*   If we do not much wonder to see a flock of rooks usually attended by a train of daws, yet it is strange that the former should so frequently have a flight of starlings for their satellites. †   Is it because rooks have a more

* There is nothing more strange in starlings and rooks being seen in company, than for the short-eared owl to be seen amongst flights of woodcocks.   Pennant mentions simultaneous migrations of cuckoos and turtle-doves having been noticed in Greece.

† The author of the *Journal of a Naturalist*, speaking of the readiness with which rooks detect the places where grubs are sure to be found, says, " I have often observed them alight on a pasture of uniform verdure, and exhibiting no sensible appearance of feathering or decay, and immediately commence staking up the ground.   Upon investigating the object of their operations, I have found the heads of plantains, the little autumnal

discerning scent than their attendants, and can lead them to spots more productive of food? Anatomists say that rooks, by reason of two large nerves which run down between the eyes into the upper mandible, have a more delicate feeling in their beaks than other round-billed birds, and can grope for their meat when out of sight. Perhaps, then, their associates attend them on the motive of interest, as greyhounds wait on the motions of their finders, and as lions are said to do on the yelpings of jackals. Lapwings and starlings sometimes associate. *

dandelions, and other plants, drawn out of the ground and scattered about, their roots having been eaten off by a grub, leaving only a crown of leaves upon the surface. This grub beneath, in the earth, the rooks had detected in their flight, and descended to feed on it, first pulling up the plant which concealed it, and then drawing the larvæ from their holes."

A correspondent, in the *Magazine of Natural History*, proves that the rook is occasionally a predatory bird. He says, " As I was passing through Chandos Street, Cavendish Square, London, soon after six o'clock this morning, my attention was attracted to a rook flying low, near the walls of some out-buildings, in which were many holes occupied by sparrows' nests. He directed his flight to one of these holes, into which he thrust himself as far as possible. It was evident that he was attempting to reach something with his bill; but apparently he did not succeed, for he shortly withdrew himself from this hole, and flew to another, into which he intruded himself in the same manner. From this second hole he retired almost immediately, bearing in his beak one of the callow brood. He flew with his spoil to a high chimney at the corner house, followed for a short distance by ten or twelve sparrows, clamouring loudly at such an atrocious robbery; and one sparrow, probably the parent, ventured to pursue even to the chimney-top, as if determined to assail the fell destroyer; but both the rook and the sparrow quickly disappeared behind the chimney-pot, and prevented my farther observation."

Colonel Montagu records an instance of great sagacity in rooks. He noticed two of them by the sea shore, after having satisfied the calls of hunger, busy in removing small fish beyond the flux of the tide, and depositing them just above high water mark under the broken rocks. — ED.

* Lapwings are invariably gregarious, assembling in very large flocks in the autumn. At this time they are esteemed excellent food.

The starlings also congregate in autumn. We saw a flight of these birds in the autumn of 1814, in Kings County, Ireland, which literally darkened the air, and must have consisted of at least a hundred thousand; they were flying near the immense marshy plain near Banacher, through which the Shannon flows. " In the autumnal and hyemal months," says Selby, " these birds gather in immense flocks, and are particularly abundant in the fenny parts of Nottinghamshire and Lincolnshire, where they roost among the reeds. Before they retire to rest, they perform various manœuvres in the air, the whole frequently describing rapid revolutions round a common centre. This peculiar flight will sometimes continue for nearly half an hour before they become finally settled for the night. Upon the approach of spring they spread themselves over the whole country."—ED.

LETTER XLIX.

TO THE HON. DAINES BARRINGTON.

March 9, 1772.

DEAR SIR, — As a gentleman and myself were walking, on
the 4th of last November, round the sea-banks at Newhaven,
near the mouth of the Lewes river, in pursuit of natural
knowledge, we were surprised to see three house swallows
gliding very swiftly by us. That morning was rather chilly,
with the wind at north-west; but the tenor of the weather, for
some time before, had been delicate, and the noons remarkably
warm. From this incident, and from repeated accounts which
I meet with, I am more and more induced to believe, that
many of the swallow kind do not depart from this island, but
lay themselves up in holes and caverns, and do, insect-like,
and bat-like, come forth at mild times, and then retire again to
their *latebræ*. Nor make I the least doubt but that, if I lived
at Newhaven, Seaford, Brighthelmstone, or any of those towns
near the chalk cliffs of the Sussex coast, by proper observations,
I should see swallows stirring at periods of the winter, when
the noons were soft and inviting, and the sun warm and invi-
gorating. And I am the more of this opinion, from what I
have remarked during some of our late springs, and though
some swallows did make their appearance about the usual
time, viz. the 13th or 14th of April, yet, meeting with a harsh
reception, and blustering, cold, north-east winds, they immediately withdrew, absconding for several days, till the weather
gave them better encouragement.

LETTER L.

TO THOMAS PENNANT, ESQ.

April 12, 1772.

DEAR SIR, — While I was in Sussex last autumn, my residence was at the village near Lewes, from whence I had
formerly the pleasure of writing to you. On the 1st of
November, I remarked that the old tortoise, formerly mentioned, began first to dig the ground, in order to the forming
of its hybernaculum, which it had fixed on just beside a great
turf of hepaticas. It scrapes out the ground with its fore
feet, and throws it up over its back with its hind; but the

motion of its legs is ridiculously slow, little exceeding the hour hand of a clock, and suitable to the composure of an animal said to be a whole month in performing one feat of copulation. Nothing can be more assiduous than this creature night and day in scooping the earth, and forcing its great body into the cavity; but, as the noons of that season proved unusually warm and sunny, it was continually interrupted, and called forth, by the heat in the middle of the day ; and, though I continued there till the 13th of November, yet the work remained unfinished. Harsher weather, and frosty mornings, would have quickened its operations.

No part of its behaviour ever struck me more than the extreme timidity it always expresses with regard to rain ; for though it has a shell that would secure it against the wheel of a loaded cart, yet does it discover as much solicitude about rain as a lady dressed in all her best attire, shuffling away on the first sprinklings, and running its head up in a corner. If attended to, it becomes an excellent weather-glass ; for as sure as it walks elate, and as it were on tiptoe, feeding with great earnestness in a morning, so sure will it rain before night. It is totally a diurnal animal, and never pretends to stir after it becomes dark. The tortoise, like other reptiles, has an arbitrary stomach, as well as lungs ; and can refrain from eating as well as breathing for a great part of the year. When first awakened it eats nothing ; nor again in the autumn, before it retires ; through the height of the summer, it feeds voraciously, devouring all the food that comes in its way. I was much taken with its sagacity in discerning those that do it kind offices ; for, as soon as the good old lady comes in sight who has waited on it for more than thirty years, it hobbles towards its benefactress with awkward alacrity ; but remains inattentive to strangers. Thus not only " the ox knoweth his owner, and the ass his master's crib," * but the most abject reptile and torpid of beings distinguishes the hand that feeds it, and is touched with the feelings of gratitude.

P. S.— In about three days after I left Sussex, the tortoise retired into the ground under the hepatica. †

---

* Isaiah, i. 3.

† A singular circumstance occurred at Ludlow with a tortoise, the property of Mr Jones, which was put in a convenient place to spend the winter. It was soon attacked by rats, which ate away its eyes, tongue, and all the under parts of its throat, together with the windp pe. In that mutilated state it is supposed it had continued for about three weeks prior to its being discovered. The most remarkable circumstance

LETTER LI.

TO THOMAS PENNANT, ESQ.

SELBORNE, *March* 15, 1773.

DEAR SIR,— By my journal for last autumn, it appears that the house-martens bred very late, and staid very late in these parts ; for, on the 1st of October, I saw young martens in their nests, nearly fledged ; and again, on the 21st of October, we had, at the next house, a nest full of young martens just ready to fly, and the old ones were hawking for insects with great alertness. The next morning, the brood forsook their nest, and were flying round the village. From this day, I never saw one of the swallow kind till November the 3d ; when twenty, or perhaps thirty, house-martens were playing all day long by the side of the Hanging Wood, and over my fields. Did these small weak birds, some of which were nestlings twelve days ago, shift their quarters at this late season of the year, to the other side of the northern tropic ? Or rather, is it not more probable, that the next church, ruin, chalk-cliff, steep covert, or perhaps sand-bank, lake, or pool, (as a more northern naturalist would say,) may become their hybernaculum, and afford them a ready and obvious retreat ? *

attending this is, that the animal did not exhibit the least signs of decomposition, nor was animation perceptible. It is, however, quite evident it was alive, otherwise putridity would have ensued. The extreme slow motion of the limbs of tortoises, mentioned by White, is depicted in Homer's *Hymn to Hermes*, which has been thus translated : —

> Feeding far off from man, the flowery herb
> Slow moving with his feet.

* The young of the swifts, before leaving their nests, are quite prepared for an aërial excursion of almost any extent. At one time, we were detached, at Holy Island, coast of Northumberland, in command of the castle. A pair of martens built in a hole over the window of our apartment. We were generally disturbed at the early dawn by these birds feeding their young. We had the curiosity to take all the young, four in number, out of the nest for examination. We found them in full feather, although they had never yet attempted to leave their nest. After having satisfied our curiosity, we were preparing to replace them in their nest, when the one we had just taken in our hand for that purpose took to its wings, and was immediately followed by the others. These little birds, accompanied by their parents, disported in the sun for upwards of two hours over the deep valley beneath our windows. They returned to the nest in the afternoon, and left it early next morning, never to return. The parents, on the following day, commenced anew the business of incubation. — ED.

We now begin to expect our vernal migration of ringousels every week. Persons worthy of credit assure me, that ringousels were seen at Christmas, 1770, in the forest of Bere, on the southern verge of this county. Hence we may conclude, that their migrations are only internal, and not extended to the continent southward, if they do at first come at all from the northern parts of this island only, and not from the north of Europe. Come from whence they will, it is plain, from the fearless disregard that they shew for men or guns, that they have been little accustomed to places of much resort. Navigators mention, that, in the Isle of Ascension, and other such desolate districts, birds are so little acquainted with the human form, that they settle on men's shoulders, and have no more dread of a sailor than they would have of a goat that was grazing. A young man at Lewes, in Sussex, assured me, that, about seven years ago, ringousels abounded so about that town in the autumn, that he killed sixteen himself in one afternoon : he added farther, that some had appeared since in every autumn ; but he could not find that any had been observed before the season in which he shot so many. I myself have found these birds in little parties in the autumn, cantoned all along the Sussex downs, wherever there were shrubs and bushes, from Chichester to Lewes ; particularly in the autumn of 1770.

LETTER LII.

TO THE HON. DAINES BARRINGTON.

SELBORNE, *March* 26, 1773.

DEAR SIR,— The more I reflect on the στοργή of animals, the more I am astonished at its effects. Nor is the violence of this affection more wonderful than the shortness of its duration. Thus, every hen is in her turn the virago of the yard, in proportion to the helplessness of her brood ; and will fly in the face of a dog or a sow in defence of those chickens, which, in a few weeks, she will drive before her with relentless cruelty.*

---

* The hen will attack any animal whatever in defence of her chickens ; and has been known to lose her own life in attempting to save the life, as she thought, of a brood of young ducklings which she had hatched, on their entering the water.

A singular instance of strong affection in the feathered tribe is related by Mr Jesse : — "A gentleman in my neighbourhood," says he, " had

This affection sublimes the passions, quickens the invention, and sharpens the sagacity of the brute creation. Thus a hen, just become a mother, is no longer that placid bird she used to be ; but, with feathers standing on end, wings hovering, and clucking note, she runs about like one possessed. Dams will throw themselves in the way of the greatest danger in order to avert it from their progeny. Thus a partridge will tumble along before a sportsman, in order to draw away the dogs from her helpless covey. In the time of nidification, the most feeble birds will assault the most rapacious. All the hirundines of a village are up in arms at the sight of a hawk, whom they will persecute till he leaves that district.* A very

directed one of his wagons to be packed with sundry hampers and boxes, intending to send it to Worthing, where he was going himself. For some time his going was delayed, and he therefore directed that the wagon should be placed in a shed in his yard, packed as it was, till it should be convenient for him to send it off. While it was in the shed, a pair of robins built their nest among some straw in the wagon, and had hatched their young just before it was sent away. One of the old birds, instead of being frightened away by the motion of the wagon, only left its nest from time to time for the purpose of flying to the nearest hedge for food for its young ; and thus, alternately affording warmth and nourishment to them, it arrived at Worthing. The affection of this bird having been observed by the wagoner, he took care in unloading not to disturb the robin's nest, and my readers will, I am sure, be glad to hear, that the robin and its young ones returned in safety to Walton Heath, being the place from whence they had set out. The distance the wagon went in going and returning could not have been less than one hundred miles." —ED.

* A curious example of this was manifested by a wren in opposition to martens. Mr Simpson mentions, that, during his residence at Welton, North America, he one morning heard a loud noise from a pair of martens that were flying from tree to tree near his dwelling. They made several attempts to get into a box fixed against the house, which they had before occupied as a breeding place ; but they always appeared to fly from it again with the utmost dread, at the same time repeating their usual loud cries. Curiosity led the gentleman to watch their motions. After some time, a small wren came from the box, and perched on a tree near it, when her shrill notes seemed to amaze her antagonists. Having remained a short time, she flew away, when the martens took an opportunity of returning to the box, but their stay was of short duration; for their diminutive adversary returned, and made them retreat with the greatest precipitation. They continued manœuvering in this way the whole day ; but the following morning, on the wren quitting the box, the martens immediately returned, took possession of their mansion, broke up their own nest, went to work afresh with much diligence and ingenuity, and soon barricaded their door. The wren returned, but could not now re-enter. She made some bold efforts to storm the nest, but was unsuccessful. The martens abstained from food for nearly two

exact observer has often remarked, that a pair of ravens, nesting in the rock of Gibraltar, would suffer no vulture or eagle to rest near their station, but would drive them from the hill with an amazing fury: even the blue thrush, at the season of breeding, would dart out from the clefts of the rocks to chase away the kestrel, or the sparrow-hawk. If you stand near the nest of a bird that has young, she will not be induced to betray them by an inadvertent fondness, but will wait about at a distance, with meat in her mouth, for an hour together.

Should I farther corroborate what I have advanced above, by some anecdotes which I probably may have mentioned before in conversation, yet you will, I trust, pardon the repetition for the sake of the illustration.

The fly-catcher of the *Zoology* (the *stoparola* of Ray) builds every year in the vines that grow on the walls of my house.* A pair of these little birds had one year inadvertently placed their nest on a naked bough, perhaps in a shady time, not being aware of the inconvenience that followed. But a hot sunny season coming on before the brood was half fledged, the reflection of the wall became insupportable, and must inevitably have destroyed the tender young, had not affection suggested an expedient, and prompted the parent birds to hover over the nest all the hotter hours, while, with wings expanded, and mouths gaping for breath, they screened off the heat from their suffering offspring.

A farther instance I once saw of notable sagacity in a willow-wren, which had built in a bank in my fields. This bird a friend and myself had observed as she sat in her nest, but were particularly careful not to disturb her, though we saw she eyed us with some degree of jealousy. Some days after, as we passed that way, we were desirous of remarking how this brood went on ; but no nest could be found, till I happened to take up a large bundle of long green moss, as it were carelessly thrown over the nest, in order to dodge the eye of any impertinent intruder.

A still more remarkable mixture of sagacity and instinct occurred to me one day, as my people were pulling off the lining of a hot-bed, in order to add some fresh dung. From out of the side of this bed leaped an animal with great agility,

days, persevering during the whole of that time in defending the entrance ; and the wren, after many fruitless attempts to force the works, raised the siege, quitted her intentions, and left the martens in quiet possession of their dwelling. — ED.

* The beam bird, *muscicapa grisola* of Linnæus. — ED.

that made a most grotesque figure; nor was it without great difficulty that it could be taken, when it proved to be a large white-bellied field-mouse, with three or four young clinging to her teats by their mouths and feet. It was amazing that the desultory and rapid motions of this dam should not oblige her litter to quit their hold, especially when it appeared that they were so young as to be both naked and blind! *

To these instances of tender attachment, many more of which might be daily discovered, by those that are studious of nature, may be opposed that rage of affection, that monstrous perversion of the στοργη, which induces some females of the brute creation to devour their young, because their owners have handled them too freely, or removed them from place to place! Swine, and sometimes the more gentle race of dogs and cats, are guilty of this horrid and preposterous murder.† When I hear now and then of an abandoned mother that destroys her offspring, I am not so much amazed; since reason perverted, and the bad passions let loose, are capable of any enormity; but why the parental feelings of brutes, that usually flow in one most uniform tenor, should sometimes be so extravagantly diverted, I leave to abler philosophers than myself to determine.

LETTER LIII.

TO THE HON. DAINES BARRINGTON.

SELBORNE, *July* 8, 1773.

DEAR SIR,—Some young men went down lately to a pond on the verge of Wolmer Forest, to hunt flappers, or young wild ducks, many of which they caught, and, among the rest, some very minute yet well-fledged wild fowls alive, which, upon examination, I found to be teals. I did not know till then that teals ever bred in the south of England, and was

---

* Bats fly with their young adhering to their teats. —ED.

† There are a few species, and but a few, of the brute creation which occasionally destroy their offspring immediately on their birth, an anomaly in the law of nature commonly followed by another, that of devouring them. But as the latter usually takes place among domestic animals, it is obvious that hunger has no share in the transaction, and that it may rather be ascribed to some temporary derangement (occasioned, perhaps, by agonizing pain) of the instinctive solicitude, interwoven with the constitution and existence of every living creature, to protect and preserve its young. — ED.

much pleased with the discovery : this I look upon as a great stroke in natural history.*

We have had, ever since I can remember, a pair of white owls that constantly breed under the eaves of this church. As I have paid good attention to the manner of life of these birds during their season of breeding, which lasts the summer through, the following remarks may not perhaps be unacceptable. About an hour before sunset, (for then the mice begin to run,) they sally forth in quest of prey, and hunt all round the hedges of meadows and small enclosures for them, which seem to be their only food. In this irregular country, we can stand on an eminence and see them beat the fields over like a setting-dog, and often drop down in the grass or corn. I have minuted these birds with my watch for an hour together, and have found, that they return to their nest, the one or the other of them, about once in five minutes ; reflecting, at the same time, on the adroitness that every animal is possessed of, as far as regards the well-being of itself and offspring.† But a piece of address, which they shew when they return loaded, should not, I think, be passed over in silence. As they take their prey with their claws, so they carry it in their claws to their nest ; but, as the feet are necessary in their ascent under the tiles, they constantly perch first on the roof of the chancel, and shift the mouse from their claws to their bill, that the feet may be at liberty to take hold of the plate on the wall, as they are rising under the eaves.

White owls seem not (but in this I am not positive) to hoot at all ;‡ all that clamorous hooting appears to me to come from the wood kinds. The white owl does indeed snore and hiss in a tremendous manner ; and these menaces well answer the intention of intimidating, for I have known a whole village up in arms on such an occasion, imagining the church-yard to be full of goblins and spectres.§ White owls also often scream

---

* Dr Haysham says, that the teal is now known to breed in the mosses about Carlisle. — ED.

† Colonel Montagu has remarked, that the wren returns with food to its offspring once in two minutes. The swallow generally feeds its young every second or third minute. — ED.

‡ Sir William Jardine says white owls do hoot, and that he has shot them in the act ; and a correspondent in Loudon's *Magazine* says, " Owls which build in Attenborough Church, in this parish, sit on the turrets and hoot fearfully. An old white owl used to frequent a dovecot, not two hundred yards from where I am writing this, and, late in the evening, would sit at the top and utter its doleful cries." — ED.

§ Dr Richardson, in speaking of the great Virginian horned owl,

horribly as they fly along : from this screaming probably arose
the common people's imaginary species of screech-owl, which
they superstitiously think attends the windows of dying
persons.   The plumage of the remiges of the wings, of every
species of owl that I have yet examined, is remarkably soft
and pliant.   Perhaps it may be necessary that the wings of
these birds should not make much resistance or rushing, that
they may be enabled to steal through the air unheard upon a
nimble and watchful quarry.

    While I am talking of owls, it may not be improper to
mention what I was told by a gentleman of the county of
Wilts : As they were grubbing a vast hollow pollard ash,
that had been the mansion of owls for centuries, he discovered
at the bottom a mass of matter that at first he could not
account for.   After some examination, he found that it was
a congeries of the bones of mice, (and perhaps of birds and
bats,) that had been heaping together for ages, being cast up
in pellets out of the crops of many generations of inhabitants.
For owls cast up the bones, fur, and feathers of what they

gives the following animated picture of its dismal unearthly cry. He
says, " It is found in almost every quarter of the United States, and
occurs in all parts of the fur countries.   Its loud and full nocturnal cry,
issuing from the gloomy recesses of the forest, bear some resemblance to
the human voice, uttered in a hollow, sepulchral tone, and has been
frequently productive of alarm to the traveller, of which an instance
occurred within my own knowledge.   A party of Scottish Highlanders,
in the service of the Hudson's Bay Company, happened, in a winter
journey, to encamp after nightfall in a dense clump of trees, whose dark
tops and lofty stems, the growth of centuries, gave a solemnity to the
scene that had strongly tended to excite the superstitious feelings of the
Highlanders.   The effect was heightened by the discovery of a tomb,
which, with a natural taste often exhibited by the Indians, had been placed
in this secluded spot.   Our travellers, having finished their supper, were
trimming their fire, preparatory to retiring to rest, when the slow and
dismal notes of the horned owl fell on the ear with a startling nearness.
None of them being acquainted with the sound, they at once concluded,
that so unearthly a voice must be the moaning of the spirit of the
departed, whose repose they supposed they had disturbed, by inadvertently
making a fire of the wood of which the tomb had been constructed.
They passed a tedious night of fear, and with the first dawn of day
hastily quitted the ill-omened spot." Audubon describes the cry of this owl
as fearful.   He says, " It suddenly alights on the top of a fern-stake or a
dead stump, shakes its feathers, arranges them, and utters a shriek so
horrid that the woods around echo to its dismal sound.   Now, it seems
as if you heard the barking of a cur-dog ; again, the notes are so rough
and mingled together, that they might be mistaken for the last gurglings
of a murdered person, striving in vain to call for assistance."—ED.

devour, after the manner of hawks. He believes, he told me, that there were bushels of this kind of substance.

When brown owls hoot, their throats swell as big as a hen's egg. I have known an owl of this species live a full year without any water. Perhaps the case may be the same with all birds of prey.* When owls fly, they stretch out their legs behind them, as a balance to their large heavy heads; for, as most nocturnal birds have large eyes and ears, they must have large heads to contain them. Large eyes, I presume, are necessary to collect every ray of light, and large concave ears to command the smallest degree of sound or noise.

The *hirundines* are a most inoffensive, harmless, entertaining, social, and useful tribe of birds; they touch no fruit in our gardens; delight, all except one species, in attaching themselves to our houses; amuse us with their migrations, songs, and marvellous agility; and clear our outlets from the annoyances of gnats and other troublesome insects. Some districts in the South Seas, near Guiaquil,† are desolated, it seems, by the infinite swarms of venomous mosquitoes, which fill the air, and render those coasts insupportable. It would be worth inquiring, whether any species of *hirundines* is found in these regions. Whoever contemplates the myriads of insects that sport in the sunbeams of a summer evening in this country, will soon be convinced to what a degree our atmosphere would be choked with them were it not for the friendly intercourse of the swallow tribe. ‡

---

* Predatory birds are endowed with the power of existing for a great length of time without food or water. In them, digestion seems to be carried on in a slow manner; and very different from this function in most other birds, as it is extremely rapid in the smaller species. Vultures after feeding may be seen in one unvaried position, patiently waiting till the work of digestion is completed, and the stimulus of hunger is renewed. If violently disturbed after a full meal, they are quite incapable of flight, until they have disgorged the contents of their stomach. — ED.

† See Ulloa's *Travels*.

‡ The wanton destruction of the swallow tribe is not only an act of great inhumanity, but also very impolitic, and can only be practised by persons who are defective either in the head or heart. The author of the *Journal of a Naturalist* expresses himself thus feelingly on the subject: — " The sportsman's essaying his skill on the swallow race, that ' skim the dimpled pool,' or harmless glide along the flowery mead, when, if successful, he consigns whole nests of infant broods to famine and to death, is pitiable indeed! No injury, no meditated crime, was ever imputed to these birds; they free our dwelling from multitudes of insects; their unsuspicious confidence and familiarity with man merit

Many species of birds have their peculiar lice ; but the *hirundines* alone seem to be annoyed with *dipterous* insects, *
which infest every species, and are so large, in proportion to
themselves, that they must be extremely irksome and injurious
to them. These are the *hippoboscæ hirundines*, with narrow
subulated wings, abounding in every nest ; and are hatched
by the warmth of the bird's own body during incubation, and
crawl about under its feathers.

A species of them is familiar to horsemen in the south of
England, under the name of forest-fly, and, to some, of side-
fly, from its running sideways, like a crab. It creeps under
the tails and about the groins of horses, which, at their first

protection, not punishment from him. The sufferings of their broods,
when the parents are destroyed, should excite humanity and demand
forbearance. I supplicate from the youthful sportsman his consideration for these most useful creatures. The positive good they do, the
beneficial services they perform for us, by clearing the air of innumerable insects, ought to render them sacred, and secure them from our
molestation. Without their friendly aid, the atmosphere we live in would
scarcely be habitable by man. They feed entirely on insects, which, if
not kept under by their means, would swarm and torment us like another
Egyptian plague. The immense quantity of flies destroyed in a short
space of time by one individual bird is scarcely to be credited by those
who have not actual experience of the fact. I was once present when a
swift was shot — I may as well confess the truth — I myself (then a
thoughtless youth) the perpetrator of the deed : I acknowledge the fault
in contrition, and will never be guilty of the like again. It was in the
breeding season, when the young were hatched, at which time the parent
birds, it is well known, are in the habit of making little excursions into
the country, to a considerable distance from the breeding places, for the
purpose of collecting flies, which they bring home to their infant progeny.
On picking up my hopeless and ill-gotten prey, I observed a number of
flies, some mutilated, others scarcely injured, crawling out of the bird's
mouth ; the throat and pouch seemed absolutely stuffed with them, and
an incredible number was at length disgorged. I am sure I speak within
compass when I state, that there was a mass of flies, just caught by this
single swift, larger than, when pressed close, could conveniently be contained in the bowl of an ordinary tablespoon ! Thus was a whole brood
of young birds deprived of one of their nursing parents, by an act of the
most wanton cruelty."— Ed.

* This insect is the *craterina hirundines* of Olfers, which has the
instinct to deposit its cocoons in the well sheltered and warm nest of the
swallow tribe, heat being so necessary to its existence. The fly, when
hatched, lives by sucking the blood of the swallow. So tormenting are
these insects to swallows, that they sometimes render the poor animals
quite stupid, and unfit for their aërial excursions. The *hippobosca equina*,
is the insect which sucks the blood of horses, and known in England by
the name of the forest-fly : it belongs to the same natural family with
that above described. — Ed.

coming out of the north, are rendered half frantic by the tickling sensation ; while our own breed little regards them.

The curious Reaumur discovered the large eggs, or rather *pupæ*, of these flies, as big as the flies themselves, which he hatched in his own bosom.   Any person that will take the trouble to examine the old nests of either species of swallows, may find in them the black shining cases, or skins, of the *pupæ* of these insects ; but, for other particulars, too long for this place, we refer the reader to *L'Histoire d'Insectes* of that admirable entomologist, tom. iv. pl. 11.

LETTER LIV.

TO THOMAS PENNANT, ESQ.

SELBORNE, *November* 9, 1773.

DEAR SIR, — As you desire me to send you such observations as may occur, I take the liberty of making the following remarks, that you may, according as you think me right or wrong, admit or reject what I here advance, in your intended new edition of the *British Zoology*.

The osprey * was shot about a year ago at Frinsham Pond, a great lake, at about six miles from hence, while it was sitting on the handle of a plough and devouring a fish ; it used to precipitate itself into the water, and so take its prey by surprise. †

---

* *British Zoology*, vol. i. p. 128.
† Wilson beautifully describes the manœuvres of the osprey, *pandion haliæetus* of Savigney, while in search of his prey : " In leaving the nest, he usually flies direct till he comes to the sea, then sails around in easy curving lines, turning sometimes in the air on a pivot, apparently without the least exertion, rarely moving the wings, his legs extended in a straight line behind, and his remarkable length and curvature, or bend of wing, distinguishes him from all other hawks.   The height at which he thus elegantly glides is various, from one hundred to one hundred and fifty, and two hundred feet, sometimes much higher, all the while calmly reconnoitring the face of the deep below.   Suddenly he is seen to check his course, as if struck by a particular object, which he seems to survey for a few moments with such steadiness, that he appears fixed in air, flapping his wings.   This object, however, he abandons, or rather the fish he had in his eye has disappeared, and he is again seen sailing around as before.   Now his attention is again arrested, and he descends with great rapidity ; but ere he reaches the surface, shoots off on another course, as if ashamed that a second victim had escaped him. He now sails at a short height above the surface, and by a zigzag descent, and without seeming to dip his feet in the water, seizes a fish, which,

A great ash-coloured* butcher-bird was shot last winter in Tisted Park, and a red-backed butcher-bird at Selborne. They are *raræ aves* in this country.

Crows† go in pairs the whole year round.

Cornish choughs‡ abound, and breed on Beechy Head, and on all the cliffs of the Sussex coast.

The common wild pigeon,§ or stock-dove, is a bird of passage in the south of England, seldom appearing till towards the end of November ; ‖ is usually the latest winter bird of passage. Before our beechen woods were so much destroyed, we had myriads of them, reaching in strings for a mile together, as they went out in a morning to feed. They leave us early in spring : where do they breed?

The people of Hampshire and Sussex call the missel-bird ¶ the storm-cock, because it sings early in the spring, in blowing,

---

after carrying a short distance, he probably drops, or yields up to the bald eagle, (*falco leucocephalus*,) and again ascends by easy spiral circles, to the higher regions of the air, where he glides about in all the ease and majesty of his species. At once, from this sublime aërial height, he descends like a perpendicular torrent, plunging into the sea with a loud rushing sound, and with the certainty of a rifle. In a few moments, he emerges, bearing in his claws his struggling prey, which he always carries head foremost ; and, having risen a few feet above the surface, shakes himself as a water spaniel would do, and directs his heavy and laborious course straightway to the land."

Mr Lloyd mentions, that in Sweden, the eagle sometimes strikes so large a pike, and so firmly do his talons hold their grasp, that he is carried under water by the superior gravity of the pike, and drowned. Dr Mullenbog says, he himself saw an enormous pike with an eagle fixed to its back by his talons, lying dead on a piece of ground which had been overflowed by a river, and from which the water had subsided.

This naturalist also gives an account of a conflict between an eagle and a pike, which a gentleman saw on the river Gotha, near Wenersborg. In this case, when the eagle first seized the pike, he soared a short distance into the air, but the weight and struggling of the fish together, soon obliged the eagle to descend. Both fell into the water and disappeared. Presently, however, the eagle again came to the surface, uttering the most piercing cries, and making apparently every endeavour to extricate his talons, but in vain ; and, after a violent struggle, was carried under water.

Montagu tell us, an osprey was seen to stoop and carry off a half-grown duck from the surface of the water, at Slapton Ley. In the struggle, the duck fell from the talons of the eagle, but was recovered before it reached the water. — Ed.

* *British Zoology*, vol. i. p. 161.   † *Ibid.* p. 167.
‡ *Ibid.* p. 198.   § *Ibid.* p. 216.
‖ See our note, p. 112. — Ed.
¶ *British Zoology*, vol. i. p. 224.

showery weather. Its song often commences with the year : with us it builds much in orchards.

A gentleman assures me he has taken the nests of ring-ousels * on Dartmoor : they build in banks on the sides of streams.

Titlarks † not only sing sweetly as they sit on trees, but also as they play and toy about on the wing; and particularly while they are descending, and sometimes as they stand on the ground. ‡

Adanson's § testimony seems to me to be a very poor evidence that European swallows migrate during our winter to Senegal; he does not talk at all like an ornithologist, and probably saw only the swallows of that country, which I know build within Governor O'Hara's hall against the roof. Had he known European swallows, would he not have mentioned the species ?

The house-swallow washes by dropping into the water as it flies ; this species appears commonly about a week before the house-marten, and about ten or twelve days before the swift.

In 1772, there were young house-martens ‖ in their nest till October the 23d.

The swift ¶ appears about ten or twelve days later than the house-swallow ; viz. about the 24th or 26th of April.

Whin-chats ** and stone-chatters †† stay with us the whole year.

Some wheatears ‡‡ continue with us the winter through. §§ Wagtails, all sorts, remain with us all the winter. ‖‖

---

* *British Zoology*, vol. i. p. 229. † *Ibid.* vol. ii. p. 237.

‡ This must have been the tree pipet, *anthus arboreus*, as the titlark generally sits on the ground. — Ed.

§ *British Zoology*, vol. ii. p. 242.

‖ *Ibid.* p. 244. ¶ *Ibid.* p. 245.

** This is a migratory species, appearing in Britain about the middle of April. — Ed.

†† *British Zoology*, vol. ii. p. 270, 271. ‡‡ *Ibid.* p. 269.

§§ Wheatears are migratory, and some few do remain. Montagu mentions the fact, and Mr Sweet says, " I observed a pair on the 17th November, near the gravel pit in Hyde-Park, which were quite lively, and flying about after the insects, as brisk as if it had been the middle of summer." They generally migrate in September. — Ed.

‖‖ There are three species of wagtails in Britain, — the pied, gray, and yellow. The pied wagtail is to be found in the south of England, during the whole year ; but, in the northern parts, it is migratory, retiring to the southward about the middle of October, and returning to the north about the beginning of March. The gray wagtail is only known

Bullfinches,[*] when fed on hempseed, often become wholly black.

We have vast flocks of female chaffinches[†] all the winter, with hardly any males among them.

When you say that, in breeding time, the cock snipes[‡] make a bleating noise, and a drumming, (perhaps I should have rather said a humming,) I suspect we mean the same thing. However, while they are playing about on the wing, they certainly make a loud piping with their mouths; but whether that bleating or humming is ventriloquous, or proceeds from the motion of their wings, I cannot say; but this I know, that when this noise happens, the bird is always descending, and his wings are violently agitated.

Soon after the lapwings[§] have done breeding, they congregate, and, leaving the moors and marshes, betake themselves to downs and sheep walks.

Two years ago[||] last spring, the little auk was found alive and unhurt, but fluttering and unable to rise, in a lane a few miles from Alresford, where there is a great lake; it was kept a while, but died.

I saw young teals[¶] taken alive in the ponds of Wolmer Forest in the beginning of July last, along with flappers, or young wild ducks.

Speaking of the swift,[**] that page says, " *its drink the dew;*" whereas it should be, " it drinks on the wing;" for all the swallow kind sip their water as they sweep over the face of pools or rivers : like Virgil's bees, they drink flying, — "*flumina summa libant.*" In this method of drinking, perhaps this genus may be peculiar.

Of the sedge-bird,[††] be pleased to say, it sings most part of the night; its notes are hurrying, but not unpleasing, and imitative of several birds, as the sparrow, swallow, skylark.[‡‡]

as an equatorial migrant in the southern counties of England, but is a regular summer visitant in the northern parts of the kingdom, arriving in April, and departing in the end of September, or beginning of October. The yellow wagtail, *motacilla flava* of Linnæus, is also migratory, appearing about the end of March: it leaves Britain in September, in search of a warmer residence for winter. — Ed.

[*] *British Zoology*, vol. ii. p. 300.   [†] *Ibid.* p. 306.
[‡] *Ibid.* p. 358.   [§] *Ibid.* p. 360.   [||] *Ibid.* p. 409.
[¶] *Ibid.* p. 475.   [**] *Ibid.* p. 15.   [††] *Ibid.* p. 16.
[‡‡] In Loudon's *Magazine*, a correspondent says, "The sedge-bird has a variety of notes, which partake of that of the skylark and the swallow,

When it happens to be silent in the night, by throwing a stone or clod into the bushes where it sits, you immediately set it a-singing, or, in other words, though it slumbers sometimes, yet, as soon as it is awakened, it reassumes its song.

It will be proper to premise here, that the fifty-fifth, fifty-seventh, fifty-ninth, and sixty-first letters have been published already in the *Philosophical Transactions;* but, as nicer observation has furnished several corrections and additions, it is hoped that the republication of them will not give offence; especially as these sheets would be very imperfect without them, and as they will be new to many readers who had no opportunity of seeing them when they made their first appearance.

LETTER LV.

TO THE HON. DAINES BARRINGTON.

SELBORNE, *November*, 20, 1773.

DEAR SIR,—In obedience to your injunctions, I sit down to give you some account of the house-marten, or martlet; and, if my monography of this little domestic and familiar bird should happen to meet with your approbation, I may probably soon extend my inquiries to the rest of the British *hirundines,* —the swallow, the swift, and the bank-marten.

A few house-martens begin to appear about the 16th of April; usually some few days later than the swallow. For some time after they appear, the *hirundines* in general pay no attention to the business of nidification, but play and sport about, either to recruit from the fatigue of their journey, if

as well as that of the house-sparrow. I have heard it imitate, in succession, (intermixed with its own note of *chur chur,*) the swallow, the house-marten, the greenfinch, the chaffinch, and lesser redpole, the redstart, the willow-wren, the whinchat, the pied and spring wagtails; yet its imitations are confined to the notes of alarm of these birds, and so exactly does it imitate them, both in tone and modulation, that, if it were to confine itself to one, (no matter which,) and not interlard the wailings of the little redpole and the shrieks of the marten, with the curses of the house-sparrow, and the *twink twink* of the chaffinch, and its own *care-for-nought* chatter, the most practised ear would not detect the difference. After being silent for a while, it often begins with the *chur chur* of the sparrow, so exactly imitated, in every respect, that, were it not for what follows, no one would suppose it to be any other bird. It is called the mocking bird here, (Lancashire,) and it well deserves the name; for it is a real scoffer at the sorrows of other birds, which it laughs to scorn, and turns into ridicule, by parodying them so exactly."—ED.

they do migrate at all, or else that their blood may recover its true tone and texture after it has been so long benumbed by the severities of winter.* About the middle of May, if the weather be fine, the marten begins to think in earnest of providing a mansion for its family. The crust, or shell, of this nest seems to be formed of such dirt or loam as comes most readily to hand, and is tempered and wrought together with little bits of broken straws, to render it tough and tenacious. As this bird often builds against a perpendicular wall, without any projecting ledge under it, it requires its utmost efforts to get the first foundation firmly fixed, so that it may safely carry the superstructure. On this occasion the bird not only clings with its claws, but partly supports itself by strongly inclining its tail against the wall, making that a fulcrum ; and, thus steadied, it works and plasters the materials into the face of the brick or stone. But then, that this work may not, while it is soft and green, pull itself down by its own weight, the provident architect has prudence and forbearance enough not to advance her work too fast ; but, by building only in the morning, and by dedicating the rest of the day to food and amusement, gives it sufficient time to dry and harden. About half an inch seems to be a sufficient layer for a day. Thus, careful workmen, when they build mud-walls, (informed at first, perhaps, by this little bird,) raise but a moderate layer at a time, and then desist ; lest the work should become top-heavy, and so be ruined by its own weight. By this method, in about ten or twelve days, is formed an hemispheric nest, with a small aperture towards the top, strong, compact, and warm ; and perfectly fitted for all the purposes for which it was intended. But then, nothing is more common than for the house-sparrow, as soon as the shell is finished, to seize on it as its own, to eject the owner, and to line it after its own manner.†

After so much labour is bestowed in erecting a mansion, as

---

* We are surprised to find that the more our author seems to have investigated the subject of swallows and their congeners, the greater is his leaning to the side of their hybernation. We need only again refer to our notes at pages 22 and 30. The ancient authors all speak of their migratory habits. From a passage in the *Birds of Aristophanes*, we are told that the swallow pointed out the time to dress in summer attire : and agreeable to the Greek calendar of Flora, which was kept at Athens by Theophrastus, the Ornithian winds blow, and the swallow arrives, between the 28th February and the 12th March. — Ed.

† See our note at page 88. — Ed.

Nature seldom works in vain, martens will breed on for several
years together in the same nest, where it happens to be well
sheltered and secure from the injuries of weather.   The shell,
or crust, of the nest is a sort of rustic work, full of knobs and
protuberances on the outside ; nor is the inside of those that
I have examined smoothed with any exactness at all ; but is
rendered soft and warm, and fit for incubation, by a lining of
small straws, grasses, and feathers ; and sometimes by a bed
of moss, interwoven with wool.   In this nest, they tread, or
engender, frequently during the time of building ; and the hen
lays from three to five white eggs.

   At first, when the young are hatched, and are in a naked
and helpless condition, the parent birds, with tender assiduity,
carry out what comes away from their young.   Were it not
for this affectionate cleanliness, the nestlings would soon be
burnt up and destroyed, in so deep and hollow a nest, by their
own caustic excrement.   In the quadruped creation, the same
neat precaution is made use of ; particularly among dogs and
cats, where the dams lick away what proceeds from their
young.   But, in birds, there seems to be a particular provision,
that the dung of nestlings is enveloped in a tough kind of
jelly, and, therefore, is the easier conveyed off, without soiling
or daubing.   Yet, as Nature is cleanly in all her ways, the
young perform this office for themselves in a little time, by
thrusting their tails out at the aperture of their nest.   As the
young of small birds presently arrive at their $\eta\lambda\iota\kappa\iota\alpha$, or full
growth, they soon become impatient of confinement, and sit
all day with their heads out at the orifice, where the dams, by
clinging to the nest, supply them with food from morning to
night.   For a time, the young are fed on the wing by their
parents ; but the feat is done by so quick and almost imperceptible a sleight, that a person must have attended very
exactly to their motions, before he would be able to perceive
it.   As soon as the young are able to shift for themselves, the
dams immediately turn their thoughts to the business of a
second brood ; while the first flight, shaken off and rejected
by their nurses, congregate in great flocks, and are the birds
that are seen clustering and hovering, on sunny mornings and
evenings, round towers and steeples, and on the roofs of
churches and houses.   These congregatings usually begin to
take place about the first week in August ; and, therefore, we
may conclude, that by that time the first flight is pretty well
over.   The young of this species do not quit their abodes all
together ; but the more forward birds get abroad some days

before the rest. These, approaching the eaves of buildings, and playing about before them, make people think that several old ones attend one nest. They are often capricious in fixing on a nesting-place, beginning many edifices, and leaving them unfinished ; but when once a nest is completed in a sheltered place, it serves for several seasons. Those which breed in a ready finished house get the start, in hatching, of those that build new, by ten days or a fortnight. These industrious artificers are at their labours in the long days before four in the morning : when they fix their materials, they plaster them on with their chins, moving their heads with a quick vibratory motion. They dip and wash as they fly sometimes, in very hot weather, but not so frequently as swallows. It has been observed, that martens usually build to a north-east or north-west aspect, that the heat of the sun may not crack and destroy their nests : but instances are also remembered where they bred for many years in vast abundance in a hot stifled inn-yard, against a wall facing to the south.

Birds in general are wise in their choice of situation ; but, in this neighbourhood, every summer, is seen a strong proof to the contrary, at a house without eaves, in an exposed district, where some martens build year by year in the corners of the windows. * But, as the corners of these windows (which face to the south-east and south-west) are too shallow, the

---

* A gentleman residing at Blois, in France, on the 14th April, 1831, made the following curious remarks on the building of the marten : — A pair of martens commenced making their nest in the deep corner of one of his windows, which, being of French make, frame and all moved inwards every time it was opened. So close did these birds build their nest to the corner, that it became attached to the frame of the window ; the nest was consequently carried away every time the window was opened ; but they recommenced building every morning, and so perseveringly did they adhere to the spot, that nothing would make them desist from their fruitless labour, until a piece of paper was nailed up at the corners of the window. When this was done, they removed to the next window, and there, with wonderful sagacity, commenced and carried on the business of building their nest, out of reach of the motion of the window frame. It is surprising to see animals thus exhibit such strong proofs of thought and skill out of the ordinary sphere of their habits.

Mr Clement Jackson, of East Looe, observed, in the same year, in a cavern near Falmouth, numbers of martens building their nests, and says, the roof was quite studded with them. But what renders the circumstance still more remarkable is, that while these birds colonized in the upper part of the cave, a pair of kestrels had taken up their abode, and were rearing their brood, under a projecting ledge at the entrance. Neither party seemed to be incommoded by the neighbourhood of the other. — ED.

nests are washed down every hard rain ; and yet these birds
drudge on to no purpose, from summer to summer, without
changing their aspect or house. It is a piteous sight to see
them labouring when half their nest is washed away, and
bringing dirt " *generis lapsi sarcire ruinas.*" Thus is instinct
a most wonderfully unequal faculty ; in some instances so
much above reason, in other respects so far below it ! Martens
love to frequent towns, especially if there are great lakes and
rivers at hand ; nay, they even affect the close air of London.
And I have not only seen them nesting in the Borough, but
even in the Strand and Fleet Street : but then it was obvious,
from the dinginess of their aspect, that their feathers partook
of the filth of that sooty atmosphere. Martens are by far the
least agile of the four species ; their wings and tails are short,
and therefore they are not capable of such surprising turns,
and quick and glancing evolutions as the swallow. Accordingly, they make use of a placid, easy motion, in a middle
region of the air, seldom mounting to any great height, and
never sweeping along together over the surface of the ground
or water. They do not wander far for food, but affect sheltered
districts, over some lake, or under some hanging wood, or in
some hollow vale, especially in windy weather. They breed
the latest of all the swallow kind : in 1772, they had nestlings
on to October twenty-first, and are never without unfledged
young as late as Michaelmas.

As the summer declines, the congregating flocks increase
in numbers daily by the constant accession of the second
broods : till at last they swarm in myriads upon myriads round
the villages on the Thames, darkening the face of the sky as
they frequent the aits of that river, where they roost. They
retire, the bulk of them I mean, in vast flocks together, about
the beginning of October ; but have appeared of late years,
in a considerable flight, in this neighbourhood, for one day or
two, as late as November the third and sixth, after they were
supposed to have been gone for more than a fortnight. They,
therefore, withdraw with us the latest of any species. Unless
these birds are very short-lived, indeed, or unless they do not
return to the district where they are bred, they must undergo
vast devastations somehow, and somewhere ; for the birds that
return yearly bear no manner of proportion to the birds that
retire. [*]

[*] Inscrutable are the ways of Him who is the director of all things.
He has, in his infinite wisdom, so nicely regulated the increase of animal
life, that there shall be no superabundance. But for this, there would

House-martens are distinguished from their congeners by having their legs covered with soft downy feathers down to their toes. They are no songsters, but twitter in a pretty, inward, soft manner in their nests. During the time of breeding, they are often greatly molested with fleas.

LETTER LVI.

TO THE HON. DAINES BARRINGTON.

RINGMER, near LEWES, *December* 9, 1773.

DEAR SIR,— I received your last favour just as I was setting out for this place; and am pleased to find that my monography met with your approbation. My remarks are the result of many years' observation; and are, I trust, true on the whole; though I do not pretend to say that they are perfectly void of mistake, or that a more nice observer might not make many additions, since subjects of this kind are inexhaustible.

If you think my letter worthy the notice of your respectable Society, you are at liberty to lay it before them; and they will consider it, I hope, as it was intended, as an humble attempt to promote a more minute inquiry into natural history, —into the life and conversation of animals. Perhaps, hereafter, I may be induced to take the house-swallow under consideration; and from that proceed to the rest of the British *hirundines*.

Though I have now travelled the Sussex Downs upwards of thirty years, yet I still investigate that chain of majestic mountains with fresh admiration, year by year; and I think I see new beauties every time I traverse it. This range, which runs from Chichester eastward, as far as East Bourn, is about sixty miles in length, and is called the South Downs, properly speaking, only round Lewes. As you pass along, you command a noble view of the wold, or weald, on one hand, and the broad downs and sea, on the other. Mr Ray used to

---

not be at this moment a vacant acre of ground in our globe, so thickly studded would it have been with the human race, and its surface would have been more then covered by even any one species of animal which is more prolific than man; the atmosphere would have been a solid mass of insects, and the mighty ocean incapable of containing its tenants. But how differently is every thing ordered, and we behold nothing but harmony of design, and a wise regulation of every object, which fits it for the ends it is destined to fulfil in the scale of being. —ED

visit a family* just at the foot of these hills, and was so ravished with the prospect from Plympton-plain, near Lewes, that he mentions those capes in his *Wisdom of God in the Works of the Creation,* with the utmost satisfaction, and thinks them equal to any thing he had seen in the finest parts of Europe.

For my own part, I think there is somewhat peculiarly sweet and amusing in the shapely-figured aspect of chalk hills, in preference to those of stone, which are rugged, broken, abrupt, and shapeless.

Perhaps I may be singular in my opinion, and not so happy as to convey to you the same idea, but I never contemplate these mountains, without thinking I perceive somewhat analogous to growth, in their gentle swellings, and smooth fungus-like protuberances, their fluted sides, and regular hollows and slopes, that carry at once the air of vegetative dilatation and expansion; or, was there ever a time when these immense masses of calcareous matter were thrown into fermentation by some adventitious moisture, — were raised and leavened into such shapes, by some plastic power, and so made to swell and heave their broad backs into the sky, so much above the less animated clay of the wild below?

By what I can guess, from the admeasurements of the hills that have been taken round my house, I should suppose that these hills surmount the wild, at an average, at about the rate of five hundred feet.

One thing is very remarkable as to the sheep: from the westward, till you get to the river Adur, all the flocks have horns, and smooth white faces, and white legs; and a hornless sheep is rarely to be seen. But as soon as you pass that river eastward, and mount Beeding-hill, all the flocks at once become hornless, or, as they call them, poll-sheep; and have, moreover, black faces, with a white tuft of wool on their foreheads, and speckled and spotted legs : so that, you would think that the flocks of Laban were pasturing on one side of the stream, and the variegated breed of his son-in-law, Jacob, were cantoned along on the other. And this diversity holds good respectively on each side, from the valley of Bramber and Beeding to the eastward, and westward all the whole length of the downs. If you talk with the shepherds on this subject, they tell you that the case has been so from time immemorial; and smile at your simplicity if you ask them, whether the

---

* Mr Courthope, of Danny.

K

·situation of these two different breeds might not be reversed?
·(However, an intelligent friend of mine near Chichester is
determined to try the experiment; and has, this autumn, at
the hazard of being laughed at, introduced a parcel of black-
faced hornless rams among his horned western ewes.) The
black-faced poll-sheep have the shortest legs and the finest
wool.*

As I had hardly ever before travelled these downs at so late
a season of the year, I was determined to keep as sharp a look-
out as possible so near the southern coast, with respect to the
summer short-winged birds of passage. We make great
inquiries concerning the withdrawing of the swallow kind,
without examining enough into the causes why this tribe is
never to be seen in winter; for, *entre nous,* the disappearing
of the latter is more marvellous than that of the former, and
much more unaccountable. The *hirundines,* if they please,
are certainly capable of migration; and yet, no doubt, are
often found in a torpid state: but redstarts, nightingales,
white-throats, black-caps, &c. &c. are very ill provided for long
flights; have never been once found, as I ever heard of, in a
torpid state, and yet can never be supposed, in such troops,
from year to year, to dodge and elude the eyes of the curious
and inquisitive, which, from day to day, discern the other small
birds that are known to abide our winters. But, notwithstanding
all my care, I saw nothing like a summer bird of passage; and
what is more strange, not one wheatear, though they abound

---

* There are ten or twelve distinct *varieties* of the common sheep,
which will all breed with each other. In the mountainous districts of
Wales and in the Highlands of Scotland, the kind preferred is the small,
horned, black-faced breed, remarkable for the very fine flavour of its flesh.
There are four distinct *species;* the bearded sheep of Barbary, the argali,
which ranges the mountains and steeps of Northern Asia, the American
argali, which inhabits Canada, and the musmon of Corsica and Sardinia.
With regard to colour, Southey, in his *Letters from Spain,* says, the sheep
of that peninsula are nearly all black. Geraldus Cambrensis informs us
that the Irish in his time were usually clothed in black habiliments,
made from wool which did not require dying. Much has been done
within the last century to improve the breed in Ireland, but still, in many
districts, black sheep are numerous. The cloth peculiar to Scotland,
called *hodden grey,* was a manufacture from the natural fleece; and
throughout the domestic farming districts, the housewives still use their
influence to have one black lamb retained among the flock, as the wool
takes on the dye more kindly and is indeed often spun into thread for
the stockings of the family, without receiving any artificial tinge. Individuals with a black covering are very common in black-faced flocks, and
occasionally occur among the Cheviot breed. — ED.

THE PARROT CROSSBILL.

so in the autumn as to be a considerable perquisite to the shepherds that take them ; and though many are to be seen to my knowledge all the winter through, in many parts of the south of England. The most intelligent shepherds tell me, that some few of these birds appear on the downs in March, and then withdraw to breed, probably, in warrens and stone quarries : now and then a nest is ploughed up in a fallow on the downs, under a furrow ; but it is thought a rarity. At the time of wheat-harvest, they begin to be taken in great numbers ; are sent for sale in vast quantities to Brighthelmstone and Tunbridge ; and appear at the tables of all the gentry that entertain with any degree of elegance. About Michaelmas they retire, and are seen no more till March. Though these birds are, when in season, in great plenty on the South Downs round Lewes, yet at East Bourn, which is the eastern extremity of those downs, they abound much more. One thing is very remarkable, that, though in the height of the season so many hundreds of dozens are taken, yet they never are seen to flock ; and it is a rare thing to see more than three or four at a time : so that there must be a perpetual flitting and constant progressive succession. It does not appear that any wheatears are taken to the westward of Houghton-bridge, which stands on the river Arun. *

I did not fail to look particularly after my new migration of ringousels, and to take notice whether they continued on the downs to this season of the year ; as I had formerly remarked them in the month of October all the way from Chichester to Lewes, wherever there were any shrubs and covert : but not one bird of this sort came within my observation. I only saw a few larks and whinchats, some rooks, and several kites and buzzards.

About midsummer, a flight of crossbills comes to the pine-groves about this house, but never makes any long stay. †

The old tortoise, that I have mentioned in a former letter

---

* Mr White is mistaken when he says that the wheatear is not to be found farther west than Houghton-bridge, as they have frequently been taken many miles west of the point mentioned. — ED.

† This bird but seldom visits this kingdom : it is a native of the extensive pine forests of the Rhine. Mr Knapp knew one instance of it breeding in England ; he says, " That rare bird the crossbill occasionally visits the orchards in our neighbourhood, coming in little parties to feed on the seeds of the apple, and, seldom as it appears, it is always noticed by the mischief it does to fruit, cutting it asunder with its well-constructed mandibles, in order to obtain the kernels." — ED.

still continues in this garden ; and retired under ground about the 20th of November, and came out again for one day on the 30th : it lies now buried in a wet swampy border under a wall facing to the south, and is enveloped at present in mud and mire !

Here is a large rookery round this house, the inhabitants of which seem to get their livelihood very easily ; for they spend the greatest part of the day on their nest-trees when the weather is mild. These rooks retire every evening, all the winter, from this rookery, where they only call by the way, as they are going to roost in deep woods : at the dawn of day, they always revisit their nest-trees,* and are preceded a few minutes by a flight of daws, that act, as it were, as their harbingers. †

* Rooks are not easily driven from the trees on which they were bred. Two striking instances of this have recently been witnessed in Edinburgh, on the grounds of the Earl of Moray, which have all been lately converted into magnificent streets and squares. Several rooks continue on the few remaining trees at the end of Ainslie Place ; and at St Bernard's Crescent, which is surrounded on both sides with houses, the rooks still incubate.

Mr Jesse makes the following curious remarks, illustrative of the attachment of this bird to its old accustomed haunts, and to the established usages of its tribe : — " The average number of rooks' nests, during the last four years, in the avenue of Hampton-Court Park, has been about seven hundred and fifty. Allowing three young birds and a pair of old ones to each nest, the number would amount to three thousand seven hundred and fifty. They are very particular that none of their society build away from the usual line of trees. A pair of rooks did so this spring, 1832, and when their nest was nearly finished, at least fifty others came and demolished it in a few minutes."

Differently from all other birds, rooks exhibit much sympathy when one of their fraternity has been killed, or hurt by a shot. They hover over their wounded companion, uttering cries of distress, and endeavouring all in their power to render him assistance. If he be able to flutter along, they animate him with their voices, and by advancing a little in front, try to induce him by their example to follow. — ED.

† The jack-daw is a bird of great intelligence ; is easily domesticated, and becomes very familiar. We had a pair in Fife, which flew about all our grounds, and even to the villages around, yet never strayed. They slept in a box, at a back window of the house. They entered the house, and even allowed themselves to be handled. They caught in their bill with great adroitness pieces of bread which were thrown to them. They followed the different members of our family through all the walks of the garden and shrubbery, and would perch on a tree, near the seats, and chatter while any person rested. One of them pronounced several words very distinctly ; such as *wee kaeie,* (little *kae,* the Scottish provincial name,) and *come here.* They were much addicted to stealing, and carried

LETTER LVII.

TO THE HON. DAINES BARRINGTON.

SELBORNE, *January* 29, 1774.

DEAR SIR,—The house-swallow, or chimney-swallow, is, undoubtedly, the first comer of all the British *hirundines ;* and appears in general on or about the thirteenth of April, as I have remarked from many years' observation.* Not but now and then a straggler is seen much earlier : and, in particular, when I was a boy, I observed a swallow for a whole day together on a sunny warm Shrove Tuesday, which day could not fall out later than the middle of March, and often happened early in February.

It is worth remarking, that these birds are seen first about lakes and mill-ponds ; and it is also very particular, that, if these early visitors happen to find frost and snow, as was the case of the two dreadful springs of 1770 and 1771, they immediately withdraw for a time ; a circumstance this, much more in favour of hiding than migration ; since it is much more probable that a bird should retire to its hybernaculum just

---

off to their box every thing they could get hold of. Besides this, they were very mischievous : they would attend the gardener at his work, and as soon as he removed to another part of the garden, they pulled up by the roots every thing he had planted ; such as young cabbages, or leeks. They had particular pleasure in turning over the leaves of a book, or pulling the whole thread off a bobbin. — ED.

* The following beautiful and vivid reflections on the swallow are from the pen of the late Sir Humphry Davy : — " I delight in this living landscape ! the swallow is one of my favourite birds, and a rival of the nightingale ; for he glads my sense of hearing. He is the joyous prophet of the year, the harbinger of the best season ; he has a life of enjoyment amongst the loveliest forms of nature ; winter is unknown to him, and he leaves the green meadows of England in autumn for the myrtle and orange groves of Italy, and for the palms of Africa ; he has always objects of pursuit, and his success is secure. Even the beings selected for his prey are poetical, beautiful, and transient. The ephemeræ are saved by his means from a slow and lingering death in the evening, and killed in a moment when they have known nothing of life but pleasure. *He is the constant destroyer of insects, the friend of man ; and with the stork and the ibis, may be regarded as a sacred bird.* This instinct, which gives him his appointed seasons, and which teaches him always when and where to move, may be regarded as flowing from a Divine source, and he belongs to the oracles of nature, which speak the awful and intelligible language of a present Deity."—ED.

at hand, than return for a week or two only to warmer latitudes. *

The swallow, though called the chimney-swallow, by no means builds altogether in chimneys, but often within barns and out-houses, against the rafters ; and so she did in Virgil's time,—

———— Ante
  - Garrula quàm tignis nidos suspendat hirundo.

In Sweden, she builds in barns, and is called *ladu swala,* (the barn-swallow.)   Besides, in the warmer parts of Europe, there are no chimneys to houses, except they are English built ; in these countries, she constructs her nest in porches, and gateways, and galleries, and open halls.†

---

* That the migration of the swallow elicited attention in the earliest times, is evident from the manner in which it is noticed by the prophet Jeremiah.   From that migration also, Cicero has drawn the following simile : " As swallows are present with us in summer, but are gone in winter, so false friends attend us in the sunshine of prosperity, but in the winter of affliction they all flee away."   The ancients usually mention this bird as wintering in Africa ; which is distinctly stated in Anacreon, λγ. Edn. Brunck. p. 38.   So great a favourite was the swallow among the Greeks, particularly at Rhodes, that they had a festival called χελιδὸνια, which was a holyday for the Greek boys, when they carried about young swallows, and sung a song, which is preserved in the works of Meursius.   It has been thus rendered in English :—

He comes ! He comes ! who loves to hear
Soft sunny hours, and seasons fair ;
The swallow hither comes, to rest
His sable wing, and snowy breast. *

These young mendicants (like Eton scholars at the *Montem*) used to levy contributions from the good nature of their fellow-citizens.

It is remarkable that most countries have a similar proverb relating to the swallow's accidental appearance before its usual time.   The French have, *Une hirondelle ne fait pas le printemps ;* the Germans, *Eine Sheval bemacht keinen Fruhling ;* the Dutch, *Eeu swalaw maak geen zomer ;* the Italians, *Una rodine non fa primevera ;* the Swedes, *En svala gor ingen sommar ;* which may be all literally translated by the English proverb, " *One swallow doth not make a summer.*"   The story is well known of a thin brass plate having been fixed on a swallow, with this inscription,—" Prithee, swallow, whither goest thou in winter ?" The bird returned next spring, with the answer subjoined, " To *Anthony of Athens.*   Why dost thou inquire ?"—ED.

† Dr Richardson gives a curious example of the cliff-swallow (*hirundo lunifrons*) building in houses.   " On the 25th of June, in the year 1825," says he, " a number of them made their first appearance at Fort Chepewyan, North America, and built their nests under the eaves of the dwelling-house, which are about six feet above a balcony that extends the

* Vol iii. p. 974, folio edition.

.' Here and there a bird may affect some odd, peculiar place ;. as we have known a swallow build down the shaft of an old well, through which chalk had been formerly drawn up, for the purpose of manure ; but, in general, with us this *hirundo* breeds in chimneys, and loves to haunt those stacks where there is a constant fire—no doubt for the sake of warmth. Not that it can subsist in the immediate shaft where there is a fire ; but prefers one adjoining to that of the kitchen, and disregards the perpetual smoke of that funnel, as I have often observed with some degree of wonder.

, Five or six, or more feet down the chimney, does this little bird begin to form her nest, about the middle of May, which

whole length of the building, and is a frequented promenade. They had thus to graze the heads of the passengers on entering their nests, and were, moreover, exposed to the depredations of the children, to whom they were novelties; yet they preferred the dwelling-house to the more lofty eaves of the storehouses, and, on the following season, returned with augmented numbers to the same spot. Fort Chepewyan has existed for many years, and trading posts, though far distant from each other, have been established in the fur countries for a century and a half; yet this, as far as I could learn, is the first instance of this species of swallow placing itself under the protection of man within the widely extended lands north of the great lakes. What cause could have thus suddenly called into action that confidence in the human race, with which the Framer of the universe has endowed this species, in common with others of the swallow tribe? It has been supposed that birds, frequenting desert countries, and unaccustomed to annoyance from man, would approach him fearlessly, or at least be less shy than those inhabiting the thickly peopled districts where they are daily exposed to the attacks of the great destroyer of their tribes. But although this may be true of some families of birds, it is far from being generally the case. On the contrary, the small birds of the fur countries, which are never objects of pursuit, and scarcely even of notice, to the Indian hunter, are shy, retiring, and distrustful, their habits contrasting strongly with the boldness and familiarity of sparrows, that are persecuted to death by every idle boy in Europe. Nay, some species which are bold enough during their winter residence in the United States, evince great timidity in the northern regions, where the raising their progeny occupies the whole time. In like manner, the redbreast of Europe, familiar as it is in winter, sequesters itself with the greatest care in the breeding season. The question, however, recurs, What is the peculiarity of economy which leads one species of bird to conceal its nest with the most extraordinary care and address, and another to place its offspring in the most exposed situation it can select?"

In the cabinet of the Lycæum, Governor De Witt Clinton has given an account of the fulvous swallow, *il folva*, which is nearly allied to the preceding species, having built its nest in the walls of houses in the Western States; and which has, every succeeding year, been advancing farther to the eastward. —Ed.

consists, like that of the house-marten, of a crust, or shell, composed of dirt, or mud, mixed with short pieces of straw, to render it tough and permanent ; with this difference, that whereas the shell of the marten is nearly hemispheric, that of the swallow is open at the top, and like half a deep dish : this nest is lined with fine grasses, and feathers, which are often collected as they float in the air.

Wonderful is the address which this adroit bird shews all day long, in ascending and descending with security through so narrow a pass. When hovering over the mouth of the funnel, the vibrations of her wings, acting on the confined air, occasion a rumbling like thunder. It is not improbable that the dam submits to this inconvenient situation so low in the shaft, in order to secure her broods from rapacious birds, and particularly from owls, which frequently fall down chimneys, perhaps in attempting to get at these nestlings. *

The swallow lays from four to six white eggs, dotted with red specks ; and brings out her first brood about the last week in June, or the first week in July. The progressive method by which the young are introduced into life is very amusing : first they emerge from the shaft with difficulty enough, and often fall down into the rooms below ; for a day or so, they are fed on the chimney top, and then are conducted to the dead leafless bough of some tree, where, sitting in a row, they are attended with great assiduity, and may then be called perchers. In a day or two more, they become fliers, but are still unable to take their own food ; therefore, they play about near the place where the dams are hawking for flies ; and when a mouthful is collected, at a certain signal given, the dam and the nestling advance, rising towards each other, and meeting at an angle ; the young one all the while uttering

---

* Swallows have a strong attachment to places where they once found security, and sometimes make their nests in curious situations. At Blois, in France, a chimney, which had a moving iron top placed over it to prevent smoking, became, in consequence of the fireplace being bricked up, a safe place for building in ; and, no doubt, the birds discovered that it was such. Within the very *hood*, or top of this machine, swinging about with every wind, and making a most hideous noise, swallows have built their nests for the last two years, 1830 and 1831 ; and often, for five minutes or more, when the wind was high, they have been noticed in vain attempting to get into it, the constant motion preventing them from entering their airy dwelling. The force of habit must be very strong indeed to induce birds to choose so inconvenient a situation for incubation. No doubt, however, the feelings of security overcome many considerations. — ED.

such a little quick note of gratitude and complacency, that a person must have paid very little regard to the wonders of Nature that has not often remarked this feat.

The dam betakes herself immediately to the business of a second brood, as soon as she is disengaged from her first; which at once associates with the first broods of house-martens, and with them congregates, clustering on sunny roofs, towers, and trees. This *hirundo* brings out her second brood towards the middle and end of August.

All the summer long is the swallow a most instructive pattern of unwearied industry and affection; for, from morning to night, while there is a family to be supported, she spends the whole day in skimming close to the ground, and exerting the most sudden turns and quick evolutions. Avenues, and long walks, under hedges, and pasture fields, and mown meadows where cattle graze, are her delight, especially if there are trees interspersed; because in such spots insects most abound. When a fly is taken, a smart snap from her bill is heard, resembling the noise at the shutting of a watch case; but the motion of the mandibles is too quick for the eye.

The swallow, probably the male bird, is the excubitor to house-martens, and other little birds, announcing the approach of birds of prey. For as soon as a hawk appears, with a shrill alarming note, he calls all the swallows and martens about him; who pursue in a body, and buffet and strike their enemy, till they have driven him from the village, darting down from above on his back, and rising in a perpendicular line in perfect security. This bird also will sound the alarm, and strike at cats when they climb on the roofs of houses, or otherwise approach the nests.* Each species of *hirundo* drinks as it

---

* The swallow is well known to be a very intrepid bird, and will attack animals of a size superior to itself, and which larger birds would not dare to face. While a gentleman was walking through a retired village lane, near Lynn Regis, in 1830, a stoat, *mustela erminea*, issued from the hedge a few paces before him, on the footpath. A swallow, flying over the place, immediately discovered the animal, fearlessly pounced upon him, and forced him to retire to his hiding-place. In a minute afterwards, however, the stoat again ventured out, when the swallow, having taken another round in the air, again obliged him to retreat. This was repeated four several times, after which the stoat disappeared, and was not again seen.

A swallow has been seen to attack a cat, in the same manner as above described. A writer in Loudon's *Magazine* says, — " Swallows were and are allowed to build in out-houses belonging to my father; the house cat would often bask in the sun, beside the out-houses, when the swallows testified their detestation of her by flying over her head in a

flies along, sipping the surface of the water; but the swallow
alone, in general, washes on the wing, by dropping into a pool
for many times together: in very hot weather, house-martens
and bank-martens dip and wash a little.

, The swallow is a delicate songster, and, in soft, sunny
weather, sings both perching and flying; on trees in a kind of
concert, and on chimney tops; is also a bold flier, ranging to
distant downs and commons, even in windy weather, which
the other species seem much to dislike; nay, even frequenting
exposed seaport towns, and making little excursions over the
salt water. Horsemen on wide downs are often closely
attended by a little party of swallows for miles together, which
plays before and behind them, sweeping around, and collecting
all the skulking insects that are roused by the trampling of
the horses' feet. When the wind blows hard, without this
expedient, they are often forced to settle to pick up their
lurking prey

. This species feeds much on little *coleoptera*, as well as on
gnats and flies, and often settles on dug ground, or paths, for
gravels to grind and digest its food. Before they depart, for
some weeks, to a bird they forsake houses and chimneys, and
roost in trees, and usually withdraw about the beginning of
October, though some few stragglers may appear on, at times,
till the first week in November.

rapid, sweeping curve, almost touching her in its lowest inclination; and
they shrieked their hatred as they flew. Now and then, as if enraged by
their pertinacity, and her own want of success, she would spring up in
the air at them, as they passed, with her best vigour and agility; but I
never knew her catch one." Another correspondent mentions a cat which
was more successful. He says, " The thing is, *a priori*, nearly impossible,
and yet we stake our credit on the authenticity of the fact, having seen
the whole process of grimalkin's wonderful cunning, and almost miraculous
rapidity. It was in the early part of May, 1832, when insects, in consequence of the cold, fly low, and, of course, the swallows are forced to
hawk for their prey by skimming the surface of the ground. The wily
cat, taking advantage of this, stretches herself upon the sunny grass-plot,
with her legs extended, as if she were dead; the flies collect about her,
as flies always do when they can find any animal as patient as my Uncle
Toby, to endure their tickling and buzzing; the simple swallows, dream-
ing of no harm, and thinking they can make good a meal, dip down from
the barren air, dart with free will upon the flies, when puss, perceiving
her prey within reach, makes a spring like a flash of lightning, and
strikes down with her paw the poor thoughtless swallow. The best
marksmen know how difficult it is to shoot a swallow on the wing; but
the cat found her patience, cunning, and rapidity, well rewarded, by
her unerring success whenever a swallow ventured within her reach."—
ED.

Some few pairs haunt the new and open streets of London next the fields, but do not enter, like the house-marten, the close and crowded parts of the city.*

Both male and female are distinguished from their congeners by the length and forkedness of their tails. They are undoubtedly the most nimble of all the species; and when the male pursues the female in amorous chase, they then go beyond their usual speed, and exert a rapidity almost too quick for the eye to follow.

After this circumstantial detail of the life and discerning στοργή of the swallow, I shall add, for your farther amusement, an anecdote or two, not much in favour of her sagacity:—

A certain swallow built, for two years together, on the handles of a pair of garden shears, that were stuck up against the boards in an out-house, and therefore must have her nest spoiled whenever that implement was wanted. And, what is stranger still, another bird of the same species built its nest on the wings and body of an owl, that happened by accident to hang, dead and dry, from the rafter of a barn. This owl, with the nest on its wings, and with eggs in the nest, was brought as a curiosity worthy the most elegant private museum in Great Britain. The owner, struck with the oddity of the sight, furnished the bringer with a large shell, or conch, desiring him to fix it just where the owl hung. The person did as he was ordered; and the following year, a pair, probably the same pair, built their nest in the conch, and laid their eggs.†

The owl and the conch make a strange, grotesque appearance, and are not the least curious specimens in that wonderful collection of art and nature.‡

* In 1819, we noticed the nest of a chimney-swallow, under the coping of a stack of chimneys, in Hyde Street, Bloomsbury, the very heart of London. — ED.

† The following interesting circumstance is mentioned in Kalm's Travels:—" A pair of swallows built their nest in the stable belonging to a lady; the female laid eggs in the nest, and was about to breed them. Some days after, the people saw the female sitting on the eggs, but the male flying about the nest, and, sometimes sitting on a nail, he was heard to utter a very plaintive note, which betrayed his uneasiness. On a nearer examination, the female was found dead in the nest, and the people flung her body away. The male went to sit upon the eggs; but, after being about two hours on them, and perhaps finding the business too troublesome, he went out, and returned in the afternoon with another female, which sat upon the nest, and afterwards fed the young ones, till they were able to provide for themselves." There seems to have been displayed in this a degree of intelligence higher than mere instinct. — ED.

‡ Sir Ashton Lever's Museum.

Thus is instinct in animals, taken the least out of its way,
an undistinguishing, limited faculty, and blind to every circumstance that does not immediately respect self-preservation, or
lead at once to the propagation or support of their species.

LETTER LVIII.

TO THE HON. DAINES BARRINGTON.

SELBORNE, *February* 14, 1774.

DEAR SIR,—I received your favour of the eighth, and am
pleased to find that you read my little history of the swallow
with your usual candour; nor was I the less pleased to find
that you made objections where you saw reason.

As to the quotations, it is difficult to say precisely which
species of *hirundo* Virgil might intend, in the lines in question,
since the ancients did not attend to specific differences, like
modern naturalists; yet somewhat may be gathered, enough
to incline me to suppose, that, in the two passages quoted, the
poet had his eye on the swallow.

In the first place, the epithet *garrula* suits the swallow well,
who is a great songster, and not the marten, which is rather a
mute bird, and when it sings, is so inward as scarce to be
heard. Besides, if *tignum* in that place signifies a rafter, rather
than a beam, as it seems to me to do, then I think it must be
the swallow that is alluded to, and not the marten, since the
former does frequently build within the roof, against the
rafters, while the latter always, as far as I have been able to
observe, builds without the roof, against eaves and cornices.*

As to the simile, too much stress must not be laid on it;
yet the epithet *nigra* speaks plainly in favour of the swallow,
whose back and wings are very black; while the rump of the
marten is milk-white, its back and wings blue, and all its under
part white as snow. Nor can the clumsy motions (comparatively clumsy) of the marten well represent the sudden and
artful evolutions, and quick turns, which Juturna gave to her
brother's chariot, so as to elude the eager pursuit of the enraged

---

* We have seen that the marten and cliff-swallow of America have
changed their habits, so far as their breeding places are concerned. The
former has been known to breed in caverns, as mentioned in our note at
page 142, and the latter has deserted the cliff of the desert for the abode
of man, as noticed in our note, pages 150, 151: so that the argument
made use of by our author is no evidence in favour of the point he wishes to
establish. — ED.

Æneas. The verb *sonat*, also, seems to imply a bird that is somewhat loquacious. *

We have had a very wet autumn and winter, so as to raise the springs to a pitch beyond any thing since 1764, which was a remarkable year for floods and high waters. The land-springs, which we call levants, break out much on the downs of Sussex, Hampshire, and Wiltshire. The country people say, when the levants rise, corn will always be dear; meaning, that when the earth is so glutted with water as to send forth springs on the downs and uplands, that the corn vales must be drowned: and so it has proved for these ten or eleven years past; for land-springs have never obtained more since the memory of man than during that period, nor has there been known a greater scarcity of all sorts of grain, considering the great improvements of modern husbandry. Such a run of wet seasons, a century or two ago, would, I am persuaded, have occasioned a famine. Therefore, pamphlets and newspaper letters that talk of combinations, tend to inflame and mislead, since we must not expect plenty till Providence sends us more favourable seasons.

The wheat of last year, all round this district, and in the county of Rutland, and elsewhere, yields remarkably bad; and our wheat on the ground, by the continual late sudden vicissitudes from fierce frost to pouring rains, looks poorly, and the turnips rot very fast.

LETTER LIX.

TO THE HON. DAINES BARRINGTON.

SELBORNE, *February 26*, 1774.

DEAR SIR,— The sand-marten, or bank-marten, is by much the least of any of the British *hirundines*, and, as far as we have ever seen, the smallest known *hirundo;* though Brisson asserts that there is one much smaller, and that is the *hirundo esculenta.*†

* *Nigra* velut magnas domini cum divitis ædes
  Pervolat, et pennis alta atria lustrat hirundo,
  Pabula parva legens, nidisque loquacibus escas:
  Et nunc porticibus vacuis, nunc humida circum
  Stagna *sonat.*

† The edible nest of this species constitutes one of the luxuries of an Indian banquet. The Nicobar swallow builds in fissures and cavities of rocks, especially such as are open to the south. In the latter situation, the finest and whitest nests are found. Sometimes fifty pounds weight of them are gathered in a nest-hunting excursion. They are small, and

But it is much to be regretted, that it is scarce possible for any observer to be so full and exact as he could wish, in reciting the circumstances attending the life and conversation of this little bird, since it is *fera naturâ*, at least in this part of the kingdom, disclaiming all domestic attachments, and haunting wild heaths and commons where there are large lakes ; while the other species, especially the swallow and house-marten, are remarkably gentle and domesticated, and never seem to think themselves safe but under the protection of man.*

Here are in this parish, in the sand-pits and banks of the lake of Wolmer Forest, several colonies of these birds ; and yet they are never seen in the village, nor do they at all frequent the cottages that are scattered about in that wild district. The only instance I ever remember where this species haunts any building, is at the town of Bishop's Waltham, in this county, where many sand-martens nestle and breed in the scaffold holes of the back wall of William of Wykeham's stables ; but then this wall stands in a very sequestered and retired enclosure, and faces upon a large and beautiful lake,

shaped like the nest of a window-swallow. If these are perfect, seventy-two of them will go to a *catty*, or one pound and three quarters. They bring a very high price in China. They are composed of a substance resembling amber, and probably the gum of the Nicobar cedar, which grows abundantly in all the islands. From December to May, it is covered with blossoms, and bears a fruit somewhat resembling a cedar or pine apple, but more like a large berry full of pustules, discharging a gum or resinous fluid. The hen constructs a neat, large nest, for laying and hatching her eggs, and the cock contrives to fix another smaller, and rather more clumsy, close to his mate ; for they are not only built for the purpose of incubation, but also for resting places. If they are robbed of them, they immediately fall to work to build others, and being remarkably active, are able in a day to finish enough to support the weight of their bodies, although they take about three weeks to complete a nest. During the north-east trade-wind, they are all alive, and fly about briskly ; but as soon as the wind comes round to the south-west, they sit or lie in their nests, in a state of stupor, and shew animation only by a kind of tremulous motion over their whole body. If the nests were taken away at this season, the poor birds must inevitably perish. — ED.

* If the sand-martens of Selborne were solitary, as Mr White states, they have been different from all others we have heard of or seen. In many situations the excavations are so near each other, that the entrance to one of their holes is frequently close to that of the other. Professor Rennie tells us that he has noticed them not three inches apart, and the whole face of a bank thickly studded over with them. We have seen them in an indurated sandbank, on the side of a stream called the Lothrie, near Leslie, in Fife, very numerous, and not above fifteen inches from each other.— ED.

And, indeed, this species seems so to delight in large waters, that no instance occurs of their abounding, but near vast pools or rivers ; and, in particular, it has been remarked that they swarm in the banks of the Thames, in some places below London Bridge.

It is curious to observe with what different degrees of architectonic skill Providence has endowed birds of the same genus, and so nearly correspondent in their general mode of life ; for, while the swallow and the house-marten discover the greatest address in raising and securely fixing crusts, or shells, of loam, as cunabula for their young, the bank-marten terebrates a round and regular hole in the sand or earth, which is serpentine, horizontal, and about two feet deep. At the inner end of this burrow does this bird deposit, in a good degree of safety, her rude nest, consisting of fine grasses and feathers, usually goose feathers, very inartificially laid together.

Perseverance will accomplish any thing : though at first one would be disinclined to believe that this weak bird, with her soft and tender bill and claws, should ever be able to bore the stubborn sand bank, without entirely disabling herself ; * yet, with these feeble instruments, have I seen a pair of them make great despatch, and could remark how much they had scooped that day, by the fresh sand which ran down the bank, and was of a different colour from that which lay loose and bleached in the sun.

In what space of time these little artists are able to mine and finish these cavities, I have never been able to discover, for reasons given above; but it would be a matter worthy of observation, where it falls in the way of any naturalist, to make his remarks. This I have often taken notice of, that several holes of different depths are left unfinished at the end of summer. To imagine that these beginnings were intentionally made, in order to be in the greater forwardness for next spring, is allowing perhaps, too much foresight and *rerum prudentia* to a simple bird. May not the cause of these *latebræ* being left unfinished arise from their meeting in those places with strata too harsh, hard, and solid for their purpose, which they relinquish, and go to a fresh spot that works more freely ? or may they not in other places fall in with a soil as much too loose and mouldering, liable to founder, and threatening to overwhelm them and their labours ?

* The bill is rather hard and sharp, well adapted for digging; and its shortness adds greatly to its strength. — ED.

One thing is remarkable, that, after some years, the old holes are forsaken, and new ones bored ; perhaps because the old habitations grow foul and fetid from long use, or because they may so abound with fleas as to become untenantable. This species of swallow, moreover, is strangely annoyed with fleas ; and we have seen fleas, bed-fleas, (*pulex irritans,* *) swarming at the mouths of these holes like bees on the stools of their hives.

The following circumstance should by no means be omitted, —that these birds do not make use of their caverns by way of hybernacula, as might be expected ; since banks so perforated have been dug out with care in the winter, when nothing was found but empty nests.

The sand-marten arrives much about the same time with the swallow, and lays, as she does, from four to six white eggs. But, as this species is *cryptogame,* carrying on the business of nidification, incubation, and the support of its young, in the dark, it would not be easy to ascertain the time of breeding, were it not for the coming forth of the broods, which appear much about the time, or rather somewhat earlier, than those of the swallow.   The nestlings are supported, in common, like those of their congeners, with gnats and other small insects, and sometimes they are fed with *libellulæ,* (dragon-flies,) almost as long as themselves.   In the last week in June, we have seen a row of these sitting on a rail, near a great pool, as perchers, and so young and helpless, as easily to be taken by hand ; but whether the dams ever feed them on the wing, as swallows and house-martens do, we have never yet been able to determine ; nor do we know whether they pursue and attack birds of prey.

When they happen to breed near hedges and enclosures, they are dispossessed of their breeding holes by the house-sparrow, which is, on the same account, a fell adversary to house-martens.

These *hirundines* are no songsters, but rather mute, making only a little harsh noise when a person approaches their nests. They seem not to be of a sociable turn, never with us congregating with their congeners in the autumn.   Undoubtedly they breed a second time, like the house-marten and swallow, and withdraw about Michaelmas.

Though, in some particular districts, they may happen to

---

* Our author is wrong in supposing these insects to be the common bed-flea ; it is the swallow-flea, (*pulex hirundinis* of Stephens,) by which they are infested.— ED.

abound, yet, on the whole, in the south of England at least, is this much the rarest species ; for there are few towns or large villages but what abound with house-martens ; few churches, towers, or steeples, but what are haunted by some swifts ; scarce a hamlet or single cottage chimney that has not its swallow ; while the bank-martens, scattered here and there live a sequestered life among some abrupt sand hills, and in the banks of some few rivers. *

These birds have a peculiar manner of flying, flitting about with odd jerks and vacillations, not unlike the motions of a butterfly. Doubtless the flight of all *hirundines* is influenced by, and adapted to, the peculiar sort of insects which furnish their food. Hence it would be worth inquiry to examine what particular genus of insects affords the principal food of each respective species of swallow.

Notwithstanding what has been advanced above, some few sand-martens, I see, haunt the skirts of London, frequenting the dirty pools in St George's Fields, and about Whitechapel. The question is, where these build, since there are no banks or bold shores in that neighbourhood ? Perhaps they nestle in the scaffold-holes of some old or new deserted building. They dip and wash as they fly sometimes, like the house-marten and swallow.

* Professor Rennie says, " We can hardly bring ourselves to believe that he meant the same species, or at least that he spoke in this instance from his own observation. A more decidedly social bird we are not acquainted with ; since it not only nestles in numerous colonies, but also hunts for insects in troops of from thirty to fifty, and, as Buffon correctly remarks, associates freely with other swallows." La Vaillant, Montagu, and Wilson, all agree on this point ; the latter says, it " appears to be the most social of its kind of all our swallows, living together in large communities of sometimes three or four hundred. Several of their holes," he adds, " are often within a few inches of each other, and extend in various strata along the front of a precipice, sometimes for eighty or a hundred yards. They are particularly fond of the shores of rivers, and in several places along the Ohio and the Kentucky river, they congregate in immense multitudes." Although it may be true, according to the remarks of these naturalists, that the sand-marten has been found in much frequented situations, we do not think that any proof of the inaccuracy of our author, as the Professor seems desirous of establishing. We have already pointed out, in our note at page 150, on the respectable authority of Dr Richardson, that one of the congeners of this bird, the cliff-swallow, has entirely changed its habits within these very few years ; and this may be the case with the sand-marten also. These birds may have been in Mr White's time much more rare in this country than at present. As far as our own observation goes, we have always noticed this species in remote and rather sequestered situations. — Ed.

Sand-martens differ from their congeners in the diminutiveness of their size, and in their colour, which is what is usually called a mouse-colour. Near Valencia, in Spain, they are taken, says Willoughby, and sold in the markets for the table, and are called by the country people, probably from their desultory, jerking manner of flight, *Papillon de Montagna.**

LETTER LX.

TO THOMAS PENNANT, ESQ.

SELBORNE, *September* 2, 1774.

DEAR SIR, — Before your letter arrived, and of my own accord, I had been remarking and comparing the tails of the male and female swallow, and this ere any young broods appeared ; so that there was no danger of confounding the dams with their *pulli* ; and, besides, as they were then always in pairs, and busied in the employ of nidification, there could be no room for mistaking the sexes, nor the individuals of different chimneys, the one for the other. From all my observations, it constantly appeared that each sex has the long feathers in its tail that give it that forked shape ; with this difference, that they are longer in the tail of the male than in that of the female.

Nightingales, when their young first come abroad, and are helpless, make a plaintive and a jarring noise ; and also a snapping or cracking, pursuing people along the hedges as they walk : these last sounds seem intended for menace and defiance.†

* Dr Richardson considers the sand-marten of the fur countries of North America, as identical with the European bird ; and, from all accounts, it is the same in every quarter of the globe. It breeds but once in the fur countries, generally late, and takes its departure about the middle of August with the rest of the swallow tribe ; which confirms the fact that they live in societies. That traveller says, " We observed thousands of these sand-martens fluttering at the entrance of their burrows, near the mouth of the Mackenzie, in the sixty-eighth parallel, on the 4th July ; and it is probable, from the state of the weather, that they had arrived at least a fortnight prior to that date. They are equally numerous in every district of the fur countries, wherein banks suitable for burrowing exist."— ED.

† It has been generally believed that the migratory songsters, both old and young, return to their native haunts in the breeding season. From this circumstance it is believed, that if any of these could be bred beyond the ordinary limits of their incubation, they would return in the following season to their birth place. Impressed with this belief, Sir John

The grasshopper-lark chirps all night in the height of summer.

Swans turn white the second year, and breed the third.

Weasels prey on moles, as appears by their being sometimes caught in mole-traps.*

Sparrow-hawks sometimes breed in old crows' nests ; and the kestrel in churches and ruins.

There are supposed to be two sorts of eels in the island of Ely. The threads sometimes discovered in eels are perhaps their young : the generation of eels is very dark and mysterious.†

Sinclair, Bart. long known for his patriotism, commissioned the late Mr Dickson of Covent Garden, to purchase for him as many nightingales' eggs as he could procure, at a shilling each. This was accordingly done, the eggs carefully packed in wool, and transmitted to Sir John by the mail. Sir John employed several men to find, and take care of, the nests of several robins, in places where the eggs might be deposited and hatched with security. The robins' eggs were removed, and replaced by those of the nightingale, which were all sat upon, hatched in due time, and the young brought up by the foster-parents. The songsters flew, when fully fledged, and were observed, for some time afterwards, near the places where they were incubated. In September, the usual migratory period, they disappeared, and never returned to the place of their birth. The nightingale is usually silent on the 1st of July. — ED.

* A man of acute observation, who had set a common spring mole-trap, perceived that a mole was taken. He took the trap from the ground, allowing the mole to continue suspended in it. He was working in the neighbourhood, and chancing to look at the trap, he perceived a weasel actively engaged in attempting to get the mole out of the wires which held it. The weasel ran up the stick, which formed the spring of the trap, and descended on the captive, which he seized, and, tried by wriggling, twisting, and hanging by it, to disengage it from the trap, but without being able to effect his purpose. When exhausted with these fruitless efforts, he relinquished his hold, and dropt to the ground, where he rested for some time; he re-ascended the stick, and renewed his efforts with redoubled ardour. The workman, after seeing him make nearly a dozen attempts, took the mole from the trap, and threw it down as a reward for his perseverance ; but, on seeing the man, he made his escape, and never returned while he remained. — ED.

† The uncertainty on this subject has, as is usual in most cases, invested it with a degree of fable. It is a common belief among schoolboys in Scotland, that horse hairs left in the water are, in a short time, converted into young eels ; and they establish the fact, to their own full satisfaction, by experiment. Repairing to a rivulet, they stick a hair in the mud at the bottom, both because they think the incipient animal derives some nourishment from the ground, and to prevent its being swept away from their observation. On their return to the spot, next day perhaps, the admiring group gather round ; one of them with his finger touches the hair, which being by this time moistened and rendered pliable, exhibits in the rippling stream a tremulous motion, that is unhesitatingly ascribed

Hen-harriers breed on the ground, and seem never to settle on trees.

When redstarts shake their tails, they move them horizontally, as dogs do when they fawn : the tail of the wagtail, when in motion, bobs up and down, like that of a jaded horse.

Hedge-sparrows have a remarkable flirt with their wings in breeding time : as soon as frosty mornings come, they make a very piping, plaintive noise.

Many birds which become silent about midsummer, reassume their notes again in September, as the thrush, blackbird, woodlark, willow-wren, &c. ; hence August is by much the most mute month, the spring, summer, and autumn through. Are birds induced to sing again because the temperament of autumn resembles that of spring ?

Linnæus ranges plants geographically : palms inhabit the tropics ; grasses the temperate zones ; and mosses and lichens the polar circles : no doubt animals may be classed in the same manner with propriety.

House-sparrows build under eaves in the spring ; as the weather becomes hotter, they get out for coolness, and nest in plum-trees and apple-trees. These birds have been known sometimes to build in rooks' nests, and sometimes in the forks of boughs under rooks' nests. *

to animation. It is allowed to float down the current, and the urchin philosophers depart, fully persuaded of the possibility of the planting and rearing beds of eels. — ED.

* The late Mrs O'Brien, of Manor Place, Chelsea, being exceedingly fond of birds, kept a number in cages. One of them, a canary, was a great favourite, but the loudness of its song frequently obliged her to put it outside of the window, among trees trained in the front of the house. During breakfast one morning, a sparrow was observed to fly several times round the cage, to alight upon the top, and chirp to the canary ; at length a reciprocal conversation ensued. He remained a few minutes, and then flew away, but soon returned with a worm in his bill, which he dropped into the cage, and again took his departure. The same attentions were manifested day after day, till they became so familiar, that the canary would at length receive the proffered food from the bill of his generous friend. This trait of the sparrow soon became known to the neighbours, who were frequent spectators of his acts of benevolence. Some of them, wishing to ascertain the extent of his kindly feelings, also put their birds out at the window, and he extended his attention to all of them ; but his first and longest visit was always paid to his old acquaintance, Mrs O'Brien's canary.

Notwithstanding the sociable disposition manifested by this sparrow towards his feathered companions, he was excessively shy with regard to man, for they were obliged to observe his motions at a distance, as the instant he noticed them he flew away. These visits were continued till

As my neighbour was housing a rick, he observed that his dogs devoured all the little red mice that they could catch, but rejected the common mice ; and that his cats eat the common mice, refusing the red.

Red-breasts sing all through the spring, summer, and autumn. The reason that they are called autumn songsters is, because in the two first seasons their voices are lost and drowned in the general chorus : in the latter, their song becomes distinguishable. Many songsters of the autumn seem to be the young cock red-breast of that year : notwithstanding the prejudices in their favour, they do much mischief in gardens to the summer fruits. *

The tit-mouse, which early in February begins to make two quaint notes, like the whetting of a saw,† is the marsh tit-mouse ; the great tit-mouse sings with three cheerful joyous notes, and begins about the same time.

Wrens sing all the winter through, frost excepted.

House-martens came remarkably late this year, both in Hampshire and Devonshire : Is this circumstance for or against either hiding or migration ?

Most birds drink sipping at intervals ; but pigeons take a long continued draught, like quadrupeds.

Notwithstanding what I have said in a former letter, no gray crows were ever known to breed on Dartmoor ; it was my mistake.

The appearance and flying of the *scarabæus solstitialis*, or fern-chaffer, commence with the month of July, and cease about the end of it. These scarabs are the constant food of *caprimulgi*, or fern-owls, through that period. They abound on the chalky downs, and in some sandy districts, but not in the clays.

In the garden of the Black Bear Inn, in the town of Reading, is a stream, or canal, running under the stables and out into the fields on the other side of the road : in this water are many carps, which lie rolling about in sight, being fed by travellers, who amuse themselves by tossing them bread ; but as soon as the weather grows at all severe, these fishes are no longer seen,

the commencement of winter, and he then withdrew, never to appear again. — ED.

* They eat also the berries of the ivy, the honeysuckle, and the *euonymus europæus*, or spindle-tree.
Redbreasts were very frequent here about the end of January, 1802, during the cold weather ; but, on the air becoming milder, they entirely disappeared ; nor did they again return, although the frost became pretty severe about six weeks after. — ED.

† It is the greater titmouse (*parus major* of Linnæus) which makes the sound alluded to. — ED.

because they retire under the stables, where they remain till the return of spring. Do they lie in a torpid state? if they do not, how are they supported?*

The note of the white-throat, which is continually repeated, and often attended with odd gesticulations on the wing, is harsh and displeasing. These birds seem of pugnacious disposition, for they sing with an erected crest, and attitudes of rivalry and defiance; are shy and wild in breeding time, avoiding neighbourhoods, and haunting lonely lanes and commons; nay, even the very tops of the Sussex Downs, where there are bushes and covert; but in July and August, they bring their broods into gardens and orchards, and make great havoc among the summer fruits.

The black-cap has, in common, a full, sweet, deep, loud, and wild pipe; yet that strain is of short continuance, and his motions are desultory; but, when that bird sits calmly and engages in song in earnest, he pours forth very sweet, but inward melody, and expresses great variety of soft and gentle modulations, superior perhaps to those of any of our warblers, the nightingale excepted.

Black-caps mostly haunt orchards and gardens: while they warble, their throats are wonderfully distended.

The song of the redstart is superior, though somewhat like that of the white-throat; some birds have a few more notes than others. Sitting very placidly on the top of a tall tree in a village, the cock sings from morning to night: he affects neighbourhoods, and avoids solitude, and loves to build in orchards and about houses; with us he perches on the vane of a tall maypole.

The fly-catcher is, of all our summer birds, the most mute

---

* These fishes are extremely cunning; hence their rustic name, *river fox*. They have frequently been known to leap over a net when used to take them, or to immerse themselves in the mud, that it might pass over without touching them.

In ponds carp become exceedingly tame, and will allow themselves to be handled. Sir John Hawkins was assured by a clergyman, a friend of his, that at the Abbey of St Bernard, near Antwerp, he saw one come to the edge of the water at the whistling of the person who fed it.

Carp are very long lived: there was one in the garden of Emanuel College, Cambridge, which was known to have inhabited it for upwards of seventy years. Gesner mentions an instance of one that reached the extraordinary age of a hundred years. Carp have been known to live a fortnight out of the water, being placed in a net, among wet moss, the head only left out, and hung up in a cellar. They are frequently plunged into water, and fed with white bread and milk. In this situation they even fatten, and their flesh is considered of a higher flavour than when taken fresh out of a pond. — ED.

and the most familiar; it also appears the last of any. It builds in a vine, or a sweet-brier, against the wall of a house, or in the hole of a wall, or on the end of a beam or plate, and often close to the post of a door, where people are going in and out all day long. This bird does not make the least pretension to song, but uses a little inward wailing note when it thinks its young in danger from cats, or other annoyances: it breeds but once, and retires early.*

Selborne parish alone can and has exhibited at times more than half the birds that are ever seen in all Sweden: the former has produced more than one hundred and twenty species, the latter only two hundred and twenty-one. Let me add also, that it has shewn near half the species that were ever known in Great Britain.†

On a retrospect, I observe that my long letter carries with it a quaint and magisterial air, and is very sententious; but when I recollect that you requested stricture and anecdote, hope you will pardon the didactic manner for the sake of the information it may happen to contain.

LETTER LXI.

TO THE HON. DAINES BARRINGTON.

SELBORNE, *September* 28, 1774.

DEAR SIR,—As the swift, or black-marten, is the largest of the British *hirundines*, so it is undoubtedly the latest comer: for I remember but one instance of its appearing before the last week in April; and in some of our late frosty harsh springs, it has not been seen till the beginning of May. This species usually arrives in pairs.

The swift, like the sand-marten, is very defective in architecture, making no crust, or shell, for its nest, but forming it of dry grasses and feathers, very rudely and inartificially put together. With all my attention to these birds, I have never been able once to discover one in the act of collecting or carrying in materials: so that I have suspected (since their nests are exactly the same) that they sometimes

---

* The beam-bird, (*muscicapa grisola*, Linn.) It is very rare in Scotland. The nest is neatly constructed, of long green moss, intermixed with the catkins of the hazel and filbert, the interior lined with straw and wool. — ED.

† Sweden 221, Great Britain 252 species. — There are now 368, including the occasional visitants. — ED.

usurp upon the house-sparrows, and expel them, as sparrows do the house and sand-marten — well remembering that I have seen them squabbling together at the entrance of their holes, and the sparrows up in arms, and much disconcerted at these intruders; and yet, I am assured by a nice observer in such matters, that they do collect feathers for their nests in Andalusia, and that he has shot them with such materials in their mouths.

Swifts, like sand-martens, carry on the business of nidification quite in the dark, in crannies of castles, and towers, and steeples, and upon the tops of the walls of churches, under the roof, and therefore cannot be so narrowly watched as those species that build more openly; but, from what I could ever observe, they begin nesting about the middle of May; and I have remarked, from eggs taken, that they have sat hard by the 9th of June. In general, they haunt tall buildings, churches, and steeples, and breed only in such; yet, in this village, some pairs frequent the lowest and meanest cottages, and educate their young under those thatched roofs. We remember but one instance where they breed out of buildings, and that is in the sides of a deep chalk pit near the town of Odiham, in this county, where we have seen many pairs entering the crevices, and skimming and squeaking round the precipices.

As I have regarded these amusive birds with no small attention, if I should advance something new and peculiar with respect to them, and different from all other birds, I might perhaps be credited, especially as my assertion is the result of many years' exact observation. The fact that I would advance is, that swifts tread, or copulate, on the wing; and I would wish any nice observer, that is startled at this supposition, to use his own eyes, and I think he will soon be convinced. In another class of animals, viz. the insect, nothing is so common as to see the different species of many genera, in conjunction as they fly. The swift is almost continually on the wing; and, as it never settles on the ground, on trees, or roofs, would seldom find opportunity for amorous rites, were it not enabled to indulge them in the air. If any person would watch these birds of a fine morning in May, as they are sailing round, at a great height from the ground, he would see, every now and then, one drop on the back of another, and both of them sink down together for many fathoms, with a loud, piercing shriek. This I take to be the juncture when the business of generation is carrying on.

As the swift eats, drinks, collects materials for its nest, and,

as it seems, propagates on the wing, it appears to live more in
the air than any other bird, and to perform all functions there,
save those of sleeping and incubation.

This *hirundo* differs widely from its congeners, in laying
invariably but two eggs at a time, which are milk-white, long,
and peaked at the small end; whereas the other species lay
at each brood from four to six.* It is a most alert bird, rising
very early, and retiring to roost very late, and is on the wing
in the height of summer, at least sixteen hours. In the longest
days it does not withdraw to rest till a quarter before nine in
the evening, being the latest of all day birds. Just before
they retire, whole groups of them assemble high in the air, and
squeak and shoot about with wonderful rapidity. But this
bird is never so much alive as in sultry thundery weather,
when it expresses great alacrity, and calls forth all its powers.
In hot mornings, several, getting together into little parties,
dash round the steeples and churches, squeaking as they go,
in a very clamorous manner: these, by nice observers, are
supposed to be males serenading their sitting hens; and not
without reason, since they seldom squeak till they come close
to the walls or eaves, and since those within utter at the same
time, a little inward note of complacency.†

When the hen has sat hard all day, she rushes forth just as
it is almost dark, and stretches and relieves her weary limbs,
and snatches a scanty meal for a few minutes, and then returns
to her duty of incubation.‡ Swifts, when wantonly and cruelly
shot while they have young, discover a little lump of insects
in their mouths, which they pouch and hold under their
tongue. In general, they feed in a much higher district than
the other species; a proof that gnats and other insects do

* Temminck, the greatest living ornithologist, says, that the swift
(*cypselus murarius* of Temminck) lays four eggs. — ED.

† The velocity of the swift's flight is extraordinary; the following
curious circumstance is recorded in Loudon's *Magazine of Natural
History*, for November, 1831: — " Some few months ago, being on
a visit at Hastings, I stopped, during an early morning's walk, to watch
a party of swifts dashing round the ruins of an old castle which overlook
the town. While I was thus amusing myself, and admiring the extraordinary rapidity of their flight, to my infinite astonishment, one of them
flew directly against the castle wall. My surprise was so great, that at
first I thought I was mistaken; but as the spot where the bird fell was
not very difficult of approach, I climbed up, and there found the bird
fluttering on the ground. I picked it up, but in a very few minutes it
died in my hand. It would be difficult to assign a cause for this curious
circumstance." — ED.

‡ Montagu says, that at night, both male and female sit upon the
nest. — ED.

also abound to a considerable height in the air : they also range to vast distances ; since locomotion is no labour to them, who are endowed with such wonderful powers of wing. Their powers seem to be in proportion to their levers ; and their wings are longer in proportion, than those of almost any other bird. When they mute, or ease themselves in flight, they raise their wings, and make them meet over their backs.

At some certain times in the summer, I had remarked that swifts were hawking very low, for hours together, over pools and streams ; and could not help inquiring into the object of their pursuit, that induced them to descend so much below their usual range. After some trouble, I found that they were taking *phryganeæ, ephemeræ, libellulæ*, (cadew-flies, may-flies, and dragon-flies,) that were just emerged out of their aurelia state. I then no longer wondered that they should be so willing to stoop for a prey that afforded them such plentiful and succulent nourishment.

They bring out their young about the middle or latter end of July ; but as these never become perchers, nor, that ever I could discern, are fed on the wing by their dams, the coming forth of the young is not so notorious as in the other species.

On the thirtieth of last June, I untiled the eaves of a house where many pairs build, and found in each nest only two squab, naked pulli ; on the eighth of July, I repeated the same inquiry, and found they had made very little progress towards a fledged state, but were still naked and helpless. From whence we may conclude, that birds whose way of life keeps them perpetually on the wing, would not be able to quit their nest till the end of the month. Swallows and martens, that have numerous families, are continually feeding them every two or three minutes ; while swifts, that have but two young to maintain, are much at their leisure, and do not attend on their nests for hours together.

Sometimes they pursue and strike at hawks that come in their way, but not with that vehemence and fury that swallows express on the same occasion.＊ They are out all day long on wet days, feeding about, and disregarding still rain ; from whence two things may be gathered,—first, that many insects abide high in the air, even in rain ; and next, that the feathers of these birds must be well preened to resist so much wet.†

＊ Swifts are very spirited birds, and being extremely pugnacious among themselves, they sometimes fight till the contending parties are brought to the ground, with the claws mutually clasping each other. — ED.

† Mr Henslow of St Alban's gives the following interesting proof of birds oiling their feathers,—a fact concerning which some eminent

Windy, and particularly windy weather with heavy showers, they dislike, and on such days withdraw, and are scarcely ever seen.

There is a circumstance respecting the colour of swifts, which seems not to be unworthy our attention. When they arrive in the spring, they are all over of a glossy dark soot colour, except their chins, which are white ; but, by being all day long in the sun and air, they become quite weather-beaten and bleached before they depart, and yet they return glossy again in the spring. Now, if they pursue the sun into lower latitudes, as some suppose, in order to enjoy a perpetual summer, why do they not return bleached? Do they not rather, perhaps, retire to rest for a season, and at that juncture moult and change their feathers, since all other birds are known to moult soon after the season of breeding? *

Swifts are very anomalous in many particulars, dissenting from all their congeners, not only in the number of their young, but in breeding but once in a summer ; whereas all the other British *hirundines* breed invariably twice. It is past all doubt that swifts can breed but once, since they withdraw in a short time after the flight of their young, and some time

naturalists have lately had a controversy. " Last summer," says he, " I brought up by hand a turtle dove, which I accustomed to fly about my room, till within this last month, at all times, except at night. Invariably when I had it sitting on my hand, it would begin pluming itself, (particularly while in moult, which was for about four months,) and, at such times, it was curious to see it apply its bill to the gland, or nipple just above its tail, and, by pincing it, procure something, though I could never discover what. On withdrawing its bill, it always stretched out its neck, and twisted its head about in the strangest manner, with its eyes shut, and the bill opening and shutting, as if in the act of chewing something which put it in pain, but which I always considered was for the purpose of spreading, or allowing the substance procured to circulate to all parts of the bill. This operation lasted about twelve seconds, and then it immediately applied it, quickly, to only three or four different parts of its plumage at a time, and, at its pleasure, easily enough, all over its head and neck, by rubbing them on such parts as were within a convenient distance ; for who ever saw a bird, particularly a duck, wash itself, without observing it rub its head and neck on its back, or the shoulders of its wings? This I have seen it do at least ten times in as many minutes on my hand; but confess, I could never detect what it was it procured from the gland for the purpose of spreading it over its plumage, though I could distinctly see it pinch the nipple." — ED.

* The probability is, that these birds have just arrived in this country after they have undergone the vernal moult. Birds differ considerably in colour before the renewal of their plumage ; and that they are in this state before taking their departure there can be little doubt, as they have not yet been subjected to the autumnal moult. — ED.

before their congeners bring out their second broods.   We
may here remark, that, as swifts breed but once in a summer,
and only two at a time, and the other *hirundines* twice, the
latter, who lay from four to six eggs, increase, at an average,
five times as fast as the former.

But in nothing are swifts more singular than in their early
retreat.   They retire, as to the main body of them, by the
tenth of August, and sometimes a few days sooner ; and every
straggler invariably withdraws by the twentieth : while their
congeners, all of them, stay till the beginning of October, many
of them all through that month, and some occasionally to the
beginning of November.   This early retreat is mysterious and
wonderful, since that time is often the sweetest season in the
year.   But, what is more extraordinary, they begin to retire
still earlier in the more southerly parts of Andalusia, where
they can be nowise influenced by any defect of heat, or as one
might suppose, defect of food.   Are they regulated in their
motions with us by a failure of food, or by a propensity to
moulting, or by a disposition to rest after so rapid a life, or by
what ?   This is one of those incidents in natural history that
not only baffles our researches, but almost eludes our guesses !

These *hirundines* never perch on trees or roofs, and so never
congregate with their congeners.   They are fearless while
haunting their nesting places, and are not to be scared with
a gun, and are often beaten down with poles and cudgels as
they stoop to go under the eaves.   Swifts are much infested
with those pests to the genus, called *hippoboscæ hirundinis*,[*]
and often wriggle and scratch themselves, in their flight, to
get rid of that clinging annoyance.

Swifts are no songsters, and have only one harsh, screaming
note ; yet there are ears to which it is not displeasing, from
an agreeable association of ideas, since that note never occurs
but in the most lovely summer weather.

They never settle on the ground but through accident, and
when down can hardly rise, on account of the shortness of
their legs, and the length of their wings : neither can they
walk, but only crawl ; but they have a strong grasp with their
feet, by which they cling to walls.   Their bodies being flat,
they can enter a very narrow crevice ; and where they cannot
pass on their bellies, they will turn up edgewise.

The particular formation of the foot discriminates the swift
from all the British *hirundines*, and, indeed, from all other

* *Craterina hirundinis* of Olfers. — Ed.

known birds, the *hirundo melba*, or great white-bellied swift of
Gibraltar, excepted; for it is so disposed as to carry " *omnes
quatuor digitos anticos*," all its four toes forward : besides, the
least toe, which should be the back toe, consists of one bone
alone, and the other three only of two apiece,—a construction
most rare and peculiar, but nicely adapted to the purposes in
which their feet are employed. This, and some peculiarities
attending the nostrils and under mandible, have induced a
discerning naturalist* to suppose that this species might con-
stitute a genus *per se.*†

In London, a party of swifts frequent the Tower, playing
and feeding over the river just below the Bridge ; others haunt
some of the churches of the Borough next the fields, but do
not venture, like the house-marten, into the close, crowded
part of the town.

The Swedes have bestowed a very pertinent name on this
swallow, calling it *ring-swala*, from the perpetual rings, or
circles, that it takes round the scene of its nidification.

Swifts feed on *coleoptera*, or small beetles with hard cases
over their wings, as well as on the softer insects ; but it does
not appear how they can procure gravel to grind their food,
as swallows do, since they never settle on the ground. Young
ones, overrun with *hippoboscæ*, are sometimes found, under
their nests, fallen to the ground, the number of vermin rendering their abode insupportable any longer. They frequent,
in this village, several abject cottages ; yet a succession still
haunts the same unlikely roofs—a good proof this that the
same birds return to the same spots. As they must stoop very
low to get up under these humble eaves, cats lie in wait, and
sometimes catch them on the wing.

On the 5th of July, 1775, I again untiled part of a roof
over the nest of a swift. The dam sat in the nest; but so
strongly was she affected by natural στοργή for her brood,
which she supposed to be in danger, that, regardless of her
own safety, she would not stir, but lay sullenly by them, per-
mitting herself to be taken in hand. The squab young we
brought down, and placed on the grass-plot, where they
tumbled about, and were as helpless as a new-born child.
While we contemplated their naked bodies, their unwieldy,

* John Antony Scopoli, of Carniola, M.D.

† This difference of character from that of the swallow tribe, has been
laid hold of as a generic distinction by Illiger, under the name of *cypselus.* — ED.

disproportioned abdomina, and their heads too heavy for their necks to support, we could not but wonder when we reflected that these shiftless beings, in a little more than a fortnight, would be able to dash through the air almost with the inconceivable swiftness of a meteor, and, perhaps, in their emigration, must traverse vast continents and oceans as distant as the equator. So soon does Nature advance small birds to their ἡλικία, or state of perfection ; while the progressive growth of men and large quadrupeds is slow and tedious !

LETTER LXII.

TO THE HON. DAINES BARRINGTON.

SELBORNE, *September*, 1774.

DEAR SIR, — By means of a straight cottage chimney, I had an opportunity this summer of remarking, at my leisure, how swallows ascend and descend through the shaft ; but my pleasure in contemplating the address with which this feat was performed, to a considerable depth in the chimney, was somewhat interrupted by apprehensions lest my eyes might undergo the same fate with those of Tobit.*

Perhaps it may be some amusement to you to hear at what times the different species of *hirundines* arrived this spring in three very distant counties of this kingdom. With us, the swallow was seen first on April the 4th ; the swift on April the 24th ; the bank-marten on April the 12th ; and the house-marten not till April the 30th. At South Zele, Devonshire, swallows did not arrive till April the 25th ; swifts, in plenty, on May the 1st ; and house-martens not till the middle of May. At Blackburn, in Lancashire, swifts were seen April the 28th ; swallows, April the 29th ; house-martens, May the 1st. Do these different dates, in such distant districts, prove any thing for or against migration ?

A farmer near Weyhill fallows his land with two teams of asses, one of which works till noon, and the other in the afternoon. When these animals have done their work, they are penned all night, like sheep, on the fallow. In the winter, they are confined and foddered in a yard, and make plenty of dung.

Linnæus says, that hawks " *paciscuntur inducias cum avibus, quamdiu cuculus cuculat ;*" but it appears to me, that, during

* Tobit, ii. 10.

that period, many little birds are taken and destroyed by birds of prey, as may be seen by their feathers left in lanes and under hedges.

The missel-thrush is, while breeding, fierce and pugnacious, driving such birds as approach its nest, with great fury, to a distance.   The Welsh call it *pen y llwyn*, the head, or master of the coppice.   He suffers no magpie, jay, or blackbird, to enter the garden where he haunts ; and is, for the time, a good guard to the new-sown legumens.   In general, he is very successful in the defence of his family : but once I observed in my garden, that several magpies came determined to storm the nest of a missel-thrush ; the dams defended their mansion with great vigour, and fought resolutely *pro aris et focis ;* but numbers at last prevailed, they tore the nest to pieces, and swallowed the young alive.*

In the season of nidification, the wildest birds are comparatively tame.   Thus the ring-dove breeds in my fields, though they are continually frequented ; † and the missel-thrush, though most shy and wild in the autumn and winter, builds in my garden, close to a walk where people are passing all day long.

Wall-fruit abounds with me this year ; but my grapes, that used to be forward and good, are at present backward beyond all precedent : and this is not the worst of the story ; for the same ungenial weather, the same black cold solstice, has injured the more necessary fruits of the earth, and discoloured and blighted our wheat.   The crop of hops promises to be very large.

Frequent returns of deafness incommode me sadly, and half

* No kind of animal food is despised by this carnivorous depredator. Young lambs, poultry, eggs, fish, carrion, insects, and fruit, — all come within the range of his voracious appetite.   He is a great enemy to all young birds; and, in many places, commits extensive ravages on the brood and eggs of game.   In various places of England and Ireland, a reward is given for their heads, at the quarter sessions.   The jay is another beautiful bird; but, like his congener, the magpie, is a most destructive knave amongst smaller birds and their eggs. — ED.

† During our residence in Fife, a pair of ring-doves incubated in a larch tree, close to a walk in the garden, and not more than twenty-five yards from the house, although this walk was frequented many times during the day, and there brought up a brood.   These young doves built in a tree not far distant from the others.   The old birds returned in the following summer, and continued to breed there every season while I remained ; as did also part of their progeny, for we had three nests within the flower garden alone, which was next to the house, and without any wall or hedge intervening. — ED.

disqualify me for a naturalist; for, when those fits are upon me, I lose all the pleasing notices and little intimations arising from rural sounds; and May is to me as silent and mute, with respect to the notes of birds, &c. as August.   My eyesight is, thank God, quick and good; but with respect to the other sense, I am, at times, disabled,

> And Wisdom at one entrance quite shut out.

LETTER LXIII.

TO THOMAS PENNANT, ESQ.

IT is matter of curious inquiry to trace out how those species of soft-billed birds, that continue with us the winter through, subsist during the dead months.   The imbecility of birds seems not to be the only reason why they shun the rigour of our winters; for the robust wry-neck (so much resembling the hardy race of woodpeckers) migrates, while the feeble little golden-crowned wren, that shadow of a bird, braves our severest frosts, without availing himself of houses or villages, to which most of our winter birds crowd in distressful seasons, while he keeps aloof in fields and woods; but perhaps this may be the reason why they may often perish, and why they are almost as rare as any bird we know. *

I have no reason to doubt, but that the soft-billed birds, which winter with us, subsist chiefly on insects in their aurelia state.   All the species of wagtails, in severe weather, haunt shallow streams, near their spring-heads, where they never freeze; and, by wading, pick out the aurelias of the genus *phryganeæ*,† &c.

Hedge-sparrows frequent sinks and gutters in hard weather, where they pick up crumbs and other sweepings; and in mild weather, they procure worms, which are stirring every month in the year, as any one may see, that will only be at the trouble of taking a candle to a grass-plot on any mild winter's night.   Redbreasts and wrens, in the winter, haunt out-houses, stables, and barns, where they find spiders and flies, that have laid themselves up during the cold season.‡   But

---

* This bird inhabits Britain, from the Landsend to the Shetland Islands, as also Ireland and the Isle of Man.   It is sometimes migratory. See our note, page 42. — ED.

† See Derham's *Physico-Theology*, p. 235.

‡ Both redbreasts and wrens approach villages and towns in winter, and will eat crumbs of bread, and other farinaceous substances.   We

the grand support of the soft-billed birds in winter is that infinite profusion of aureliæ of the *lepidoptera ordo*, which is fastened to the twigs of trees and their trunks; to the pales and walls of gardens and buildings; and is found in every cranny and cleft of rock or rubbish, and even in the ground itself.

Every species of titmouse winters with us; they have what I call a kind of intermediate bill, between the hard and the soft, between the Linnæan genera of *fringilla* and *motacilla*. One species alone spends its whole time in the woods and fields, never retreating for succour, in the severest seasons, to houses and neighbourhoods,—and that is the delicate long-tailed titmouse,* which is almost as minute as the golden-crowned wren: but the blue titmouse, or nun, (*parus cæruleus,*) the cole-mouse, (*parus ater,*) the great black-headed titmouse, (*fringillago,*) and the marsh titmouse, (*parus palustris,*) all resort, at times, to buildings; and in hard weather particularly. The great titmouse, driven by stress of weather, much frequents houses; and, in deep snows, I have seen this bird, while it hung with its back downwards, (to my no small delight and admiration,) draw straws lengthwise from out the eaves of thatched houses, in order to pull out the flies that were concealed between them, and that in such numbers that they quite defaced the thatch, and gave it a ragged appearance.†

The blue titmouse, or nun, is a great frequenter of houses, and a general devourer. Besides insects, it is very fond of

---

have seen these birds feeding along with domestic poultry, during snow storms, and even in frosty weather; on which occasions they become very tame.—ED.

* We have never heard of this beautiful little bird approaching the habitations of man during storms, although its congeners are as familiar as the robin during a nard winter, and will feed on bread, or other farinaceous diet. In the severe spring of 1824, great numbers, of various species, visited our grounds, and remained close to the house during the time the snow lay, mixing and feeding with the poultry. We have more than once seen a little hero of a blue titmouse disputing the right of a hen to feed from the same dish with him. In Loudon's *Magazine*, a correspondent says that this species destroys bees, "which it effects by rapping with its bill at the entrance of the hive, and killing the insects as they come out. I was informed that a whole hive was in this manner quickly destroyed."—ED.

† Mr Gavin Inglis, of Strathendry Bleachfield, near Leslie, Fife, informed us, that he saw sparrows similarly employed on the thatch of one of his stacks; and that, finding their efforts ineffectual when exerted singly, they accomplished their end by uniting their strength,—several of them hung to one straw, and thus pulled it out.—ED.

M

flesh ; for it frequently picks bones on dunghills ; it is a vast admirer of suet, and haunts butchers' shops.   When a boy, I have known twenty in a morning caught with snap mouse-traps, baited with tallow or suet.   It will also pick holes in apples left on the ground, and be well entertained with the seeds on the head of a sunflower.   The blue, marsh, and great titmice will, in very severe weather, carry away barley and oat straws from the sides of ricks.

How the wheatear and whin-chat support themselves in winter, cannot be so easily ascertained, since they spend their time on wild heaths and warrens ; the former especially, where there are stone quarries : most probable it is, that their maintenance arises from the aureliæ of the *lepidoptera ordo*, which furnish them with a plentiful table in the wilderness.

LETTER LXIV.

TO THOMAS PENNANT, ESQ.

SELBORNE, *March* 9, 1775.

DEAR SIR,—Some future faunist, a man of fortune, will, I hope, extend his visits to the kingdom of Ireland ; a new field, and a country little known to the naturalist. *   He will not, it is to be wished, undertake that tour unaccompanied by a botanist, because the mountains have scarcely been sufficiently examined ; and the southerly counties of so mild an island may possibly afford some plants little to be expected within the British dominions.†   A person of a thinking turn of mind will draw many just remarks from the modern improvements of that

* Among the newly described species indigenous to these kingdoms, is Sabine's snipe, *scolopax Sabini*, which was discovered in Ireland. It has now been identified as a native of that country. — ED.

† In Cunnemara, a wild district of Galway, Ireland, Mr Mackay of Dublin discovered the *erica Mediterranea*, growing on a declivity, by a stream, in boggy ground, at the foot of Urrisbeg mountain, occupying a space of about half a mile ; and also the *Menzièsia polifolia*.   These two plants had not before been found in Britain or Ireland, being only known to the botanist as indigenous to the south of Europe ; and Mr Bree discovered the *iris tuberosa* near Cork.   The *eriocaulon septangulare* abounds in all the small lakes of Cunnemara.   The rare *arabis ciliata*, the *Menzièsia polifolia*, the *saxifraga umbrosa*, so well known as London pride, are also reckoned among its natives ; the *arenaria ciliata* has been found on Ben Bulbew, and the *rosa Hibernica* in the vicinity of Belfast. The *arbutus unedo*, or snowberry tree, contributes much to the beauty of Killarney, where the elegant *pinguicula grandiflora* is also found, and to be met with nowhere else. — ED.

country, both in arts and agriculture, where premiums obtained long before they were heard of with us. The manners of the wild natives, their superstitions, their prejudices, their sordid way of life, will extort from him many useful reflections. He should also take with him an able draughtsman : for he must, by no means, pass over the noble castles and seats, the extensive and picturesque lakes and waterfalls, and the lofty, stupendous mountains, so little known, and so engaging to the imagination, when described and exhibited in a lively manner. Such a work would be well received.

As I have seen no modern map of Scotland, I cannot pretend to say how accurate or particular any such may be : but this I know, that the best old maps of that kingdom are very defective.

The great obvious defect that I have remarked in all maps of Scotland that have fallen in my way is, a want of a coloured line, or stroke, that shall exactly define the just limits of that district called the Highlands.* Moreover, all the great avenues

---

* The Highlands of Scotland are separated from that portion of North Britain termed the Lowlands, by a lofty range of granitic mountains, called the Grampians, which is the only line of demarkation between these distinct divisions of the kingdom. The physical structure of this chain is as remarkable as the general direction is striking, regular, and continuous, forming a grand natural boundary of sublime and romantic peaks, commencing north of the river Don, in the county of Aberdeen, and intersecting the kingdom in a diagonal direction, till it terminates in the south-west, beyond Ardmore, in the county of Dunbarton. This barrier presents a bold, rocky, and precipitous aspect. Many places of the south front consist of a species of breccia. In the centre, and following the range, is a bed of limestone, of vast extent, which contains many strata of slate, and a marble which takes a fine polish, the prevailing colours of which are blue, green, and brown, intermixed with streaks of pure white. A very valuable quarry of green marble has been recently wrought in Glentilt. In the districts of Fortingall, Strathfillan, and Glenlyon, quantities of lead and silver ore have been found. Over the whole of this great range of mountains are numerous detached masses of red and blue granite, containing garnets, amethysts, aqua-marines, rock-crystals, and pebbles of great beauty and variety.

In this fine chain, there are many summits of considerable altitude, as Benlomond, Schiehallion, and Benlawers. From these, the views are extensive, wild, and magnificent :

> There the boundless eye might sail,
> O'er a sea of mountains borne.

Here you have a wide fertile valley, and there the rugged and precipitous fastness of some sublime cliffs, on whose tops the golden eagle holds undisputed sway, with nought to disturb the repose of the solitude but the notes of the ptarmigan ; while the white hare may be noticed stealing slowly along the bottom of the cliff. — Ed.

to that mountainous and romantic country want to be well distinguished. The military roads formed by General Wade, are so great and Roman-like an undertaking, that they well merit attention. My old map, Moll's map, takes notice of Fort William ; but could not mention the other forts, that have been erected long since; therefore, a good representation of the chain of forts should not be omitted.

The celebrated zigzag up the Coryarich must not be passed over. Moll takes notice of Hamilton and Drumlanrig, and such capital houses ; but a new survey, no doubt, should represent every seat and castle remarkable for any great event, or celebrated for its paintings, &c. Lord Breadalbane's seat and beautiful policy are too curious and extraordinary to be omitted.

The seat of the Earl of Eglintoun, near Glasgow, is worthy of notice. The pine plantations of that nobleman are very grand and extensive indeed.

LETTER LXV.

TO THE HON. DAINES BARRINGTON.

SELBORNE, *June* 8, 1775.

DEAR SIR, — On September the 21st, 1741, being then on a visit, and intent on field diversions, I rose before daybreak ; when I came into the enclosures, I found the stubbles and clover grounds matted all over with a thick coat of cobweb, in the meshes of which, a copious and heavy dew hung so plentifully that the whole face of the country seemed, as it were, covered with two or three setting-nets drawn one over another. When the dogs attempted to hunt, their eyes were so blinded and hoodwinked that they could not proceed, but were obliged to lie down and scrape the encumbrances from their faces with their fore feet ; so that, finding my sport interrupted, I returned home, musing in my mind on the oddness of the occurrence.

As the morning advanced, the sun became bright and warm, and the day turned out one of those most lovely ones which no season but the autumn produces, — cloudless, calm, serene, and worthy of the south of France itself.

About nine, an appearance very unusual began to demand our attention, — a shower of cobwebs falling from very elevated regions, and continuing, without any interruption, till the close of the day.

These webs were not single filmy threads, floating in the air in all directions, but perfect flakes, or rags : some near an inch broad, and five or six long, which fell with a degree of velocity, that shewed they were considerably heavier than the atmosphere.

On every side, as the observer turned his eyes, he might behold a continual succession of fresh flakes falling into his sight, and twinkling like stars, as they turned their sides towards the sun.

How far this wonderful shower extended, would be difficult to say; but we know that it reached Bradley, Selborne, and Alresford, three places which lie in a sort of triangle, the shortest of whose sides is about eight miles in extent.

At the second of those places, there was a gentleman, (for whose veracity and intelligent turn we have the greatest veneration,) who observed it the moment he got abroad; but concluded that, as soon as he came upon the hill above his house, where he took his morning rides, he should be higher than this meteor, which he imagined might have been blown, like thistle-down, from the common above; but, to his great astonishment, when he rode to the most elevated part of the down, three hundred feet above his fields, he found the webs, in appearance, still as much above him as before; still descending into sight in constant succession, and twinkling in the sun, so as to draw the attention of the most incurious.

Neither before nor after, was any such fall observed; but on this day, the flakes hung in the trees and hedges so thick, that a diligent person sent out might have gathered baskets full.

The remark that I shall make on these cobweb-like appearances, called gossamer, is, that strange and superstitious as the notions about them were formerly, nobody in these days doubts but that they are the real production of small spiders, which swarm in the fields in fine weather in autumn, and have a power of shooting out webs from their tails, so as to render themselves buoyant and lighter than air. But why these apterous insects should that day take such a wonderful aërial excursion, and why their webs should at once become so gross and material as to be considerably more weighty than air, and to descend with precipitation, is a matter beyond my skill. If I might be allowed to hazard a supposition, I should imagine that those filmy threads, when first shot, might be entangled in the rising dew, and so drawn up, spiders and all, by a brisk evaporation, into the regions where clouds are formed; and if the spiders have a power of coiling and thickening their webs in the air, as Dr Lister says they have, [see his *Letters* to Mr Ray,] then, when they were become heavier than the air, they must fall.

Every day in fine weather, in autumn chiefly, do I see those spiders shooting out their webs and mounting aloft : they will go off from your finger, if you will take them into your hand. Last summer, one alighted on my book as I was reading in the parlour ; and, running to the top of the page, and shooting out a web, took its departure from thence. But what I most wondered at was, that it went off with considerable velocity in a place where no air was stirring ; and I am sure that I did not assist it with my breath. So that these little crawlers seem to have, while mounting, some locomotive power without the use of wings, and to move in the air faster than the air itself.*

* Gossamer has been long noticed both by poets and naturalists. It is now known to be produced by several different kinds of spiders, particularly the flying ones. Mr Murray, who has given much attention to the economy of these insects, says, they have the power of projecting their threads to a considerable distance, and by this means transporting themselves from the ground to any elevation in the atmosphere, or from the apex of one object to another. He is of opinion that the threads of their web are electric, or so influenced by that subtle element, that buoyancy is imparted, and the baseless shrouds of this aërial voyager are, together with their fabricator, raised into the higher regions of the air.

Most spiders, when crawling over uneven surfaces, leave behind them a thread, serving as a cable, or line of suspension, lest they should fall, or be blown from their eminence ; so that nearly the whole surface of the ground is covered with the net work of these singular animals. Besides the ground spiders, other wanderers contribute to these accumulations, which, however delicate, are at the same time durable. That this tissue is always on the increase, may be noticed by following a plough for a short space ; for no sooner has it finished one ridge, than the fresh mould turned up is equally interlaced with innumerable threads, which glisten in the sun's rays, and can only be accounted for by the circumstance mentioned by Mr Murray, that during fine weather the air is filled with these excursive webs of the *aranea aeronautica.* The spider is often seen at the end of its thread, with extended limbs, balancing itself like a bird, and invariably floating before the wind. The same gentleman, however, says, he has seen threads projected in a close room, where there was no current of air to carry them in a direct line, which is an interesting fact.

Mr Murray thinks that electricity, either positive or negative, is an active agent in the movement of the spiders' webs ; which opinion has been combated by Mr Blackwall, who asserts, that they have not the power of propelling their webs without assistance from the wind, and that the cobwebs seen floating in the air are raised from the surface of the ground by the action of air, highly rarified by a cloudless sun. — Ed.

LETTER LXVI.

TO THE HON. DAINES BARRINGTON.

SELBORNE, *August* 15, 1775.

DEAR SIR, — There is a wonderful spirit of sociality in the brute creation, independent of sexual attachment : the congregating of gregarious birds in the winter is a remarkable instance.

Many horses, though quiet with company, will not stay one minute in a field by themselves ; the strongest fences cannot restrain them. My neighbour's horse will not only not stay by himself abroad, but he will not bear to be left alone in a strange stable, without discovering the utmost impatience, and endeavouring to break the rack and manger with his fore feet. He has been known to leap out at a stable window, through which dung was thrown, after company ; and yet, in other respects, is remarkably quiet. Oxen and cows will not fatten by themselves ; but will neglect the finest pasture that is not recommended by society. It would be needless to instance in sheep, which constantly flock together. *

---

* There were two Hanoverian horses, which had assisted in drawing the same gun during the whole Peninsular War, in the German brigade of artillery. One of them met his death in an engagement ; after which the survivor was picqueted as usual, and his food was brought to him. He refused to eat, and kept constantly turning his head round to look for his companion, and sometimes calling him by a neigh. Every care was taken, and all means that could be thought of were adopted, to make him eat, but without effect. Other horses surrounded him on all sides, but he paid no attention to them ; his whole demeanour indicated the deepest sorrow, and he died from hunger, not having tasted a bit from the time his companion fell.

Lord Kaimes relates a circumstance of a canary which fell dead in singing to his mate, while in the act of incubation. The female quitted her nest, and finding him dead, rejected all food, and died by his side.

Mr Charles Hall, of Englishbatch, had a beagle bitch which suckled a kitten, to whom she shewed the most devoted attachment.

"M. Antoine," says Professor Rennie, "relates the following anecdote of a lapwing which a clergyman kept in his garden : — It lived chiefly on insects, but, as the winter drew on, these failed, and necessity compelled the poor bird to approach the house, from which it had previously remained at a wary distance; and a servant, hearing its feeble cry, as if it were asking charity, opened for it the door of the back kitchen. It did not venture far at first, but it became daily more familiar and imboldened as the cold increased, till at length it actually entered the kitchen, though already occupied by a dog and a cat. By degrees it at

But this propensity seems not to be confined to animals of the same species ; for we know a doe, still alive, that was brought up from a little fawn with a dairy of cows ; with them it goes afield, and with them it returns to the yard.   The dogs of the house take no notice of this deer, being used to her ; but, if strange dogs come by, a chase ensues ; while the master smiles to see his favourite securely leading her pursuers over hedge, or gate, or stile, till she returns to the cows, who, with fierce lowings, and menacing horns, drive the assailants quite out of the pasture.

Even great disparity of kind and size does not always prevent social advances and mutual fellowship.   For a very intelligent and observant person has assured me, that, in the former part of his life, keeping but one horse, he happened also on a time to have but one solitary hen.   These two incongruous animals spent much of their time together, in a lonely orchard, where they saw no creature but each other. By degrees, an apparent regard began to take place between these two sequestered individuals.   The fowl would approach the quadruped with notes of complacency, rubbing herself gently against his legs ; while the horse would look down with satisfaction, and move with the greatest caution and circumspection, lest he should trample on his diminutive companion. Thus, by mutual good offices, each seemed to console the vacant hours of the other ; so that Milton, when he puts the

length came to so good an understanding with these animals, that it entered regularly at nightfall, and established itself at the chimney corner, where it remained snugly beside them for the night ; but, as soon as the warmth of spring returned, it preferred roosting in the garden, though it resumed its place at the chimney corner the ensuing winter.   Instead of being afraid of its two old acquaintances, the dog and the cat, it now treated them as inferiors, and arrogated to itself the place which it had previously obtained by humble solicitation.   This interesting pet was at last choked by a bone which it had swallowed."

The following singular presentiment in a goose is related by Mr C. A. Brew, of Ennis :— " An old goose, that had been for a fortnight hatching in a farmer's kitchen, was perceived on a sudden to be taken violently ill. She soon after left the nest, and repaired to an outhouse, where there was a young goose of the past year, which she brought with her into the kitchen. The young one immediately scrambled into the old one's nest, sat, hatched, and afterwards brought up the brood.   The old goose, as soon as the young one had taken her place, sat down by the side of the nest, and shortly after died.   As the young goose had never been in the habit of entering the kitchen before, it would be difficult to account for this fact, except by supposing that the old one had some way of communicating her anxieties, which the other was perfectly able to understand."— ED.

following sentiment in the mouth of Adam, seems to be
somewhat mistaken : —

> Much less can bird with beast, or fish with fowl,
> So well converse, nor with the ox the ape.

LETTER LXVII.

TO THE HON. DAINES BARRINGTON.

SELBORNE, *October* 2, 1775.

DEAR SIR, — We have two gangs, or hordes of gipsies,
which infest the south and west of England, and come round
in their circuit two or three times in the year.   One of these
tribes calls itself by the noble name of Stanley, of which I
have nothing particular to say ; but the other is distinguished
by an appellative somewhat remarkable.   As far as their harsh
gibberish can be understood, they seem to say that the name
of their clan is Curleople : now the termination of this word
is apparently Grecian ; and, as Mezeray and the gravest
historians all agree that these vagrants did certainly migrate
from Egypt and the East, two or three centuries ago, * and so

---

* The gipsies first attracted notice in the beginning of the fifteenth
century, and, within a few years afterwards, they had spread themselves
all over the Continent.   The earliest mention which is made of them
was in the years 1414 and 1417, when they were observed in Germany.
In 1418, they were found in Switzerland ; in 1422, in Italy ; and, in
1427, they are mentioned as having been seen in the neighbourhood of
Paris, and about the same time in Spain.   In England they were not
known till some time after.   One remarkable part of their history is, their
continuing the same unsettled mode of life, and rigidly keeping apart
from all other people.   It is impossible to find a greater similarity in
the traits of character, and the manners exhibited by different tribes of
the same family, than that which is observable amongst the gipsies of the
different countries of Europe, under whatever appellation they are known.
The habits of the *cygani* of Hungary, the *gitano* of Spain, the *zigenners*
of Transylvania, the *zingari* of Italy, the *bohemien* of France, the *gipsy*
of England, and the *tinkler* of Scotland, are identical ; whether we regard
their physical distinction, or their mode of subsistence.

Their features and complexion mark them of eastern origin.   Grell-
man thinks them Hindoos of the lowest class ; and a comparison of
the language of that people with a list of about four hundred words possessed by him goes far to prove a national connection.   There is, besides,
some striking coincidences in the construction of the languages.   He
attributes their appearance to the cruel war of devastation carried on by
Timur-Beg in 1408-9, and supposes them to be fugitives from their native
land, and that they passed through the desert of Persia, and along the
Gulf of Persia, through Arabia Petrea, over the Isthmus of Suez, into

spread by degrees over Europe, may not this family name, a little corrupted, be the very name they brought with them

· Egypt, and, entering Europe from thence, have brought with them the name Egyptians, which has been corrupted in England into gipsies.

This opinion seems to have been early entertained, but soon forgotten ; for we find that Hieronymus Foroliviensis, in the nineteenth volume of Muratori, says, that, on the 7th day of August, A.D. 1432, two hundred of the *cingari* came to his native town, and halted there two days on their journey to Rome, and that some of them said they came from India— "et, ut audivi, aliqui dicebant quod erant Indiâ." Munster, who, in 1524, conversed with one of the *cingari*, found that his belief was, the tribe had come from that country.

The Abbé Dubois says, that in every country of the Peninsula, great numbers of families are to be found, whose ancestors were obliged to emigrate thither in times of trouble or famine from their native land, and to establish themselves amongst strangers. But the most remarkable feature in their history is, that these colonists preserve their own language, from generation to generation, as well as their national peculiarities. Many families might be pointed out who have continued four or five hundred years in particular districts without approximating in the least to the manners, fashions, or language, of the tribes among whom they have been naturalized.

Leaving this species of evidence, we shall proceed to one which seems to afford more conclusive proofs than any other of the Hindoo origin of the gipsies ; namely, a short vocabulary of words, collected from the gipsy of England, the giatano of Spain, and the cygani of Hungary; and if we make allowance for the corruptions, which must necessarily have crept in amongst people wandering through countries whose language was not only distinct from their own, but also unconnected with each other, we shall not wonder at the slight difference, seeing the great variety of provincial dialect spoken even in Britain itself :

	English Gypsy.	Hungarian.	Hindoo.	Spanish.
Cow,	Gourumin.	Gourumin,	Goru.	—
Old woman,	Puromaneshe.	—	Peer.	Pari.
Ox,	Gocero.	Gouro.	—	—
Soul,	—	—	Jee, Javo.	Ochi.
Bed,	—	(Bedstead.)	Charpoai.	Choripey.
Face,	Mui.	—	Mooh.	—
Duck,	Heretz.	—	Haunse.	—
Worm,	Kirma.	—	Keerak.	—
Fork,	Kassoni.	Kastoni.	Kaunta.	—
Scissors,	Catsaw.	—	Quinchee.	—
Knife,	Churi.	Schluri.	Chorah.	Churi.
Drunk,	Motto.	—	Mad-walla.	Matocino.
Red,	—	—	Laul.	Olajo.
Salt,	Lone.	Lhon.	Loon.	Lon.
Key,	Kesin.	Klucko.	Koonjee.	Clachi.

Besides these, we may mention, that the gipsies use the word banduk, for a musket, which, in the Hindoo, is bundooq ; and kahngeree English, cangri Spanish, and kahngeri Hungarian, all signify church. Could a

from the Levant? It would be matter of some curiosity could one meet with an intelligent person among them, to inquire whether, in their jargon, they still retain any Greek words: the Greek radicals will appear in hand, foot, head, water, earth, &c. It is possible, that, amidst their cant and corrupted dialect, many mutilated remains of their native language might still be discovered.

With regard to those peculiar people, the gipsies, one thing is very remarkable, and especially as they came from warmer climates; and that is, that while other beggars lodge in barns, stables, and cow-houses, these sturdy savages seem to pride themselves in braving the severities of winter, and in living *sub dio* the whole year round. Last September was as wet a month as ever was known; and yet, during those deluges, did a young gipsy girl lie in the midst of one of our hop-gardens, on the cold ground, with nothing over her but a piece of a blanket, extended on a few hazel rods bent hoop fashion, and stuck into the earth at each end, in circumstances too trying for a cow in the same condition: yet within this garden there was a large hop-kiln, into the chambers of which she might have retired, had she thought shelter an object worthy her attention.

Europe itself, it seems, cannot set bounds to the rovings of these vagabonds; for Mr Bell, in his return from Peking, met a gang of these people on the confines of Tartary, who were endeavouring to penetrate those deserts, and try their fortune in China.*

Gipsies are called in French, *Bohemiens;* in Italian and modern Greek, *Zingani.*

vocabulary be formed of the dialect used by gipsies, the era and route by which they entered Europe might possibly be traced by an ingenious linguist.

Ludolf, in the seventeenth century, collected from certain wandering tribes, which he met in Æthiopia and Nubia, a vocabulary of thiry-eight words. These were so fortunately selected, that a counterpart has, in almost every instance, offered itself, both from the language of Hindostan, and from that of the European gipsy. This fact recalls an observation made by Sir William Jones, though it may bear but little upon the question — that the ancient Egyptian and Sanscrit are probably the same. — ED.

* See Bell's *Travels in China.*

LETTER LXVIII

TO THE HON. DAINES BARRINGTON.

SELBORNE, *November* 1, 1775.

DEAR SIR,

> HIC —— tædæ pingues, hic plurimus ignis
> Semper, et assiduâ postes fuligine nigri.

I shall make no apology for troubling you with the detail of a very simple piece of domestic economy, being satisfied that you think nothing beneath your attention that tends to utility: the matter alluded to is the use of rushes instead of candles, which I am well aware prevails in many districts besides this; but as I know there are countries also where it does not obtain, and as I have considered the subject with some degree of exactness, I shall proceed in my humble story, and leave you to judge of the expediency.

The proper species of rush for this purpose seems to be the *juncus conglomeratus*, or common soft rush, which is to be found in most moist pastures, by the sides of streams, and under hedges.* These rushes are in best condition in the height of summer; but may be gathered, so as to serve the purpose well, quite on to autumn. It would be needless to add, that the largest and longest are best. Decayed labourers, women, and children, make it their business to procure and prepare them. As soon as they are cut, they must be flung into water, and kept there; for otherwise they will dry and shrink, and the peel will not run. At first, a person would find it no easy matter to divest a rush of its peel, or rind, so as to leave one regular, narrow, even rib, from top to bottom, that may support the pith; but this, like other feats, soon becomes familiar, even to children; and we have seen an old woman, stone blind, performing this business with great despatch, and seldom failing to strip them with the nicest

---

* In many of the northern parts of Scotland rushes were formerly used in place of cotton for wicks to lamps, which, in Perthshire and the adjoining counties, are termed crozeys. They are much more durable than cotton. In Zetland, a shell, the *fusus antiquus* of Lamark, suspended horizontally by a cord, was formerly used as a lamp, the canal of the shell serving as a cavity for the reception of the rush-wick. In various places of the same districts, ropes for *tethering* cattle were formed of rushes by the peasantry during their idle hours, and also by herd boys. If firmly platted, they were pretty durable. We have seen them often used in the north. — ED.

regularity. When these *junci* are thus far prepared, they must lie out on the grass to be bleached, and take the dew for some nights, and afterwards be dried in the sun.

Some address is required in dipping these rushes in the scalding fat, or grease; but this knack also is to be attained by practice. The careful wife of an industrious Hampshire labourer obtains all her fat for nothing, for she saves the scummings of her bacon-pot for this use; and, if the grease abounds with salt, she causes the salt to precipitate to the bottom, by setting the scummings in a warm oven. Where hogs are not much in use, and especially by the sea-side, the coarser animal oils will come very cheap. A pound of common grease may be procured for fourpence; and about six pounds of grease will dip a pound of rushes; and one pound of rushes may be bought for one shilling; so that a pound of rushes, medicated and ready for use, will cost three shillings. If men that keep bees will mix a little wax with the grease, it will give it a consistency, and render it more cleanly, and make the rushes burn longer: mutton suet would have the same effect.

A good rush, which measured in length two feet four inches and a half, being minuted, burnt only three minutes short of an hour; and a rush of still greater length has been known to burn one hour and a quarter.

These rushes give a good, clear light. Watch-lights, (coated with tallow,) it is true, shed a dismal one — " darkness visible ;" but then the wicks of those have two ribs of the rind, or peel, to support the pith, while the wick of the dipped rush has but one. The two ribs are intended to impede the progress of the flame, and make the candle last.

In a pound of dry rushes, avoirdupois, which I caused to be weighed and numbered, we found upwards of one thousand six hundred individuals. Now, suppose each of these burns, one with another, only half an hour, then a poor man will purchase eight hundred hours of light, a time exceeding thirty-three entire days, for three shillings. According to this account, each rush, before dipping, costs one thirty-third of a farthing, and one-eleventh afterwards. Thus a poor family will enjoy five and a half hours of comfortable light for a farthing. An experienced old housekeeper assures me, that one pound and a half of rushes completely supplies his family the year round, since working people burn no candle in the long days, because they rise and go to bed by daylight.

Little farmers use rushes much in the short days, both

morning and evening, in the dairy and kitchen; but the very poor, who are always the worst economists, and therefore must continue very poor, buy a halfpenny candle every evening, which, in their blowing, open rooms, does not burn much more than two hours. Thus have they only two hours' light for their money, instead of eleven.

While on the subject of rural economy, it may not be improper to mention a pretty implement of housewifery that we have seen nowhere else; that is, little neat besoms which our foresters make from the stalks of the *polytricum commune*, or great golden maiden-hair, which they call silk-wood, and find plenty in the bogs.* When this moss is well combed and dressed, and divested of its outer skin, it becomes of a beautiful bright chestnut colour; and, being soft and pliant, is very proper for the dusting of beds, curtains, carpets, hangings, &c. If these besoms were known to the brushmakers in town, it is probable they might come much in use for the purpose above mentioned. †

LETTER LXIX

TO THE HON. DAINES BARRINGTON.

SELBORNE, *December* 12, 1775.

DEAR SIR, — We had in this village, more than twenty years ago, an idiot boy, whom I well remember, who, from a child, shewed a strong propensity to bees; they were his food, his amusement, his sole object. And as people of this cast have seldom more than one point in view, so this lad exerted all his few faculties on this one pursuit. In the winter, he dozed away his time, within his father's house, by the fire-side, in a kind of torpid state, seldom departing from the chimney corner; but in the summer he was all alert, and in quest of his game in the fields, and on sunny banks. Honey-bees, humble-bees, and wasps, were his prey wherever he found them: he had no apprehensions from their stings, but would seize them *nudis manibus*, and at once disarm them of their weapons, and suck their bodies for the sake of their honey-bags. Sometimes he would fill his bosom, between his shirt and skin, with a number of these captives; and sometimes would confine them

---

* These besoms are common in the south of Scotland. From the same substance mats and rugs are plaited. In Ireland large mats of this kind are used by the peasantry for beds. — ED.

† A besom of this sort is to be seen in Sir Ashton Lever's museum.

In bottles. He was a very *merops apiaster*, or bee-bird, and very injurious to men that kept bees ; for he would slide into their bee-gardens, and, sitting down before the stools, would rap with his finger on the hives, and so take the bees as they came out. He has been known to overturn hives for the sake of honey, of which he was passionately fond. Where metheglin was making, he would linger round the tubs and vessels, begging a draught of what he called bee-wine. As he ran about, he used to make a humming noise with his lips, resembling the buzzing of bees. This lad was lean and sallow, and of a cadaverous complexion ; and, except in his favourite pursuit, in which he was wonderfully adroit, discovered no manner of understanding. Had his capacity been better, and directed to the same object, he had perhaps abated much of our wonder at the feats of a more modern exhibiter of bees ; and we may justly say of him now,

Thou,

Had thy presiding star propitious shone,
Shouldst Wildman be.

When a tall youth, he was removed from hence to a distant village, where he died, as I understand, before he arrived at manhood.

LETTER LXX.

TO THE HON. DAINES BARRINGTON.

SELBORNE, January 8, 1776.

DEAR SIR,— It is the hardest thing in the world to shake off superstitious prejudices : they are sucked in, as it were, with our mother's milk ; and, growing up with us at the time when they take the fastest hold, and make the most lasting impressions, become so interwoven into our very constitutions, that the strongest good sense is required to disengage ourselves from them. No wonder, therefore, that the lower people retain them their whole lives through, since their minds are not invigorated by a liberal education, and therefore not enabled to make any efforts adequate to the occasion.

Such a preamble seems to be necessary before we enter on the superstitions of this district, lest we should be suspected of exaggeration in a recital of practices too gross for this enlightened age.

But the people of Tring, in Hertfordshire, would do well to remember, that no longer ago than the year 1751, and within twenty miles of the capital, they seized on two superannuated wretches, crazed with age, and overwhelmed with infirmities, on a suspicion of witchcraft; and, by trying experiments, drowned them in a horse-pond.

In a farm-yard, near the middle of this village, stands, at this day, a row of pollard-ashes, which, by the seams and long cicatrices down their sides, manifestly shew that, in former times, they have been cleft asunder. These trees, when young and flexible, were severed and held open by wedges, while ruptured children, stripped naked, were pushed through the apertures, under a persuasion that, by such a process, the poor babes would be cured of their infirmity. As soon as the operation was over, the tree in the suffering part was plastered with loam, and carefully swathed up. * If the parts coalesced

---

* Among the popular superstitions of Britain trees have always held a conspicuous place. There is hardly a county in the kingdom, or indeed a parish, that has not had its witch's thorn, or some such ominously named tree. Among the peasantry of Scotland, the mountain ash, which is termed the rowan tree, was considered a complete antidote against the effects of witchcraft; and, in consequence, a twig of it was very commonly carried in the pocket: but that it might have complete efficacy, it was necessary that it should be accompanied by the following couplet, written on paper, wrapped round the wood, and secured by a *red* silk thread:

Rowan tree and red thread
Keeps the witches at their speed.

An amber bead was supposed to have precisely the same effect; if the red silk thread was attached to it with the above couplet, only the words "lammar bead" were substituted for rowan tree. Among the higher classes, amber beads were worn, and always strung with red silk thread.

The Hindoos have a similar superstition, as remarked by Bishop Heber, near Boitpoor, in Upper Nilia. "I passed a fine tree of the mimosa, with leaves, at a little distance, so much resembling those of the mountain ash, that I was for a moment deceived, and asked if it did not bring fruit? They answered, no; but that it was a very noble tree, being called 'the imperial tree,' for its excellent properties; that it slept all night, and wakened and was alive all day, withdrawing its leaves if any one attempted to touch them. Above all, however, it was useful as a preservative against magic; a sprig worn in the turban, or suspended over the bed, was a perfect security against all spells, evil eye, &c. insomuch that the most formidable wizard would not, if he could help it, approach its shade. One, indeed, they said, who was very renowned for his power (like Loorinite in the *Kehama*) of killing plants and drying up their sap with a look, had come to this very tree, and gazed on it intently; 'but,' said the old man, who told me this, with an air of triumph, 'look as he might, he could do the tree no harm;' a fact of which I make no question. I was amused and surprised to find the superstition, which, in England and Scotland, attaches to the rowan tree, was applied to a tree of nearly similar form. Which nation has been, in this case, the

and soldered together, as usually fell out where the feat was performed with any adroitness at all, the party was cured ; but where the cleft continued to gape, the operation, it was supposed, would prove ineffectual. Having occasion to enlarge my garden not long since, I cut down two or three such trees, one of which did not grow together.

We have several persons now living in the village, who, in their childhood, were supposed to be healed by this super-stitious ceremony, derived down, perhaps, from our Saxon ancestors, who practised it before their conversion to Chris-tianity. *

imitator ? or from what common centre are all these common notions derived ?"— ED.

* It would be difficult to trace at what time these superstitions crept in ; there can be little doubt, however, that they prevailed long before the light of Christianity shed its rays on mankind. They exist amongst all nations ; and the less informed the people, the greater their influence on the human mind. Even to the present hour, we find persons in the highest ranks of society whose minds are deeply tinctured with them.

If a magpie *cross* our path, when we first go out of a morning, it is considered a bad omen. Anglers, in spring, seeing a single magpie, augur a bad day's sport ; but if there are two, the case is otherwise. We have no doubt the observation may generally hold true, as in cold weather the prudent magpies only leave their nests, one at a time, in search of food, the other remaining to keep the eggs warm. It is, therefore, only in mild weather that two are to be seen together ; and fish never take well, except in such weather. The magpie has always been esteemed an ominous bird ; the following old distich tells what the numbers of those seen at a time forebodes : —

> One sorrow, two mirth,
> Three a wedding, four death.

The feathers or the pigeon are never used for stuffing beds or pillows, because it is said they would prolong the deathbed sufferings. The reason assigned is, that " the bird has no gall."

When the aurora borealis is seen in great quantity, and very luminous, it is said to be the precursor of some great and terrible events. In the autumn of 1830, this phenomenon caused much consternation amongst the inhabitants of Weardale, as appears from the Newcastle Chronicle. They imagined they saw the figure of a man on a white horse, holding in his hand a *red sword*, moving across the heavens, and that it foretold the present eventful times, — " wars and rumours of wars." Sailors for the most part will not whistle at sea, because, they say, it will raise the wind. When, however, they are becalmed, and wish to have a breeze, they invite its approach by frequent whistling as they tread the deck with impatient steps.

Insects also assert an important place amongst the superstitions of all countries. The following amusing passage is quoted from a *Tour in Brit-tany* : — " If there are bees kept in the house where a marriage feast is celebrated, care is always taken to dress up their hives in red, which is done by placing upon them pieces of scarlet cloth, or of some such bright

At the south corner of the Plestor, or area, near the church, there stood, about twenty years ago, a very old, grotesque, hollow, pollard-ash, which for ages had been looked on with no small veneration as a shrew-ash. Now, a shrew-ash is an ash whose twigs or branches, when gently applied to the limbs of cattle, will immediately relieve the pains which a beast suffers from the running of a shrew-mouse over the part affected : for it is supposed that a shrew-mouse is of so baneful and deleterious a nature, that wherever it creeps over a beast, be it horse, cow, or sheep, the suffering animal is afflicted with cruel anguish, and threatened with the loss of the use of the limb. Against this accident, to which they were continually liable, our provident forefathers always kept a shrew-ash at hand, which, when once medicated, would maintain its virtue for ever. A shrew-ash was made thus : * — Into the body of the tree, a deep hole was bored with an auger, and a poor devoted shrew-mouse was thrust in alive, and plugged in, no doubt, with several quaint incantations, long since forgotten. As the ceremonies necessary for such a consecration are no longer understood, all succession is at an end, and no such tree is known to subsist in the manor or hundred.

As to that on the Plestor,

> The late vicar stubb'd and burnt it,

when he was way-warden, regardless of the remonstrances of the bystanders, who interceded in vain for its preservation, urging its power and efficacy, and alleging that it had been

> Religione patrum multos servata per annos.

LETTER LXXI.

TO THE HON. DAINES BARRINGTON.

SELBORNE, *February* 7, 1776.

DEAR SIR, — In heavy fogs, on elevated situations especially, trees are perfect alembics : and no one that has not attended to such matters, can imagine how much water one tree will distil in a night's time, by condensing the vapour, which

colour; the Bretons imagining that the bees would forsake their dwellings if they were not made to participate in the rejoicings of their owners: in like manner, they are all put into mournings when a death occurs in the family."

Innumerable illustrations of similar superstitions might be quoted; but we conceive the above sufficient for our purpose. — ED.

* For a similar practice, see Plot's *Staffordshire.*

trickles down the twigs and boughs, so as to make the ground below quite in a float. In Newton-lane, in October, 1775, on a misty day, a particular oak in leaf dropped so fast that the cart-way stood in puddles, and the ruts ran with water, though the ground in general was dusty.*

In some of our smaller islands in the West Indies, if I mistake not, there are no springs or rivers ; but the people are supplied with that necessary element, water, merely by the dripping of some large tall trees, which, standing in the bosom of a mountain, keep their heads constantly enveloped with fogs and clouds, from which they dispense their kindly, never-ceasing moisture ; and so render those districts habitable by condensation alone. †

* The house in which we resided in Fife was built on a greenstone rock, on the south brow of the high ground overlooking the beautiful river Leven, about two hundred feet above its level, and five hundred feet distant from it. We there remarked, that, even in closets in the garrets, shoes, and all kinds of leather, soon became mouldy, which could be produced only by the moisture generated by the trees, which in thick groves closely surrounded the house. — ED.

† There are no rivulets, or springs, in the island of Ferro, the westmost of the Canaries, except on a part of the beach, which is nearly inaccessible. To supply the place of a fountain, however, Nature, ever bountiful, has bestowed upon this island a species of tree, unknown to all other parts of the world. It is of moderate size, and its leaves are straight, long, and evergreen. Around its summit a small cloud perpetually rests, which so drenches the leaves with moisture, that they continually distil upon the ground a stream of fine clear water. To these trees, as to perennial springs, the inhabitants of Ferro resort ; and are thus supplied with an abundance of water for themselves and for their cattle.

The trunk of this tree is about nine feet in circumference ; the top branches are not higher than thirty feet from the ground ; the circumference of all the branches together is one hundred and twenty feet ; the branches are thick, and extended, the leaves being about three feet nine inches from the ground. Its fruit is shaped like that of the oak, but tastes like the kernel of a pine apple, and the leaves resemble those of the laurel, but are longer, wider, and curved.

Trees require a great quantity of water to supply their organs. This is given off in perspiration by their leaves. In the experiments of Hales on the quantity of water taken up by plants, it was found that a pear-tree, which weighed seventy-one pounds, absorbed fifteen pounds of water in six hours ; and that branches of an inch diameter, and from five to six feet high, sucked up from fifteen to thirty ounces in twelve hours. When these were stript of their leaves, they only sucked up one ounce in twelve hours.

The white birch tree, *betula alba*, is noted on account of the wine that is extracted from it, and is said to possess the medical qualities of an anti-scorbutic, deobstruent, and diuretic. The method of bleeding the tree is performed thus : —About the beginning of March, an oblique cut is

Trees in leaf have such a vast proportion more of surface than those that are naked, that, in theory, their condensations should greatly exceed those that are stripped of their leaves : but, as the former imbibe also a great quantity of moisture, it is difficult to say which drip most : but this I know, that deciduous trees, that are entwined with much ivy, seem to distil the greatest quantity. Ivy leaves are smooth, and thick, and cold, and therefore condense very fast ; and besides, ever-greens imbibe very little. * These facts may furnish the intelligent with hints concerning what sorts of trees they should plant round small ponds that they would wish to be perennial ; and shew them how advantageous some trees are in preference to others.

Trees perspire profusely, condense largely, and check evaporation so much, that woods are always moist ; no

made, almost as deep as the pith, under some well spreading branch, into which a small stone or chip is inserted to keep the lips of the wound open.   To this orifice a bottle is attached to collect the flowing juice, which is limpid, watery, and sweetish, but retains something of both the taste and odour of the tree.   One tree affords two or three gallons a day ; at the same time, it receives no perceptible injury from being thus bled, from which it would appear, that much of its moisture has at other times been given off through its leaves ; and, in all proba-bility, it acquires an increased action to supply the extra quantity which is thus drained from it. — Ed.

* There can be little doubt, that the moisture of climate is greatly influenced by trees.   It has been remarked, after cutting down forests, particularly on high grounds, that the quantity of rain has been lessened, by diminishing, it is supposed, the attraction between the earth and the clouds.   This fact has been experienced on a large scale in America. In Kentucky there are many brooks, now completely dry in summer, which afforded an abundant supply of water all the year round about twenty-five or thirty years ago ; and, in some parts of the state of New Jersey, where the woods have been extensively cleared away, many streams have altogether disappeared.

The climate of Britain, it is very generally believed, has deteriorated by becoming much more changeable than it was sixty years ago.   This has, with much probability, been attributed to the extent of planting, to the introduction of green crops, and abolition of fallows in an improved sys-tem of agriculture.   Mr Murray is of opinion, that trees, by condensing the moisture of the air in foggy weather, materially affect the climate, and that thickly wooded countries must necessarily be colder, and more humid than naked savannahs.   Trees are, therefore, it would seem, ready conductors of aërial electricity, the climate being improved when woods are cleared away, and becoming more moist by planting.   This fact receives corroboration from the history of our own country, as well as from that of North America. — Ed.

wonder, therefore, that they contribute much to pools and streams.

That trees are great promoters of lakes and rivers, appears from a well-known fact in North America; for, since the woods and forests have been grubbed and cleared, all bodies of water are much diminished: so that some streams, that were very considerable a century ago, will not now drive a common mill.* Besides, most woodlands, forests, and chases, with us, abound with pools and morasses, no doubt for the reason given above.†

To a thinking mind, few phenomena are more strange than the state of little ponds on the summits of chalk hills, many of which are never dry in the most trying droughts of summer; on chalk hills, I say, because in many rocky and gravelly soils, springs usually break out pretty high on the sides of elevated grounds and mountains; but no person acquainted with chalky districts will allow that they ever saw springs in such a soil but in valleys and bottoms, since the waters of so pervious a stratum as chalk all lie on one dead level, as well-diggers have assured me again and again.‡

Now, we have many such little round ponds in this district; and one in particular on our sheep-down, three hundred feet above my house; which, though never above three feet deep in the middle, and not more than thirty feet in diameter, and

* Vide Kalm's *Travels to North America.*

† For the diminution of some of the lakes and rivers of America, we must seek other causes. About a thousand rivers and streams empty themselves into Lake Superior, sweeping into it earth, primitive boulder stones, and drift timber, which sometimes accumulate so much as to form islands in the estuaries. A lignite formation, indeed, is said to be now in progress, similar to that of Bovey in Devonshire. Within a mile of the shore, the water is about seventy fathoms; within eight miles, one hundred and thirty-six fathoms; and the greatest depth of the lake, farther from the shore, is unknown. Lake Erie, from similar causes, is gradually becoming shallower. Long Point, for example, has, in three years, gained no less than three miles on the water. — ED.

‡ In making wells at Modena, in Italy, the workmen dig through several strata of soils, till they come to a very hard kind of earth, much resembling chalk; here they begin the mason-work, and build a wall, which they carry on at their leisure till they finish it, without being interrupted with one drop of water, and without any apprehension of not finding it when they come to make the experiment. The wall being completed, they bore through the bed of chalk, at the bottom, with a long auger, but take care to ascend from the pit before they draw out the instrument again: which when they have done, the water springs up into the well, and in a little time rises to the brim — nay, sometimes overflows the neighbouring grounds. — ED.

containing pernaps not more than two or three hundred hogsheads of water, yet never is known to fail, though it affords
drink for three hundred or four hundred sheep, and for at
least twenty head of large cattle besides. This pond, it is true,
is overhung with two moderate beeches, that, doubtless, at
times, afford it much supply; but then we have others as
small, that, without the aid of trees, and in spite of evaporation
from sun and wind, and perpetual consumption by cattle, yet
constantly maintain a moderate share of water, without over-
flowing in the wettest seasons, as they would do if supplied
by springs. By my journal of May, 1775, it appears that
" the small and even considerable ponds on the vales are now
dried up, while the small ponds on the very tops of hills are
but little affected."   Can this difference be accounted for
from evaporation alone, which certainly is more prevalent in
bottoms ? or rather have not those elevated pools some
unnoticed recruits, which in the night-time counterbalance
the waste of the day; without which, the cattle alone must
soon exhaust them ? And here it will be necessary to enter
more minutely into the cause.   Dr Hales, in his *Vegetable
Statics*, advances, from experiment, that " the moister the earth
is, the more dew falls on it in a night ; and more than a double
quantity of dew falls on an equal surface of moist earth."
Hence we see that water, by its coolness, is enabled to assimi-
late to itself a large quantity of moisture nightly by condensation ;
and that the air, when loaded with fogs and vapours, and even
with copious dews, can alone advance a considerable and never-
failing resource. *   Persons that are much abroad, and travel
early and late, such as shepherds, fishermen, &c. can tell what
prodigious fogs prevail in the night on elevated downs, even
in the hottest parts of summer; and how much the surfaces of
things are drenched by those swimming vapours, though, to the
senses, all the while, little moisture seems to fall.

* Fogs are much more frequent in cold seasons, and cold countries, than
in such as are warm ; because, in the former, the aqueous particles, being
condensed almost as soon as they proceed from the surface of the earth, are
incapable of rising into the higher portions of the atmosphere. If the
cold be augmented, the fog freezes, attaching itself in small icicles to the
branches of trees, and to the hair and clothes of persons exposed to it, to
the blades of grass, and other substances.— ED.

LETTER LXXII.

TO THE HON. DAINES BARRINGTON.

SELBORNE, *April* 3, 1776.

DEAR SIR, — Monsieur Herissant, a French anatomist, seems persuaded that he has discovered the reason why cuckoos do not hatch their own eggs ; the impediment, he supposes, arises from the internal structure of their parts, which incapacitates them for incubation. According to this gentleman, the crop, or craw, of a cuckoo, does not lie before the sternum at the bottom of the neck, as in the *gallinæ, columbæ,* &c. but immediately behind it, on and over the bowels, so as to make a large protuberance in the belly. *

Induced by this assertion, we procured a cuckoo ; and, cutting open the breast-bone, and exposing the intestines to sight, found the crop lying as mentioned above. This stomach was large and round, and stuffed hard, like a pin-cushion, with food, which, upon nice examination, we found to consist of various insects ; such as small scarabs, spiders, and dragon-flies ; the last of which we have seen cuckoos catching on the wing, as they were just emerging out of the aurelia state. Among this farrago also were to be seen maggots, and many seeds, which belonged either to gooseberries, currants, cranberries, or some such fruit ; so that these birds apparently subsist on insects and fruits ; nor was there the least appearance of bones, feathers, or fur, to support the idle notion of their being birds of prey.†

The sternum in this bird seemed to us to be remarkably short, between which and the anus lay the crop, or craw, and, immediately behind that, the bowels against the back-bone.

It must be allowed, as this anatomist observes, that the crop, placed just below the bowels, must, especially when full, be in a very uneasy situation during the business of incubation ; yet the test will be, to examine whether birds that are actually known to sit for certain are not formed in a similar manner.

* *Histoire de l'Academie Royale,* 1752.

† Sir William Jardine says, that when cuckoos have fed much on some of the large hairy caterpillars so common on the northern moors, the stomach becomes coated with the short hairs, which may have given rise to the opinion that they are predatory. But has not Sir William mistaken the fibrous structure of the stomach for these hairs? Its American congeners, the yellow-billed cuckoo, and the black-billed cuckoo, rob birds of their eggs ; and the latter feeds on fresh water shell-fish. — ED.

This inquiry I proposed to myself to make with a fern-owl, or goat-sucker, as soon as opportunity offered : because, if their formation proves the same, the reason for incapacity in the cuckoo will be allowed to have been taken up somewhat hastily.

Not long after, a fern-owl was procured, which, from its habits and shape, we suspected might resemble the cuckoo in its internal construction. Nor were our suspicions ill grounded ; for, upon the dissection, the crop, or craw, also lay behind the sternum, immediately on the viscera, between them and the skin of the belly. It was bulky, and stuffed hard with large *phalænæ*, moths of several sorts, and their eggs, which, no doubt, had been forced out of these insects by the action of swallowing.

Now, as it appears that this bird, which is so well known to practise incubation, is formed in a similar manner with cuckoos, Monsieur Herissant's conjecture, that cuckoos are incapable of incubation from the disposition of their intestines, seems to fall to the ground : and we are still at a loss for the cause of that strange and singular peculiarity in the instance of the *cuculus canorus.*

We found the case to be the same with the ring-tail hawk, in respect to formation ; and, as far as I can recollect, with the swift ; and probably it is so with many more sorts of birds that are not granivorous.

LETTER LXXIII.

TO THE HON. DAINES BARRINGTON.

SELBORNE, *April* 29, 1776.

DEAR SIR, — On August the 4th, 1775, we surprised a large viper, which seemed very heavy and bloated, as it lay in the grass, basking in the sun. When we came to cut it up, we found that the abdomen was crowded with young, fifteen in number ; the shortest of which measured full seven inches, and were about the size of full-grown earth-worms. This little fry issued into the world with the true viper spirit about them, shewing great alertness as soon as disengaged from the belly of the dam : they twisted and wriggled about, and set themselves up, and gaped very wide, when touched with a stick, shewing manifest tokens of menace and defiance, though as yet they had no manner of fangs that we could find, even with the help of our glasses.

To a thinking mind, nothing is more wonderful than that early instinct which impresses young animals with the notion of the situation of their natural weapons, and of using them properly in their own defence, even before those weapons subsist or are formed. * Thus a young cock will spar at his adversary before his spurs are grown ; and a calf or lamb will push with their heads before their horns are sprouted.   In the same manner did these young adders attempt to bite before their fangs were in being.   The dam, however, was furnished with very formidable ones, which we lifted up, (for they fold down when not used,) and cut them off with the point of our scissars.

There was little room to suppose that this brood had ever been in the open air before, and that they were taken in for refuge, at the mouth of the dam, when she perceived that danger was approaching; because then, probably, we should have found them somewhere in the neck, and not in the abdomen.

LETTER LXXIV.

TO THE HON. DAINES BARRINGTON.

CASTRATION has a strange effect : it emasculates both man, beast, and bird, and brings them to a near resemblance of the other sex.   Thus, eunuchs have smooth unmuscular arms, thighs, and legs ; and broad hips, and beardless chins, and squeaking voices.   Gelt stags and bucks have hornless heads, like hinds and does.   Thus wethers have small horns, like ewes ; and oxen large bent horns, and hoarse voices when they low, like cows : for bulls have short straight horns ; and though they mutter and grumble in a deep tremendous tone, yet they low in a shrill high key.   Capons have small combs and gills, and look pallid about the head like pullets; they also walk without any parade, and hover chickens like hens. Barrow-hogs have also small tusks like sows. †

* An adder with two distinct heads, which lived three days, taken with five others from the body of an old one, found in a ditch at Drumlanrig, Dumfriesshire, is now in the museum of Mr Thomas Grierson, Baitford, near Thornhill. — ED.

† After castration animals generally lose their spirit, although, in the instance of horses, this is by no means always the case.   The following fact is a strong evidence of this : — The horse of a nobleman in Ireland ran at a man, seized him with his teeth by the arm, which he broke; he then threw him down, and lay upon him. Every effort to get him off

Thus far it is plain, that the deprivation of masculine vigour puts a stop to the growth of those parts or appendages that are looked upon as its insignia. But the ingenious Mr Lisle, in his book on husbandry, carries it much farther; for he says, that the loss of those insignia alone has sometimes a strange effect on the ability itself. He had a boar so fierce and venereous that, to prevent mischief, orders were given for his tusks to be broken off. No sooner had the beast suffered this injury than his powers forsook him, and he neglected those females to whom before he was passionately attached, and from whom no fences could restrain him.

LETTER LXXV.

TO THE HON. DAINES BARRINGTON.

THE natural term of a hog's life is little known, and the reason is plain,—because it is neither profitable nor convenient to keep that turbulent animal to the full extent of its time; however, my neighbour, a man of substance, who had no occasion to study every little advantage to a nicety, kept a half-bred Bantam sow, who was as thick as she was long, and whose belly swept on the ground, till she was advanced to her seventeenth year; at which period, she shewed some tokens of age by the decay of her teeth, and the decline of her fertility.

For about ten years, this prolific mother produced two litters in the year, of about ten at a time, and once above twenty at a litter; but, as there were near double the number of pigs to that of teats, many died. From long experience in the world, this female was grown very sagacious and artful. When she found occasion to converse with a boar, she used to open all the intervening gates, and march, by herself, up to a distant farm where one was kept, and when her purpose was served, would return by the same means. At the age of about fifteen, her litters began to be reduced to four or five; and such a litter she exhibited when in her fatting-pen. She proved, when fat, good bacon, juicy, and tender; the rind, or sward, was remarkably thin. At a moderate computation, she was allowed to have been the fruitful parent of three

proved unavailing, and they were forced to shoot nim. The only reason could be assigned for such ferocity was, that he had been castrated by this man some time before, which the animal seems to have remembered. — ED.

hundred pigs,—a prodigious instance of fecundity in so large a quadruped! She was killed in spring, 1775. *

LETTER LXXVI.

TO THE HON. DAINES BARRINGTON.

SELBORNE, *May* 9, 1776.

—— Admorunt ubera tigres.

DEAR SIR,—We have remarked in a former letter how much incongruous animals, in a lonely state, may be attached to each other from a spirit of sociality ; in this, it may not be amiss to recount a different motive, which has been known to create as strange a fondness.

My friend had a little helpless leveret brought to him, which the servants fed with milk in a spoon, and, about the same time, his cat kittened, and the young were despatched and buried. The hare was soon lost, and supposed to be gone the way of most foundlings, to be killed by some dog or cat. However, in about a fortnight, as the master was sitting in his garden, in the dusk of the evening, he observed his cat, with tail erect, trotting towards him, and calling with little short inward notes of complacency, such as they use towards their kittens, and something gamboling after, which proved to be the leveret that the cat had supported with her milk, and continued to support with great affection.

Thus was a graminivorous animal nurtured by a carnivorous and predaceous one ! †

* The hog is a very prolific animal, and where persons have the proper means of feeding, it turns out very profitable. The following is the produce of a sow fed near Drogheda, for the short space of nine months :

July, 1813.	A litter of eleven, seven sold at 30s. . .	£10 10 . 0
July, 1814.	A litter of eleven, nine sold at 40s. . .	18 0 0
March,	Three of first litter, sold in market at .	31 0 0
April,	Sow sold fat, ...	20 5 5

£79 15 5

And a breeding sow was kept, valued at £20. A sow, belonging to Mr Thomas Richdale, Leicestershire, had produced, in the year 1797, three hundred and fifty pigs in twenty litters ; four years before, it brought two hundred and five in twelve litters. A sow, the property of George Baillie, butcher, in Hospital Street, Perth, on the 22d of August, 1829, littered the amazing number of *twenty-nine pigs.* Suaban is of opinion, that in twelve generations, a single pair would produce as many as Europe could support. — ED.

† Of incongruous attachments formed by animals, there is perhaps none more remarkable than the following, which proves that even the strongest of nature's laws may be altered by circumstances : Mr Cross,

Why so cruel and sanguinary a beast as a cat, of the ferocious genus of *felis*, the *murium leo*, as Linnæus calls it, should be affected with any tenderness towards an animal which is its natural prey, is not so easy to determine. *

This strange affection probably was occasioned by that desiderium, those tender maternal feelings, which the loss of her kittens had awakened in her breast; and by the complacency and ease she derived to herself from procuring her teats to be drawn, which were too much distended with milk; till, from habit, she became as much delighted with this foundling, as if it had been her real offspring.

This incident is no bad solution of that strange circumstance which grave historians, as well as the poets, assert, of exposed children being sometimes nurtured by female wild beasts that probably had lost their young. For it is not one whit more marvellous that Romulus and Remus, in their infant state, should be nursed by a she-wolf, than that a poor little sucking leveret should be fostered and cherished by a bloody grimalkin:

> —— Viridi fœtam Mavortis in antro
> Procubuisse lupam: geminos huic ubera circum
> Ludere pendentes pueros, et lambere matrem
> Impavidos: illam tereti cervice reflexam
> Mulcere alternos, et corpora fingere linguâ.

In Exeter Change, had, for some years, within one cage, the snake called the hooded snake, *cobra di capello*, and a canary bird; they appeared most affectionately attached to each other. — Ed.

* A cat, belonging to a person in Taunton, in May, 1822, having lost her kittens, transferred her affection to two ducklings, which were kept in the yard adjoining. She led them out every day to feed; seemed quite pleased to see them eat; returned with them to their usual nest, and evinced for them as much attachment as she could have shewn to her lost young ones.

The following is a still more extraordinary proof of the kindly feelings of the cat: — A short time ago, a young girl, daughter of Mr John Anderson, farmer at Collin, on the road to Annan, brought home early one morning two fine larks, which she had taken from the nest in a neighbouring field. Soon afterwards, the girl discovered that one of the larks had been taken out of the cage, and, on searching for it, found that the cat, whose only kitten died a day or two before, had carried the bird to the place where she usually nurtured her offspring, and was trying every method to make it suckle her; and when the lark attempted to get away, she still detained it, evincing the utmost anxiety for its safety. The girl, however, caught the bird, and placed it in the cage, which she hung in a situation beyond the reach of the cat. A few days after, several more birds were brought to the house, one of which the persevering cat also stole, and again tried, by all the endearing acts in her power, to make this likewise accept of her nourishment. Neither of the birds suffered the least injury from the animal. — Ed.

LETTER LXXVII.

TO THE HON. DAINES BARRINGTON.

SELBORNE, *May* 20, 1777.

DEAR SIR, — Lands that are subject to frequent inundations, are always poor ; and, probably, the reason may be, because the worms are drowned. The most insignificant insects and reptiles are of much more consequence, and have much more influence in the economy of Nature, than the incurious are aware of ; and are mighty in their effect, from their minuteness, which renders them less an object of attention ; and from their numbers and fecundity. * Earth-worms, though in appearance a small and despicable link in the chain of Nature, yet, if lost, would make a lamentable chasm. For to say nothing of half the birds, and some quadrupeds, which are almost entirely supported by them, worms seem to be the great promoters of vegetation, which would proceed but lamely without them, by boring, perforating, and loosening the soil, and rendering it pervious to rains and the fibres of plants, by drawing straws and stalks of leaves into it ; and, most of all, by throwing up such infinite numbers of lumps of earth, called worm-casts,

---

* The earth-worm has been long considered a viviparous animal, but M. Léon Dufour seems to have determined that it is oviparous. The eggs are of a very peculiar structure, being long, tapering, and terminated at each end by a pencil of fringed membranaceous substance. They have more the appearance, indeed, of a chrysalis or cocoon than of an egg ; but their pulp, &c. prove them to be true eggs. The worms, when hatched, are very agile, and, when disturbed, will sometimes retreat for safety within the shell, which they have just quitted, or instinctively dig into the clay.

Reaumur computes, though from what data it is difficult to conjecture, that the number of worms lodged in the bosom of the earth exceeds that of the grains of all kinds of corn collected by man.

A narrative in the *Times* newspaper of the disinterment of the body of the patriot Hampden, in Hampden Church, in July, 1828, contains some curious facts respecting the worm of corruption. Hampden was interred in June, 1643. It is stated in the *Times*, that "the skull was in some places perfectly bare, whilst in others the skin remained nearly entire, upon which we discovered a number of maggots, and small red worms, feeding with great activity. This was the only spot where-any symptoms of life were apparent, as if the brain contained a vital principle within it which engendered its own destruction ; otherwise, how can we account, after a lapse of nearly two centuries, for finding living creatures preying upon the seat of intellect, when they were nowhere else to be found — in no other part of the body?" — ED.

which, being their excrement, is a fine manure for grain and grass. Worms probably provide new soil for hills and slopes where the rain washes the earth away ; and they affect slopes, probably, to avoid being flooded. Gardeners and farmers express their detestation of worms ; the former, because they render their walks unsightly, and make them much work : and the latter, because, as they think, worms eat their green corn. But these men would find, that the earth without worms would soon become cold, hard-bound, and void of fermentation, and consequently steril : and, besides, in favour of worms it should be hinted, that green corn, plants, and flowers are not so much injured by them as by many species of *coleoptera* (scarabs) and *tipulæ* (long-legs,) in their larva or grub state ; and by unnoticed myriads of small shell-less snails, called slugs, which silently and imperceptibly make amazing havoc in the field and garden. *

These hints we think proper to throw out, in order to set the inquisitive and discerning to work.

A good monography of worms would afford much entertainment, and information at the same time ; and would open a large and new field in natural history. Worms work most in the spring, but by no means lie torpid in the dead months ; are out every mild night in the winter, as any person may be convinced that will take the pains to examine his grass plots with a candle ; are hermaphrodites, and much addicted to venery, and consequently very prolific.

LETTER LXXVIII.

TO THE HON. DAINES BARRINGTON.

SELBORNE, *November* 22, 1777.

DEAR SIR,— You cannot but remember, that the twenty-sixth and twenty-seventh of last March were very hot days ; so sultry, that every body complained, and were restless under those sensations to which they had not been reconciled by gradual approaches.

The sudden summer-like heat was attended by many summer coincidences ; for, on those two days, the thermometer rose to sixty-six in the shade ; many species of insects revived

---

* Farmer Young, of Norton-farm, says, that this spring, about four acres of his wheat, in one field, was entirely destroyed by slugs, which swarmed on the blades of corn, and devoured it as fast as it sprang.

and came forth ; some bees swarmed in this neighbourhood ; the old tortoise, near Lewes, awakened, and came forth out of its dormitory ; and, what is most to my present purpose, many house-swallows appeared, and were very alert in many places, and particularly at Cobham, in Surrey.*

But as that short warm period was succeeded as well as preceded by harsh, severe weather, with frequent frosts and ice, and cutting winds, the insects withdrew, the tortoise retired again into the ground, and the swallows were seen no more until the tenth of April, when, the rigour of the spring abating, a softer season began to prevail.

Again, it appears by my journals for many years past, that house-martens retire, to a bird, about the beginning of October ; so that a person not very observant of such matters would conclude that they had taken their last farewell ; but then it may be seen in my diaries, also, that considerable flocks have discovered themselves again in the first week of November, and often on the fourth day of that month, only for one day ; and that not as if they were in actual migration, but playing about at their leisure, and feeding calmly, as if no enterprise of moment at all agitated their spirits. And this was the case in the beginning of this very month ; for, on the fourth of November, more than twenty house-martens, which, in appearance,

---

* We are still unable to account for the reappearance of swallows after they seem to have taken their departure ; but, at the same time, we are not inclined to believe in their general torpidity during the winter. We must have proof on this subject.

A curious fact respecting the swallow was mentioned by our late worthy friend and intelligent naturalist, Captain Dougal Carmichael. It appears that swallows are birds of passage at the southern extremity of Africa, as well as in other parts of the world. They return to the Cape of Good Hope in September, and quit it again in March and April. A pair of these birds (*hirundo capensis*) fixed their flask-shaped nest against the angle formed by the wall with the board which supported the eaves. This nest had a single aperture, by which the birds went in and out. It fell down after the young quitted it. On the February following, these birds built in the same place ; but on this occasion Captain Carmichael remarked, in the construction of the nest, an improvement which can hardly be referred to the dictates of mere instinct. It was formed with an opening at both sides, and the swallows invariably entered at the one, and came out at the other. One advantage obtained by this arrangement was, that its occupants were saved the trouble of turning round in the nest, and thus avoided the risk of any derangement in its internal economy. But the chief object appeared to be, to facilitate their escape from the attacks of serpents, which harbour in the roofs of thatched houses, or crawl up along the wall, and not unfrequently devour both the mother and her young. — ED.

had all departed about the seventh of October, were seen again, for that one morning only, sporting between my fields and the Hanger, and feasting on insects which swarmed in that sheltered district. The preceding day was wet and blustering, but the fourth was dark, and mild, and soft, the wind at south-west, and the thermometer at 58½; a pitch not common at that season of the year. Moreover, it may not be amiss to add in this place, that whenever the thermometer is above 50, the bat comes flitting out in every autumnal and winter month.

From all these circumstances laid together, it is obvious that torpid insects, reptiles, and quadrupeds, are awakened from their profoundest slumbers by a little untimely warmth ; and, therefore, that nothing so much promotes this deathlike stupor as a defect of heat. And farther, it is reasonable to suppose, that two whole species, or at least many individuals of these two species of British *hirundines*, do never leave this island at all, but partake of the same benumbed state ; for we cannot suppose that, after a month's absence, house-martens can return from southern regions to appear for one morning in November, or that house-swallows should leave the districts of Africa to enjoy, in March, the transient summer of a couple of days.

LETTER LXXIX.

TO THE HON. DAINES BARRINGTON.

SELBORNE, *January* 8, 1778.

DEAR SIR,— There was, in this village, several years ago, a miserable pauper, who, from his birth, was afflicted with a leprosy, as far as we are aware, of a singular kind, since it affected only the palms of his hands and the soles of his feet. This scaly eruption usually broke out twice in the year, at the spring and fall ; and by peeling away, left the skin so thin and tender, that neither his hands nor feet were able to perform their functions ; so that the poor object was half his time on crutches, incapable of employ, and languishing in a tiresome state of indolence and inactivity. His habit was lean, lank, and cadaverous. In this sad plight, he dragged on a miserable existence, a burden to himself and his parish, which was obliged to support him, till he was relieved by death, at more than thirty years of age.

The good women, who love to account for every defect in

children by the doctrine of longing, said that his mother felt a violent propensity for oysters, which she was unable to gratify, and that the black rough scurf on his hands and feet were the shells of that fish. We knew his parents, neither of whom were lepers : his father, in particular, lived to be far advanced in years.

In all ages, the leprosy has made dreadful havoc among mankind. The Israelites seem to have been greatly afflicted with it from the most remote times, as appears from the peculiar and repeated injunctions given them in the Levitical law. *
Nor was the rancour of this foul disorder much abated in the last period of their commonwealth, as may be seen in many passages of the New Testament.

Some centuries ago, this horrible distemper prevailed all over Europe ; and our forefathers were by no means exempt, as appears by the large provision made for objects labouring under this calamity. There was an hospital for female lepers in the diocese of Lincoln, a noble one near Durham, three in London and Southwark, and perhaps many more in or near our great towns and cities. Moreover, some crowned heads, and other wealthy and charitable personages, bequeathed large legacies to such poor people as languished under this hopeless infirmity.

It must, therefore, in these days, be, to a humane and thinking person, a matter of equal wonder and satisfaction, when he contemplates how nearly this pest is eradicated, and observes that a leper is now a rare sight. He will, moreover, when engaged in such a train of thought, naturally inquire for the reason. This happy change, perhaps, may have originated and been continued from the much smaller quantity of salted meat and fish now eaten in these kingdoms — from the use of linen next the skin — from the plenty of better bread — and from the profusion of fruits, roots, legumes, and greens, so common in every family. † Three or four centuries ago, before there were any' enclosures, sown grasses, field turnips, or field carrots, or hay, all the cattle that had grown fat in summer, and were not killed for winter use, were turned out soon after Michaelmas to shift as they could through the dead months ;

* See Leviticus, chap. xiii. and xiv.
† In former times many affections of the skin, especially impetiginous eruptions, were mistaken for leprosy, and confounded with scurvy, which is also a different disease. The disuse of salted provisions as a daily article of diet, and the employment of vegetables, sugar, and diluting drinks, have caused the rare occurrence of these diseases in the present day. —ED.

so that no fresh meat could be had in winter or spring. Hence the marvellous account of the vast stores of salted flesh found in the larder of the eldest Spencer,* in the days of Edward the Second, even so late in the spring as the third of May. It was from magazines like these that the turbulent barons supported in idleness their riotous swarms of retainers, ready for any disorder or mischief. But agriculture has now arrived at such a pitch of perfection, that our best and fattest meats are killed in the winter; and no man needs eat salted flesh, unless he prefer it, that has money to buy fresh.

One cause of this distemper might be, no doubt, the quantity of wretched fresh and salt fish consumed by the commonalty at all seasons, as well as in Lent, which our poor now would hardly be persuaded to touch.

The use of linen changes, shirts or shifts, in the room of sordid or filthy woollen, long worn next the skin, is a matter of neatness comparatively modern, but must prove a great means of preventing cutaneous ails. At this very time, woollen instead of linen prevails among the poorer Welsh, who are subject to foul eruptions.

The plenty of good wheaten bread that now is found among all ranks of people in the south, instead of that miserable sort which used in old days to be made of barley or beans, may contribute not a little to the sweetening their blood and correcting their juices; for the inhabitants of mountainous districts, to this day, are still liable to the itch and other cutaneous disorders, from a wretchedness and poverty of diet.

As to the produce of a garden, every middle-aged person of observation may perceive, within his own memory, both in town and country, how vastly the consumption of vegetables is increased. Green stalls in cities now support multitudes in a comfortable state, while gardeners get fortunes. Every decent labourer, also, has his garden, which is half his support, as well as his delight; and common farmers provide plenty of beans, pease, and greens, for their hinds to eat with their bacon; and those few that do not are despised for their sordid parsimony, and looked upon as regardless of the welfare of their dependents. Potatoes have prevailed in this little district, by means of premiums, within these twenty years only, and are much esteemed here now by the poor, who would scarce have ventured to taste them in the last reign.

---

* Namely, six hundred bacons, eighty carcasses of beef, and six hundred muttons.

Our Saxon ancestors certainly had some sort of cabbage, because they call the month of February sprout-cale; * but long after their days, the cultivation of gardens was little attended to. The religious, being men of leisure, and keeping up a constant correspondence with Italy, were the first people among us who had gardens and fruit trees in any perfection, within the walls of their abbeys† and priories. The barons neglected every pursuit that did not lead to war, or tend to the pleasure of the chase.

It was not till gentlemen took up the study of horticulture themselves that the knowledge of gardening made such hasty advances. Lord Cobham, Lord Ila, and Mr Waller of Beaconsfield, were some of the first people of rank that promoted the elegant science of ornamenting, without despising the superintendence of the kitchen quarters and fruit walls.‡

A remark made by the excellent Mr Ray, in his *Tour of Europe*, at once surprises us, and corroborates what has been advanced above; for we find him observing, so late as his days, that " the Italians use several herbs for salads, which are not yet, or have not been but lately, used in England, viz. *selleri*, (celery,) which is nothing else but the sweet smallage, the young shoots whereof, with a little of the head of the root cut off, they eat raw with oil and pepper." And farther, he adds, " curled endive, blanched, is much used beyond seas, and, for a raw salad, seemed to excel lettuce itself." Now this journey was undertaken no longer ago than in the year 1663.

---

* The Saxons derived the names of their months from similar causes. —March was called stormy month; May, Trimilki, from cows being milked thrice a day in that month; June was called diet and weed month; and September barley month.— ED.

† " In monasteries, the lamp of knowledge continued to burn, however dimly. In them, men of business were formed for the state. The art of writing was cultivated by the monks; they were the only proficients in mechanics, *gardening*, and architecture."— See DALRYMPLE's *Annals of Scotland.*

‡ Horticulture has made great progress in Britain since our author's time. Societies have been established, experimental gardens formed, premiums awarded for the best vegetables produced, and an excellent magazine, exclusively devoted to horticultural science, has been published for some years, under the able direction of Mr J. C. Loudon.— ED.

LETTER LXXX.

TO THE HON. DAINES BARRINGTON.

SELBORNE, *February* 12, 1778.

Fortè puer, comitum seductus ab agmine fido,
Dixerat, ecquis adest ? et, adest, responderat echo.
Hic stupet ; utque aciem partes divisit in omnes ;
Voce, veni clamat magnâ. Vocat illa vocantem.

DEAR SIR,—In a district so diversified as this, so full of hollow vales and hanging woods, it is no wonder that echoes should abound. Many we have discovered, that return the cry of a pack of dogs, the notes of a hunting horn, a tunable ring of bells, or the melody of birds, very agreeably ; but we were still at a loss for a polysyllabical articulate echo, till a young gentleman, who had parted from his company in a summer evening walk, and was calling after them, stumbled upon a very curious one, in a spot where it might least be expected. At first, he was much surprised, and could not be persuaded but that he was mocked by some boy ; but repeating his trials in several languages, and finding his respondent to be a very adroit polyglot, he then discerned the deception.

This echo, in an evening before rural noises cease, would repeat ten syllables most articulately and distinctly, especially if quick dactyls were chosen. The last syllables of

Tityre, tu patulæ recubans——

were as audibly and intelligibly returned as the first; and there is no doubt, could trial have been made, but that at midnight, when the air is very elastic, and a dead stillness prevails, one or two syllables more might have been obtained ; but the distance rendered so late an experiment very inconvenient.

Quick dactyls, we observed, succeeded best ; for when we came to try its powers in slow, heavy, embarrassed spondees, of the same number of syllables,

Monstrum horrendum, informe, ingens——

we could perceive a return but of four or five.*

* There is a very extraordinary echo at a ruined fortress near Lourain in France. If a person sings, he only hears his own voice, without any repetition ; on the contrary, those who stand at some distance, hear the echo, but not the voice ; but then they hear it with surprising variations, sometimes louder, sometimes softer, now more near, then more distant.

All echoes have some one place to which they are returned stronger and more distinct than to any other; and that is always the place that lies at right angles with the object of repercussion, and is not too near, nor too far off. Buildings, or naked rocks, re-echo much more articulately than hanging woods or vales; because, in the latter, the voice is, as it were, entangled, and embarrassed in the covert, and weakened in the rebound.

The true object of this echo, as we found by various experiments, is the stone-built, tiled hop-kiln in Gally Lane, which measures in front forty feet, and from the ground to the eaves, twelve feet. The true *centrum phonicum*, or just distance, is one particular spot in the King's Field, in the path to Nore-hill, on the very brink of the steep balk above the hollow cart-way. In this case, there is no choice of distance; but the path, by mere contingency, happens to be the lucky, the identical spot, because the ground rises or falls so immediately, if the speaker either retires or advances, that his mouth would at once be above or below the object.

We measured this polysyllabical echo with great exactness, and found the distance to fall very short of Dr Plot's rule for distinct articulation; for the Doctor, in his *History of Oxford-shire*, allows one hundred and twenty feet for the return of each syllable distinctly; hence this echo, which gives ten distinct syllables, ought to measure four hundred yards, or one hundred and twenty feet to each syllable; whereas our distance is only two hundred and fifty-eight yards, or near seventy-five feet to each syllable.* Thus our measure falls short of the Doctor's as five to eight; but then it must be acknowledged, that this candid philosopher was convinced afterwards, that some latitude must be admitted of in the distance of echoes, according to time and place.

When experiments of this sort are making, it should always be remembered, that weather and the time of day have a vast

There is an account in the *Memoirs of the French Academy* of a similar echo near Rouen. The building which returns it is a semicircular court-yard; yet every one of the same form does not produce a similar effect.—ED.

* A knowledge of the progression of sound is not an article of mere steril curiosity, but in several instances useful; for by this means we are enabled to determine the distance of ships, or other moving bodies. Suppose, for example, that a vessel fires a gun, the sound of which is heard five seconds after the flash is seen, as sound moves one thousand one hundred and forty-two English feet in a second, this number, multiplied by five, gives the distance of five thousand seven hundred and ten feet. The same principle is applicable in storms of lightning and thunder.—ED.

influence on an echo; for a dull, heavy, moist air deadens and clogs the sound; and hot sunshine renders the air thin and weak, and deprives it of all its springiness; and a ruffling wind quite defeats the whole. In a still, clear, dewy evening, the air is most elastic; and perhaps the later the hour the more so.

Echo has always been so amusing to the imagination, that the poets have personified her; and, in their hands, she has been the occasion of many a beautiful fiction. Nor need the gravest man be ashamed to appear taken with such a phenomenon, since it may become the subject of philosophical or mathematical inquiries.

One should have imagined that echoes, if not entertaining, must at least have been harmless and inoffensive: yet Virgil advances a strange notion, that they are injurious to bees. After enumerating some probable and reasonable annoyances, such as prudent owners would wish far removed from their bee-gardens, he adds,

——— Aut ubi concava pulsu
Saxa sonant, vocisque offensa resultat imago.

This wild and fanciful assertion will hardly be admitted by the philosophers of these days, especially as they all now seem agreed that insects are not furnished with any organs of hearing at all.* But if it should be urged, that, though they cannot hear, yet perhaps they may feel the repercussion of sounds, I grant it is possible they may. Yet that these impressions are distasteful or hurtful I deny, because bees, in good summers, thrive well in my outlet, where the echoes are very strong; for this village is another Anathoth, a place of responses, or echoes. Besides, it does not appear from experiment that bees are in any way capable of being affected by sounds: for I have often tried my own with a large speaking trumpet held close to their hives, and with such an exertion of voice as would have hailed a ship at the distance of a mile, and still these insects pursued their various employments undisturbed, and without shewing the least sensibility or resentment.

* The organs of hearing in insects are the antennæ, or horn-like processes, which stand out from the forehead. If these organs do not convey sound, in the same manner as the ears of other animals, they are, at least, very sensible of any concussion produced in the atmosphere by sounds, and if not the ears themselves, are, at least, analogous to them. The reflected sound of an echo cannot take place at less than fifty-five feet; because it is necessary that the distance should be such, and the reverberated or reflected sound so long in arriving, that the ear may distinguish clearly between that and the original sound. — ED.

Some time since its discovery, this echo is become totally silent, though the object, or hop-kiln, remains : nor is there any mystery in this defect, for the field between is planted as a hop-garden, and the voice of the speaker is totally absorbed and lost among the poles and entangled foliage of the hops. And when the poles are removed in autumn, the disappointment is the same ; because a tall quick-set hedge, nurtured up for the purpose of shelter to the hop-ground, entirely interrupts the impulse and repercussion of the voice : so that, till those obstructions are removed, no more of its garrulity can be expected.

Should any gentleman of fortune think an echo in his park or outlet a pleasing incident, he might build one at little or no expense. For, whenever he had occasion for a new barn, stable, dog-kennel, or the like structure, it would be only needful to erect this building on the gentle declivity of a hill, with a like rising opposite to it, at a few hundred yards' distance ; and perhaps success might be the easier ensured could some canal, lake, or stream, intervene. From a seat at the *centrum phonicum*, he and his friends might amuse themselves sometimes of an evening with the prattle of this loquacious nymph ; of whose complacency and decent reserve, more may be said than can with truth of every individual of her sex ; since she is

> Quæ nec *reticere* loquenti,
> Nec *prior* ipsa loqui, didicit resonabilis echo.

P.S. The classic reader will, I trust, pardon the following lovely quotation, so finely describing echoes, and so poetically acccounting for their causes from popular superstition : —

> Quæ benè quom videas, rationem reddere possis
> Tute tibi atque aliis, quo pacto per loca sola
> Saxa pareis formas verborum ex ordine reddant,
> Palanteis comites quom monteis inter opacos
> Quærimus, et magnâ dispersos voce ciemus.
> Sex etiam, aut septem loca vidi reddere voces
> Unam quom jaceres : ita colles collibus ipsis
> Verba repulsantes iterabant dicta referre.
> Hæc loca capripedes Satyros, Nymphasque tenere
> Finitimi fingunt, et Faunos esse loquuntur ;
> Quorum noctivago strepitu, ludoque jocanti
> Adfirmant volgo taciturna silentia rumpi,
> Chordarumque sonos fieri, dulceisque querelas,
> Tibia quas fundit digitis pulsata canentum ;
> Et genus agricolûm latè sentiscere, quom Pan
> Pinea semiferi capitis velamina quassans,
> Unco sæpe labro calamos percurrit hianteis,
> Fistula silvestrem ne cesset fundere musam.
> LUCRETIUS, lib. iv.

LETTER LXXXI.

TO THE HON. DAINES BARRINGTON.

SELBORNE, *May* 13, 778.

DEAR SIR,— Among the many singularities attending those amusing birds, the swifts, I am now confirmed in the opinion that we have every year the same number of pairs invariably; at least the result of my inquiry has been exactly the same for a long time past. The swallows and martens are so numerous, and so widely distributed over the village, that it is hardly possible to recount them ; while the swifts, though they do not all build in the church, yet so frequently haunt it, and play and rendezvous round it, that they are easily enumerated. The number that I constantly find are eight pairs, about half of which reside in the church, and the rest build in some of the lowest and meanest thatched cottages. * Now, as these eight pairs — allowance being made for accidents — breed yearly eight pairs more, what becomes annually of this increase ? and what determines, every spring, which pairs shall visit us, and re-occupy their ancient haunts ?

Ever since I have attended to the subject of ornithology, I have always supposed that the sudden reverse of affection, that strange ανπσπορρη, which immediately succeeds in the feathered kind to the most passionate fondness, is the occasion of an equal dispersion of birds over the face of the earth. Without this provision, one favourite district would be crowded with inhabitants, while others would be destitute and forsaken. But the parent birds seem to maintain a jealous superiority, and to oblige the young to seek for new abodes ; and the rivalry of the males in many kinds prevents their crowding the one on the other. Whether the swallows and house-martens return in the same exact number annually it is not easy to say, for reasons given above; but it is apparent, as I have remarked before in my *Monographies,* that the numbers returning bear no manner of proportion to the numbers retiring.

* We do not mean to dispute the accuracy of the fact here mentioned ; but we have seen many instances where the number of nests were trebled, during three or four years, in one locality. —ED.

LETTER LXXXII.

TO THE HON. DAINES BARRINGTON.

SELBORNE, *June* 2, 1778.

DEAR SIR,— The standing objection to botany has always been, that it is a pursuit that amuses the fancy and exercises the memory, without improving the mind, or advancing any real knowledge ; and, where the science is carried no farther than a mere systematic classification, the charge is but too true. But the botanist that is desirous of wiping off this aspersion, should be by no means content with a list of names ; he should study plants philosophically, should investigate the laws of vegetation, should examine the powers and virtues of efficacious herbs, should promote their cultivation, and graft the gardener, the planter, and the husbandman on the phytologist. Not that system is by any means to be thrown aside — without system the field of Nature would be a pathless wilderness — but system should be subservient to, not the main object of, pursuit.

Vegetation is highly worthy of our attention, and in itself is of the utmost consequence to mankind, and productive of many of the greatest comforts and elegancies of life. To plants we owe timber, bread, beer, honey, wine, oil, linen, cotton, &c.—what not only strengthens our hearts, and exhilarates our spirits, but what secures us from inclemencies of weather, and adorns our persons. Man, in his true state of nature, seems to be subsisted by spontaneous vegetation ; in middle climes, where grasses prevail, he mixes some animal food with the produce of the field and garden ; and it is towards the polar extremes only, that, like his kindred bears and wolves, he gorges himself with flesh alone, and is driven to what hunger has never been known to compel the very beasts,—to prey upon his own species.*

The productions of vegetation have had a vast influence on the commerce of nations, and have been the great promoters of navigation, as may be seen in the articles of sugar, tea, tobacco, opium, ginseng, betel, pepper, &c. As every climate has its peculiar produce, our natural wants bring on a mutual intercourse ; so that by means of trade, each distant part is supplied with the growth of every latitude. But, without the knowledge of plants and their culture, we must have been

* See the late voyages to the South Seas.

content with our hips and haws, without enjoying the delicate fruits of India, and the salutiferous drugs of Peru.

Instead of examining the minute distinctions of every various species of each obscure genus, the botanist should endeavour to make himself acquainted with those that are useful. You shall see a man readily ascertain every herb of the field, yet hardly know wheat from barley, or at least one sort of wheat or barley from another.*

But of all sorts of vegetation, the grasses seem to be most neglected : neither the farmer nor the grazier seem to distinguish the annual from the perennial, the hardy from the tender, nor the succulent and nutritive from the dry and juiceless.†

The study of grasses would be of great consequence to a northerly and grazing kingdom. The botanist that could improve the sward of the district where he lived, would be a useful member of society : to raise a thick turf on a naked soil, would be worth volumes of systematic knowledge ; and he would be the best commonwealth's man that could occasion the growth of "two blades of grass where one alone was seen before."

LETTER LXXXIII.

TO THE HON. DANIES BARRINGTON.

SELBORNE, *July* 3, 1778.

DEAR SIR,— In a district so diversified with such a variety of hill and dale, aspects and soils, it is no wonder that great choice of plants should be found. Chalks, clays, sands, sheep-walks and downs, bogs, heaths, woodlands, and champaign fields, cannot but furnish an ample *flora*. The deep rocky lanes abound with *filices*, and the pastures and moist woods with *fungi*. If in any branch of botany we may seem to be wanting, it must be in the large aquatic plants, which are not

---

 * The observations and experiments of one generation after another, have enabled us progressively to improve, by culture, the *cereal* grasses, into those valuable plants wheat and barley, which now maintain millions of our fellow men. — ED.

† Of late not only the attention of the naturalist, but also of the farmer, has been directed to the study of grasses, to the preference of particular species, and to the relative produce of the different kinds. Among the works which have most contributed to the advancement of this highly important department of agriculture, we would mention Curtis on *British Grasses*, and the splendid and valuable *Hortus Gramineus Woburnensis;* and in Young's *Farmer's Magazine* many interesting experiments have been recorded. — ED.

to be expected on a spot far removed from rivers, and lying
up amidst the hill country at the spring-heads. To enumerate
all the plants that have been discovered within our limits,
would be a needless work; but a short list of the more rare,
and the spots where they are to be found, may neither be
unacceptable nor unentertaining.

Helleborus fœtidus, stinking hellebore, bear's-foot, or setter-
wort,—all over the Highwood and Coney-croft-hanger. This
continues a great branching plant the winter through, blossoming about January, and is very ornamental in shady walks and
shrubberies. The good women give the leaves powdered to
children troubled with worms; but it is a violent remedy, and
ought to be administered with caution.

Helleborus viridis, green hellebore,—in the deep stony lane,
on the left hand, just before the turning to Norton Farm, and
at the top of Middle Dorton, under the hedge. This plant dies
down to the ground early in autumn, and springs again about
February, flowering almost as soon as it appears above ground.

Vaccinium oxycoccus, creeping bilberries, or cranberries,—
in the bogs of Bin's-pond:

Vaccinium myrtillus, whortle, or bilberries,—on the dry hillocks of Wolmer Forest:

Drosera rotundifolia, round-leaved sundew,—in the bogs of
Bin's-pond:

Drosera longifolia, long-leaved sundew,—in the bogs of Bin's-
pond:

Comarum palustre, purple comarum, or marsh cinque-foil,—
in the bogs of Bin's-pond:

Hypericum androsæmum, Tutsan, St John's wort,—in the
stony hollow lanes:

Vinca minor, less periwinkle,—in Selborne-hanger or Shrubwood:

Monatropa hypopithys, yellow monotropa, or bird's-nest,—
in Selborne-hanger under the shady beeches, to whose roots it
seems to be parasitical—at the north-west end of the Hanger:

Chlora perfoliata, *Blackstonia perfoliata*, *Hudsoni*, perfoliated
yellow-wort,—on the banks in the King's Field:

Paris quadrifolia, herb Paris, true-love, or one-berry,—in
the Church-litten-coppice:

Chrysosplenium oppositifolium, opposite golden saxifrage,—
in the dark and rocky hollow lanes:

Gentiana amarella, autumnal gentian, or fellwort,—on the
Zig-zag and Hanger:

Lathræa squammaria, tooth-wort,—in the Church-litten-coppice, under some hazels near the foot-bridge, in Trimming's garden hedge, and on the dry wall opposite Grange-yard:

Dipsacus pilosus, small teasel,—in the Short and Long Lith:

Lathyrus sylvestris, narrow-leaved, or wild lathyrus,—in the bushes at the foot of the Short Lith, near the path:

Ophrys spiralis, ladies' traces,—in the Long Lith, and towards the south corner of the common:

Ophrys nidus avis, bird's-nest ophrys,—in the Long Lith, under the shady beeches among the dead leaves, in Great Dorton among the bushes, and on the Hanger plentifully:

Serapias latifolia, helleborine,—in the Highwood under the shady beeches:

Daphne laureola, spurge laurel,—in Selborne-hanger and the High-wood:

Daphne mezereum, the mezereon,—in Selborne-hanger, among the shrubs at the south-east end, above the cottages:

Lycoperdon tuber, truffles,—in the Hanger and High-wood:

Sambucus ebulus, dwarf elder, walwort, or danewort,—among the rubbish and ruined foundations of the Priory.

Of all the propensities of plants, none seem more strange than their different periods of blossoming. Some produce their flowers in the winter, or very first dawnings of spring; many when the spring is established; some at midsummer, and some not till autumn. When we see the *helleborus fœtidus* and *helleborus niger* blowing at Christmas, the *helleborus hyemalis* in January, and the *helleborus viridis* as soon as ever it emerges out of the ground, we do not wonder, because they are kindred plants that we expect should keep pace the one with the other; but other congenerous vegetables differ so widely in their time of flowering, that we cannot but admire. I shall only instance at present in the *crocus sativus*, * the

* Two species are generally admitted by botanists, the *crocus sativus* of Linnæus, or saffron crocus, and the *crocus vernus*, the vernal crocus. Besides good specific differences, these two plants are distinct in their properties, the highly odoriferous stigmas of the *crocus sativus* alone furnishing the saffron of commerce. The stigma of the *crocus vernus* is inodorous.

The similarity of climate and weather that characterizes vernal and autumnal days, often produces, towards the latter end of September, a vegetation vying with that of May in profusion and variety of tints.

Many plants, generally considered as exclusively vernal, bloom a second time. Of this, the *viola canina* and *odorata* are striking examples; and the sweet *gentiana verna*, or spring gentian, often unfolds its azure blossoms for the second time, late in October, studding the verdant sward with a blue that rivals in intensity the ultramarine. — ED.

vernal and the autumnal crocus, which have such an affinity, that the best botanists only make them varieties of the same genus, of which there is only one species, not being able to discern any difference in the corolla, or in the internal structure. Yet the vernal crocus expands its flowers by the beginning of March at farthest, and often in very rigorous weather; and cannot be retarded but by some violence offered; while the autumnal (the saffron) defies the influence of the spring and summer, and will not blow till most plants begin to fade and run to seed. This circumstance is one of the wonders of the creation, little noticed because a common occurrence; yet ought not to be overlooked on account of its being familiar, since it would be as difficult to be explained as the most stupendous phenomenon in nature.

> Say, what impels, amidst surrounding snow
> Congeal'd, the crocus' flamy bud to glow?
> Say, what retards, amidst the summer's blaze,
> Th autumnal bulb, till pale, declining days?
> The GOD OF SEASONS, whose pervading power
> Controls the sun, or sheds the fleecy shower:
> He bids each flower his quickening word obey,
> Or to each lingering bloom enjoins delay.

LETTER LXXXIV.

TO THE HON. DAINES BARRINGTON.

SELBORNE, *August* 7, 1778.

Omnibus animalibus reliquis certus et uniusmodi, et in suo cuique genere incessus est; aves solæ vario meatu feruntur, et in terrâ, et in aere. PLIN. *Hist. Nat.* lib. x. cap. 38.

DEAR SIR,—A good ornithologist should be able to distinguish birds by their air as well as their colours and shape, on the ground as well as on the wing, and in the bush as well as in the hand. For, though it must not be said that every species of birds has a manner peculiar to itself, yet there is somewhat in most genera at least that at first sight discriminates them, and enables a judicious observer to pronounce upon them with some certainty. Put a bird in motion,

Et vera incessu patuit.

Thus kites and buzzards sail round in circles, with wings expanded and motionless; and it is from their gliding manner that the former are still called, in the north of England, gleads, from the Saxon verb *glidan*, to glide. The kestrel, or windhover, has a peculiar mode of hanging in the air in one place, his wings all the while being briskly agitated. Hen-harriers fly low over heaths or fields of corn, and beat the ground regularly like a pointer or setting-dog. Owls move in a buoyant manner, as if lighter than the air ; they seem to want ballast. There is a peculiarity belonging to ravens that must draw the attention even of the most incurious, — they spend all their leisure time in striking and cuffing each other on the wing in a kind of playful skirmish ; and when they move from one place to another, frequently turn on their backs with a loud croak, and seem to be falling to the ground. When this odd gesture betides them, they are scratching themselves with one foot, and thus lose the centre of gravity. Rooks sometimes dive and tumble in a frolicsome manner ; crows and daws swagger in their walk ; woodpeckers fly *volatu undoso*, opening and closing their wings at every stroke, and so are always rising and falling in curves. All of this genus use their tails, which incline downward, as a support while they run up trees. Parrots, like all other hooked-clawed birds, walk awkwardly, and make use of their bill as a third foot, climbing and descending with ridiculous caution. All the *gallinæ* parade and walk gracefully, and run nimbly ; but fly with difficulty, with an impetuous whirring, and in a straight line. Magpies and jays flutter with powerless wings, and make no despatch ; herons seem encumbered with too much sail for their light bodies ; but these vast hollow wings are necessary in carrying burdens, such as large fishes, and the like ; pigeons, and particularly the sort called smiters, have a way of clashing their wings, the one against the other, over their backs with a loud snap ; another variety, called tumblers, turn themselves over in the air. * Some birds have movements peculiar to the season of love : thus ring-doves, though strong and rapid at other times, yet, in the spring, hang about on the wing in a toying and playful manner; thus the cock snipe, while breeding, forgetting his former flight, fans the air like the windhover ; and the greenfinch, in particular, exhibits such languishing and faltering gestures as to appear like a wounded and dying bird ; the king-fisher darts along like an arrow ; fern-owls, or goat-suckers, glance in the dust over the tops of trees like a meteor ; starlings, as it were, swim along, while missel-thrushes use a wild and desultory flight ; swallows

* Mr Swainson is of opinion, that this movement is indicative of pleasure or excitement.—ED.

sweep over the surface of the ground and water, and distinguish
themselves by rapid turns and quick evolutions : swifts dash
round in circles ; and the bank-marten moves with frequent
vacillations like a butterfly.   Most of the small birds fly by
jerks, rising and falling as they advance.   Most small birds
hop ; but wagtails and larks walk, moving their legs alternately.   Sky-larks rise and fall perpendicularly as they sing ; *
woodlarks hang poised in the air ; and titlarks rise and fall
in large curves, singing in their descent.   The white-throat
uses odd jerks and gesticulations over the tops of hedges and
bushes.   All the duck kind waddle ; divers and auks walk as
if fettered, and stand erect on their tails ; these are the
compedes of Linnæus.   Geese and cranes, and most wild
owls, move in figured flights, often changing their position.
The secondary remiges of *tringæ*, wild ducks, and some others,
are very long, and give their wings, when in motion, a hooked
appearance.   Dabchicks, moor-hens, and coots, fly erect,
with their legs hanging down, and hardly make any despatch :
the reason is plain, their wings are placed too forward out of
the true centre of gravity ; as the legs of auks and divers are
situated too backward.

LETTER LXXXV.

TO THE HON. DAINES BARRINGTON.

SELBORNE, *September* 9, 1778.

DEAR SIR,—From the motion of birds, the transition is
natural enough to their notes and language, of which I shall
say something.   Not that I would pretend to understand their
language like the vizier, who, by the recital of a conversation
which passed between two owls, reclaimed a sultan,† before
delighting in conquest and devastation ; but I would be thought
only to mean, that many of the winged tribes have various
sounds and voices adapted to express their various passions,
wants, and feelings, such as anger, fear, love, hatred, hunger,
and the like.   All species are not equally eloquent ; some are
copious and fluent, as it were, in their utterance, while others
are confined to a few important sounds ; no bird, like the fish

---

* The male of the yellow breasted chat, *icteria polyglotta* of Swainson, while the female is sitting, sometimes mounts up into the air almost
perpendicularly, to the height of thirty or forty feet, with his legs hanging,
descending, as he rose, by repeated jerks, as if highly irritated. —ED.

† See *Spectator*, No. 512.

kind, is quite mute,* though some are rather silent.   The language of birds is very ancient, and like other ancient modes of speech, very elliptical; little is said, but much is meant and understood. †

The notes of the eagle kind are shrill and piercing; and about the season of nidification much diversified, as I have been often assured by a curious observer of nature, who long resided at Gibraltar, where eagles abound.   The notes of our hawks much resemble those of the king of birds.   Owls have very expressive notes; they hoot in a fine vocal sound, much resembling the *vox humana*, and reducible by a pitch-pipe to a musical key.   This note seems to express complacency and rivalry among the males; they use also a quick call and an horrible scream; and can snore and hiss when they mean to menace.   Ravens, besides their loud croak, can exert a deep and solemn note that makes the woods to echo; the amorous sound of a crow is strange and ridiculous; rooks, in the breeding season, attempt sometimes, in the gaiety of their hearts, to sing, but with no great success; the parrot kind have many modulations of voice, as appears by their aptitude to learn human sounds; doves coo in an amorous and mournful manner, and are emblems of despairing lovers; the woodpecker sets up a sort of loud and hearty laugh; the fern-owl, or goat-sucker, from the dusk till daybreak, serenades his mate with the clattering of castanets.   All the tuneful *passeres* express their

---

* Mr John Thomson of Hull says, "Some tench, which I caught in ponds, made a croaking like a frog for a full half hour, whilst in the basket at my shoulder." It is well known that when the herring is just caught in the net, and brought into the boat, it utters a shrill cry like a mouse. The gurnard grunts or croaks when taken and freed from the hook. — Ed.

† Mr J. Murray says, "I once heard the cuckoo's note at midnight. This occurred some years ago, as I was coming from Charleton to Douglas, in the Isle of Man. It was moonlight, and I enjoyed a delightful walk *en solitaire*, my reveries being frequently interrupted by this interesting note, unusual, if I mistake not, for the 'witching hour.'" Mr W. H. White says, "During the summer of 1830, the days were wet and chilly, and the nights clear and calm, so that the night was in fact more pleasant than the day; so much so, that I frequently went out after supper, and as frequently heard the cuckoo and the nightingale from ten till eleven o'clock; but on two succeeding evenings, the 4th and 5th of June, the moon being about full, and shining with 'unclouded majesty,' I heard, about the 'witching hour of night,' both the cuckoo and the nightingale; and on the 9th was highly gratified in hearing a trio, with all the native melody of the grove, performed by the cuckoo, the nightingale, and the sedge-warbler, a little after midnight." — Ed.

complacency by sweet modulations, and a variety of melody. The swallow, as has been observed in a former letter, by a shrill alarm, bespeaks the attention of the other *hirundines*, and bids them be aware that the hawk is at hand.* Aquatic and gregarious birds, especially the nocturnal, that shift their quarters in the dark, are very noisy and loquacious,—as cranes, wild-geese, wild-ducks, and the like : their perpetual clamour prevents them from dispersing and losing their companions.

In so extensive a subject, sketches and outlines are as much as can be expected ; for it would be endless to instance in all the infinite variety of the feathered nation. We shall, therefore, confine the remainder of this letter to the few domestic fowls of our yards, which are most known, and, therefore, best understood. And first, the peacock, with his gorgeous train, demands our attention ; but, like most of the gaudy birds, his notes are grating and shocking to the ear: the yelling of cats, and the braying of an ass, are not more disgustful. The voice of the goose is trumpet-like, and clanking ; and once saved the Capitol at Rome, as grave historians assert: the hiss, also, of the gander is formidable, and full of menace, and " protective of his young." Among ducks, the sexual distinction of voice is remarkable ; for, while the quack of the female is loud and sonorous, the voice of the drake is inward, and harsh, and feeble, and scarce discernible. The cock turkey struts and gobbles to his mistress in a most uncouth manner : he hath also a pert and petulant note when he attacks his adversary. When a hen turkey leads forth her young brood, she keeps a watchful eye ; and if a bird of prey appear, though ever so high in the air, the careful mother announces the enemy with a little inward moan, and watches him with a

* Syme makes the following judicious remarks upon the songs of birds : — " The notes of soft-billed birds are finely toned, mellow, and plaintive ; those of the hard-billed species are sprightly, cheerful, and rapid. This difference proceeds from the construction of the larynx ; as a large pipe of an organ produces a deeper and more mellow-toned note than a small pipe ; so the trachea of the nightingale, which is wider than that of the canary, sends forth a deeper and more mellow-toned note. Soft-billed birds, also, sing more from the lower part of their throat than the hard-billed species. This, together with the greater width of the larynx of the nightingale and other soft-billed warblers, fully accounts for their soft, round, mellow notes, compared with the shrill, sharp, and clear notes of the canary and other hard-billed songsters. In a comprehensive sense, the complete song of birds includes all the notes they are capable of uttering, and, taken in this sense, it is analogous to the speech of man." — Ed.

steady and attentive look; but, if he approach, her note becomes earnest and alarming, and her outcries are redoubled.

No inhabitants of a yard seem possessed of such a variety of expression, and so copious a language, as common poultry. Take a chicken of four or five days old, and hold it up to a window where there are flies, and it will immediately seize its prey with little twitterings of complacency; but if you tender it a wasp or a bee, at once its note becomes harsh, and expressive of disapprobation and a sense of danger. When a pullet is ready to lay, she intimates the event by a joyous and easy soft note. Of all the occurrences of their life, that of laying seems to be the most important; for no sooner has a hen disburdened herself, than she rushes forth with a clamorous kind of joy, which the cock and the rest of his mistresses immediately adopt. The tumult is not confined to the family concerned, but catches from yard to yard, and spreads to every homestead within hearing, till at last the whole village is in an uproar. As soon as a hen becomes a mother, her new relation demands a new language; she then runs clucking and screaming about, and seems agitated as if possessed. The father of the flock has also a considerable vocabulary: if he finds food, he calls a favourite concubine to partake; and if a bird of prey passes over, with a warning voice, he bids his family beware. The gallant chanticleer has, at command, his amorous phrases, and his terms of defiance. But the sound by which he is best known is his crowing: by this he has been distinguished in all ages as the countryman's clock or larum,— as the watchman that proclaims the divisions of the night. Thus the poet elegantly styles him

> —— the crested cock, whose clarion sounds
> The silent hours.

A neighbouring gentleman, one summer, had lost most of his chickens by a sparrow-hawk, that came gliding down, between a fagot pile and the end of his house, to the place where the coops stood. The owner, inwardly vexed to see his flock thus diminishing, hung a setting net adroitly between the pile and the house, into which the caitiff dashed, and was entangled. Resentment suggested the law of retaliation; he, therefore, clipped the hawk's wings, cut off his talons, and, fixing a cork on his bill, threw him down among the brood-hens. Imagination cannot paint the scene that ensued; the expressions that fear, rage, and revenge inspired, were new, or at least such as had been unnoticed before. The exasperated matrons upbraided — they execrated — they insulted — they triumphed. In a word, they never desisted from buffeting their adversary till they had torn him in a hundred pieces.

LETTER LXXXVI.

TO THE HON. DAINES BARRINGTON.

SELBORNE.

——— monstrent

Quid tantùm Oceano properent se tingere soles
Hyberni; vel quæ tardis mora noctibus obstet.

GENTLEMEN who have outlets might contrive to make ornament subservient to utility; a pleasing eye-trap might also contribute to promote science: an obelisk in a garden or park might be both an embellishment and a heliotrope.

Any person that is curious, and enjoys the advantage of a good horizon, might, with little trouble, make two heliotropes, the one for the winter, the other for the summer solstice; and these two erections might be constructed with very little expense; for two pieces of timber frame-work, about ten or twelve feet high, and four feet broad at the base, and close lined with plank, would answer the purpose.

The erection for the former should, if possible, be placed within sight of some window in the common sitting parlour; because men, at that dead season of the year, are usually within doors at the close of the day; while that for the latter might be fixed for any given spot in the garden or outlet, whence the owner might contemplate, in a fine summer's evening, the utmost extent that the sun makes to the northward at the season of the longest days. Now nothing would be necessary but to place these two objects with so much exactness, that the westerly limb of the sun, at setting, might but just clear the winter heliotrope to the west of it, on the shortest day, and that the whole disc of the sun, at the longest day, might exactly, at setting, also clear the summer heliotrope to the north of it. *

---

* Mr Mark Watt has invented a very curious and interesting instrument, which he calls the heliastron, or solar compass. Having observed the daily variation of barometers and the magnetic needle, and remarking that a similar series of alternate changes were more or less observable in every instrument capable of indicating a slight alteration of the impressions made on them, and that these diurnal changes bore a proportionate

By this simple expedient, it would soon appear, that there is no such thing, strictly speaking, as a solstice; for, from the shortest day, the owner would, every clear evening, see the disc advancing, at its setting, to the westward of the object; and, from the ongest day, observe the sun retiring backwards every evening, at its setting, towards the object westward, till, in a few nights, it would set quite behind it, and so by degrees to the west of it; for when the sun comes near the summer solstice, the whole disc of it would at first set behind the object: after a time, the northern limb would first appear, and so every night gradually more, till at length the whole diameter would set northward of it for about three nights; but, on the middle night of the three, sensibly more remote than the former or following. When beginning its recess from the summer tropic, it would continue more and more to be hidden every night, till at length it would descend quite behind the object again; and so nightly more and more to the westward.

relation to the latitude in which the instruments were placed, or to the degrees of solar influence that might exist in the regions in which they were used, and of which they would partake; he also noticed, in coincidence with these movements, the daily expansion and contraction of the petals and leaves of most plants, and that the different species of the heliotropium and chrysanthemum, turned their corollæ round toward the sun for many hours during the day. Hence he concluded that an instrument might be constructed upon principles nearly similar to the laws which regulate these motions in plants.

This instrument he formed of a circular ring of cork, three inches in diameter. Into this is fixed twenty-five needles fully impregnated with the magnetic fluid, and these are placed at equal distances round the circumference of the circle, with their north and south poles placed outwards alternately. This circle is affixed to a light slip of wood, five inches long, and one-fourth of an inch broad, by a piece of copper wire, of a semicircular form, the extremities of which are passed through the opposite sides of the cork's circle; and the slip of wood attached to the centre of the wire. Into the centre of the bar is fixed an agate cup; and the whole traverses like a compass needle upon a fine steel point, the bar of wood being equipoised by a small weight at the end of it, equivalent to the weight of the needles. This instrument, when placed with a disc of purple velvet across the needles, in the sun's rays, continued to revolve nearly the whole day, moving always in the direction from east to west by south, in the course of the sun's apparent motion. It moves forty or fifty degrees to the light of a single candle held close to the side of the circle. A piece of clear amber, formed into a convex lens, if fixed into a circle of cork, and suspended by a fine hair or filament, under a glass cover, will also be arrested by the incidence of the solar rays, and will continue to present its surface to the sun, if unclouded, as long as he is invisible above the horizon.

It is, perhaps, not generally known, that the conducting power of living plants, in favouring the rapid distribution of electricity, has been reckoned three millions of times greater than that of water. — ED.

LETTER LXXXVII.

TO THE HON. DAINES BARRINGTON.

SELBORNE.

——— Mugire videbis
Sub pedibus terram, et descendere montibus ornos.

WHEN I was a boy, I used to read, with astonishment and
implicit assent, accounts in Baker's *Chronicle* of walking hills
and travelling mountains. John Philips, in his *Cyder,* alludes
to the credit that was given to such stories with a delicate but
quaint vein of humour, peculiar to the author of the *Splendid
Shilling :*

> I nor advise, nor reprehend, the choice
> Of Marcley Hill ; * the apple no where finds
> A kinder mould : yet 'tis unsafe to trust
> Deceitful ground : who knows but that, once more,
> This mount may journey, and, his present site
> Forsaking, to thy neighbour's bounds transfer
> The goodly plants, affording matter strange
> For law debates !

But, when I came to consider better, I began to suspect
that, though our hills may never have journeyed far, yet that
the ends of many of them have slipped and fallen away at
distant periods, leaving the cliffs bare and abrupt. This seems
to have been the case with Nore and Whetham Hills, and
especially with the ridge between Harteley Park and Ward-
le-ham, where the ground has slid into vast swellings and
furrows, and lies still in such romantic confusion as cannot be
accounted for from any other cause. A strange event, that
happened not long since, justifies our suspicions ; which,
though it befell not within the limits of this parish, yet as it
was within the hundred of Selborne, and as the circumstances
were singular, may fairly claim a place in a work of this nature.

---

* Marcley Hill is near the confluence of the Lug and Wye, about six
miles east of Hereford. In the year 1595, it was, after roaring and shaking
in a terrible manner for three days together, about six o'clock on Sunday
evening, put in motion, and continued moving for eight hours, in which
time it advanced upwards of two hundred feet from its first situation, and
mounted twelve fathoms higher than it was before. In the place where
it set out, it left a gap four hundred feet long, and three hundred and
twenty broad ; and in its progress it overthrew a chapel, together with
trees and houses that stood in its way. — ED.

The months of January and February in the year 1774, were remarkable for great melting snows and vast gluts of rain, so that, by the end of the latter month, the land-springs, or levants, began to prevail, and to be near as high as in the memorable winter of 1764. The beginning of March also went on in the same tenor, when, in the night between the 8th and 9th of that month, a considerable part of the great woody hanger at Hawkley was torn from its place, and fell down, leaving a high freestone cliff naked and bare, and resembling the steep side of a chalk-pit. It appears that this huge fragment, being, perhaps, sapped and undermined by waters, foundered, and was ingulfed, going down in a perpendicular direction; for a gate, which stood in the field on the top of the hill, after sinking with its posts for thirty or forty feet, remained in so true and upright a position, as to open and shut with great exactness, just as in its first situation. Several oaks also are still standing, and in a state of vegetation, after taking the same desperate leap. That great part of this prodigious mass was absorbed in some gulf below, is plain also from the inclining ground at the bottom of the hill, which is free and unencumbered, but would have been buried in heaps of rubbish, had the fragment parted and fallen forward. About an hundred yards from the foot of this hanging coppice stood a cottage by the side of a lane; and two hundred yards lower, on the other side of the lane, was a farm-house, in which lived a labourer and his family; and just by, a stout new barn. The cottage was inhabited by an old woman and her son, and his wife. These people, in the evening, which was very dark and tempestuous, observed that the brick floors of their kitchens began to heave and part, and that the walls seemed to open, and the roofs to crack; but they all agree that no tremor of the ground, indicating an earthquake, was ever felt, only that the wind continued to make a most tremendous roaring in the woods and hangers. The miserable inhabitants, not daring to go to bed, remained in the utmost solicitude and confusion, expecting every moment to be buried under the ruins of their shattered edifices. When daylight came, they were at leisure to contemplate the devastations of the night. They then found that a deep rift, or chasm, had opened under their houses, and torn them, as it were, in two, and that one end of the barn had suffered in a similar manner: that a pond near the cottage had undergone a strange reverse, becoming deep at the shallow end, and so *vice versa*: that many large oaks were removed out of their perpendicular some thrown down, and some fallen into the heads of neighbouring trees ; and that a gate was thrust forward, with its hedge, full six feet, so as to require a new track to be made to it. From the foot of the cliff, the general course of the ground, which is pasture, inclines in a moderate descent for half a mile, and is interspersed with some hillocks, which were rifted in every direction, as well towards the great woody hanger as from it. In the first pasture the deep clefts began, and, running across the lane and under the buildings, made such vast shelves that the road was impassable for some time ; and so over to an arable field on the other side, which was strangely torn and disordered. The second pasture field, being more soft and springy, was protruded forward without many fissures in the turf, which was raised in long ridges resembling graves, lying at right angles to the motion. At the bottom of this enclosure, the soil and turf rose many feet against the bodies of some oaks that obstructed their farther course, and terminated this awful commotion. *

* There are numerous instances on record of mountain slips of this kind, in various places of the world ; indeed, they are almost of daily occurrence, to a greater or lesser extent. That which is recorded by our author, is trifling when compared to some others. We may particularize the fall of Mount Rusfi, in Switzerland, which took place in 1806. " Here," says Saussure, writing on the spot, " but three weeks ago, was one of the most delightfully fertile valleys of all Switzerland, green and luxuriant, adorned with little villages, full of secure and happy farmers. Now, three of these villages are for ever erased from the face of the earth, and an extended desolation, burying alive several hundred peasants, overspreads the valley of Lowertz."

Early in the evening of the second of September, an immense projection of the mountain of Rusfi gave way, and was precipitated into the valley. In four minutes, it completely overwhelmed three villages, and part of two others. The torrent of earth and stones was more rapid than that of lava, and its effects as irresistible and terrible. The mountain, in its tremendous descent, carried trees, rocks, houses, and every thing before it ; the mass spread in every direction, so as to bury completely a space of charming country, more than three miles square. The force of the earth was so great, that it not only overspread the hollow of the valley, but even ascended to a considerable height on the side of the opposite mountain.

Part of the falling mass rolled into the lake of Lowertz, filling a fifth part of it up ; and raised the water so much, that two islands within it, and the village of Sever, were, for a time, completely overwhelmed by the swell. By this frightful catastrophe, four hundred and thirty-four individuals lost their lives ; and there were also lost one hundred and seventy cows and horses, and one hundred and three goats and sheep ; eighty-seven meadows destroyed, sixty meadows damaged ; ninety-three houses entirely destroyed, eight houses damaged, and uninhabitable ; one hundred and sixty-six cow-houses, barns, &c. destroyed, and nineteen damaged. — Ed.

The perpendicular height of the precipice, in general, is twenty-three yards ; the length of the lapse, or slip, as seen from the fields below, one hundred and eighty-one ; and a partial fall, concealed in the coppice, extends seventy yards more : so that the total length of this fragment that fell was two hundred and fifty-one yards.　About fifty acres of land suffered from this violent convulsion ; two houses were entirely destroyed ; one end of a new barn was left in ruins, the walls being cracked through the very stones that composed them ; a hanging coppice was changed to a naked rock ; and some grass grounds and an arable field so broken and rifted by the chasms, as to be rendered, for a time, neither fit for the plough, nor safe for pasturage, till considerable labour and expense had been bestowed in levelling the surface, and filling in the gaping fissures.

LETTER LXXXVIII.

TO THE HON. DAINES BARRINGTON.

SELBORNE.

Resonant arbusta.

THERE is a steep abrupt pasture field, interspersed with furze, close to the back of this village, well known by the name of the Short Lithe, consisting of a rocky dry soil, and inclining to the afternoon sun.　This spot abounds with the *gryllus campestris*, or field-cricket ;* which, though frequent in these parts, is by no means a common insect in many other counties.

As their cheerful summer cry cannot but draw the attention of a naturalist, I have often gone down to examine the economy of these *grylli*, and study their mode of life ; but they are so shy and cautious that it is no easy matter to get a sight of them ; for, feeling a person's footsteps as he advances, they stop short in the midst of their song, and retire backward nimbly into their burrows, where they lurk till all suspicion of danger is over.

At first, we attempted to dig them out with a spade, but without any great success ; for either we could not get to the bottom of the hole, which often terminated under a great stone, or else, in breaking up the ground, we inadvertently squeezed the poor insect to death.　Out of one so bruised, we

---

* *Acheta campestris,* Fabricius. — ED.

took a multitude of eggs, which were long and narrow, of a yellow colour, and covered with a very tough skin. By this accident, we learned to distinguish the male from the female; the former of which is shining black, with a golden stripe across his shoulders; the latter is more dusky, more capacious about the abdomen, and carries a long sword-shaped weapon at her tail, which probably is the instrument with which she deposits her eggs in crannies and safe receptacles.

Where violent methods will not avail, more gentle means will often succeed; and so it proved in the present case: for, though a spade be too boisterous and rough an implement, a pliant stalk of grass, gently insinuated into the caverns, will probe their windings to the bottom, and quickly bring out the inhabitant; and thus the humane inquirer may gratify his curiosity without injuring the object of it.* It is remarkable, that, though these insects are furnished with long legs behind, and brawny thighs for leaping, like grasshoppers, yet, when driven from their holes, they shew no activity, but crawl along in a shiftless manner, so as easily to be taken; and again, though provided with a curious apparatus of wings, yet they never exert them when there seems to be the greatest occasion. The males only make that shrilling noise, perhaps out of rivalry and emulation, as is the case with many animals which exert some sprightly note during their breeding time: it is raised by a brisk friction of one wing against the other. They are solitary beings, living singly male or female, each as it may happen; but there must be a time when the sexes have some intercourse, and then the wings may be useful, perhaps, during the hours of night. When the males meet, they will fight fiercely, as I found by some which I put into the crevices of a dry stone wall, where I should have been glad to have made them settle; for though they seemed distressed by being taken out of their knowledge, yet the first that got possession of the chinks would seize on any that were obtruded upon them, with a vast row of serrated fangs. With their strong jaws,

---

* The children in France amuse themselves in the fields hunting the field-cricket. They put into the hole of that insect an ant, to which a long hair is attached, and allowing the little animal to penetrate to the bottom of the burrow, they then draw it out, and the cricket always follows it, and in this manner is captured. Pliny informs us of a simple method of taking this insect, which is, by thrusting a slender piece of stick to the bottom of their burrow, when the cricket immediately gets upon it to know the reason of the intrusion, and is thus easily secured. This simplicity of the animal no doubt gave rise to the proverb *stultior grillo*, — more foolish than a cricket. — ED.

toothed like the shears of a lobster's claws, they perforate and round their curious regular cells, having no fore-claws to dig, like the mole-cricket. When taken in hand, I could not but wonder that they never offered to defend themselves, though armed with such formidable weapons. Of such herbs as grow before the mouths of their burrows, they eat indiscriminately; and, on a little platform, which they make just by, they drop their dung; and never in the day-time seem to stir more than two or three inches from home. Sitting in the entrance of their caverns, they chirp all night as well as day, from the middle of the month of May to the middle of July; and, in hot weather, when they are most vigorous, they make the hills echo; and, in the still hours of darkness, may be heard to a considerable distance. In the beginning of the season, their notes are more faint and inward; but become louder as the summer advances, and so die away again by degrees.

Sounds do not always give us pleasure according to their sweetness and melody; nor do harsh sounds always displease. We are more apt to be captivated or disgusted with the associations which they promote, than with the notes themselves. Thus the shrilling of the field-cricket, though sharp and stridulous, yet marvellously delights some hearers, filling their minds with a train of summer ideas of every thing that is rural, verdurous, and joyous.

About the 10th of March, the crickets appear at the mouths of their cells, which they then open and bore, and shape very elegantly. All that ever I have seen at that season were in their pupa state, and had only the rudiments of wings lying under a skin, or coat, which must be cast before the insect can arrive at its perfect state;* from whence I should suppose that the old ones of last year do not always survive the winter. In August, their holes begin to be obliterated, and the insects are seen no more till spring.

Not many summers ago, I endeavoured to transplant a colony to the terrace in my garden, by boring deep holes in the sloping turf. The new inhabitants staid some time, and fed and sung; but wandered away by degrees, and were heard at a farther distance every morning; so that it appears that, on this emergency, they made use of their wings in attempting to return to the spot from which they were taken.

One of these crickets, when confined in a paper cage, and

---

* We have observed that they cast these skins in April, which are then seen lying at the mouths of their holes.

set in the sun, and supplied with plants moistened with water, will feed and thrive, and become so merry and loud as to be irksome in the same room where a person is sitting : if the plants are not wetted, it will die.

LETTER LXXXIX.

TO THE HON. DAINES BARRINGTON.

SELBORNE.

Far from all resort of mirth
Save the cricket on the hearth.
MILTON's *Il Penseroso.*

DEAR SIR,—While many other insects must be sought after in fields, and woods, and waters, the *gryllus domesticus,* * or house-cricket, resides altogether within our dwellings, intruding itself upon our notice whether we will or no. This species delights in new-built houses, being, like the spider, pleased with the moisture of the walls ; and, besides, the softness of the mortar enables them to burrow and mine between the joints of the bricks or stones, and to open communications from one room to another. They are particularly fond of kitchens and bakers' ovens, on account of their perpetual warmth. †

Tender insects that live abroad either enjoy only the short period of one summer, or else doze away the cold uncomfortable months in profound slumbers ; but these, residing as it were in a torrid zone, are always alert and merry ; a good Christmas fire is to them like the heats of the dog-days. Though they are frequently heard by day, yet is their natural time of motion only in the night. As soon as it grows dusk, the chirping increases, and they come running forth, and are from the size of a flea to that of their full stature. As one should suppose,

* *Acheta domestica,* Fabricius. — ED.

† These animals are exceedingly pugnacious, and fight desperately with each other. We have frequently captured crickets, and, having put them into a tumbler covered with paper, have witnessed their battles. Upon more than one occasion we have known them eat each other. We left three of them together in a tumbler, along with some pieces of bread, and, on examining them on the following day, two had been completely devoured, except three of the limbs and the antennæ. The survivor was quite brisk and lively. In return for his misdeeds, we terminated the existence of this insect cannibal, and placed him in our cabinet. Latreille informs us that this cricket eats only insects, and certainly thrives well in houses infested by cockroches. We had always supposed that they lived upon bread, until we discovered them devouring each other. — ED.

from the burning atmosphere which they inhabit, they are a thirsty race, and shew a great propensity for liquids, being found frequently drowned in pans of water, milk, broth, or the like.   Whatever is moist they affect ; and, therefore, often gnaw holes in wet woollen stockings and aprons that are hung .o the fire ; they are the housewife's barometer, foretelling-her when it will rain ; and are prognostics sometimes, she thinks, of ill or good luck ; of the death of a near relation, or the approach of an absent lover.   By being the constant companions of her solitary hours, they naturally become the objects of her superstition. *   These crickets are not only very thirsty, but very voracious; for they will eat the scummings of pots, and yeast, salt, and crumbs of bread ; and any kitchen offal or sweepings.   In the summer we have observed them to fly, when it became dusk, out of the windows, and over the neighbouring roofs.   This feat of activity accounts for the sudden manner in which they often leave their haunts, as it does for the method by which they come to houses where they were not known before.   It is remarkable, that many sorts of insects seem never to use their wings but when they have a mind to shift their quarters and settle new colonies.   When in the air, they move *volatu undoso*, in waves, or curves, like woodpeckers, opening and shutting their wings at every stroke, and so are always rising or sinking.

When they increase to a great degree, as they did once in the house where I am now writing, they become noisome pests, flying into the candles, and dashing into people's faces ; but may be blasted and destroyed by gunpowder discharged into their crevices and crannies.   In families, at such times, they are, like Pharaoh's plague of frogs, " in their bed-chambers, and upon their beds, and in their ovens, and in their kneading-troughs." †   Their shrilling noise is occasioned by a brisk attrition of their wings.   Cats catch hearth-crickets, and, playing with them as they do with mice, devour them. Crickets may be destroyed, like wasps, by phials half filled with beer, or any liquid, and set in their haunts ; for, being always eager to drink, they will crowd in till the bottles are full.

* Sir William Jardine says, that, in Dumfriesshire, it is considered lucky to have crickets in a house ; but if they disappear from one which they have long inhabited, it is looked upon as foreboding some calamity to the family. — ED.
† Exod. viii. 3.

LETTER XC.

TO THE HON. DAINES BARRINGTON.

SELBORNE.

How diversified are the modes of life, not only of incongruous, but even of congenerous animals! and yet their specific distinctions are not more various than their propensities. Thus, while the field-cricket delights in sunny, dry banks, and the house-cricket rejoices amidst the glowing heat of the kitchen hearth or oven, the *gryllus gryllotalpa* (the mole-cricket) haunts moist meadows, and frequents the sides of ponds, and banks of streams, performing all its functions in a swampy wet soil. With a pair of fore-feet, curiously adapted to the purpose, it burrows and works under ground like the mole, raising a ridge as it proceeds, but seldom throwing up hillocks.*

As mole-crickets often infest gardens by the sides of canals, they are unwelcome guests to the gardener, raising up ridges in their subterraneous progress, and rendering the walks unsightly. If they take to the kitchen quarters, they occasion great damage among the plants and roots, by destroying whole beds of cabbages, young legumes, and flowers. When dug out, they seem very slow and helpless, and make no use of their wings by day; but at night they come abroad, and make long excursions, as I have been convinced by finding stragglers, in a morning, in improbable places. In fine weather, about the middle of April, and just at the close of day, they begin to solace themselves with a low, dull, jarring note, continued for a long time without interruption, and not unlike the chattering of the fern-owl, or goat-sucker, but more inward.

---

* This is the *gryllotalpa vulgaris* of Latreille; the structure of its arms and fore-feet fit it in a peculiar manner for these operations, being of great strength, and moved by a set of muscles admirably fitted for the purpose of digging, giving vigour to these parts. The breast consists of a hard and thick horny substance, strengthened within by a double frame-work of tough gristle, in the front edge of which the shoulder-blades are firmly articulated. This structure seems intended to prevent the breast from being injured by the powerful muscles of the arms during the operation of digging. The arms are powerfully formed, and of great breadth, in proportion to the size of the animal; the feet are shaped like two broad hands, and provided with four large broad-based and sharp claws, pointing somewhat obliquely outwards, like the hands of the mole, this being the direction in which the animal digs, throwing the earth on both sides as it advances. — ED.

About the beginning of May, they lay their eggs, as I was once an eye-witness; for a gardener, at a house where I was on a visit, happening to be mowing, on the 6th of that month, by the side of a canal, his scythe struck too deep, pared off a large piece of turf, and laid open to view a curious scene of domestic economy :—

> ———— ingentem lato dedit ore fenestram ;
> Apparet domus intus, et atria longa patescunt :
> Apparent ———————— penetralia.

There were many caverns and winding passages leading to a kind of chamber, neatly smoothed and rounded, and about the size of a moderate snuff-box.   Within the secret nursery were deposited near an hundred eggs, of a dirty yellow colour, and enveloped in a tough skin ; but too lately excluded to contain any rudiments of young, being full of a viscous substance. The eggs lay but shallow, and within the influence of the sun, just under a little heap of fresh moved mould, like that which is raised by ants.

When mole-crickets fly, they move *cursu undoso*, rising and falling in curves, like the other species mentioned before.   In different parts of this kingdom, people call them fen-crickets, churr-worms, and eve-churrs, — all very apposite names.

Anatomists, who have examined the intestines of these insects, astonish me with their accounts : for they say, that from the structure, position, and number of their stomachs, or maws, there seems to be good reason to suppose that this and the two former species ruminate, or chew the cud like many quadrupeds !

LETTER XCI.

TO THE HON. DAINES BARRINGTON.

SELBORNE, *May* 7, 1779.

It is now more than forty years that I have paid some attention to the ornithology of this district, without being able to exhaust the subject : new occurrences still arise as long as any inquiries are kept alive.

In the last week of last month, five of those most rare birds, too uncommon to have obtained an English name, but known to naturalists by the terms of *himantopus*, or *loripes*, and *charadrius himantopus*,* were shot upon the verge of Frinsham Pond,

* This is the long-legged plover of Bewick, and other British authors. — ED.

a large lake belonging to the Bishop of Winchester, and lying between Wolmer Forest and the town of Farnham, in the county of Surrey. The pond-keeper says there were three brace in the flock; but that, after he had satisfied his curiosity, he suffered the sixth to remain unmolested. One of these specimens I procured, and found the length of the legs to be so extraordinary, that, at first sight, one might have supposed the shanks had been fastened on to impose on the credulity of the beholder: they were legs in *caricatura;* and had we seen such proportions on a Chinese or Japan screen, we should have made large allowances for the fancy of the draughtsman. These birds are of the plover family, and might, with propriety, be called the stilt-plovers. Brisson, under that idea, gives them the apposite name of *l'échasse*. My specimen, when drawn, and stuffed with pepper, weighed only four ounces and a quarter, though the naked part of the thigh measured three inches and a half, and the legs four inches and a half : Hence we may safely assert, that these birds exhibit, weight for inches, incomparably the greatest length of legs of any known bird. The flamingo, for instance, is one of the most long-legged birds, and yet it bears no manner of proportion to the himantopus; for a cock flamingo weighs, at an average, about four pounds avoirdupois; and his legs and thighs measure usually about twenty inches. But four pounds are fifteen times and a fraction more than four ounces and one quarter : and if four ounces and a quarter have eight inches of legs, four pounds must have one hundred and twenty inches and a fraction of legs, viz. somewhat more than ten feet,—such a monstrous proportion as the world never saw! If you should try the experiment in still larger birds, the disparity would still increase. It must be matter of great curiosity to see the stilt-plover move; to observe how it can wield such a length of lever with such feeble muscles as the thighs seem to be furnished with. At best, one should expect it to be but a bad walker : but what adds to the wonder is, that it has no back toe. Now, without that steady prop to support its steps, it must be liable, in speculation, to perpetual vacillations, and seldom able to preserve the true centre of gravity.

The old name of *himantopus* is taken from Pliny; and, by an awkward metaphor, implies that the legs are as slender and pliant as if cut out of a thong of leather. Neither Willughby nor Ray, in all their curious researches, either at home or abroad, ever saw this bird. Mr Pennant never met with it in all Great Britain, but observed it often in the cabinets of the curious at Paris. Hasselquist says, that it migrates to Egypt in the autumn ; and a most accurate observer of nature has assured me, that he has found it on the banks of the streams in Andalusia.

Our writers record it to have been found only twice in Great Britain. From all these relations it plainly appears, that these long-legged plovers are birds of South Europe, and rarely visit our island ; and when they do, are wanderers and stragglers, and impelled to make so distant and northern an excursion, from motives or accidents, for which we are not able to account. One thing may fairly be deduced, that these birds come over to us from the Continent, since nobody can suppose that a species not noticed once in an age, and of such a remarkable make, can constantly breed unobserved in this kingdom.*

LETTER XCII.

TO THE HON. DAINES BARRINGTON.

SELBORNE, *April* 21; 1780.

DEAR SIR,— The old Sussex tortoise, that I have mentioned to you so often, is become my property. I dug it out of its winter dormitory in March last, when it was enough awakened to express its resentments by hissing ; and, packing it in a box with earth, carried it eighty miles in post chaises. The rattle and hurry of the journey so perfectly roused it, that when I turned it out on a border, it walked twice down to the bottom of my garden : however, in the evening, the weather being cold, it buried itself in the loose mould, and continues still concealed.

As it will be under my eye, I shall now have an opportunity of enlarging my observations on its mode of life, and propensities ; and perceive already, that, towards the time of coming forth, it opens a breathing-place in the ground near its head, requiring, I conclude, a freer respiration as it becomes more alive. This creature not only goes under the earth from the middle of November to the middle of April, but sleeps great part of the summer ; for it goes to bed, in the longest days, at four in the afternoon, and often does not stir in the morning

---

* This bird is a widely diffused species, being common in Egypt, the shores of the Caspian Sea, the southern deserts of Independent Tartary, and Madras, in the East Indies. — ED.

till late. Besides, it retires to rest for every shower, and does not move at all in wet days. *

When one reflects on the state of this strange being, it is a matter of wonder, to find that Providence should bestow such a profusion of days, such a seeming waste of longevity, on a reptile that appears to relish it so little as to squander more than two-thirds of its existence in a joyless stupor, and be lost to all sensation for months together in the profoundest of slumbers.

While I was writing this letter, a moist and warm afternoon, with the thermometer at 50, brought forth troops of shell-snails ; and, at the same juncture, the tortoise heaved up the mould and put out its head ; and the next morning came forth, as it were raised from the dead, and walked about till four in the afternoon. This was a curious coincidence — a very amusing occurrence — to see such a similarity of feelings between two φερσοικοι,—for so the Greeks call both the shell-snail and the tortoise. †

Summer birds are, this cold and backward spring, unusually

---

* Dr Bright mentions that land-tortoises are used as food in Hungary. He says, " In the evening I was taken to see another object of curiosity, —the garden kept for the rearing and preservation of land-tortoises. The *testudo orbicularis* is the species most common about the lake, and the river Szala, which falls into it. Tortoises, likewise, occur in great numbers in various parts of Hungary, more particularly about Füxes Gyarmath, and the marshes of the river Theiss ; and being deemed a delicacy for the table, are caught and kept in preserves. That of Keszthely encloses about an acre of land, intersected by trenches and ponds, in which the animals feed and enjoy themselves. In one corner was a space separated from the rest by boards two feet high, forming a pen for snails, which here, as well as in Germany, are in request as an article of food. The upper edge of the boards were spiked with nails an inch in height, and at intervals of half an inch, over which, I was assured, these animals never attempt to make their way. This snail, the *helix pomatia,* is in great demand in Vienna, where sacks of them are regularly exposed for sale in the markets, alternating with sacks of beans, lentils, kidney-beans, and truffles." The *helix pomatia* is now ranked among the British land snails. It is the largest of our land shells ; is pretty abundant in some of the southern counties of England ; and was introduced by the luxurious Romans, during their residence in Britain. — Ed.

† Snail shells remain in a torpid state during the winter, in the holes of walls, in the ground, or under large stones. They, however, sometimes make their appearance in winter, if the weather should be very mild, and particularly in moist or rainy days. These animals have a wonderful faculty of living, for a great length of time, without food. They have been known to exist in a drawer, or box, without nutriment of any kind, for two or three years. — Ed.

late : I have seen but one swallow yet. This conformity with the weather convinces me more and more that they sleep in the winter.

MORE PARTICULARS RESPECTING THE OLD FAMILY TORTOISE.

BECAUSE we call this creature an abject reptile, we are too apt to undervalue his abilities, and depreciate his powers of instinct. Yet he is, as Mr Pope says of his lord,

Much too wise to walk into a well ;

and has so much discernment as not to fall down a haha, but to stop and withdraw from the brink with the readiest precaution.

Though he loves warm weather, he avoids the hot sun; because his thick shell, when once heated, would, as the poet says of solid armour, " scald with safety." He therefore spends the more sultry hours under the umbrella of a large cabbage leaf, or amidst the waving forests of an asparagus bed.

But as he avoids the heat in summer, so, in the decline of the year, he improves the faint autumnal beams, by getting within the reflection of a fruit wall ; and, though he never has read that planes inclining to the horizon receive a greater share of warmth,* he inclines his shell, by tilting it against the wall, to collect and admit every feeble ray.

Pitiable seems the condition of this poor embarrassed reptile ; to be cased in a suit of ponderous armour, which he cannot lay aside ; to be imprisoned, as it were, within his own shell, must preclude, we should suppose, all activity and disposition for enterprise. Yet there is a season of the year (usually the beginning of June) when his exertions are remarkable. He then walks on tiptoe, and is stirring by five in the morning ; and, traversing the garden, examines every wicket and interstice in the fences, through which he will escape if possible ; and often has eluded the care of the gardener, and wandered to some distant field. The motives that impel him to undertake these rambles seem to be of the amorous kind : his fancy then becomes intent on sexual attachments, which transport him beyond his usual gravity, and induce him to forget for a time his ordinary solemn deportment.

---

* Several years ago a book was written entitled, "Fruit walls improved by inclining them to the horizon ; " in which the author has shewn, by calculation, that a much greater number of the rays of the sun will fall on such walls than on those which are perpendicular.

LETTER XCIII.

TO THOMAS PENNANT, ESQ.

A PAIR of honey-buzzards, *buteo apivorus, sive vespivorus,* Raii, built them a large shallow nest, composed of twigs, and lined with dead beechen leaves, upon a tall slender beech near the middle of Selborne hanger, in the summer of 1780. In the middle of the month of June, a bold boy climbed this tree, though standing on so steep and dizzy a situation, and brought down an egg, the only one in the nest, which had been sat on for some time, and contained the embryo of a young bird. The egg was smaller, and not so round, as those of the common buzzard; was dotted at each end with small red spots, and surrounded in the middle with a broad bloody zone.

The hen bird was shot, and answered exactly to Mr Ray's description of that species: had a black cere, short thick legs, and a long tail. When on the wing, this species may be easily distinguished from the common buzzard, by its hawk-like appearance, small head, wings not so blunt, and longer tail. This specimen contained in its craw some limbs of frogs, and many gray snails without shells. The irides of the eyes of this bird were of a beautiful bright yellow colour.

About the tenth of July, in the same summer, a pair of sparrow-hawks bred in an old crow's nest on a low beech in the same hanger;* and as their brood, which was numerous, began to grow up, became so daring and ravenous, that they were a terror to all the dames in the village that had chickens or ducklings under their care. A boy climbed the tree, and found the young so fledged that they all escaped from him; but discovered that a good house had been kept; the larder was well stored with provisions; for he brought down a young blackbird, jay, and house-marten, all clean picked, and some

---

* Professor Rennie says, "Although I have known this bird frequently take possession of the abandoned nest of a crow or a magpie, without making any additional repairs, I have also known it breed in the holes of precipitous rocks, as at Howford, near Mauchline, in Ayrshire, and Cartlan Crags, near Lanark."

The sparrow-hawk is a bold, audacious bird, and builds frequently in the most frequented situations. Some years ago, when on a visit to Lord Douglas, at Douglas Castle, Lanarkshire, we discovered a nest close to the approach, and not far distant from the east gate. We were desirous to possess the birds, and his lordship gave orders to the gamekeeper to shoot them, but he only killed the female. — ED.

half devoured.* The old birds had been observed to make sad havoc for some days among the new-flown swallows and martens, which, being but lately out of their nests, had not acquired those powers and command of wing that enable them, when more mature, to set such enemies at defiance.

LETTER XCIV.

TO THOMAS PENNANT, ESQ.

SELBORNE, *November* 30, 1780.

DEAR SIR,—Every incident that occasions a renewal of our correspondence will ever be pleasing and agreeable to me.

As to the wild wood-pigeon, the *oenas*, or *vinago*, of Ray, I am much of your mind; and see no reason for making it the origin of the common house-dove: but suppose those that have advanced that opinion may have been misled by another appellation, often given to the *oenas*, which is that of stock-dove.

Unless the stock-dove in the winter varies greatly in manners from itself in summer, no species seems more unlikely to be domesticated, and to make a house-dove. We very rarely see the latter settle on trees at all, nor does it ever haunt the woods; but the former, as long as it stays with us, from November perhaps to February, lives the same wild life with the ring-dove, (*palumbus torquatus ;*) frequents coppices and groves, supports itself chiefly by mast, and delights to roost in the tallest beeches. Could it be known in what manner stock-doves build, the doubt would be settled with me at once, provided they construct their nests on trees, like the ring-dove, as I much suspect they do.

You received, you say, last spring, a stock-dove from Sussex ; and are informed that they sometimes breed in that country. But why did not your correspondent determine the place of its nidification, whether on rocks, cliffs, or trees? If he was not an adroit ornithologist. I should doubt the fact, because people

---

* Speaking of the cruel propensities of this bird, Montagu says, " The more generous hawks, we have frequently observed, kill their prey as soon as caught, by eating the head first ; whereas the buzzards, in particular, begin eating their prey indiscriminately. We have several times taken partridges and other birds from them, which had one side of the breast or a thigh devoured, and the bird still alive."— ED.

with us perpetually confound the stock-dove with the ring-
dove. *

For my own part, I readily concur with you in supposing
that house-doves are derived from the small blue rock-pigeon,
for many reasons.   In the first place, the wild stock-dove is
manifestly larger than the common house-dove, against the
usual rule of domestication, which generally enlarges the
breed.   Again, those two remarkable black spots on the
remiges of each wing of the stock-dove, which are so characteristic of the species, would not, one should think, be totally
lost by its being reclaimed ; but would often break out among
its descendants.   But what is worth a hundred arguments, is
the instance you give in Sir Roger Mostyn's house-doves in
Caernarvonshire ; which, though tempted by plenty of food
and gentle treatment, can never be prevailed on to inhabit
their cote for any time; but, as soon as they begin to breed,
betake themselves to the fastnesses of Ormshead, and deposit
their young in safety amidst the inaccessible caverns and
precipices of that stupendous promontory.

Naturam expellas furcâ . . . tamen usque recurret.

I have consulted a sportsman, now in his seventy-eighth
year, who tells me, that fifty or sixty years back, when the
beechen woods were much more extensive than at present, the
number of wood-pigeons was astonishing ; that he has often
killed near twenty in a day ; and that, with a long wild-fowl
piece, he has shot seven or eight at a time on the wing, as
they came wheeling over his head : he moreover adds, which
I was not aware of, that often there were among them little
parties of small blue doves, which he calls rockiers.   The
food of these numberless emigrants was beech-mast and some
acorns ; and particularly barley, which they collected in the
stubbles.   But of late years, since the vast increase of turnips,
that vegetable has furnished a great part of their support in

---

* There are three species of wild pigeon in Britain, besides the turtle-
dove,— the ring-dove, *columba palumbus*, the stock-dove, *columba aenas*,
and the rock-dove, *columba livia*. The two latter are very nearly allied ;
but a very strong distinctive mark is, that the stock-dove is larger than
the rock-dove, and the latter is white on the lower part of the back,
whereas the stock-dove is ash-coloured.   It is now generally believed
that the rock-dove is the progenitor of all our domestic breeds of pigeons.
There is one circumstance which renders this opinion pretty conclusive,
and that is, we never find the domestic pigeon taking to trees to build,
when they become wild, but always resorting to old ruins, or to rocks.
The ring-dove is much larger than the other two species. — ED.

hard weather ; and the holes they pick in these roots greatly
damage the crop. From this food their flesh has contracted
a rancidness which occasions them to be rejected by nicer
judges of eating, who thought them before a delicate dish.
They were shot not only as they were feeding in the fields, and
especially in snowy weather, but also at the close of the evening, by men who lay in ambush among the woods and groves
to kill them as they came in to roost. * These are the principal
circumstances relating to this wonderful internal migration,
which with us takes place towards the end of November, and
ceases early in the spring. Last winter we had, in Selborne
High-wood, about an hundred of these doves ; but in former
times the flocks were so vast, not only with us, but all the
district around, that on mornings and evenings they traversed
the air, like rooks, in strings, reaching for a mile together.
When they thus rendezvoused here by thousands, if they
happened to be suddenly roused from their roost-trees on an
evening,

> Their rising all at once was like the sound
> . Of thunder heard remote.

It will by no means be foreign to the present purpose to
add, that I had a relation in this neighbourhood who made it
a practice for a time, whenever he could procure the eggs of a
ring-dove, to place them under a pair of doves that were sitting
in his own pigeon-house, hoping thereby, if he could bring
about a coalition, to enlarge his breed, and teach his own
doves to beat out into the woods, and to support themselves
by mast. The plan was plausible, but something always
interrupted the success ; for though the birds were usually
hatched, and sometimes grew to half their size, yet none ever
arrived at maturity. I myself have seen these foundlings in
their nest displaying a strange ferocity of nature, so as scarcely
to bear to be looked at, and snapping with their bills by way
of menace. In short, they always died, perhaps for want of
proper sustenance ; but the owner thought that by their fierce
and wild demeanour they frighted their foster-mothers, and so
were starved.

Virgil, as a familiar occurrence, by way of simile, describes
a dove haunting the cavern of a rock, in such engaging
numbers, that I cannot refrain from quoting the passage ; and

---

. * Some old sportsmen say, that the main part of these flocks used to
withdraw as soon as the heavy Christmas frosts were over.

John Dryden has rendered it so happily in our language, that without farther excuse, I shall add his translation also :

Qualis spelunca subitò commota columba,
Cui domus, et dulces latebroso in pumice nidi,
Fertur in arva volans, plausúmque exterrita pennis
Dat tecto ingentem: mox aëre lapsa quieto
Radit iter liquidum, celeres neque commovet alas.

As when the dove her rocky hold forsakes,
Roused in a fright, her sounding wings she shakes ;
The cavern rings with clattering ; out she flies,
And leaves her callow care, and cleaves the skies :
At first she flutters ; but at length she springs
To smoother flight, and shoots upon her wings.

LETTER XCV.

TO THE HON. DAINES BARRINGTON.

SELBORNE, *September* 3, 1781.

I HAVE now read your *Miscellanies* through with much care and satisfaction ; and am to return you my best thanks for the honourable mention made in them of me as a naturalist, which I wish I may deserve.

In some former letters, I expressed my suspicions that many of the house-martens do not depart in the winter far from this village. I therefore determined to make some search about the south-east end of the hill, where I imagined they might slumber out the uncomfortable months of winter. But supposing that the examination would be made to the best advantage in the spring, and observing that no martens had appeared by the 11th of April last, on that day I employed some men to explore the shrubs and cavities of the suspected spot. The persons took pains, but without any success ; however, a remarkable incident occurred in the midst of our pursuit, — while the labourers were at work, a house-marten, the first that had been seen this year, came down the village in the sight of several people, and went at once into a nest, where it staid a short time, and then flew over the houses ; for some days after, no martens were observed, not till the 16th of April, and then only a pair. Martens in general were remarkably late this year. *

* These early birds may be such as have hastened hither, by coming within the range of a favouring gale of wind. — ED.

LETTER XCVI.

TO THE HON. DAINES BARRINGTON.

SELBORNE, *September* 9, 1781.

I HAVE just met with a circumstance respecting swifts, which furnishes an exception to the whole tenor of my observations ever since I have bestowed any attention on that species of *hirundines.* Our swifts, in general, withdrew this year about the first day of August, all save one pair, which in two or three days was reduced to a single bird. The perseverance of this individual made me suspect that the strongest of motives, that of an attachment to her young, could alone occasion so late a stay. I watched therefore till the twenty-fourth of August, and then discovered that, under the eaves of the church, she attended upon two young, which were fledged, and now put out their white chins from a crevice. These remained till the twenty-seventh, looking more alert every day, and seeming to long to be on the wing. After this day, they were missing at once; nor could I ever observe them with their dam coursing round the church in the act of learning to fly, as the first broods evidently do. On the thirty-first, I caused the eaves to be searched; but we found in the nest only two callow, dead, stinking swifts, on which a second nest had been formed. This double nest was full of the black shining cases of the *hippoboscæ hirundinis.*

The following remarks on this unusual incident are obvious: The first is, that though it be disagreeable to swifts to remain beyond the beginning of August, yet that they can subsist longer is undeniable. The second is, that this uncommon event, as it was owing to the loss of the first brood, so it corroborates my former remark, that swifts breed regularly but once; since, was the contrary the case, the occurrence above could neither be new nor rare.

P.S. One swift was seen at Lyndon, in the county of Rutland, in 1782, so late as the 3d of September.

LETTER XCVII.

TO THE HON. DAINES BARRINGTON.

As I have sometimes known you make inquiries about several kinds of insects, I shall here send you an account of one sort which I little expected to have found in this kingdom. I had often observed that one particular part of a vine, growing on the walls of my house, was covered in the autumn with a black, dust-like appearance, on which the flies fed eagerly; and that the shoots and leaves thus affected did not thrive, nor did the fruit ripen. To this substance I applied my glasses, but could not discover that it had any thing to do with animal life, as I at first expected; but upon a closer examination behind the larger boughs, we were surprised to find that they were coated over with husky shells, from whose sides proceeded a cotton-like substance, surrounding a multitude of eggs. This curious and uncommon production put me upon recollecting what I have heard and read concerning the *coccus vitis viniferæ* of Linnæus, which, in the south of Europe, infests many vines, and is a horrid and loathsome pest. As soon as I had turned to the accounts given of this insect, I saw at once that it swarmed on my vine : and did not appear to have been at all checked by the preceding winter, which had been uncommonly severe.

Not being then at all aware that it had any thing to do with England, I was much inclined to think that it came from Gibraltar, among the many boxes and packages of plants and birds which I had formerly received from thence ; and especially as the vine infested grew immediately under my study window, where I usually kept my specimens.* True it is, that I had received nothing from thence for some years : but as insects, we know, are conveyed from one country to another in a very unexpected manner, and have a wonderful power of maintaining their existence till they fall into a *nidus* proper

---

* Most of the species of *coccus*, which are found in and infest the green-houses and conservatories of Britain, have been introduced with exotic plants. They are now very common in this country, and are a very prolific race. The females fix themselves, and tenaciously and immoveably adhere, to the branches of plants. Some of them lose entirely the form of insects: their bodies swell, their skin stretches, and becomes smooth, and they so closely resemble some of the galls, or excrescences, found on plants, as to be taken for such by people unacquainted with the subject. After this change, the abdomen serves only as a kind of shell, or covering, under which the eggs are concealed. Others, although they are also thus fixed, preserve their insect form till they have laid their eggs, and then die. A kind of downy substance grows on their abdomen, which serves for the formation of the nest in which they deposit their eggs. The males differ considerably from the females, being provided with wings, and are small, but very active insects. It is from one of this tribe, the *coccus cacti*, or American cochineal, that the celebrated red dye called cochineal is made. — ED.

for their support and increase, I cannot but suspect still that these *cocci* came to me originally from Andalusia. Yet, all the while, candour obliges me to confess, that Mr Lightfoot has written me word, that he once, and but once, saw these insects on a vine at Weymouth, in Dorsetshire; which, it is here to be observed, is a seaport town to which the *coccus* might be conveyed by shipping.

As many of my readers may possibly never have heard of this strange and unusual insect, I shall here transcribe a passage from a *Natural History of Gibraltar*, written by the Reverend John White, late vicar of Blackburn, in Lancashire, but not yet published :—

" In the year 1770, a vine, which grew on the east side of my house, and which had produced the finest crops of grapes for years past, was suddenly overspread, on all the woody branches, with large lumps of a white fibrous substance, resembling spiders' webs, or rather raw cotton. It was of a very clammy quality, sticking fast to every thing that touched it, and capable of being spun into long threads. At first I suspected it to be the product of spiders, but could find none. Nothing was to be seen connected with it, but many brown oval husky shells, which by no means looked like insects, but rather resembled bits of the dry bark of the vine. The tree had a plentiful crop of grapes set, when this pest appeared upon it ; but the fruit was manifestly injured by this foul encumbrance. It remained all the summer, still increasing, and loaded the woody and bearing branches to a vast degree. I often pulled off great quantities by handfuls ; but it was so slimy and tenacious that it could by no means be cleared. The grapes never filled to their natural perfection, but turned watery and vapid. Upon perusing the works afterwards of M. de Reaumur, I found this matter perfectly described and accounted for. Those husky shells which I had observed, were no other than the female *coccus*, from whose sides this cotton-like substance exudes, and serves as a covering and security for their eggs."

To this account I think proper to add, that, though the female *cocci* are stationary, and seldom remove from the place to which they stick, yet the male is a winged insect ; and that the black dust which I saw was undoubtedly the excrement of the females, which is eaten by ants as well as flies. Though the utmost severity of our winter did not destroy these insects, yet the attention of the gardener, in a summer or two, has entirely relieved my vine from this filthy annoyance.

As we have remarked above, that insects are often conveyed from one country to another in a very unaccountable manner, I shall here mention an emigration of small *aphides*, which was observed in the village of Selborne, no longer ago than August the 1st, 1785.

At about three o'clock in the afternoon of that day, which was very hot, the people of this village were surprised by a shower of *aphides*, or smother-flies, which fell in these parts. * Those that were walking in the street at that juncture, found themselves covered with these insects, which settled also on the hedges and gardens, blackening all the vegetables where they alighted. My annuals were discoloured with them, and the stalks of a bed of onions were quite coated over for six days after. These armies were then, no doubt, in a state of emigration, and shifting their quarters ; and might have come, as far as we know, from the great hop plantations of Kent or Sussex, the wind being all that day in the easterly quarter. They were observed, at the same time, in great clouds about Farnham, and all along the vale from Farnham to Alton. †

LETTER XCVIII.

TO THE HON. DAINES BARRINGTON.

DEAR SIR,— When I happen to visit a family where gold and silver fishes ‡ are kept in a glass bowl, I am always pleased

---

* There are several species of these troublesome, although minute, animals ; the loftiest tree is as liable to their attacks as the most humble plant. Their numbers are incalculably great. They prefer the young and tender shoots, and frequently insinuate themselves into the very heart of the plants, where they commit much havoc. Some feed indiscriminately on every kind of plant, while others confine their ravages to one species of plant only. The *aphis* of the rose tree too frequently despoil this delightful flower. The *aphides* afford a very striking deviation from the general laws of nature,— one impregnation of the female is sufficient for nine generations. — ED.

† For various methods by which several insects shift their quarters, see Derham's *Physico-Theology*.

‡ The gold and silver fishes are but one species, the *cyprinus auratus* of Linnæus. The young fry, when first produced, are perfectly black, but they afterwards change to white, and then to gold colour ; the latter colours appear first about the tail, and extend upwards. The smallest fish are the most beautiful, being of a fine orange red, appearing as if sprinkled over with gold dust: some are silvery white, and others white,

with the occurrence, because it offers me an opportunity of observing the actions and propensities of those beings with whom we can be little acquainted in their natural state. Not long since, I spent a fortnight at the house of a friend, where there was such a *vivary*, to which I paid no small attention, taking every occasion to remark what passed within its narrow limits. It was here that I first observed the manner in which fishes die. As soon as the creature sickens, the head sinks lower and lower, and it stands, as it were, on its head; till, getting weaker, and losing all poise, the tail turns over, and, at last, it floats on the surface of the water, with its belly uppermost. The reason why fishes, when dead, swim in that manner, is very obvious; because, when the body is no longer balanced by the fins of the belly, the broad muscular back preponderates by its own gravity, and turns the belly uppermost, as lighter, from its being a cavity, and because it contains the swimming bladders, which contribute to render it buoyant. Some that delight in gold and silver fishes, have adopted a notion that they need no aliment. True it is, that they will subsist for a long time without any apparent food but what they can collect from pure water frequently changed; yet they must draw some support from animalcula, and other nourishment, supplied by the water; because, though they seem to eat nothing, yet the consequences of eating often drop from them. That they are best pleased with such jejune diet may easily be confuted, since, if you toss them crumbs, they will seize them with great readiness, not to say greediness: however, bread should be given sparingly, lest, turning sour, it corrupt the water. They will also feed on the water plant called *lemna*, (duck's meat,) and also on small fry.

When they want to move a little, they gently protrude themselves with their *pinnæ pectorales*; but it is with their strong muscular tails only that they, and all fishes, shoot along with such inconceivable rapidity. It has been said, that the eyes of fishes are immoveable; but these apparently turn them forward or backward, in their sockets, as their occasions require. They take little notice of a lighted candle, though applied close to their heads, but flounce, and seem much frightened by a sudden stroke of the hand against the support whereon the bowl is hung; especially when they have been

spotted with red. When kept in ponds, they are frequently taught to rise to the surface of the water, at the sound of a bell, to be fed. They are said to have been first introduced into England in 1691. — Ed.

motionless, and perhaps asleep. As fishes have no eyelids, it is not easy to discern when they are sleeping or not, because their eyes are always open.

Nothing can be more amusing than a glass bowl containing such fishes: the double refractions of the glass and water represent them, when moving, in a shifting and changeable variety of dimensions, shades, and colours; while the two mediums, assisted by the concavo-convex shape of the vessel, magnify and distort them vastly; not to mention that the introduction of another element and its inhabitants into our parlours engages the fancy in a very agreeable manner.

Gold and silver fishes, though originally natives of China and Japan, yet are become so well reconciled to our climate, as to thrive and multiply very fast in our ponds and stews. Linnæus ranks this species of fish under the genus of *cyprinus*, or carp, and calls it *cyprinus auratus*.

Some people exhibit this sort of fish in a very fanciful way; for they cause a glass bowl to be blown with a large hollow space within, that does not communicate with it. In this cavity they put a bird occasionally, so that you may see a goldfinch or a linnet hopping, as it were, in the midst of the water, and the fishes swimming in a circle round it. The simple exhibition of the fishes is agreeable and pleasant; but in so complicated a way, becomes whimsical and unnatural, and liable to the objection due to him,

Qui variare cupit rem prodigialitèr unam.

LETTER XCIX.

TO THE HON. DAINES BARRINGTON.

October 10, 1781.

DEAR SIR,—I think I have observed before, that much the most considerable part of the house-martens withdraw from hence about the first week in October; but that some, the latter broods, I am now convinced, linger on till towards the middle of that month; and that at times—once perhaps in two or three years—a flight, for one day only, has shewn itself in the first week in November.

Having taken notice, in October, 1780, that the last flight was numerous, amounting perhaps to one hundred and fifty, and that the season was soft and still, I was resolved to pay uncommon attention to these late birds, to find, if possible, where they roosted, and to determine the precise time of their retreat. The mode of life of these latter *hirundines* is very favourable to such a design, for they spend the whole day in the sheltered district between me and the Hanger, sailing about in a placid easy manner, and feasting on those insects which love to haunt a spot so secure from ruffling winds. As my principal object was to discover the place of their roosting, I took care to wait on them before they retired to rest, and was much pleased to find that, for several evenings together, just at a quarter past five in the afternoon, they all scudded away in great haste towards the south-east, and darted down among the low shrubs above the cottages at the end of the hill.* This

---

* Our author is most desirous to establish the opinion, that some of the *hirundines* and their congeners live with us during the winter. In addition to the mass of evidence which we have brought forward regarding the migration of the swallow tribe, we shall conclude this subject with the interesting observations of Audubon, the celebrated American ornithologist, on the republican, or cliff-swallow. " Being extremely desirous of settling the long-agitated question respecting the migration or supposed torpidity of swallows, I embraced every opportunity of examining their habits, carefully noted their arrival and disappearance, and recorded every fact connected with their history. After some years' constant observation and reflection, I remarked, that, among all the species of migratory birds, those that remove farthest from us depart sooner than those which retire only to the confines of the United States; and, by a parity of reasoning, those that remain later return earlier in the spring. These remarks were confirmed as I advanced towards the south-west on the approach of winter, for I there found numbers of warblers, thrushes, &c. in full feather and song. It was also remarked, that the *hirundo viridis* of Wilson remained about the city of New Orleans later than any other swallow. As immense numbers of them were seen during the month of November, I kept a diary of the temperature from the 3d of that month, until the arrival of the *hirundo purpurea*. The following notes are taken from my journal, and, as I had excellent opportunities, during a residence of many years in the country, of visiting the lakes to which these swallows were said to resort during transient frosts, I present them with confidence : —

" *November* 11. — Weather very sharp, with a heavy white frost. Swallows in abundance during the whole day. On inquiring of the inhabitants if this was an unusual occurrence, I was answered in the affirmative by all the French and Spaniards. From this date to the twenty-second the thermometer averaged sixty-five degrees, the weather generally a drizzly fog. Swallows playing over the city in thousands.

" *November* 25. — Thermometer this morning at thirty degrees. Ice in New Orleans a quarter of an inch thick. The swallows resorted to the lee of the cypress swamp in the rear of the city. Thousands were flying in different flocks. Fourteen were killed at a single shot, all in perfect plumage and very fat. The markets were abundantly supplied with these tender, juicy, and delicious birds. Saw swallows every day, but remarked them more plentiful the stronger the breeze blew from the sea.

spot in many respects seems to be well calculated for their
winter residence, for, in many parts, it is as steep as the roof
of any house, and therefore secure from the annoyances of
water; and it is, moreover, clothed with beechen shrubs, which,
being stunted and bitten by sheep, make the thickest covert
imaginable, and are so entangled as to be impervious to the
smallest spaniel; besides, it is the nature of underwood beech
never to cast its leaf all the winter, so that, with the leaves on
the ground and those on the twigs, no shelter can be more
complete. I watched them on to the thirteenth and fourteenth
of October, and found their evening retreat was exact and
uniform; but after this they made no regular appearance. Now
and then a straggler was seen; and, on the twenty-second of
October, I observed two, in the morning, over the village, and
with them my remarks for the season ended.

· From all these circumstances put together, it is more than
probable that this lingering flight, at so late a season of the
year, never departed from the island. Had they indulged
me that autumn with a November visit, as I much desired, I
presume that, with proper assistants, I should have settled the
matter past all doubt; but though the third of November was

"*December* 20. — The weather continues much the same. Foggy and
drizzly mist. Thermometer averaging sixty-three degrees.

"*January* 14. — Thermometer forty-two degrees. Weather continues
the same. My little favourites constantly in view.

"*January* 28. — Thermometer at forty degrees. Having seen the
hirundo viridis continually, and the *hirundo purpurea*, or purple marten,
beginning to appear, I discontinued my observations.

"During the whole winter, many of them retired to the holes about the
houses, but the greater number resorted to the lakes, and spent the night
among the branches of *myrica cerifera*, the *cirier*, as it is termed
by the French settlers. At sunset they began to flock together, calling
to each other for that purpose, and, in a short time, presented the appearance of clouds moving towards the lakes, or the mouth of the Mississippi,
as the weather and wind suited. Their aërial evolutions, before they
alight, are truly beautiful. They appear at first as if reconnoitering the
place, when, suddenly throwing themselves into a vortex of apparent
confusion, they descend spirally with astonishing quickness, and very
much resemble a *trombe*, or water spout. When within a few feet of the
ciriers, they disperse in all directions, and settle in a few moments.
Their twittering, and the motions of their wings, are, however, heard
during the whole night. As soon as the day begins to dawn, they rise,
flying low over the lakes, almost touching the water for some time, and
then rising, gradually move off in search of food, separating in different
directions. The hunters who resort to these places destroy great numbers
of them, by knocking them down with light paddles, used in propelling
their canoes." — Ed.

a sweet day, and in appearance exactly suited to my wishes, yet not a marten was to be seen, and so I was forced, reluctantly, to give up the pursuit.

I have only to add, that were the bushes, which cover some acres, and are not my own property, to be grubbed and carefully examined, probably those late broods, and perhaps the whole aggregate body of the house-martens of this district, might be found there in different secret dormitories; and that, so far from withdrawing into warmer climes, it would appear that they never depart three hundred yards from the village.

LETTER C.

TO THE HON. DAINES BARRINGTON.

THEY who write on natural history, cannot too frequently advert to instinct, that wonderful limited faculty, which, in some instances, raises the brute creation, as it were, above reason, and in others, leaves them so far below it. Philosophers have defined instinct to be that secret influence by which every species is impelled naturally to pursue, at all times, the same way, or track, without any teaching or example; whereas reason, without instruction, would often vary, and do that by many methods which instinct effects by one alone. Now, this maxim must be taken in a qualified sense, for there are instances in which instinct does vary and conform to the circumstances of place and convenience.

It has been remarked, that every species of bird has a mode of nidification peculiar to itself, so that a schoolboy would at once pronounce on the sort of nest before him. This is the case among fields, and woods, and wilds; but in the villages round London, where mosses, and gossamer and cotton from vegetables, are hardly to be found, the nest of the chaffinch has not that elegant finished appearance, nor is it so beautifully studded with lichens, as in a more rural district; and the wren is obliged to construct its house with straws and dry grasses, which do not give it that rotundity and compactness so remarkable in the edifices of that little architect. Again, the regular nest of the house-marten is hemispheric; but where a rafter, or a joist, or a cornice, may happen to stand in the way, the nest is so contrived as to conform to the obstruction, and becomes flat, or oval, or compressed.

In the following instances, instinct is perfectly uniform and consistent. There are three creatures, the squirrel, the field-mouse, and the bird called the nut-hatch, (*sitta europæa,*) which live much on hazel-nuts, and yet they open them each in a different way. The first, after rasping off the small end, splits the shell into two with his long fore teeth, as a man does with his knife ; the second nibbles a hole with his teeth, so regular as if drilled with a wimble, and yet so small that one would wonder how the kernel can be extracted through it ; while the last picks an irregular ragged hole with its bill ; but as this artist has no paws to hold the nut firm while he pierces it, like an adroit workman, he fixes it as it were in a vice, in some cleft of a tree, or in some crevice, when, standing over it, he perforates the stubborn shell. We have often placed nuts in the chink of a gate-post, where nut-hatches have been known to haunt, and have always found that those birds have readily penetrated them. While at work, they make a rapping noise that may be heard at a considerable distance.*

You that understand both the theory and practical part of music, may best inform us why harmony or melody should so

---

* Instinct is not invariably infallible, as Professor Rennie justly observes, for we can discover many mistakes of this faculty. For example, when Dr Arnold discovered that wonderful vegetable production, the *rafflesia Arnoldii*, in Sumatra, which is said to smell like tainted beef, he observed a swarm of flies gathered around it, for the purpose, as he supposed, of depositing their eggs upon it, as they no doubt imagined it to be tainted carrion.

The circumstance of insects mistaking the rafflesia for putrid meat, is not a singular one, as we have similar mistakes happening in this country. The common flesh fly (*musca vomitorea*) often lays its eggs in the fetid sorts of *phalli* and *agarici*, apparently supposing them genuine flesh.

The earth-worm, which is instinctively afraid of moles, flies to the surface of the earth whenever it finds the ground shaking, whether by man or animals. Boys who wish to capture these poor animals, take advantage of this natural dread of an enemy, and by sinking a spade or stake into the ground, move it backwards and forwards, and the alarmed worms ascend to the surface. It is mentioned by Dr Anderson, in his *Bee*, that the lapwing (*tringa vanellus*) is aware of this instinctive fear of the earth-worm, and when other food is scarce, it pats the ground with its feet, till the earth-worms, mistaking it for a mole approaching, ascend to the surface, when they are immediately devoured by the cunning bird.

The flight of the cuckoo being very like that of a hawk, it is frequently pursued by small birds, thinking it one of these fell destroyers.

Linnæus mentions that at Tornea, there is a meadow, or bog, which abounds with water hemlock, (*cicuta virosa*,) which the cattle eat, and are poisoned ; from fifty to a hundred head of cattle die annually from this cause.—ED.

strangely affect some men, as it were by recollection, for days after a concert is over. What I mean, the following passage will most readily explain : —

" Præhabebat porrò vocibus humanîs, instrumentisque harmonicis, musicam illam avium : non quod aliâ quoque non delectaretur ; sed quod ex musicâ humanâ relinqueretur in animo continens quædam, attentionemque et somnum conturbans agitatio : dum ascensus, exscensus, tenores, ac mutationes illæ sonorum et consonantiarum, euntque, redeuntque per phantasiam : — cum nihil tale relinqui possit ex modulationibus avium, quæ, quod non sunt perinde a nobis imitabiles, non possunt perinde internam facultatem commovere."— GASSENDUS, *in Vitâ Peireskii.* *

This curious quotation strikes me much by so well representing my own case, and by describing what I have so often felt, but never could so well express. When I hear fine music, I am haunted with passages therefrom night and day, and especially at first waking ; which, by their importunity, give me more uneasiness than pleasure : elegant lessons still tease my imagination, and recur irresistibly to my recollection at seasons, and even when I am desirous of thinking of more serious matters. †

---

* As this striking passage can be only understood by the classical scholar, we offer a translation for the use of those who are not so : — " He preferred, besides, the music of birds to the human voice, and to musical instruments ; not because he derived no pleasure from the last, but because, after music from the human voice there was left in the mind a certain continual agitation, disturbing attention and sleep, while the risings and fallings, the tones and changes, of sound and concords, pass and repass through the fancy ; whereas nothing of this kind can remain after the warblings of birds, which, as they cannot be imitated by us, cannot therefore affect the faculty of imagination within us."— ED.

† A similar impulse was felt by Alfieri, who, in his life, written by himself, describes his sensations on hearing music, as of a very powerful kind. He thus speaks of the first opera he witnessed when he was only twelve years of age, — " This varied and enchanting music sank deep into my soul, and made the most astonishing impression on my imagination : it agitated the inmost recesses of my heart to such a degree, that for several weeks I experienced the most profound melancholy, which was not, however, wholly unattended with pleasure. I became tired and disgusted with my studies, while, at the same time, the most wild and whimsical ideas took such possession of my mind as would have led me to portray them in the most impassioned verses, had I not been wholly unacquainted with my own feelings. It was the first time music had produced such a powerful effect on my mind. I had never experienced any thing similar, and it long remained engraven on my memory. When I recollect the feelings excited by the representation of

LETTER CI.

TO THE HON. DAINES BARRINGTON.

A RARE, and I think a new, little bird frequents my garden, which I have great reason to think is the pettichaps: it is common in some parts of the kingdom; and I have received formerly several dead specimens from Gibraltar. This bird much resembles the white-throat, but has a more white, or rather silvery, breast and belly; is restless and active, like the willow-wrens, and hops from bough to bough, examining every part for food; it also runs up the stems of the crown-imperials, and, putting its head into the bells of those flowers, sips the liquor which stands in the nectarium of each petal. Sometimes it feeds on the ground like the hedge-sparrow, by hopping about on the grass-plots and mown walks.

One of my neighbours, an intelligent and observing man, informs me, that, in the beginning of May, and about ten minutes before eight o'clock in the evening, he discovered a great cluster of house-swallows, thirty at least, he supposes, perching on a willow that hung over the verge of James

the grand operas, at which I was present, during several carnivals, and compare them with those which I now experience, on returning from the performance of a piece I have not witnessed for some time, I am fully convinced that nothing acts so powerfully on my mind as all species of music, and particularly the sound of female voices, and of contralto. Nothing excites more various or terrific sensations in my mind. Thus the plots of the greatest number of my tragedies were either formed while listening to music, or a few hours afterwards." In a subsequent passage he remarks, — "My greatest pleasure consisted in attending the opera buffa, though the gay and lively music left a deep and melancholy impression on my mind. A thousand gloomy and mournful ideas assailed my imagination, in which I delighted to indulge by wandering alone on the shores of the Chiaja Portici."

Associations of ideas, awakened by music, have also a powerful effect upon the sensitive mind. The following quotation from the *London Magazine* strikingly illustrates this fact: — "I knew, at Paris, the widow of an Irish patriot, who could not hear the 'Exile of Erin' sung without being overpowered to such a degree, that it would have been truly alarming, had not a flood of tears come to her relief. What is wonderful, so far from having a fine musical ear, she had not even a common-place relish for music. The same effect was produced on her by the 'Minstrel Boy' of Moore. A young friend of the writer, who has no taste for music, is similarly overpowered, even in a crowded theatre, when 'Home, sweet Home, is sung."— ED.

Knight's upper pond. His attention was first drawn by the twittering of these birds, which sat motionless in a row on the bough, with their heads all one way, and, by their weight, pressing down the twig, so that it nearly touched the water. In this situation, he watched them till he could see no longer. Repeated accounts of this sort, spring and fall, induce us greatly to suspect, that house-swallows have some strong attachment to water, independent of the matter of food ; and, though they may not retire into that element, yet they may conceal themselves in the banks of pools and rivers during the uncomfortable months of winter.

One of the keepers of Wolmer Forest sent me a peregrine falcon, which he shot on the verge of that district, as it was devouring a wood-pigeon. The *falco peregrinus*, or haggard falcon, is a noble species of hawk, seldom seen in the southern counties. In winter 1767, one was killed in the neighbouring parish of Faringdon, and sent by me to Mr Pennant into North Wales. * Since that time, I have met with none till now. The specimen mentioned above was in fine preservation, and not injured by the shot : it measured forty-two inches from wing to wing, and twenty-one from beak to tail, and weighed two pounds and a half standing weight. This species is very robust, and wonderfully formed for rapine ; its breast was plump and muscular ; its thighs long, thick, and brawny ; and its legs remarkably short and well set ; the feet were armed with most formidable, sharp, long talons ; the eyelids and cere of the bill were yellow ; but the irides of the eyes dusky ; the beak was thick and hooked, and of a dark colour, and had a jagged process near the end of the upper mandible on each side ; its tail, or train, was short in proportion to the bulk of its body ; yet the wings, when closed, did not extend to the end of the train. From its large and fair proportions, it might be supposed to have been a female ; but I was not permitted to cut open the specimen. For one of the birds of prey, which are usually lean, this was in high case : in its craw were many barley-corns, which probably came from the crop of the wood-pigeon, on which it was feeding when shot : for voracious birds do not eat grain ; but, when devouring their quarry, with undistinguishing vehemence, swallow bones and feathers, and all matters, indiscriminately. † This falcon was probably driven

* See Letters X. XI. to Thomas Pennant, Esq.

† The bones and feathers which are swallowed along with the flesh by birds of prey, tend to assist digestion. — Ed.

from the mountains of North Wales or Scotland, where they are known to breed, by rigorous weather and deep snows that had lately fallen.

LETTER CII.

TO THE HON. DAINES BARRINGTON.

My near neighbour, a young gentleman in the service of the East India Company, has brought home a dog and a bitch of the Chinese breed from Canton ; such as are fattened in that country for the purpose of being eaten : they are about the size of a moderate spaniel ; of a pale yellow colour, with coarse bristling hair on their backs ; sharp, upright ears, and peaked heads, which give them a very fox-like appearance. Their hind legs are unusually straight, without any bend at the hock, or ham, to such a degree as to give them an awkward gait when they trot. When they are in motion, their tails are curved high over their backs, like those of some hounds, and have a bare place each on the outside, from the tip midway, that does not seem to be matter of accident, but somewhat singular. Their eyes are jet black, small, and piercing ; the insides of their lips and mouths of the same colour, and their tongues blue. The bitch has a dew-claw on each hind leg ; the dog has none. When taken out into a field, the bitch shewed some disposition for hunting, and dwelt on the scent of a covey of partridges till she sprung them, giving her tongue all the time. The dogs in South America are dumb ;* but these bark much in a short, thick manner, like foxes ; and have a surly, savage demeanour, like their ancestors, which are not domesticated, but bred up in sties, where they are fed for the table with rice-meal and other farinaceous food. These dogs, having been taken on board as soon as weaned, could not learn much from their dam ; yet they did not relish flesh when they came to England. In the islands of the Pacific Ocean, the dogs are bred up on vegetables, and would not eat flesh when offered them by our circumnavigators.

We believe that all dogs, in a state of nature, have sharp, upright, fox-like ears ; and that hanging ears, which are esteemed so graceful, are the effect of choice breeding and

---

* The dogs which Captain Franklin brought from the Arctic Regions were dumb, and are never known to bark in their native country ; but a young one, that was whelped here, has learnt to imitate his fellows.— ED.

cultivation. Thus in the Travels of Ysbrandt Ides from Muscovy to China, the dogs which draw the Tartars on snow sledges near the river Oby, are engraved with prick-ears, like those from Canton. The Kamtschatdales also train the same sort of sharp-eared, peak-nosed dogs to draw their sledges ; as may be seen in an elegant print engraved for Captain Cook's last voyage round the world.

Now we are upon the subject of dogs, it may not be impertinent to add, that spaniels, as all sportsmen know, though they hunt partridges and pheasants, as it were, by instinct, and with much delight and alacrity, yet will hardly touch their bones when offered as food ; nor will a mongrel dog of my own, though he is remarkable for finding that sort of game. But, when we came to offer the bones of partridges to the two Chinese dogs, they devoured them with much greediness, and licked the platter clean.

No sporting dogs will flush woodcocks till inured to the scent, and trained to the sport, which they then pursue with vehemence and transport ; but then they will not touch their bones, but turn from them with abhorrence, even when they are hungry. *

Now, that dogs should not be fond of the bones of such birds as they are not disposed to hunt, is no wonder ; but why they reject and do not care to eat their natural game, is not so easily accounted for, since the end of hunting seems to be, that the chase pursued should be eaten. Dogs, again, will not devour the more rancid water-fowls ; nor indeed the bones of any wild-fowls ; nor will they touch the fetid bodies of birds that feed on offal and garbage ; and indeed there may be somewhat of providential instinct in this circumstance of dislike ; for vultures,† and kites, and ravens, and crows, &c. were intended to be messmates with dogs‡ over their carrion ; and seem to be appointed by Nature as fellow-scavengers, to remove all cadaverous nuisances from the face of the earth.

---

* Pointers are frequently known to set game the first time they are taken into a field, and to preserve their point with the steadiness of an old well-trained dog.—ED.

† Hasselquist, in his *Travels to the Levant*, observes, that the dogs and vultures at Grand Cairo maintain such a friendly intercourse, as to bring up their young together in the same place.

‡ The Chinese word for a dog, to a European ear, sounds like *quihloh*.

LETTER CIII.

TO THE HON. DAINES BARRINGTON.

THE fossil wood buried in the bogs of Wolmer Forest, is not yet all exhausted ; for the peat-cutters now and then stumble upon a log. I have just seen a piece which was sent by a labourer of Oakhanger to a carpenter of this village : this was the butt end of a small oak, about five feet long, and about five inches in diameter. It had apparently been severed from the ground by an ax, was very ponderous, and as black as ebony. Upon asking the carpenter for what purpose he had procured it, he told me that it was to be sent to his brother, a joiner at Farnham, who was to make use of it in cabinet work, by inlaying it along with whiter woods.

Those that are much abroad on evenings after it is dark, in spring and summer, frequently hear a nocturnal bird passing by on the wing, and repeating often a short quick note. This bird I have remarked myself, but never could make out till lately. I am assured now, that it is the stone-curlew, (*charadrius oedicnemus.*) Some of them pass over or near my house almost every evening after it is dark, from the uplands of the hill and Northfield, away down towards Dorton ; where, among the streams and meadows, they find a greater plenty of food. Birds that fly by night are obliged to be noisy ; their notes, often repeated, become signals, or watch-words, to keep them together, that they may not stray or lose each other in the dark.

The evening proceedings and manœuvres of the rooks are curious and amusing in the autumn. Just before dusk, they return in long strings from the foraging of the day, and rendezvous by thousands over Selborne-down, where they wheel round in the air, and sport and dive in a playful manner, all the while exerting their voices, and making a loud cawing, which, being blended and softened by the distance that we at the village are below them, becomes a confused noise or chiding ; or rather a pleasing murmur, very engaging to the imagination, and not unlike the cry of a pack of hounds in hollow, echoing woods, or the rushing of the wind in tall trees, or the tumbling of the tide upon a pebbly shore. When this ceremony is over, with the last gleam of day, they retire for the night to the deep beechen woods of Tisted and Ropley. We remember a little girl, who, as she was going to bed, used to remark on such an occurrence, in the true spirit of physico-theology, that the rooks were saying their prayers ; and yet this child was much too young to be aware that the Scriptures have said of the Deity—that " He feedeth the ravens who call upon him."*

LETTER CIV.

TO THE HON. DAINES BARRINGTON.

In reading Dr Huxham's *Observationes de Aëre*, &c. written at Plymouth, I find, by those curious and accurate remarks, which contain an account of the weather from the year 1727 to the year 1748, inclusive, that though there is frequent rain in that district of Devonshire, yet the quantity falling is not great; and that some years it has been very small ; for in 1731, the rain measured only 17^{inch}.—266^{thou}.; and in 1741, 20—354 ; and again, in 1743, only 20—908. Places near the sea have frequent scuds, that keep the atmosphere moist, yet do not reach far up into the country ; making thus the maritime situations appear wet, when the rain is not considerable. In the wettest years at Plymouth, the Doctor measured only once 36 ; and again once, viz. 1734, 37—114 ; a quantity of rain that has twice been exceeded at Selborne in the short period of my observations. Dr Huxham remarks, that frequent small rains keep the air moist ; while heavy ones render it more dry, by beating down the vapours.† He is also of opinion,

---

* Rooks have undoubtedly a language of their own, which is understood by the whole community ; and a bird set to watch by them has a peculiar note, by which it warns its fellows of approaching danger, and upon the sound of which they all take flight, and always in a direction opposite to where the danger is apprehended. — ED.

† Mr Spence remarks, on this subject, — "The superior dryness of the air in Italy in summer, compared with that of England, and many parts of the north of Europe, is well known ; but I was not aware that the difference is equally striking even in the rainy part of winter, judging, for want of a better hygrometer, from the condensation of moisture on the inside of windows in rooms without a fire, which I have always observed to be very considerable in winter, both in England, and in Brussels, during a three years' residence there, whenever a cold night succeeds a rainy or warm day, the condensed moisture often even running down to the floor ; whereas at Florence, under precisely similar circumstances, I have never but once observed more than a slight condensation in the middle of the panes, as if breathed on, even in rooms with a north aspect, and only once during the frost, any appearance, and that but slight, of that thick crust of ice formed on the inside of the panes in England, and at Brussels, whenever

that the dingy smoky appearance in the sky, in very dry seasons, arises from the want of moisture sufficient to let the light through, and render the atmosphere transparent; because he had observed several bodies more diaphanous when wet than dry; and did never recollect that the air had that look in rainy seasons.

My friend, who lives just beyond the top of the Down, brought his three swivel guns to try them in my outlet, with their muzzles towards the Hanger, supposing that the report would have had a great effect; but the experiment did not answer his expectation. He then removed them to the alcove on the Hanger; when the sound, rushing along the Lythe and Comb-wood, was very grand: but it was at the Hermitage that the echoes and repercussions delighted the hearers; not only filling the Lythe with a roar, as if all the beeches were tearing up by the roots, but, turning to the left, they pervaded the vale above Comb-wood ponds; and, after a pause, seemed to take up the crash again, and to extend round Harteley Hangers, and to die away at last among the coppices and coverts of Ward-le-ham. It has been remarked before, that this district is an *Anathoth*, a place of responses, or echoes, and therefore proper for such experiments; we may farther add, that the pauses in echoes, when they cease and yet are taken up again, like the pauses in music, surprise the hearers, and have a fine effect on the imagination.

The gentleman above mentioned has just fixed a barometer in his parlour at Newton Valence. The tube was first filled here (at Selborne) twice with care, when the mercury agreed, and stood exactly with my own; but being filled again twice at Newton, the mercury stood, on account of the great elevation of that house, three-tenths of an inch lower than the barometers at this village, and so continues to do, be the weight of the atmosphere what it may. The plate of the barometer at Newton is figured as low as twenty-seven; because, in stormy weather, the mercury there will sometimes descend below twenty-eight. We have supposed Newton house to stand two hundred feet higher than this house: but if the rule holds good, which says that mercury in a barometer sinks

a hard frost sets in. Among many other proofs of the greater dryness of the air in winter, one is afforded by the profusion in which grapes are to be had, at less than twopence a pound, at the corners of every street, up to the end of March, quite free from all mouldiness, though cut full four months, and kept merely by being hung at the top of rooms without a fire."—ED.

one-tenth of an inch for every hundred feet elevation, then the Newton barometer, by standing three-tenths lower than that of Selborne, proves that Newton house must be three hundred feet higher than that in which I am writing, instead of two hundred.

It may not be impertinent to add, that the barometers at Selborne stand three-tenths of an inch lower than the barometers at South Lambeth ; whence we may conclude, that the former place is about three hundred feet higher than the latter ; and with good reason, because the streams that rise with us run into the Thames at Weybridge, and so to London. Of course, therefore, there must be lower ground all the way from Selborne to South Lambeth ; the distance between which, all the windings and indentings of the streams considered, cannot be less than an hundred miles. *

LETTER CV.

TO THE HON. DAINES BARRINGTON.

SINCE the weather of a district is undoubtedly part of its natural history, I shall make no farther apology for the four following letters, which will contain many particulars concerning some of the great frosts, and a few respecting some very hot summers, that have distinguished themselves from the rest during the course of my observations.

As the frost in January, 1768, was, for the small time it lasted, the most severe that we had then known for many years, and was remarkably injurious to evergreens, some account of its rigour, and reason of its ravages, may be useful, and not unacceptable to persons that delight in planting and ornamenting ; and may particularly become a work that professes never to lose sight of utility.

For the last two or three days of the former year, there were considerable falls of snow, which lay deep and uniform on the ground without any drifting, wrapping up the more

---

* The best instrument now in use for determining the pressure of the atmosphere, the altitude of any place above another, or above the level of the sea, is the barometer invented and made by Mr Adie, 58, Princes Street, Edinburgh, and named by him the sympiesometer. The great simplicity of this instrument is a high recommendation, as it gives the altitudes by a single process of subtraction and multiplication, whereas to obtain the altitude with the common barometer, the use of the barometrical tables is indispensable.—ED.

humble vegetation in perfect security. From the first day to the fifth of the new year, more snow succeeded ; but from that day, the air became entirely clear, and the heat of the sun about noon had a considerable influence in sheltered situations.

It was in such an aspect, that the snow on the author's evergreens was melted every day, and frozen intensely every night; so that the laurustines, bays, laurels, and arbutuses, looked, in three or four days, as if they had been burnt in the fire ; while a neighbour's plantation of the same kind, in a high, cold situation, where the snow was never melted at all, remained uninjured.*

From hence I would infer, that it is the repeated melting and freezing of the snow that is so fatal to vegetation, rather than the severity of the cold. Therefore, it highly behoves every planter, who wishes to escape the cruel mortification of losing in a few days the labour and hopes of years, to bestir himself on such emergencies ; and, if his plantations are small, to avail himself of mats, cloths, pease-haum, straw, reeds, or any such covering, for a short time ; or if his shrubberies are extensive, to see that his people go about with prongs and forks, and carefully dislodge the snow from the boughs ; since the naked foliage will shift much better for itself, than where the snow is partly melted and frozen again.

It may perhaps appear at first like a paradox, but doubtless the more tender trees and shrubs should never be planted in hot aspects ; not only for the reason assigned above, but also because, thus circumstanced, they are disposed to shoot earlier in the spring, and to grow on later in the autumn than they would otherwise do, and so are sufferers by lagging or early frosts. For this reason, also, plants from Siberia will hardly endure our climate ; because, on the very first advances of spring, they shoot away, and so are cut off by the severe night of March or April.

Dr Fothergill and others have experienced the same inconvenience with respect to the more tender shrubs from North America : which they therefore plant under north walls. There

* The effect of shade, in preventing, or rather neutralizing, terrestrial radiation, was strikingly exhibited at Florence, in January, 1830, after the second and longest frost. While all the rest of the surrounding exposed grass looked bare and withered, that under a group of old evergreen oaks had made a shoot of from one to two inches, and was of a fine vivid green, distinguishable at a great distance. Groundsel, the daisy, shepherd's purse, *veronica arvensis,calendula arvensis,*&c. were in flower the whole winter, their blossoms expanding in bright warm days during the frost.—ED.

should also, perhaps, be a wall to the east, to defend them
from the piercing blasts from that quarter.

This observation might, without any impropriety, be carried
into animal life; for discerning bee-masters now find that
their hives should not, in the winter, be exposed to the hot
sun, because such unseasonable warmth awakens the inhabitants too early from their slumbers; and, by putting their
juices into motion too soon, subjects them afterwards to
inconveniencies when rigorous weather returns.

The coincidents attending this short but intense frost, were,
that the horses fell sick with an epidemic distemper, which
injured the winds of many, and killed some; that colds and
coughs were general among the human species; that it froze
under people's beds for several nights; that meat was so hard
frozen that it could not be spitted, and could not be secured
but in cellars;* that several redwings and thrushes were
killed by the frost; and that the large titmouse continued to
pull straws lengthwise from the eaves of thatched houses and
barns in a most adroit manner, for a purpose that has been
explained already.†

On the third of January, Benjamin Martin's thermometer,
within doors, in a close parlour where there was no fire, fell
in the night to 20, and on the fourth to 18, and on the seventh
to 17½, a degree of cold which the owner never since saw in
the same situation; and he regrets much that he was not able
at that juncture to attend his instrument abroad. All this time,
the wind continued north and north-east; and yet on the
eighth, roost-cocks, which had been silent, began to sound
their clarions, and crows to clamour, as prognostic of milder
weather; and, moreover, moles began to heave and work, and
a manifest thaw took place. From the latter circumstance, we
may conclude, that thaws often originate under ground from
warm vapours which arise, else how should subterraneous
animals receive such early intimations of their approach?
Moreover, we have often observed that cold seems to descend
from above;‡ for when a thermometer hangs abroad in a

* Meat thus frozen will keep any length of time. At St Petersburgh,
there is a market of frozen meat. A species of extinct elephant was
found in the ice of the North Seas, where it must have remained for many
centuries, and when discovered, part of the flesh was yet preserved, and
untainted. — Ed.

† See Letter LXIII. to Thomas Pennant, Esq.

‡ This may be explained, on the principle that the radiation of caloric
proceeds more rapidly from the earth's surface, when the sky is clear, and
is interrupted by the intervention of a cloud. — Ed.

frosty night, the intervention of a cloud shall immediately raise the mercury ten degrees; and a clear sky shall again compel it to descend to its former gage.

And here it may be proper to observe, on what has been said above, that though frosts advance to their utmost severity by somewhat of a regular gradation, yet thaws do not usually come on by as regular a declension of cold; but often take place immediately from intense freezing; as men in sickness often mend at once from a paroxysm. *

To the great credit of Portugal laurels and American junipers, be it remembered, that they remained untouched amidst the general havoc: hence men should learn to ornament chiefly with such trees as are able to withstand accidental severities, and not subject themselves to the vexation of a loss which may befall them once perhaps in ten years, yet may hardly be recovered through the whole course of their lives.

As it appeared afterwards, the ilexes were much injured, the cypresses were half destroyed, the arbutuses lingered on, but never recovered; and the bays, laurustines, and laurels, were killed to the ground; and the very wild hollies, in hot aspects, were so much affected, that they cast all their leaves.†

* About the middle of November, 1831, the winter set in at Edinburgh with considerable severity, and was followed up by a fall of snow. It lay on the ground for some days, and had been raked up in heaps along the sides of the street. It continued freezing hard, on the evening of the twenty-first, at six o'clock, when we were out of doors. We had occasion to be out again a little after midnight, and, the moment we set our face out of doors, we were astonished at the extreme warmth of the atmosphere, which felt like a genial summer mid-day breeze, the wind blowing gently from the south, and the whole snow had disappeared. So rapid was the thaw, that the atmosphere seemed incapable of properly taking up the moist vapour, and next day the walls of all the houses in Edinburgh ran down with condensed vapour: those which were painted with size appeared as wet as if they had been newly washed, and it was some days before they were thoroughly dry. — ED.

† The winter of 1830-31, remarkable for the great quantity of snow that fell in some parts of the kingdom, as well as for the severity of the frost, caused very great devastation among the evergreens, particularly in Ireland. At Headford, in the county of Galway, several very large trees of the *arbutus unedo*, which had already flourished for many years, and attained a diameter of nearly a foot, were destroyed down to the root. In the vicinity of Clogher, in the county of Tyrone, most of the laurustines, bays, and laurels, and many of the evergreens, were entirely destroyed; nor were the Portugal laurels entirely exempted. In one shrubbery, in particular, the decay was so rapid as to produce an almost overpowering smell. — ED.

By the fourteenth of January, the snow was entirely gone ; the turnips emerged, not damaged at all, save in sunny places ; the wheat looked delicately ; and the garden plants were well preserved ; for snow is the most kindly mantle that infant vegetation can be wrapped in : were it not for that friendly meteor, no vegetable life could exist at all in northerly regions. Yet in Sweden, the earth in April is not divested of snow for more than a fortnight before the face of the country is covered with flowers.

LETTER CVI.

TO THE HON. DAINES BARRINGTON.

THERE were some circumstances attending the remarkable frost in January, 1776, so singular and striking, that a short detail of them may not be unacceptable.

The most certain way to be exact will be to copy the passages from my journal, which were taken from time to time as things occurred. But it may be proper previously to remark, that the first week in January was uncommonly wet, and drowned with vast rains from every quarter : from whence may be inferred, as there is great reason to believe is the case, that intense frosts seldom take place till the earth is perfectly glutted and chilled with water ; and hence dry autumns are seldom followed by rigorous winters. *

January 7th. — Snow driving all the day, which was followed by frost, sleet, and some snow, till the twelfth, when a prodigious mass overwhelmed all the works of men, drifting over the tops of the gates, and filling the hollow lanes.

On the fourteenth, the writer was obliged to be much abroad ; and thinks he never before or since encountered such rugged Siberian weather. Many of the narrow roads were now filled above the tops of the hedges ; through which the snow was driven into most romantic and grotesque shapes, so striking to the imagination, as not to be seen without wonder and pleasure. The poultry dared not to stir out of their roosting places ; for cocks and hens are so dazzled and confounded by the glare of snow, that they would soon perish.

---

* The autumn preceding January, 1768, was very wet, and particularly the month of September, during which there fell at Lyndon, in the county of Rutland, six inches and a half of rain. And the terrible long. frost in 1739-40 set in after a rainy season, and when the springs were. very high.

without assistance.   The hares also lay sullenly in their seats, and would not move till compelled by hunger; being conscious, poor animals, that the drifts and heaps treacherously betray their footsteps, and prove fatal to numbers of them.

From the fourteenth, the snow continued to increase. and began to stop the road-wagons and coaches, which could no longer keep on their regular stages ; and especially on the western roads, where the fall appears to have been deeper than in the south.   The company at Bath, that wanted to attend the Queen's birth day, were strangely incommoded : many carriages of persons who got, in their way to town from Bath, as far as Marlborough, after strange embarrassments, here met with a *ne plus ultra*.   The ladies fretted, and offered large rewards to labourers, if they would shovel them a road to London ; but the relentless heaps of snow were too bulky to be removed ; and so the eighteenth passed over, leaving the company in very uncomfortable circumstances, at the Castle and other inns.

On the twentieth, the sun shone out for the first time since the frost began ; a circumstance, that has been remarked before, much in favour of vegetation.   All this time, the cold was not very intense, for the thermometer stood at twenty-nine, twenty-eight, twenty-five, and thereabout ; but on the twenty-first it descended to twenty.   The birds now began to be in a very pitiable and starving condition.   Tamed by the season, sky-larks settled in the streets of towns, because they saw the ground was bare ; rooks frequented dunghills close to houses; and crows watched horses as they passed, and greedily devoured what dropped from them ; hares now came into men's gardens, and, scraping away the snow, devoured such plants as they could find.

On the twenty-second, the author had occasion to go to London, through a sort of Laplandian scene, very wild and grotesque indeed.   But the metropolis itself exhibited a still more singular appearance than the country ; for, being bedded deep in snow, the pavement of the streets could not be touched by the wheels or the horses' feet, so that the carriages ran about without the least noise.   Such an exemption from din and clatter was strange, but not pleasant; it seemed to convey an uncomfortable idea of desolation :

Ipsa silentia terrent.

On the twenty-seventh, much snow fell all day, and in the evening, the frost became very intense.   At South Lambeth, for the four following nights, the thermometer fell to eleven, seven, six, six; and at Selborne, to seven, six, ten; and on the thirty-first of January, just before sunrise, with rime on the trees, and on the tube of the glass, the quicksilver sank exactly to zero, being thirty-two degrees below the freezing point; but by eleven in the morning, though in the shade, it sprang up to sixteen and a half,* — a most unusual degree of cold this for the south of England! During these four nights, the cold was so penetrating, that it occasioned ice in warm chambers, and under beds; and, in the day, the wind was so keen, that persons of robust constitutions could scarcely endure to face it. The Thames was at once so frozen over, both above and below bridge, that crowds ran about on the ice. The streets were now strangely encumbered with snow, which crumbled and trode dusty; and, turning gray, resembled bay salt: what had fallen on the roofs was so perfectly dry, that, from first to last, it lay twenty-six days on the houses in the city; a longer time than had been remembered by the oldest housekeepers living. According to all appearances, we might now have expected the continuance of this rigorous weather for weeks to come, since every night increased in severity; but behold, without any apparent cause, on the first of February, a thaw took place, and some rain followed before night; making good the observation above, that frosts often go off as it were, at once, without any gradual declension of cold. On the second of February, the thaw persisted; and on the third, swarms of little insects were frisking and sporting in a court-yard at South Lambeth, as if they had felt no frost. Why the juices in the small bodies and smaller limbs of such minute beings, are not frozen, is a matter of curious inquiry.†

* At Selborne, the cold was greater than at any other place that the author could hear of with certainty; though some reported at the time, that, at a village in Kent, the thermometer fell two degrees below zero, viz. thirty-four degrees below the freezing point. The thermometer used at Selborne was graduated by Benjamin Martin.

† It is surprising the degree of cold which the eggs and chrisalids of insects can endure, without destroying the vital principle; nor is it less astonishing the degree of heat they are capable of sustaining. Spallanzani, and John Hunter, have made some curious experiments on these subjects. "Intense cold," says Spallanzani, "does not destroy the eggs of insects." The year 1709 was celebrated for the intensity of its cold, and its fatal effects on animals and plants. Fahrenheit's thermometer fell to one degree. 'Who can believe,' exclaims Boerhaave, ' that the severity of this winter did not destroy the eggs of insects, especially those exposed to its influence in open fields, on the bare earth, or on the exposed branches

Severe frosts seem to be partial, or to run in currents ; for at the same juncture, as the author was informed by accurate correspondents, at Lyndon, in the county of Rutland, the thermometer stood at nineteen; at Blackburn, in Lancashire, at nineteen ; and at Manchester, at twenty-one, twenty, and eighteen. Thus does some unknown circumstance strangely overbalance latitude, and render the cold sometimes much greater in the southern than the northern parts of this kingdom.

The consequences of this severity were, that, in Hampshire, at the melting of the snow, the wheat looked well, and the turnips came forth little injured. The laurels and laurustines were somewhat damaged, but only in hot aspects. No evergreens were quite destroyed ; and not half the damage sustained that befell in January, 1768. Those laurels that were a little scorched on the south sides, were perfectly untouched on their north sides. The care taken to shake the snow day by day from the branches, seemed greatly to avail the author's evergreens. A neighbour's laurel hedge, in a high situation, and facing to the north, was perfectly green and vigorous ; and the Portugal laurels remained unhurt.

As to the birds, the thrushes and blackbirds were mostly destroyed ; and the partridges, by the weather and poachers, were so thinned, that few remained to breed the following year.

of trees! Yet the genial warmth of spring having again tempered the air, these eggs were hatched, and as numerously as in the mildest winters.' Since that time, there have been winters still more severe, for, in France, as well as in several other European states, in December, 1788, the thermometer fell considerably beneath that of 1709.

" I subjected eggs of insects to a more severe trial than in the winter of 1709. Among others were those of the silk-worm moth, and the elm butterfly, which I enclosed in a glass vessel, and buried five hours in a mixture of the ice and rock-salt, when the thermometer fell six degrees below zero; notwithstanding which, caterpillars were extruded from all the eggs, and exactly at the same time with those which had not been subjected to this experiment. In the succeeding year, I exposed them to a still greater degree of cold. I prepared a mixture of rock-salt and nitrate of ammonia, and reduced the thermometer to twenty-two degrees below zero, which was twenty-three degrees lower than the cold of 1709. They suffered nothing from this rigorous treatment, as they were all hatched in due season." From the experiments of John Hunter, we find that a hen's egg will freeze by a great degree of cold, while, at the same time, it is possessed of a principle of vitality which prevents its destruction. — Ed.

LETTER CVII.

TO THE HON. DAINES BARRINGTON.

As the frost in December, 1784, was very extraordinary, you, I trust, will not be displeased to hear the particulars; and especially when I promise to say no more about the severities of winter, after I have finished this letter.

The first week in December was very wet, with the barometer very low. On the seventh, with the barometer at twenty-eight five-tenths, came on a vast snow, which continued all that day and the next, and most part of the following night; so that, by the morning of the ninth, the works of men were quite overwhelmed, the lanes filled so as to be impassable, and the ground covered twelve or fifteen inches without any drifting. In the evening of the ninth, the air began to be so very sharp, that we thought it would be curious to attend to the motions of a thermometer; we, therefore, hung out two, one made by Martin, and one by Dolland, which soon began to shew us what we were to expect; for, by ten o'clock, they fell to twenty-one, and at eleven to four, when we went to bed. On the tenth, in the morning, the quicksilver of Dolland's glass was down to half a degree below zero, and that of Martin's, which was absurdly graduated only to four degrees above zero, sunk quite into the brass guard of the ball, so that, when the weather became most interesting, this was useless. On the tenth, at eleven at night, though the air was perfectly still, Dolland's glass went down to one degree below zero! This strange severity of the weather made me very desirous to know what degree of cold there might be in such an exalted and near situation as Newton. We had, therefore, on the morning of the tenth, written to Mr ———, and entreated him to hang out his thermometer, made by Adams, and to pay some attention to it, morning and evening, expecting wonderful phenomena, in so elevated a region, at two hundred feet or more above my house. But, behold! on the tenth, at eleven at night, it was down only to seventeen, and the next morning at twenty-two, when mine was at ten! We were so disturbed at this unexpected reverse of comparative local cold, that we sent one of my glasses up, thinking that of Mr ——— must, somehow, be wrongly constructed. But, when the instruments came to be confronted, they went exactly together, so that, for one night at least, the cold at Newton was eighteen degrees less than at Selborne, and, through the whole frost, ten or twelve degrees ;* and, indeed, when we came to observe consequences, we could readily credit this, for all my laurustines, bays, ilexes, arbutuses, cypresses, and even my Portugal laurels, and, which occasions more regret, my fine sloping laurel hedge, were scorched up, while, at Newton, the same trees have not lost a leaf!

We had steady frost on the twenty-fifth, when the thermometer, in the morning, was down to ten with us, and at Newton only to twenty-one. Strong frost continued till the thirty-first, when some tendency to thaw was observed, and by January the third, 1785, the thaw was confirmed, and some rain fell.

A circumstance that I must not omit, because it was new to us, is, that on Friday, December the tenth, being bright sunshine, the air was full of icy *spiculæ*, floating in all directions, like atoms in a sunbeam let into a dark room. We thought them, at first, particles of the rime falling from my tall hedges, but were soon convinced to the contrary, by making our observations in open places where no rime could reach us. Were they watery particles of the air frozen as

* The Rev. Mr Bree, of Allesley Rectory, made similar observations in the years 1830 and 1831. He says, " I have elsewhere observed, in the year 1830, that the effects of the frosty nights on trees seemed to differ according to the circumstances, and to be most destructive in lower situations. Several instances of the same kind presented themselves to my notice this season, during the frosts which prevailed in the month of May. The gooseberries and currants were in some cases much injured in gardens which lay low, while those in more elevated situations escaped unhurt. Many of our native plants were cut off, as *equisetum arvense, aspidium filix mas.* and *aculeatum scilla nutans,* &c. all of them lovers of low ground. But not only were the late frosts most destructive in low situations, they seem also to have had a much more injurious effect on vegetation within a few feet of the surface of the ground than they had as many yards above it. And of this I was struck with a remarkable instance in a wood in this neighbourhood, which consists chiefly of oak. For the space of several acres, I observed the opening foliage of the underwood oak, about seven or eight feet from the ground, to be entirely cut off by the frost, though the bushes were, of course, much sheltered by the overshadowing boughs of the poles and trees above them ; while, contrary to what might be expected, the foliage of the poles and trees themselves, which were exposed to the atmosphere, but elevated some yards above the underwood, remained unaffected. In the case, also, of single oak trees, in other situations, I observed the foliage of the lower boughs to be cut off by the frost, and the head of the higher branches to be unimpaired." —Ed.

they floated, or were they evaporations from the snow frozen
as they mounted ?*

We were much obliged to the thermometers for the early
information they gave us, and hurried our apples, pears, onions,
potatoes, &c. into the cellar and warm closets : while those
who had not, or neglected such warnings, lost all their stores of
roots and fruits, and had their very bread and cheese frozen.

I must not omit to tell you, that, during those two Siberian
days, my parlour cat was so electric, that had a person stroked
her, and been properly insulated, the shock might have been
given to a whole circle of people.†

* We can account for this phenomenon only by the supposition, that
these spiculæ were formed by a thin stratum of vapour passing through
the higher regions of the atmosphere; and that they were not dense
enough to have the ordinary appearance of snow. We know that snow
itself is crystallized vapour, and the distinctness and forms of these crystals
will be in proportion to the intensity of the cold at the time. The
ordinary cold in this country is seldom such as to produce these, and the
snow has usually a flaky appearance. Captain Scoresby mentions having
frequently seen snow in a highly crystallized state in the Arctic Regions.
In this country there are occasional showers of highly crystallized snow.
On the 4th of February, 1830, a fall of this kind was noticed at Cambridge, the thermometer then standing at about twenty-two degrees, and
the wind from the east-north-east. Nearly all the snow which fell was
of that beautiful stellated form called by Captain Scoresby the "lamellar
stelliform crystals." They consisted chiefly of six points, radiating from
a centre, forming with each other, at that centre, angles of sixty degrees,
and having commonly additional ramifications on the primary ones, in
the same plane with them, and forming angles of sixty degrees with the
primaries. These, however, consisted of great variety in their arrangement. Some were regular in all their parts, while others were quite
eccentric. Some of these were fashioned by the obliteration of the
alternate rays, so as to form angles of one hundred and twenty, instead
of one hundred and sixty, degrees; the additional ramifications still
forming angles of sixty degrees with the primaries. The size of these
crystals varied from one-eighth to one-third of an inch in diameter.
Scoresby says, that the time when the greatest quantity of crystals fell in
the Arctic Seas, was when the thermometer stood between sixteen and
twenty-two degrees, and the wind was north-east or north-north-east,
which corresponded with what was observed at Cambridge. — ED.

† Some animals have the voluntary power of communicating electricity,
The torpedo, and electric eel, may be mentioned as well known instances.
In the *Magazine of Natural History,* a correspondent mentions having
received several shocks from a caterpillar of the *cerura vinula,* or puss-
moth. These he found on a young poplar. He says, — " The *cerura*
shewed decided symptoms of irritation, which particularly drew my attention. It began to contract its body, drawing itself closely together, and,
by degrees, elevated and extended its bifurcated tail. There were slowly
protruded from out of the points bright red filaments, and irregularly
bent to one side. In a short time I felt a sudden tingle along my arms,

I forgot to mention before, that, during the two severe days, two men, who were tracing hares in the snow, had their feet frozen ; and two men, who were much better employed, had their fingers so affected by the frost, while they were thrashing in a barn, that mortification followed, from which they did not recover for many weeks.

This frost killed all the furze and most of the ivy, and in many places stripped the hollies of all their leaves. It came at a very early time of the year, before old November ended, and may yet be allowed, from its effects, to have exceeded any since 1739-40.*

LETTER CVIII.

TO THE HON. DAINES BARRINGTON.

As the effects of heat are seldom very remarkable in the northerly climate of England, where the summers are often so defective in warmth and sunshine, as not to ripen the fruits of the earth so well as might be wished, I shall be more concise in my account of the severity of a summer season, and so make a little amends for the prolix account of the degrees of cold, and the inconveniencies that we suffered from some late rigorous winters.

The summers of 1781 and 1783, were unusually hot and dry ; to them, therefore, I shall turn back in my journals, without recurring to any more distant period.   In the former of these years, my peach and nectarine trees suffered so much from the heat, that the rind on the bodies was scalded and came off ; since which, the trees have been in a decaying state. This may prove a hint to assiduous gardeners to fence and shelter their wall-trees with mats or boards, as they may easily do, because such annoyance is seldom of long continuance.   During that summer, also, I observed that my apples were coddled, as it were, on the trees ; so that they had no quickness of flavour, and would not keep in the winter. This

which made me stop with surprise.   Suspecting, however, that this might be imaginary, I again proceeded ; and shortly after I felt another shock, which made me almost involuntarily throw the twig with the creature upon the ground."— ED.

* Mr Miller, in his *Gardener's Dictionary*, says positively, that the Portugal laurels remained untouched in the remarkable frost of 1739-40 : so that either that accurate observer was much mistaken, or else the frost of December, 1784, was much more severe and destructive than that in the year above mentioned.

circumstance put me in mind of what I have heard travellers assert, that they never ate a good apple or apricot in the south of Europe, where the heats were so great as to render the juices vapid and insipid.

The great pests of a garden are wasps, which destroy all the finer fruits just as they are coming into perfection. In 1781, we had none; in 1783, there were myriads, which would have devoured all the produce of my garden had we not set the boys to take the nests, and caught thousands with hazel-twigs tipped with bird-lime: we have since employed the boys to take and destroy the large breeding wasps in the spring. Such expedients have a great effect on these marauders, and will keep them under. Though wasps do not abound but in hot summers, yet they do not prevail in every hot summer, as I have instanced in the two years above mentioned. *

In the sultry season of 1783, honey-dews were so frequent as to deface and destroy the beauties of my garden. My honeysuckles, which were one week the most sweet and lovely objects that eye could behold, became the next the most loathsome, being enveloped in a viscous substance, and loaded with black *aphides*, or smother-flies. The occasion of this clammy

---

* There is a wonderful provision in the economy of Nature, by which the numbers of these troublesome marauders are kept within moderate bounds, and but for which they would soon overrun the face of the earth. Every wasp's nest is peopled by several thousands of neuters, or workers. But the neuters, which are first produced, are likewise the first that perish: for not one of them survives the termination of even a mild winter.

The female wasps are, however, stronger, and can bear the rigours of winter better than either the males or neuters. But several hundreds of the females of every nest perish before the end of the winter, and, indeed, not more than ten or a dozen of each nest survive that season. These females are destined for the continuation of the species, and each of them becomes the founder of a new republic. It is quite uncertain whether any male wasps survive. Every nest, about the beginning of October, presents a strange scene of what appears anomalous cruelty. The wasps then not only desist from bringing nourishment to their young, but also drag them in the caterpillar state from their cells, and expose them to the weather, where they either die for want of food, or become a prey to birds, or, as is more generally the case, the parent wasps pinch them to death with their forceps. But instead of being cruel and unnatural, this is perhaps an act of mercy, as wasps do not lay up a store of food for the winter, and their progeny would consequently die a painful and lingering death from starvation if left in their cells. So that what appears a transgression of the predominating love of animals for their young is, in fact, a merciful effort of instinct. — ED.

appearance seems to be this, that in hot weather, the effluvia of flowers in fields, and meadows, and gardens, are drawn up in the day by a brisk evaporation, and then in the night fall down again with the dews in which they are entangled ; that the air is strongly scented, and therefore impregnated with the particles of flowers in summer weather, our senses will inform us ; and that this clammy sweet substance is of the vegetable kind, we may learn from bees, to whom it is very grateful ; and we may be assured that it falls in the night, because it is always first seen in warm still mornings. *

On chalky and sandy soils, and in the hot villages about London, the thermometer has been often observed to mount as high as eighty-three or eighty-four ; but with us, in this hilly and woody district, I have hardly ever seen it exceed eighty, nor does it often arrive at that pitch. The reason, I conclude, is, that our dense clayey soil, so much shaded by trees, is not so easily heated through as those above mentioned ; and, besides, our mountains cause currents of air and breezes ; and the vast effluvia from our woodlands temper and moderate our heats.

LETTER CIX.

TO THE HON. DAINES BARRINGTON.

THE summer of the year 1783, was an amazing and portentous one, and full of horrible phenomena ; for, besides the alarming meteors and tremendous thunder-storms, that affrighted and distressed the different counties of this kingdom, the peculiar haze, or smoky fog, that prevailed for many weeks in this island, and in every part of Europe, and even beyond its limits, was a most extraordinary appearance, unlike any thing known within the memory of man. By my journal, I find that I had noticed this strange occurrence from June twenty-third to July twentieth, inclusive, during which period the wind varied to every quarter, without making any alteration in the air. The sun, at noon, looked as blank as a clouded moon, and shed a rust-coloured ferruginous light on the ground and floors of rooms, but was particularly lurid and blood-coloured at rising and setting. All the time, the heat was so intense that butchers' meat could hardly be eaten the day after it was killed ; and the flies swarmed so in the lanes and hedges, that they rendered the horses half frantic, and riding irksome. The

* Honey dew is the excrement of the aphides. — ED.

country people began to look with a superstitious awe at the
red lowering aspect of the sun; and, indeed, there was reason
'for the most enlightened person to be apprehensive, for all
the while, Calabria and part of the isle of Sicily were torn and
convulsed with earthquakes;* and about that juncture, a
volcano sprung out of the sea on the coast of Norway.   On
this occasion, Milton's noble simile of the sun, in his first book
of Paradise Lost, frequently occurred to my mind; and it is
indeed particularly applicable, because, towards the end, it
alludes to a superstitious kind of dread, with which the minds
of men are always impressed by such strange and unusual
phenomena : —

—— As when the sun, new risen,
Looks through the horizontal, misty air,
Shorn of his beams; or, from behind the moon,
In dim eclipse, disastrous twilight sheds
On half the nations, and with fear of change
Perplexes monarchs. ——

LETTER CX.

TO THE HON. DAINES BARRINGTON.

WE are very seldom annoyed with thunder-storms; and it
is no less remarkable than true, that those which arise in the
south have hardly been known to reach this village; for, before
they get over us, they take a direction to the east or to the
west, or sometimes divide into two, and go in part to one of
those quarters, and in part to the other; as was truly the case
in summer 1783, when, though the country round was continually harassed with tempests, and often from the south, yet
we escaped them all; as appears by my journal of that summer.

* The shocks of the dreadful earthquakes here alluded to began on the
5th February, and continued, at different times, till the 1st of March,
1783; during which time, the face of the two Calabrias, lying between
the thirty-eighth and thirty-ninth degree, were entirely altered; hills
had been swallowed up, others lowered; huge mountains split asunder,
and parts of them driven to a considerable distance; valleys filled up; the
courses of rivers altered; springs dried, and new ones formed.   At
Laureana, in Calabria Ultra, two tenements, with large plantations,
situated in a level valley, were detached by the earthquake, and trans-
planted, with their trees still remaining in their places, to the distance of
about a mile from their first situation; and from the spot on which they
formerly stood, hot water, mixed with sand, sprang to a considerable
height.   It would be difficult to assign the reason why Europe generally
was much affected in the electrical condition of its atmosphere during
this remarkable summer. — ED.

The only way that I can at all account for this fact—for such it is—is, that on that quarter, between us and the sea, there are continual mountains, hill behind hill, such as Nore-hill, the Barnet, Butser-hill, and Ports-down, which somehow divert the storms, and give them a different direction. High promontories, and elevated grounds, have always been observed to attract clouds, and disarm them of their mischievous contents, which are discharged into the trees and summits, as soon as they come in contact with these turbulent meteors; while the humble vales escape, because they are so far beneath them.

But when I say I do not remember a thunder-storm from the south, I do not mean that we never have suffered from thunder-storms at all; for on June 5th, 1784, the thermometer in the morning being at sixty-four, and at noon at seventy, the barometer at twenty-nine, six-tenths one-half, and the wind north, I observed a blue mist, smelling strongly of sulphur, hang along our sloping woods, and seeming to indicate that thunder was at hand. I was called in about two in the afternoon, and so missed seeing the gathering of the clouds in the north, which they who were abroad assured me had something uncommon in its appearance. At about a quarter after two, the storm began in the parish of Harteley, moving slowly from north to south; and from thence it came over Norton-farm, and so to Grange-farm, both in this parish. It began with vast drops of rain, which were soon succeeded by round hail, and then by convex pieces of ice, which measured three inches in girth.* Had it been as extensive as it was violent, and of any continuance, (for it was very short,) it must have ravaged all the neighbourhood. In the parish of Harteley, it did some damage to one farm; but Norton, which lay

---

* On the 4th January, 1829, a violent hail-storm passed over Edmonton, near London; during which, hailstones fell of an irregular shape, and measuring three and four inches in circumference. Calamities from hail, however, are but of rare occurrence in this country, compared with the Continent. In France, hail-storms are frequent and formidable, and, in many districts, have done great injuries to corn, as also to vines and olive trees. In the years 1799, 1800, and 1801, the storms of hail in France had been more than usually prevalent, and many families had, in consequence, been reduced to ruin. This state of things suggested to M. Barrau, of Toulouse, the establishment of a mutual indemnity insurance company against hail, which has been continued ever since.

Some time ago, hailstones fell at Sterlitamak, in the government of Onesburg, which were found to contain in their centre a nucleus of small stones. These were analysed, and in one hundred, their component parts consisted of red oxide of iron 70.00, of oxide of manganese 7.50, alum 3.75, silica 7.50, sulphur and waste 5.00. —ED.

in the centre of the storm, was greatly injured; as was Grange, which lay next to it.   It did but just reach to the middle of the village, where the hail broke my north windows, and all my garden-lights and hand-glasses, and many of my neighbours' windows.   The extent of the storm was about two miles in length, and one in breadth.   We were just sitting down to dinner; but were soon diverted from our repast by the clattering of tiles, and the jingling of glass.   There fell, at the same time, prodigious torrents of rain on the farms above mentioned, which occasioned a flood as violent as it was sudden; doing great damage to the meadows and fallows, by deluging the one, and washing away the soil of the other.   The hollow lane towards Alton was so torn and disordered as not to be passable till mended, rocks being removed that weighed two hundred weight.   Those that saw the effect which the great hail had on ponds and pools, say that the dashing of the water made an extraordinary appearance, the froth and spray standing up in the air three feet above the surface.   The rushing and roaring of the hail, as it approached, was truly tremendous.

Though the clouds at South Lambeth, near London, were at that juncture thin and light, and no storm was in sight, nor within hearing, yet the air was strongly electric; for the bells of an electric machine at that place rang repeatedly, and fierce sparks were discharged.

When I first took the present work in hand, I proposed to have added an *Annus-Historico-Naturalis*, or the Natural History of the Twelve Months of the Year; which would have comprised many incidents and occurrences that have not fallen into my way to be mentioned in my series of letters; but, as Mr Aikin of Warrington has lately published somewhat of this sort, and as the length of my correspondence has sufficiently put your patience to the test, I shall here take a respectful leave of you and Natural History together.   And am,

With all due deference and regard,

Your most obliged,

And most humble Servant,

GIL. WHITE.

SELBORNE, *June* 25, 1787.

OBSERVATIONS

 on

VARIOUS PARTS OF NATURE,

FROM MR WHITE'S MSS.

WITH

REMARKS BY MR MARKWICK AND THE EDITOR.

OBSERVATIONS ON QUADRUPEDS.

SHEEP.— The sheep on the downs this winter (1769) are very ragged, and their coats much torn ; the shepherds say, they tear their fleeces with their own mouths and horns, and they are always in that way in mild wet winters, being teased and tickled with a kind of lice.

After ewes and lambs are shorn, there is great confusion and bleating, neither the dams nor the young being able to distinguish one another as before. This embarrassment seems not so much to arise from the loss of the fleece, which may occasion an alteration in their appearance, as from the defect of that *notus odor*, discriminating each individual personally ; which also is confounded by the strong scent of the pitch and tar wherewith they are newly marked ; for the brute creation recognize each other more from the smell than the sight ; and in matters of identity and diversity, appeal much more to their noses than their eyes. After sheep have been washed, there is the same confusion, from the reason given above.

RABBITS.— Rabbits make incomparably the finest turf, for they not only bite closer than larger quadrupeds, but they allow no bents to rise ; hence warrens produce much the most delicate turf for gardens. Sheep never touch the stalks of grasses.

CAT AND SQUIRRELS. — A boy has taken three little young squirrels in their nest, or drey, as it is called in these parts. These small creatures he put under the care of a cat who had lately lost her kittens, and finds that she nurses and suckles them with the same assiduity and affection as if they were her own offspring. This circumstance corroborates my suspicion, that the mention of exposed and deserted children being nurtured by female beasts of prey who had lost their young, may not be so improbable an incident as many have supposed; and therefore may be. a justification of those authors who have gravely mentioned, what some have deemed to be a wild and improbable story.

So many people went to see the little squirrels suckled by a cat, that the foster mother became jealous of her charge, and in pain for their safety ; and therefore hid them over the ceiling, where one died. This circumstance shews her affection for these fondlings, and that she supposes the squirrels to be her own young. Thus hens, when they have hatched ducklings, are equally attached to them as if they were their own chickens.

HORSE. — An old hunting mare, which ran on the common, being taken very ill, ran down into the village, as it were, to implore the help of men, and died the night following in the street.*

HOUNDS. — The king's stag hounds came down to Alton, attended by a huntsman and six yeoman prickers, with horns, to try for the stag that has haunted Harteley Wood for so long a time. Many hundreds of people, horse and foot, attended the dogs to see the deer unharboured; but though the huntsman drew Harteley Wood, and Long Coppice, and Shrubwood, and Temple Hangers, and, in their way back, Harteley and Ward-le-ham Hangers, yet no stag could be found.

---

* The Rev. Mr Bree says, " Some years ago, a quantity of peat soil was thrown down in a heap, in the corner of a small field adjoining my house, for the purpose of being used in the garden as occasion required. A horse that was turned out into the same field (which I may observe afforded a good pasture) was in the frequent habit of going to this heap of peat soil, and feeding upon it with as much apparent satisfaction as if it had been a rick of good hay. A pointer dog, also, which was usually kept tied up, on being let loose, would almost invariably go to the heap of soil, and devour lumps of it with avidity."— ED.

· The royal pack, accustomed to have the deer turned out before them, never drew the coverts with any address and spirit, as many people that were present observed; and this remark the event has proved to be a true one : for as a person was lately pursuing a pheasant that was wing-broken, in Harteley Wood, he stumbled upon the stag by accident, and ran in upon him as he lay concealed amidst a thick brake of brambles and bushes.

OBSERVATIONS ON BIRDS.

BIRDS IN GENERAL.

In severe weather, fieldfares, redwings, skylarks, and titlarks, resort to watered meadows for food ; the latter wades up to its belly in pursuit of the pupæ of insects, and runs along upon the floating grass and weeds. Many gnats are on the snow near the water : these support the birds in part.

Birds are much influenced in their choice of food by colour; for though white currants are much sweeter fruit than red, yet they seldom touch the former till they have devoured every bunch of the latter.

Redstarts, fly-catchers, and black-caps, arrive early in April. If these little delicate beings are birds of passage, (as we have reason to suppose they are, because they are never seen in winter,) how could they, feeble as they seem, bear up against such storms of snow and rain, and make their way through such meteorous turbulences, as one should suppose would embarrass and retard the most hardy and resolute of the winged nation ? Yet they keep their appointed times and seasons ; and, in spite of frost and winds, return to their stations periodically, as if they had met with nothing to obstruct them. The withdrawing and appearance of the short-winged summer birds, is a very puzzling circumstance in natural history.

When the boys bring me wasps' nests, my bantam fowls fare deliciously, and, when the combs are pulled to pieces, devour the young wasps in their maggot state, with the highest glee and delight. Any insect-eating bird would do the same; and, therefore, I have often wondered that the accurate Mr Ray should call one species of buzzard *buteo apivorus sive vespivorus*, or the *honey-buzzard*, because some combs of wasps happened to be found in one of their nests. The combs were conveyed thither, doubtless, for the sake of the maggots or nymphs, and not for their honey; since none is to be found in the combs of wasps. Birds of prey occasionally feed on insects; thus have I seen a tame kite picking up the female ants full of eggs, with much satisfaction.*

* That redstarts, fly-catchers, black-caps, and other slender-billed insectivorous small birds, particularly the swallow tribe, make their first appearance very early in the spring, is a well known fact; though the fly-catcher is the latest of them all in its visit, (as this accurate naturalist observes in another place,) for it is never seen before the month of May. If these delicate creatures come to us from a distant country, they will probably be exposed in their passage, as Mr White justly remarks, to much greater difficulties from storms and tempests, than their feeble powers appear to be able to surmount:* on the other hand, if we suppose them to pass the winter in a dormant state, in this country, concealed in caverns, or other hiding places, sufficiently guarded from the extreme cold of our winter, to preserve their life, and that, at the approach of spring, they revive from their torpid state, and reassume their usual powers of action, it will entirely remove the first difficulty, arising from the storms and tempests they are liable to meet with in their passage; but how are we to get over the still greater difficulty of their revivification from their torpid state? What degree of warmth in the temperature of the air is necessary to produce that effect, and how it operates on the functions of animal life, are questions not easily answered.

How could Mr White suppose that Ray named this species the honey-buzzard, because it fed on honey, when he not only named it in Latin, *buteo apivorus et vespivorus*, but expressly says, that " it feeds on insects, and brings up its young with the maggots, or nymphs of wasps."

That birds of prey, when in want of their proper food, flesh, sometimes feed on insects, I have little doubt, and think I have observed the common buzzard, (*falco buteo*,) to settle on the ground, and pick up insects of some kind or other.—MARKWICK.

Our author seems sceptical to the last regarding the migration of birds generally, and especially the short-winged tribes. The following observations were made by Mr Andrew Bloxam, of Glenfield, near Leicester, in a voyage from England to South America, in the years

* M. Neumann has recorded a very extraordinary fact, of a fine specimen of the little thrush, *turdus minor* of Bonaparte, being taken, on the 23d December, 1825, in a wood near Kleinzererbst, in the Duchy of Anhalt-Cœthen, Germany. It would be difficult to account for the appearance of this bird, supposed to be exclusively found in North America, as it exhibited no marks of confinement.—ED.

Rooks. — Rooks are continually fighting, and pulling each other's nests to pieces : these proceedings are inconsistent with

1824 - 5. They cannot fail to be highly interesting, as proving the great excursions frequently, if not periodically, taken by land birds : — " 1824, Oct. 11. A chaffinch flew on board ; weather stormy ; Bay of Biscay, lat. 48 deg. 33 min. north, long. 7 deg. 50 min. west. Several snipes were seen the same day. — Oct. 13. A skylark was caught ; weather stormy ; lat. 45 deg. 4 min. north, long. 10 deg. 10 min. west. — Oct. 14. A goldfinch was caught in the rigging ; this and the two former soon died from exhaustion ; at the same time, a small white owl flew round the vessel, but did not settle on board ; lat. 44 deg. 1 min. north, long. 11 deg. 19 min. west ; wind brisk ; our nearest distance from land, Cape Finisterre, one hundred and twenty miles. — Oct. 27. A hawk was seen flying about the ship, but did not settle ; distance from the Canary Islands, the nearest land, two hundred and fifty miles. — Oct. 29. In the morning, a single swallow was seen flying about the vessel, and frequently settling ; it was joined soon afterwards by another, and both continued with us the whole day ; lat. 23 deg. 11 min. north, long. 23 deg. 13 min. west. — Oct. 30. Swallows and martens in great numbers about the vessel ; they were easily captured by the sailors, as they flew close to the deck, in search of flies ; they appeared to be more in want of food than tired ; lat. 41 deg. 47 min. north, long. 25 deg. 58 min. west. — Oct. 31. Swallows and martens still continue with us in great numbers, and were seen several successive days, apparently on a south-west course ; a hen redstart was also observed about the ship ; it continued with us several days, and used to come into the ports of the after gun-room to be fed, food being purposely placed there for it ; lat. 19 deg. 54 min. north, long. 25 deg. west. — Nov. 3. Swallows still with us. — Nov. 4. The spotted gallinule was caught on deck ; lat. 8 deg. 2 min. north, long. 25 deg. 37 min. west. — Nov. 7. A fine female kestrel hawk was captured in the rigging ; it was preserved in a cage for some days, but afterwards contrived to escape, and flew off ; lat. 8 deg. 2 min. north, long. 24 deg. 40 min. west ; four hundred and twenty-four miles from land. It is remarkable, that all the above named are British ; they were verified by a reference to Bewick's Birds. — Nov. 21. A small bat, or large, dark-coloured moth, was seen flying about the top of the rigging, but soon left us ; we were three hundred miles from the nearest point of South America. — Nov. 23. A Brazilian land bird, *corvus dubius* of Linn. settled on board ; lat. 22 deg. 46 min. south, long. 37 deg. 42 min. west ; about three hundred miles from Rio Janeiro. — Dec. 30. The *fringilla australis* flew on board ; we were, at the time, exactly thirty-seven miles south of Staten Land, with a northerly breeze. — 1825, Sept. 28. A small humming-bird flew round the vessel, but did not settle on board ; we were, at the time, about ten miles from land, off the coast of Chili, opposite Conception.

" It may be remarked, that, though so many land birds were seen on our passage out, not one was met with on the return. I found swallows both at Rio Janeiro and Valparaiso ; at the latter place, rearing their young. The marten I also found at Valparaiso, and other parts of Chili." — ED.

living in such close community. And yet, if a pair offer to build on a single tree, the nest is plundered and demolished at once. Some rooks roost on their nest-trees. The twigs which the rooks drop in building, supply the poor with brush-wood to light their fires. Some unhappy pairs are not per-mitted to finish any nests till the rest have completed their building. As soon as they get a few sticks together, a party comes and demolishes the whole. As soon as rooks have finished their nests, and before they lay, the cocks begin to feed the hens, who receive their bounty with a fondling, tre-mulous voice, and fluttering wings, and all the little blandish-ments that are expressed by the young, while in a helpless state. This gallant deportment of the male is continued through the whole season of incubation. These birds do not copulate on trees, nor in their nests, but on the ground in the open fields. *

THRUSHES.—Thrushes, during long droughts, are of great service in hunting out shell snails, which they pull in pieces for their young, and are thereby very serviceable in gardens. †
Missel thrushes do not destroy the fruit in gardens like the other species of *turdi,* but feed on the berries of misseltoe,

---

* After the first brood of rooks are sufficiently fledged, they all leave their nest-trees in the day time, and resort to some distant place in search of food, but return regularly every evening, in vast flights, to their nest-trees, where, after flying round several times, with much noise and clamour, till they are all assembled together, they take up their abode for the night.—MARKWICK.

† We are aware that thrushes feed on snail shells, but think it more likely that they will find them in moist than in dry weather, at which time they generally conceal themselves in holes.

In the neighbourhood of Pitlessie, in Fife, a pair of thrushes built their nest in a cart-shed, while four wheelwrights were engaged in it as a work-shop. It was placed between one of the hulls of the harrow and the adjoining tooth. The men were busily employed at the noiseful work of joining wood all the day, yet these birds flew in and out at the door of the shed, without fear or dread, and finished their nest with mortar. On the second day, the hen laid an egg, on which she sat, and was occasionally relieved by the cock. In thirteen days the birds came out of the shells, which the old ones always carried off. They fed their young with shell-snails, such as those of the *helex nemoralis, H. arbus-torum,* and *H. aspersa,* as also butterflies and moths. The nest was robbed one Sunday, in the absence of the millwrights.

Mr E. H. Greenhow, of North Shields, mentions a similar occurrence which came under his own observation, at Whitby. This nest was also built in a shed, at a public place.—ED.

and, in the spring, on ivy berries, which then begin to ripen. In the summer, when their young become fledged, they leave neighbourhoods, and retire to sheep-walks and wild commons.

The magpies, when they have young, destroy the broods of missel thrushes, though the dams are fierce birds, and fight boldly in defence of their nests. It is probably to avoid such insults, that this species of thrush, though wild at other times, delights to build near houses, and in frequented walks and gardens.*

POULTRY.—Many creatures are endowed with a ready discernment to see what will turn to their own advantage and emolument ; and often discover more sagacity than could be expected. Thus, my neighbour's poultry watch for wagons loaded with wheat, and, running after them, pick up a number of grains which are shaken from the sheaves by the agitation of the carriages. Thus, when my brother used to take down his gun to shoot sparrows, his cats would run out before him, to be ready to catch up the birds as they fell.

The earnest and early propensity of the *gallinæ* to roost on high, is very observable ; and discovers a strong dread impressed on their spirits respecting vermin that may annoy them on the ground during the hours of darkness. Hence poultry, if left to themselves and not housed, will perch the winter through on yew trees and fir trees ; and turkeys and guinea fowls, heavy as they are, get up into apple trees : pheasants also, in woods, sleep on trees to avoid foxes ; while pea-fowls climb to the tops of the highest trees round their owner's house for security, let the weather be ever so cold or blowing. Partridges, it is true, roost on the ground, not having the faculty of perching ; but then the same fear prevails in their minds ; for, through apprehensions from polecats and stoats, they never trust themselves to coverts, but nestle

---

* Of the truth of this I have been an eye-witness, having seen the common thrush feeding on the shell snail.

In the very early part of this spring, (1797,) a bird of this species used to sit every morning on the top of some high elms close by my windows, and delight me with its charming song, attracted thither, probably, by some ripe ivy berries that grew near the place.

I have remarked something like the latter fact ; for I remember, many years ago, seeing a pair of these birds fly up repeatedly, and attack some larger bird, which I suppose disturbed their nest in my orchard, uttering, at the same time, violent shrieks. — Since writing the above, I have seen, more than once, a pair of these birds attack some magpies that had disturbed their nest, with great violence, and loud shrieks.—MARKWICK.

T

together in the midst of large fields, far removed from hedges and coppices, which they love to haunt in the day, and where, at that season, they can skulk more secure from the ravages of rapacious birds.

As to ducks and geese, their awkward, splay, web feet forbid them to settle on trees ; they therefore, in the hours of darkness and danger, betake themselves to their own element, the water, where, amidst large lakes and pools, like ships riding at anchor, they float the whole night long in peace and security. *

* Guinea fowls not only roost on high, but in hard weather resort, even in the day time, to the very tops of the highest trees.

Last winter, when the ground was covered with snow, I discovered all my guinea fowls, in the middle of the day, sitting on the highest boughs of some very tall elms, chattering and making a great clamour : I ordered them to be driven down, lest they should be frozen to death in so elevated a situation ; but this was not effected without much difficulty, they being very unwilling to quit their lofty abode, notwithstanding one of them had its feet so much frozen, that we were obliged to kill it. I know not how to account for this, unless it was occasioned by their aversion to the snow on the ground, they being birds that come originally from a hot climate.

Notwithstanding the awkward, splay, web feet, as Mr White calls them, of the duck genus, some of the foreign species have the power of settling on the boughs of trees, apparently with great ease ; an instance of which I have seen in the Earl of Ashburnham's menagerie, where the summer duck (*anas sponsa*) flew up and settled on the branch of an oak tree, in my presence ; but whether any of them roost on trees in the night, we are not informed by any author that I am acquainted with. I suppose not ; but that, like the rest of the genus, they sleep on the water, where the birds of this genus are not always perfectly secure, as will appear from the following circumstance, which happened in this neighbourhood a few years since, as I was credibly informed : A female fox was found in the morning, drowned in the same pond in which were several geese, and it was supposed, that, in the night, the fox swam into the pond to devour the geese, but was attacked by the gander, which, being most powerful in its own element, buffeted the fox with its wings about the head, till it was drowned.—MARKWICK.

In Aberdeenshire, in 1821, thirty geese deserted the pond where they were bred, and were never more heard of. A gentleman saw them in their flight eastward towards the sea, the wind blowing a gale from the north-west.

A gentleman near Huddersfield had a flock of geese, which were fed on high ground not visible from his house : they were brought home at night ; and very frequently, on seeing the house from the top of the hill, they would take wing, and fly homewards, making a circuit of about a mile. On one occasion, they were nearly alighting at a pond of water at the next farm-house, similar to one near their home ; they soon, however, discovered their mistake, and raised themselves in the

A HYBRID PHEASANT.

HEN PARTRIDGE.—A hen partridge came out of a ditch, and ran along shivering with her wings, and crying out as if wounded and unable to get from us. While the dam acted this distress, the boy who attended me saw her brood, that was small and unable to fly, run for shelter into an old fox-earth under the bank. So wonderful a power is instinct !*

air to nearly as great a height as before, alighted at their own pond, and were at it long before their driver, notwithstanding the latter went in a direct line. This was the more singular, because these geese were fat, and heavy. At Tittenhanger Green, in 1828, there was a flock of from fifteen to twenty geese. which used to indulge in aërial excursions like the above.

A hen which had, for three successive seasons, been occupied in rearing broods of ducks, became quite habituated to their taking the water. In the middle of a pond to which the ducklings resorted, there was a large stone, to which the hen would fly, and patiently await the brood, as they swam around it. On the fourth year, she sat on her own eggs, and, expecting her chickens to take to the water, as on former occasions, she flew to the stone in the middle of the pond, and called them to her with much earnestness, but they did not feel inclined to follow her dictates.

The following fact is related by Professor Scarpa:—A duck, accustomed to feed out of its owner's hand, was once offered some perfumed bread, which it at first refused to take. After several attempts, however, it at length complied, took the bread in its bill, and, carrying it to a neighbour's pond, moved it in various directions, as if to wash away the disagreeable taste and smell, and then swallowed it.

A correspondent in Loudon's *Magazine of Natural History* says, " I have lately seen a preternaturally large, but perfect goose's egg, containing a smaller one within it, the *inner one possessing its proper calcareous shell.*" This is certainly a very singular production. We have frequently known shells to have two yolks, but this is the only instance we have met with of one egg containing another entire one within it.

Our friend, Mr Andrew Shortrede, informs us, that he remembers, on his father's farm of Monklaw, near Jedburgh, a duck, which in the spring laid *black eggs.* As the season advanced, the blackness gradually went off, till, at the end of autumn, the eggs were whiter than those of an ordinary duck. This animal was of rather a longer shape than usual.

On the same farm, there was another duck which laid two eggs in a day. The fact was proved by locking the bird up, when one egg was found early in the morning, and another in the evening. This remarkable duck was killed by a servant ignorant of its virtues. — ED.

* It is not uncommon to see an old partridge feign itself wounded, and run along on the ground fluttering and crying, before either dog or man, to draw them away from its helpless unfledged young ones. I have seen it often, and once, in particular, I saw a remarkable instance of the old bird's solicitude to save its brood. As I was hunting with a young pointer, the dog ran on a brood of very small partridges; the old bird cried, fluttered, and ran tumbling along, just before the dog's nose, till she had drawn him to a considerable distance, when she took wing, and flew still

A Hybrid Pheasant. — Lord Stawell sent me, from the great lodge in the Holt, a curious bird for my inspection. It was found by the spaniels of one of his keepers in a coppice, and shot on the wing. The shape, air, and habit of the bird, and the scarlet ring round the eyes, agreed well with the appearance of a cock pheasant ; but then the head and neck, and breast and belly, were of a glossy black : and though it weighed three pounds three ounces and a half, * the weight of a large full-grown cock pheasant, yet there was no sign of any spurs on the legs, as is usual with all grown cock pheasants, who have long ones. The legs and feet were naked of feathers, and therefore it could be nothing of the grouse kind.   In the tail were no long, bending feathers, such as cock pheasants usually have, and are characteristic of the sex.   The tail was much shorter than the tail of a hen pheasant, and blunt and square at the end. The back, wing-feathers, and tail, were all of a pale russet, curiously streaked, somewhat like the upper parts of a hen partridge.   I returned it with my verdict, that it was probably a spurious, or hybrid hen-bird, bred between a cock pheasant and some domestic fowl.† When I came to talk with the keeper who brought it, he told me that some pea-hens had been known last summer to haunt the coppices and coverts where this mule was found.

Mr Elmer, of Farnham, the famous game painter, was employed to take an exact copy of this curious bird.

N.B. — It ought to be mentioned, that some good judges have imagined this bird to have been a stray grouse or black-cock ; it is, however, to be observed, that Mr W. remarks, that its legs and feet were naked, whereas those of the grouse are feathered to the toes. ‡

farther off, but not out of the field: on this the dog returned to me, near the place the young ones lay concealed in the grass, which the old bird no sooner perceived, than she flew back again to us, settled just before the dog's nose again, and, by rolling and tumbling about, drew off his attention from her young, and thus preserved her brood a second time.   I have also seen, when a kite has been hovering over a covey of young partridges, the old birds fly up at the bird of prey, screaming and fighting with all their might, to preserve their brood.— Markwick.

* Hen pheasants usually weigh only two pounds ten ounces.

† This curious *lusus naturæ* is now in the collection of the Earl of Egremont, at his seat at Petworth, and is allowed by naturalists to be a mule betwixt the black-cock and common pheasant.— Ed.

‡ Mr Latham observes, that " pea-hens, after they have done laying, sometimes assume the plumage of the male bird," and has given a figure

LAND-RAIL.— A man brought me a land-rail, or daker-hèn, a bird so rare in this district, that we seldom see more than one or two in a season, and these only in autumn. This is deemed a bird of passage by all the writers; yet, from its formation, seems to be poorly qualified for migration; for its wings are short, and placed so forward, and out of the centre of gravity, that it flies in a very heavy and embarrassed manner, with its legs hanging down; and can hardly be sprung a second time, as it runs very fast, and seems to depend more on the swiftness of its feet than on its flying.

of the male-feathered pea-hen now to be seen in the Leverian Museum; and M. Salerne remarks, that "the hen pheasant, when she has done laying and sitting, will get the plumage of the male." May not this hybrid pheasant, as Mr White calls it, be a bird of this kind? that is, an old hen pheasant, which had just begun to assume the plumage of the cock.—MARKWICK.

We have already noticed this curious subject, in our note at page 93. The facts of the female bird assuming the plumage of the male, which have been recorded by authors, are the following: pea-hen, by Hunter; turkey, by Bechstein; common pheasant, by Hunter; golden pheasant, by Blumenbach; the domestic hen, by Aristotle, Tucker, and Butter; the partridge, by Montagu; the domestic pigeon, by Tiedmann; the bustard, by Tiedmann; American pelican, by Catesby; common wild duck, by Tiedmann. Some years ago, a female golden pheasant, in the possession of the Duke of Buccleugh, assumed the male plumage. Mr Falconer of Carlowrie, member of the Wernerian Society, knew a domestic duck assume the garb of the drake; and a nobleman in Devonshire had a female wild duck, which made a similar change. Lord Glenlee lately presented to the Edinburgh College Museum a pea-hen with the male attire.

Dr Butter, who has bestowed much attention to this subject, comes to the three following conclusions: 1st, That in order to separate and distinguish the sexes, Nature has affixed certain external characters, proper to each. 2d, That in early life, the differences between the male and female are scarcely observable, but that at a certain period, the male assumes characteristic distinctions, denominated by Mr Hunter, "secondary properties," which the female then wants. 3d, That the female seldom makes an advance towards these secondary properties, until her powers of procreation are gone, when an inclination to resemble the masculine form takes place. And he considers, as this principle is common to all females, it is not a *monstrous* occurrence, as some authors have termed it.

It is not generally known, that pheasants are beneficial to the farmer. This fact was fully proved in 1821, at Whitney Court, where Tomkins Day, Esq. shot a hen pheasant, that excited the notice of the sportsmen present, from the immense size of its craw, which, on being opened, was found to contain more than half a pint of that destructive insect, the wire worm.—ED.

When we came to draw it, we found the entrails so soft and tender, that in appearance, they might have been dressed like the ropes of a woodcock. The craw, or crop, was small and lank, containing a mucus ; the gizzard thick and strong, and filled with small shell snails, some whole, and many ground to pieces through the attrition which is occasioned by the muscular force and motion of that intestine. We saw no gravels among the food ; perhaps the shell snails might perform the functions of gravels or pebbles, and might grind one another. Land-rails used to abound formerly, I remember, in the low, wet, bean fields of Christian Malford, in North Wilts, and in the meadows near Paradise Gardens, at Oxford, where I have often heard them cry, crex, crex. The bird mentioned above weighed seven ounces and a half, was fat and tender, and in flavour like the flesh of a woodcock. The liver was very large and delicate.*

FOOD FOR THE RING-DOVE. — One of my neighbours shot a ring-dove on an evening as it was returning from feed and going to roost. When his wife had picked and drawn it, she found its craw stuffed with the most nice and tender tops of turnips. These she washed and boiled, and so sat down to a choice and delicate plate of greens, culled and provided in this extraordinary manner.

Hence we may see that graminivorous birds, when grain fails, can subsist on the leaves of vegetables. There is reason to suppose that they would not long be healthy without ; for

---

* Land-rails are more plentiful with us than in the neighbourhood of Selborne. I have found four brace in an afternoon, and a friend of mine lately shot nine in two adjoining fields; but I never saw them in any other season than the autumn.

That it is a bird of passage, there can be little doubt, though Mr White thinks it poorly qualified for migration, on account of the wings being short, and not placed in the exact centre of gravity: how that may be I cannot say, but I know that its heavy sluggish flight is not owing to its inability of flying faster, for I have seen it fly very swiftly; although in general its actions are sluggish. Its unwillingness to rise proceeds, I imagine, from its sluggish disposition, and its great timidity; for it will sometimes squat so close to the ground, as to suffer itself to be taken up by the hand, rather than rise ; and yet it will at times run very fast.

What Mr White remarks respecting the small shell snails found in its gizzard, confirms my opinion, that it frequents corn fields, seed clover, and brakes or fern, more for the sake of snails, slugs, and other insects which abound in such places, than for the grain or seeds, and that it is entirely an insectivorous bird.— MARKWICK.

turkeys, though corn-fed, delight in a variety of plants, such as cabbage, lettuce, endive, &c. and poultry pick much grass ; while geese live for months together on commons by grazing alone.

> Nought is useless made : ———
> ——— On the barren heath
> The shepherd tends his flock, that daily crop
> Their verdant dinner from the mossy turf
> Sufficient : after them, the cackling *goose,*
> Close grazer, finds wherewith to ease her want.
> PHILIPS' *Cyder.* *

HEN-HARRIER. — A neighbouring gentleman sprung a pheasant in a wheat stubble, and shot at it ; when, notwithstanding the report of the gun, it was immediately pursued by the blue hawk, known by the name of the hen-harrier, but escaped into some covert.   He then sprung a second, and a third, in the same field, that got away in the same manner ; the hawk hovering round him all the while that he was beating the field, conscious, no doubt, of the game that lurked in the stubble. Hence we may conclude, that this bird of prey was rendered very daring and bold by hunger, and that hawks cannot always seize their game when they please.   We may farther observe, that they cannot pounce their quarry on the ground, where it might be able to make a stout resistance, since so large a fowl as a pheasant could not but be visible to the piercing eye of a hawk, when hovering over the field.   Hence that propensity of cowring and squatting, till they are almost trod on, which, no doubt, was intended as a mode of security : though long rendered destructive to the whole race of *gallinæ* by the invention of nets and guns.†

---

* That many graminivorous birds feed also on the herbage, or leaves of plants, there can be no doubt : partridges and larks frequently feed on the green leaves of turnips, which gives a peculiar flavour to their flesh, that is, to me, very palatable : the flavour, also, of wild ducks and geese, greatly depends on the nature of their food ; and their flesh frequently contracts a rank, unpleasant taste, from their having lately fed on strong marshy aquatic plants, as I suppose.

That the leaves of vegetables are wholesome, and conducive to the health of birds, seems probable, for many people fat their ducks and turkeys with the leaves of lettuce chopped small.—MARKWICK.

† Of the great boldness and rapacity of birds of prey, when urged on by hunger, I have seen several instances ; particularly, when shooting in the winter, in company with two friends, a woodcock flew across us,

GREAT SPECKLED DIVER, OR LOON.— As one of my neighbours was traversing Wolmer Forest, from Bramshot across the moors, he found a large uncommon bird fluttering in the heath, but not wounded, which he brought home alive. On examination it proved to be *colymbus glacialis*, Linn. the great speckled diver, or loon, which is most excellently described in Willughby's *Ornithology.**

Every part and proportion of this bird is so incomparably adapted to its mode of life, that in no instance do we see the wisdom of God in the creation to more advantage. The head

closely pursued by a small hawk; we all three fired at the woodcock instead of the hawk, which, notwithstanding the report of three guns close by it, continued its pursuit of the woodcock, struck it down, and carried it off, as we afterwards discovered.

At another time, when partridge-shooting with a friend, we saw a ring-tail hawk rise out of a pit with some large bird in its claws; though at a great distance we both fired, and obliged it to drop its prey, which proved to be one of the partridges we were in pursuit of. And lastly, in an evening, I shot at, and plainly saw that I had wounded a partridge, but, it being late, was obliged to go home without finding it again. The next morning, I walked round my land without any gun; but a favourite old spaniel followed my heels. When I came near the field where I wounded the bird the evening before, I heard the partridges call, and they seemed to be much disturbed. On my approaching the bar-way, they all rose, some on my right and some on my left hand; and just before and over my head, I perceived (though indistinctly, from the extreme velocity of their motion) two birds fly directly against each other, when instantly, to my great astonishment, down dropped a partridge at my feet: the dog immediately seized it, and, on examination, I found the blood flow very fast from a fresh wound in the head, but there were some dry clotted blood on its wings and side; whence I concluded, that a hawk had singled out my wounded bird as the object of its prey, and had struck it down the instant that my approach had obliged the birds to rise on the wing; but the space between the hedges was so small, and the motion of the birds so instantaneous and quick, that I could not distinctly observe the operation. — MARKWICK.

* Montagu, in his *Ornithological Dictionary*, relates that "A northern diver, taken alive, was kept in a pond for some months, which gave us an opportunity of attending to its manners. In a few days it became extremely docile, would come at the call, from one side of the pond to the other, and would take food from the hand. The bird had received an injury in the head, which had deprived one eye of its sight, and the other was a little impaired; but, notwithstanding, it could, by incessantly diving, discover all the fish that was thrown into the pond. In defect of fish it would eat flesh.

"It is observable that the legs of this bird are so constructed and situated, as to render it incapable of walking upon them. This is probably the case with all the divers, as well as the grebes." — ED.

is sharp, and smaller than the part of the neck adjoining, in order that it may pierce the water; the wings are placed forward, and out of the centre of gravity, for a purpose which shall be noticed hereafter; the thighs quite at the podex, in order to facilitate diving; and the legs are flat, and as sharp backwards almost as the edge of a knife, that, in striking, they may easily cut the water: while the feet are palmated and broad for swimming, yet so folded up, when advanced forward to take a fresh stroke, as to be full as narrow as the shank. The two exterior toes of the feet are longest; the nails flat and broad, resembling the human, which give strength, and increase the power of swimming. The foot, when expanded, is not at right angles to the leg or body of the bird; but the exterior part inclining towards the head, forms an acute angle with the body; the intention being, not to give motion in the line of the legs themselves, but, by the combined impulse of both in an intermediate line, the line of the body.

Most people know, that have observed at all, that the swimming of birds is nothing more than a walking in the water, where one foot succeeds the other as on the land; yet no one, as far as I am aware, has remarked that diving fowls, while under water, impel and row themselves forward by a motion of their wings, as well as by the impulse of their feet: but such is really the case, as any person may easily be convinced, who will observe ducks when hunted by dogs in a clear pond. Nor do I know that any one has given a reason why the wings of diving fowls are placed so forward: doubtless, not for the purpose of promoting their speed in flying, since that position certainly impedes it; but probably for the increase of their motion under water, by the use of four oars instead of two; yet were the wings and feet nearer together, as in land birds, they would, when in action, rather hinder than assist one another.

This *colymbus* was of considerable bulk, weighing only three drachms short of three pounds avoirdupois. It measured in length from the bill to the tail (which was very short) two feet, and to the extremities of the toes, four inches more; and the breadth of the wings expanded was forty-two inches. A person attempted to eat the body, but found it very strong and rancid, as is the flesh of all birds living on fish. Divers, or loons, though bred in the most northerly parts of Europe, yet are seen with us in very severe winters; and, on the Thames, are called sprat loons, because they prey much on that sort of fish.

The legs of the *colymbi* and *mergi* are placed so very back-ward, and so out of all centre of gravity, that these birds cannot walk at all.   They are called by Linnæus *compedes*, because they move on the ground as if shackled or fettered. *

STONE-CURLEW. — On the twenty-seventh of February, 1788, stone-curlews were heard to pipe ; and on March first, after it was dark, some were passing over the village, as might be perceived by their quick short note, which they use in their nocturnal excursions by way of watch-word, that they may not stray and lose their companions.

Thus we see, that retire whithersoever they may in the winter, they return again early in the spring, and are, as it now appears, the first summer birds that come back.   Perhaps the mildness of the season may have quickened the emigration of the curlews this year.

They spend the day in high elevated fields and sheep-walks ; but seem to descend in the night to streams and meadows, perhaps for water, which their upland haunts do not afford them.†

* These accurate and ingenious observations, tending to set forth in a proper light the wonderful works of God in the creation, and to point out his wisdom in adapting the singular form and position of the limbs of this bird to the particular mode in which it is destined to pass the greatest part of its life, in an element much denser than the air, do Mr White credit, not only as a naturalist, but as a man and as a philosopher, in the truest sense of the word, in my opinion ; for, were we enabled to trace the works of Nature minutely and accurately, we should find, not only that every bird, but every creature, is equally well adapted to the purpose for which it was intended ; though this fitness and propriety of form is more striking in such animals as are destined to any uncommon mode of life.

I have had in my possession two birds, which, though of a different genus, bear a great resemblance to Mr White's *colymbus*, in their manner of life, which is spent chiefly in the water, where they swim and dive with astonishing rapidity ; for which purpose, their fin-toed feet, placed far behind, and very short wings, are particularly well adapted, and shew the wisdom of God in the creation as conspicuously as the bird before mentioned.   These birds were the greater and lesser crested grebe, (*podiceps cristatus et auritus.*)   What surprised me most was, that the first of these birds was found alive on dry ground, about seven miles from the sea, to which place there was no communication by water.   How did it get so far from the sea, its wings and legs being so ill adapted either to flying or walking ? The lesser crested grebe was also found in a fresh water pond, which had no communication with other water, at some miles distance from the sea. — MARKWICK.

† On the thirty-first of January, 1792, I received a bird of this species, which had been recently killed by a neighbouring farmer, who said that

THE SMALLEST UNCRESTED WILLOW WREN.—The smallest uncrested willow-wren, or chiff chaf, is the next early summer bird which we have remarked; it utters two sharp, piercing notes, so loud, in hollow woods, as to occasion an echo; and is usually first heard about the 20th of March.*

FERN-OWL, OR GOAT-SUCKER.—The country people have a notion that the fern-owl, or churn-owl, or eve-jarr, which they also call a puckeridge, is very injurious to weanling calves, by inflicting, as it strikes at them, the fatal distemper known to cow-leeches by the name of puckeridge. Thus does this harmless, ill-fated bird, fall under a double imputation, which it by no means deserves,—in Italy, of sucking the teats of goats, whence it is called *caprimulgus;* and, with us, of communicating a deadly disorder to cattle. But the truth of the matter is, the malady above mentioned is occasioned by the *œstrus bovis,* a dipterous insect, which lays its eggs along the chines of kine, where the maggots, when hatched, eat their way through the hide of the beast into the flesh, and grow to a very large size. I have just talked with a man, who says he has more than once stripped calves who have died of the puckeridge: that the ail or complaint lay along the chine, where the flesh was much swelled, and filled with purulent matter. Once I myself saw a large, rough maggot of this sort squeezed out of the back of a cow. These maggots in Essex are called wornils.†

he had frequently seen it in his fields during the former part of the winter; this perhaps was an occasional straggler, which, by some accident, was prevented from accompanying its companions in their migration. — MARKWICK.

* This bird, which Mr White calls the smallest willow-wren, or chiff chaf, makes its appearance very early in the spring, and is very common with us; but I cannot make out the three different species of willow wrens, which he assures us he has discovered. Ever since the publication of his *History of Selborne,* I have used my utmost endeavours to discover his three birds, but hitherto without success. I have frequently shot the bird which "haunts only the tops of trees, and makes a sibilous noise," even in the very act of uttering that sibilous note; but it always proved to be the common willow-wren, or his chiff chaf. In short, I never could discover more than one species, unless my greater pettichaps, (*sylvia hortensis* of Latham,) is his greatest willow-wren.—MARKWICK.

The three species are the wood-wren, *sylvia sibilatrix* of Bechstein; the chiff chaf, *sylvia hippolais* of Latham, and the hay bird, *motacilla trochilus* of Latham. — ED.

† This is the maggot of the breeze-fly, *œstrus bovis* of Clark. They prove extremely troublesome to cattle. During our residence in Fife,

The least observation and attention would convince men, that these birds neither injure the goatherd nor the grazier, but are perfectly harmless, and subsist alone, being night birds, on night insects, such as *scarabæi*, and *phalænæ;* and, through the month of July, mostly on the *scarabæus solstitialis*, which in many districts abounds at that season. Those that we have opened have always had their craws stuffed with large night moths and their eggs, and pieces of chaffers; nor does it any-wise appear how they can, weak and unarmed as they seem, inflict any harm upon kine, unless they possess the powers of animal magnetism, and can affect them by fluttering over them

A fern-owl, this evening, (August 27,) shewed off in a very unusual and entertaining manner, by hawking round and round the circumference of my great spreading oak for twenty times following, keeping mostly close to the grass, but occasionally glancing up amidst the boughs of the tree. This amusing bird was then in pursuit of a brood of some particular *phalænæ* belonging to the oak, of which there are several sorts; and exhibited on the occasion a command of wing superior, I think, to that of the swallow itself.

When a person approaches the haunt of fern-owls in an evening, they continue flying round the head of the obtruder; and, by striking their wings together above their backs, in the manner that the pigeons called smiters are known to do, make a smart snap : perhaps at that time they are jealous for their young; and their noise and gesture are intended by way of menace.

Fern-owls have attachment to oaks, no doubt on account of food; for the next evening we saw one again several times among the boughs of the same tree; but it did not skim round

we frequently squeezed them out of our cows. We endeavoured to feed one on fresh killed beef, but it refused to eat, and died. In 1824, a cow had three of these in her back, which we extracted; and having put them in a basin for examination, after we had finished the operation, one of our tame jackdaws deprived us from carrying our intentions into effect, by devouring them as a lunch. One of these was an inch long, and as thick as our little finger; and the swelling which it produced in the animal's back was of the size of the largest penny-piece. This was extracted by a person pressing with a piece of wood against another piece which we held opposite. The force required to press it through the aperture (which was about an eighth of an inch in diameter) was such, that the noise resembled that of a pop-gun, and the worm was projected to a distance of twelve feet from the cow's back. — ED.

its stem over the grass, as on the evening before. In May, these birds find the *scarabæus melolontha* on the oak ; and the *scarabæus solstitialis* at midsummer. These peculiar birds can only be watched and observed for two hours in the twenty-four; and then in a dubious twilight, an hour after sunset and an hour before sunrise.

On this day, (July 14, 1789,) a woman brought me two eggs of a fern-owl, or eve-jarr, which she found on the verge of the hanger, to the left of the hermitage, under a beechen shrub. This person, who lives just at the foot of the hanger, seems well acquainted with these nocturnal swallows, and says she has often found their eggs near that place, and that they lay only two at a time on the bare ground. The eggs were oblong, dusky, and streaked somewhat in the manner of the plumage of the parent bird, and were equal in size at each end. The dam was sitting on the eggs when found, which contained the rudiments of young, and would have been hatched perhaps in a week. From hence we may see the time of their breeding, which corresponds pretty well with the swift, as does also the period of their arrival. Each species is usually seen about the beginning of May : each breeds but once in a summer : each lays only two eggs.

July 4, 1790.— The woman who brought me two fern-owl's eggs last year, on July 14, on this day produced me two more, one of which had been laid this morning, as appears plainly, because there was only one in the nest the evening before. They were found, as last July, on the verge of the down above the hermitage, under a beechen shrub, on the naked ground. Last year, those eggs were full of young, and just ready to be hatched.

These circumstances point out the exact time when these curious nocturnal migratory birds lay their eggs and hatch their young. Fern-owls, like snipes, stone-curlews, and some birds, make no nest. Birds that build on the ground do not make much of nests. *

---

* No author that I am acquainted with has given so accurate and pleasing an account of the manners and habits of the goat-sucker as Mr White, taken entirely from his own observations. Its being a nocturnal bird, has prevented my having many opportunities of observing it. I suspect that it passes the day in concealment amidst the dark and shady gloom of deep-wooded dells, or, as they are called here, gills ; having more than once seen it roused from such solitary places by my dogs, when shooting in the day-time. I have also sometimes seen it in an

SAND-MARTENS. — March 23, 1788. — A gentleman, who was this week on a visit at Waverley, took the opportunity of examining some of the holes in the sand banks with which that district abounds. As these are undoubtedly bored by bank-martens, and are the places where they avowedly breed, he was in hopes they might have slept there also, and that he might have surprised them just as they were awaking from their winter slumbers. When he had dug for some time, he found the holes were horizontal and serpentine, as I had observed before ; and that the nests were deposited at the inner end, and had been occupied by broods in former summers ; but no torpid birds were to be found. He opened and examined about a dozen holes. Another gentleman made the same search many years ago, with as little success. These holes were in depth about two feet.

March 21, 1790. — A single bank or sand-marten was seen hovering and playing round the sand pit at Short Heath, where in the summer they abound.

April 9, 1793. — A sober hind assures us, that this day, on Wish-hanger common, between Hedleigh and Frinsham, he saw several bank-martens playing in and out, and hanging before some nest holes in a sand hill, where these birds usually nestle.

This incident confirms my suspicions that this species of *hirundo* is to be seen first of any ; and gives great reason to suppose that they do not leave their wild haunts at all, but are secreted amidst the clefts and caverns of those abrupt cliffs where they usually spend their summers.

The late severe weather considered, it is not very probable that these birds should have migrated so early from a tropical region, through all these cutting winds and pinching frosts ; but it is easy to suppose that they may, like bats and flies, have been awakened by the influence of the sun, amidst their secret *latebræ*, where they have spent the uncomfortable foodless months in a torpid state, and the profoundest of slumbers.

There is a large pond at Wish-hanger, which induces these sand-martens to frequent that district : for I have ever remarked that they haunt near great waters, either rivers or lakes. *

evening, but not long enough to take notice of its habits and manners. I have never seen it but in the summer, between the months of May and September. — MARKWICK.

* Here, and in many other passages of his writings, this very ingenious

SWALLOWS, CONGREGATING AND DISAPPEARANCE OF.—During the severe winds that often prevail late in the spring, it is not easy to say how the *hirundines* subsist; for they withdraw themselves, and are hardly ever seen, nor do any insects appear for their support.   That they can retire to rest, and sleep away these uncomfortable periods, as bats do, is a matter rather to be suspected than proved : or do they not rather spend their time in deep and sheltered vales near waters, where insects are more likely to be found?   Certain it is, that hardly any individuals of this genus have at such times been seen for several days together.

September 13, 1791.— The congregating flocks of *hirundines* on the church and tower are very beautiful and amusing! When they fly off together from the roof, on any alarm, they quite swarm in the air.   But they soon settle in heaps, and, preening their feathers, and lifting up their wings to admit the sun, seem highly to enjoy the warm situation.   Thus they spend the heat of the day, preparing for their emigration, and, as it were, consulting when and where they are to go.   The flight about the church seems to consist chiefly of house-martens, above four hundred in number; but there are other places of rendezvous about the village frequented at the same time.

naturalist favours the opinion, that part at least of the swallow tribe pass their winter in a torpid state, in the same manner as bats and flies, and revive again on the approach of spring.

I have frequently taken notice of all these circumstances, which induced Mr White to suppose that some of the *hirundines* lie torpid during winter. I have seen, so late as November, on a finer day than usual at that season of the year, two or three swallows flying backwards and forwards under a warm hedge, or on the sunny side of some old building; nay, I once saw, on the 8th of December, two martens flying about very briskly, the weather being mild. I had not seen any considerable number, either of swallows or martens, for a good while before : from whence, then, could these few birds come, if not from some hole or cavern where they had laid themselves up for the winter? Surely it will not be asserted that these birds migrate back again, from some distant tropical region, merely on the appearance of a fine day or two at this late season of the year. Again, very early in the spring, and sometimes immediately after very cold, severe weather, on its growing a little warmer, a few of these birds suddenly make their appearance, long before the generality of them are seen.   These appearances certainly favour the opinion of their passing the winter in a torpid state, but do not absolutely prove the fact ; for who ever saw them reviving of their own accord from their torpid state, without being first brought to the fire, and, as it were, forced into life again; soon after which revivification they constantly die. — MARKWICK.

It is remarkable, that though most of them sit on the battlements and roofs, yet many hang or cling for some time by their claws against the surface of the walls, in a manner not practised by them at any other time of their remaining with us.

The swallows seem to delight more in holding their assemblies on trees.

November 3, 1789. — Two swallows were seen this morning at Newton vicarage house, hovering and settling on the roofs and out-buildings. None have been observed at Selborne since October 11. It is very remarkable, that after the *hirundines* have disappeared for some weeks, a few are occasionally seen again; sometimes, in the first week in November, and that only for one day. Do they not withdraw and slumber in some hiding-place during the interval? for we cannot suppose they had migrated to warmer climes, and so returned again for one day. Is it not more probable that they are awakened from sleep, and, like the bats, are come forth to collect a little food? Bats appear at all seasons through the autumn and spring months, when the thermometer is at fifty, because then *phalænæ* and moths are stirring. These swallows looked like young ones. *

WAGTAILS. — While the cows are feeding in the moist low pasture, broods of wagtails, white and gray, run round them, close up to their noses, and under their very bellies, availing themselves of the flies that settle on their legs, and probably finding worms and *larvæ* that are roused by the trampling of their feet. Nature is such an economist, that the most

---

* Of their migration, the proofs are such as will scarcely admit of a doubt. Sir Charles Wager and Captain Wright saw vast flocks of them at sea, when on their passage from one country to another. Our author, Mr White, saw what he deemed the actual migration of these birds, and which he has described at p. 78 of his *History of Selborne;* and of their congregating together on the roofs of churches and other buildings, and on trees, previous to their departure, many instances occur; particularly, I once observed a large flock of house-martens on the roof of the church here at Catsfield, which acted exactly in the manner here described by Mr White, sometimes preening their feathers, and spreading their wings to the sun, and then flying off all together, but soon returning to their former situation. The greatest part of these birds seemed to be young ones. — MARKWICK.

Wilson, Audubon, and Richardson, all attest the migration of the swallow and its congeners, in America; and every author, ancient and modern, of whatever country, describe these birds as changing their residence during winter. — ED.

incongruous animals can avail themselves of each other!
Interest makes strange friendships. *

WRYNECKS.—These birds appear on the grass-plots and
walks ; they walk a little as well as hop, and thrust their bills
into the turf, in quest, I conclude, of ants, which are their food.
While they hold their bills in the grass, they draw out their
prey with their tongues, which are so long as to be coiled round
their heads.

GROSBEAK.—Mr B. shot a cock grosbeak, which he had
observed to haunt his garden for more than a fortnight. I
began to accuse this bird of making sad havock among the
buds of the cherries, gooseberries, and wall-fruit of all the
neighbouring orchards. Upon opening its crop, or craw, no
buds were to be seen ; but a mass of kernels of the stones of
fruits. Mr B. observed, that this bird frequented the spot
where plum trees grow ; and that he had seen it with somewhat hard in its mouth, which it broke with difficulty : these
were the stones of damsons. The Latin ornithologists call
this bird *coccothraustes*, i. e. berry-breaker, because, with its
large horny beak, it cracks and breaks the shells of stone
fruits for the sake of the seed or kernel. Birds of this sort
are rarely seen in England, and only in winter. †

* Birds continually avail themselves of particular and unusual circumstances to procure their food : thus wagtails keep playing about the noses
and legs of cattle as they feed, in quest of flies and other insects which
abound near those animals; and great numbers of them will follow close
to the plough to devour the worms, &c. that are turned up by that
instrument. The red-breast attends the gardener when digging his
borders; and will, with great familiarity and tameness, pick out the
worms almost close to his spade, as I have frequently seen. Starlings
and magpies very often sit on the backs of sheep and deer to pick out their
ticks. — MARKWICK.

† I have never seen this rare bird but during the severest cold of the
hardest winters ; at which season of the year, I have had in my possession
two or three that were killed in this neighbourhood in different years. —
MARKWICK.

On the second week of September, 1832, Mr Greenhow, surgeon of
North Shields, mentions that a flock of Egyptian geese was seen beside
the Tweed, at Carham, two of which, while nibbling grass on the margin
of the river, were shot by Ralph Stephenson, gamekeeper. — ED.

OBSERVATIONS ON INSECTS AND VERMES.

INSECTS IN GENERAL.

THE day and night insects occupy the annuals alternately : the *papilios, muscæ,* and *apes,* are succeeded at the close of day oy *phalænæ,* earwigs,* woodlice, &c. In the dusk of the evening, when beetles begin to buzz, partridges begin to call : these two circumstances are exactly coincident.

Ivy is the last flower that supports the hymenopterous and dipterous insects. On sunny days, quite on to November, they swarm on trees covered with this plant ; and when they disappear, probably retire under the shelter of its leaves, concealing themselves between its fibres and the trees which it entwines.†

Spiders, woodlice, *lepismæ* in cupboards and among sugar, some *empedes,* gnats, flies of several species, some *phalænæ* in hedges, earth-worms, &c. are stirring at all times, when winters are mild ; and are of great service to those soft-billed birds that never leave us.

On every sunny day, the winter through, clouds of insects, usually called gnats, (I suppose *tipulæ* and *empedes,*) appear sporting and dancing over the tops of the evergreen trees in the shrubbery, and frisking about as if the business of generation was still going on. Hence it appears that these *diptera* (which by their sizes appear to be of different species) are not subject to a torpid state in the winter, as most winged insects are. At night, and in frosty weather, and when it rains and blows, they seem to retire into those trees. They often are out in a fog.‡

---

* Earwigs, although it is not generally known, are capable of flying. This is mentioned by Kirby and Spence; and Mr Denson, of Bayswater, establishes this fact by experiment. He says, " Each, before taking flight, aided, or effected the expansion of its snow-white membranous wings with the forceps in its tail, which it turned over its back, and used with admirable adroitness. They flew ably, and in curves of short diameters." — ED.

† This I have often observed, having seen bees and other winged insects swarming about the flowers of the ivy very late in the autumn.— MARKWICK.

‡ This I have also seen, and have frequently observed swarms of little winged insects playing up and down in the air in the middle of the winter, even when the ground has been covered with snow. — MARKWICK.

HUMMING IN THE AIR. — There is a natural occurrence to be met with upon the highest part of our down in hot summer days, which always amuses me much, without giving me any satisfaction with respect to the cause of it ; and that is, a loud audible humming of bees in the air, though not one insect is to be seen.* This sound is to be heard distinctly the whole common through, from the Money-dells, to Mr White's avenue gate. Any person would suppose that a large swarm of bees was in motion, and playing about over his head. This noise was heard last week, on June twenty-eighth.

> Resounds the living surface of the ground,
> Nor undelightful is the ceaseless *hum* —
> To him who muses — at noon. —
> Thick in yon stream of light, a thousand ways,
> Upward and downward, thwarting and convolved,
> The quivering nations sport.
>
> THOMSON'S *Seasons.*

CHAFFERS. — Cock-chaffers seldom abound oftener than once in three or four years ; when they swarm, they deface the trees and hedges. Whole woods of oaks are stripped bare by them.†

Chaffers are eaten by the turkey, the rook, and the house-sparrow.

The *scarabæus solstitialis* first appears about June twenty-six : they are very punctual in their coming out every year. They are a small species, about half the size of the May-chaffer, and are known in some parts by the name of the fern-chaffer.‡

---

* This sound does not proceed from bees, as our author supposes, but from the common gnat (*culex pipiens.*) We particularly noticed this in August, 1832, in a lane which leads from the back of Warriston Crescent, to the Newhaven road. On the third, the air was very hot, and the sound proceeded from the top of some high trees. Next day we passed the same road ; the air was more cold and somewhat moist, when these gnats were sporting in the sunbeams, close to the top of a hedge, which was not more than four feet high. This mighty congregation of gnats formed a lengthened column of two hundred yards, by about a yard in breadth, and two yards in depth ; their numbers we believe to have been greater than there have been human beings on our globe, from the creation to the present time. — ED.

† Respect being had to the size of the cock-chaffer, it is six times stronger than a horse ; and if the elephant, as Linnæus observed, was strong in proportion to the stag-beetle, it would be able to pull up rocks by the root, and to level mountains ; were the lion and tiger as strong and as swift for their magnitude, as the cicindela and the beetle, nothing could escape them by precaution, or withstand them by strength. — ED.

‡ A singular circumstance relative to the cock-chaffer, or, as it is called here, the May-bug, (*scarabæus melolontha,*) happened this year (1800.)

Ptinus Pectinicornis.—Those maggots that make worm-holes in tables, chairs, bed-posts, &c. and destroy wooden furniture, especially where there is any sap, are the *larvæ* of the *ptinus pectinicornis*. This insect, it is probable, deposits its eggs on the surface, and the worms eat their way in.

In their holes, they turn into their *pupæ* state, and so come forth winged in July: eating their way through the valances or curtains of a bed, or any other furniture that happens to obstruct their passage.

They seem to be most inclined to breed in beech ; hence beech will not make lasting utensils or furniture. If their eggs are deposited on the surface, frequent rubbing will preserve wooden furniture. *

Blatta Orientalis, (Cockroach.)— A neighbour complained to me that her house was overrun with a kind of black beetle, or, as she expressed herself, with a kind of black-bob, which swarmed in her kitchen when they got up in the morning before daybreak.

Soon after this account, I observed an unusual insect in one of my dark chimney closets, and find since, that in the night, they swarm also in my kitchen. On examination, I soon ascertained the species to be the *blatta orientalis* of Linnæus, and the *blatta molendinaria* of Mouffet. The male is winged ; the female is not, but shews somewhat like the rudiments of wings, as if in the *pupa* state.

These insects belonged originally to the warmer parts of America, and were conveyed from thence by shipping to the

---

My gardener, in digging some ground, found, about six incnes under the surface, two of these insects alive, and perfectly formed, so early as the twenty-fourth of March. When he brought them to me, they appeared to be as perfect and as much alive as in the midst of summer, crawling about as briskly as ever ; yet I saw no more of this insect till the twenty-second of May, when it began to make its appearance. How comes it, that though it was perfectly formed so early as the twenty-fourth of March, it did not shew itself above ground till nearly two months afterwards?—Markwick.

* Naturalists have observed, that the male broods of insects invariably appear earlier than the female broods. Professor Rennie notices, that upon the leaf of a poplar tree, of three eggs of the puss moth, (*cerura vinula*,) which he found, two were hatched about a fortnight before the other. The first were males, and the last a female ; thus distinctly proving, that eggs from which females are produced are longer of hatching. As they were found on the same leaf, they were of course presumed to be laid by the same parent ; at the same time, the difference in the time of hatching could not depend upon any atmospherical cause. — Ed.

East Indies ; and, by means of commerce, begin to prevail in the more northern parts of Europe, as Russia, Sweden, &c. How long they have abounded in England, I cannot say, but have never observed them in my house till lately.

They love warmth, and haunt chimney closets, and the backs of ovens. Poda says, that these and house-crickets will not associate together; but he is mistaken in that assertion, as Linnæus suspected he was. They are altogether night insects, *lucifugæ*, never coming forth till the rooms are dark and still, and escaping away nimbly at the approach of a candle.* Their antennæ are remarkably long, slender, and flexile.

October, 1790.—After the servants are gone to bed, the kitchen hearth swarms with young crickets, and young *blattæ molendinariæ* of all sizes, from the most minute growth to their full proportions. They seem to live in a friendly manner together, and not to prey the one on the other.

August, 1792.—After the destruction of many thousands of *blattæ molendinariæ*, we find that at intervals a fresh detachment of old ones arrives, and particularly during this hot season ; for the windows being left open in the evenings, the males come flying in at the casements from the neighbouring houses, which swarm with them. How the females, that seem to have no perfect wings that they can use, can contrive to get from house to house, does not so readily appear. These, like many insects, when they find their present abodes overstocked, have powers of migrating to fresh quarters. Since the *blattæ* have been so much kept under, the crickets have greatly increased in number.

GRYLLUS DOMESTICUS, (HOUSE-CRICKET.)— November.— After the servants are gone to bed, the kitchen hearth swarms with minute crickets not so large as fleas, which must have been lately hatched. So that these domestic insects, cherished by the influence of a constant large fire, regard not the season of the year, but produce their young at a time when their

---

* Although the cockroach is generally to be seen only on leaving its retreat after sunset, yet they occasionally do appear through the day. Our friend, Sir Patrick Walker, who is an excellent practical naturalist, and well skilled in entomology, informed us, that the captain of a vessel from the Mauritius told him, that during their passage from thence to Leith, cockroaches used simultaneously to come on deck, from the hold, which was infested with them, and take to their wings in myriads, fly several times round the vessel like a dense cloud, alight on the deck, and instantly retreat below. — ED.

congeners are either dead, or laid up for the winter, to pass away the uncomfortable months in the profoundest slumbers, and a state of torpidity.

When house-crickets are out and running about a room in the night, if surprised by a candle, they give two or three shrill notes, as it were for a signal to their fellows, that they may escape to their crannies and lurking holes, to avoid danger.

CIMEX LINEARIS.— August 12, 1775.— *Cimices lineares* are now in high copulation on ponds and pools. The females, who vastly exceed the males in bulk, dart and shoot along on the surface of the water with the males on their backs. When a female chooses to be disengaged, she rears, and jumps, and plunges, like an unruly colt ; the lover, thus dismounted, soon finds a new mate. The females, as fast as their curiosities are satisfied, retire to another part of the lake, perhaps to deposit their fœtus in quiet : hence the sexes are found separate, except where generation is going on. From the multitude of minute young of all gradations of sizes, these insects seem, without doubt, to be viviparous.

PHALÆNA QUERCUS. — Most of our oaks are naked of leaves, and even the Holt in general, having been ravaged by the caterpillars of a small *phalæna*, which is of a pale yellow colour. These insects, though a feeble race, yet, from their infinite numbers, are of wonderful effect, being able to destroy the foliage of whole forests and districts. At this season, they leave their *aurelia*, and issue forth in their fly state, swarming and covering the trees and hedges.

In a field near Greatham, I saw a flight of swifts busied in catching their prey near the ground; and found they were hawking after these *phalænæ*. The *aurelia* of this moth is shining, and as black as jet; and lies wrapped up in a leaf of the tree, which is rolled round it, and secured at the ends by a web, to prevent the maggot from falling out.*

EPHEMERA CAUDA BISETA, (MAY FLY.) — June 10, 1771.— Myriads of May flies appeared, for the first time, on the Alresford stream. The air was crowded with them, and the surface of the water covered. Large trouts sucked them in as they lay struggling on the surface of the stream, unable to rise till their wings were dried.

This appearance reconciled me, in some measure, to the wonderful account that Scopoli gives of the quantities emerging from the rivers of Carniola. Their motions are very peculiar, up and down for many yards almost in a perpendicular line.†

SPHYNX OCELLATA. — A vast insect appears after it is dusk, flying with a humming noise, and inserting its tongue into the

---

* I suspect that the insect here meant, is not the *phalæna quercus,* but the *phalæna viridata,* concerning which, I find the following note in my *Naturalist's Calendar* for the year 1785:—

About this time, and for a few days last past, I observed the leaves of almost all the oak trees in Denn copse, to be eaten and destroyed, and, on examining more narrowly, saw an infinite number of small beautiful pale green moths flying about the trees; the leaves of which, that were not quite destroyed, were curled up, and withinside were the *exuviæ,* or remains, of the *chrysalis,* from whence I suppose the moths had issued, and whose caterpillar had eaten the leaves.—MARKWICK.

† I once saw a swarm of these insects playing up and down over the surface of a pond in Denn Park, exactly in the manner described by this accurate naturalist. It was late in the evening of a warm summer day when I observed them.—MARKWICK.

bloom of the honeysuckle; it scarcely settles upon the plants, but feeds on the wing, in the manner of humming birds.*

WILD BEE.—There is a sort of wild bee frequenting the garden-campion for the sake of its tomentum, which probably it turns to some purpose in the business of nidification. It is very pleasant to see with what address it strips off the *pubes*, running from the top to the bottom of a branch, and shaving it bare with all the dexterity of a hoop shaver. When it has got a vast bundle, almost as large as itself, it flies away, holding it secure between its chin and its fore legs.

There is a remarkable hill on the downs near Lewes, in Sussex, known by the name of Mount Carburn, which overlooks that town, and affords a most engaging prospect of all the country round, besides several views of the sea. On the very summit of this exalted promontory, and amidst the trenches of its Danish camp, there haunts a species of wild bee, making its nest in the chalky soil. When people approach the place, these insects begin to be alarmed, and, with a sharp and hostile sound, dash and strike round the heads and faces of intruders. I have often been interrupted myself while contemplating the grandeur of the scenery around me, and have thought myself in danger of being stung.

WASPS.—Wasps abound in woody wild districts, far from neighbourhoods: they feed on flowers, and catch flies and caterpillars to carry to their young. Wasps make their nests with the raspings of sound timber; hornets, with what they

---

* I have frequently seen the large bee moth, (*sphinx stellatarum*,) inserting its long tongue, or proboscis, into the centre of flowers, and feeding on their nectar, without settling on them, but keeping constantly on the wing.—MARKWICK.

gnaw from decayed: these particles of wood are kneaded up with a mixture of saliva from their bodies, and moulded into combs.

When there is no fruit in the gardens, wasps eat flies, and suck the honey from flowers, from ivy blossoms, and umbellated plants: they carry off also flesh from butchers' shambles. *

ŒSTRUS CURVICAUDA.— This insect lays its nits, or eggs, on horses' legs, flanks, &c. each on a single hair. The maggots, when hatched, do not enter the horses' skins, but fall to the ground. It seems to abound most in moist, moorish places, though sometimes seen in the uplands. †

NOSE FLY.— About the beginning of July, a species of fly (*musca*) obtains, which proves very tormenting to horses, trying still to enter their nostrils and ears, and actually laying their eggs in the latter of those organs, or perhaps in both. When these abound, horses in woodland districts become very impatient at their work, continually tossing their heads, and rubbing their noses on each other, regardless of the driver; so that accidents often ensue. In the heat of the day, men are often obliged to desist from ploughing. Saddle-horses are also very troublesome at such seasons. Country people call this insect the nose fly. ‡

ICHNEUMON FLY.— I saw lately a small ichneumon fly attack a spider much larger than itself, on a grass walk. When the spider made any resistance, the ichneumon applied her tail to him, and stung him with great vehemence, so that he soon became dead and motionless. The ichneumon then running backward, drew her prey very nimbly over the walk into the standing grass. This spider would be deposited in some hole, where the ichneumon would lay some eggs; and as

---

* In the year 1775, wasps abounded so prodigiously in this neighbourhood, that, in the month of August, no less than seven or eight of their nests were ploughed up in one field; of which there were several instances, as I was informed.

In the spring, about the beginning of April, a single wasp is sometimes seen, which is of a larger size than usual: this, I imagine, is the queen, or female wasp, the mother of the future swarm.— MARKWICK.

† The *Œstrus hominis*, or human gadfly, is a native of the West India Islands, and deposits its eggs in the human skin, where they change to the maggot state, and occasion great pain; so many as two hundred and thirty-five have been known to be propagated in the flesh of an individual. Professor Jameson's *Journal* for April, 1830, records some curious cases of this kind.— ED.

‡ Is not this insect the *œstrus nasalis* of Linnæus, so well described by Mr Clark, in the third volume of the *Linnæan Transactions*, under the name of *œstrus veterinus*?— MARKWICK.

soon as the eggs were hatched, the carcass would afford ready
food for the maggots. *

* The eggs of insects are liable to great variety of forms, and
external markings : they are seldom oval, like those of birds. Some are
figured on one side, and plain on the other. The following are examples
of a few of these forms :—

No. 1. is an egg of the speckled wood butterfly, (*hipparchia ægeria.*)
2. the small tortoise-shell butterfly. — 3. the large tortoise-shell butterfly.

4. Angle shades moth.—5. Lackey moth.—6. Cabbage butterfly.

Nature is no less fanciful in the strange freaks which she exhibits, in
many of the caterpillars of insects ; among these may be noticed the
following figure, the lobster caterpillar, (*stauropus fagi*, of *Germar.*)

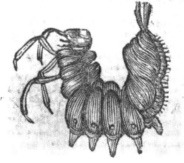

Perhaps some eggs might be injected into the body of the spider, in the act of stinging. Some ichneumons deposit their eggs in the *aurelia* of moths and butterflies. *

This singular animal is of a rich orange colour; and has frequently caused great alarm amongst the ignorant and superstitious, from the preying attitude which it assumes. The habitations of some moths display great ingenuity: and in the preparation of these, the animals manifest much intuitive foresight. The goat moth (*cossus ligniperda*) excavates for itself a hollow in a tree, fit for its reception. The following is a figure of a winter nest of one of these, formed of a fabric, consisting of the raspings of a tree, united with strong silk :

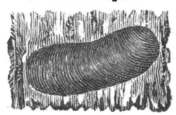

Many of the insect tribe are subject to great diversity of shape in the male and female; and in some instances are so unlike, that they might well pass for distinct species. We offer the following as not much diversified examples of this :—

1. Female vapourer moth.　　2. The male ditto.— En.

* In my *Naturalist's Calendar* for 1795, July 21st, 1 find the following note : —

It is not uncommon for some of the species of ichneumon flies to deposit their eggs in the chrysalis of a butterfly. Some time ago, I put two of the chrysalis of a butterfly into a box, and covered it with gauze, to discover what species of butterfly they would produce ; but instead of a butterfly, one of them produced a number of small ichneumon flies.

There are many instances of the great service these little insects are of to mankind in reducing the number of noxious insects, by depositing their eggs in the soft bodies of their *larvæ ;* but none more remarkable than that of the ichneumon *tipula*, which pierces the tender body, and deposits

BOMBYLIUS MEDIUS.— The *bombylius medius* is much about in March and the beginning of April, and soon seems to retire. It is a hairy insect, like a humble-bee, but with only two wings, and a long, straight beak, with which it sucks the early flowers. The female seems to lay its eggs as it poises on its wings, by striking its tail on the ground, and against the grass that stands in its way, in a quick manner, for several times together. *

MUSCÆ, (FLIES.)—In the decline of the year, when the mornings and evenings become chilly, many species of flies (*muscæ*) retire into houses, and swarm in the windows.

At first they are very brisk and alert; but, as they grow more torpid, one cannot help observing that they move with difficulty, and are scarce able to lift their legs, which seem as if glued to the glass; and by degrees, many do actually stick on till they die in the place.

It has been observed that divers flies, besides their sharp, hooked nails, have also skinny palms, or flaps to their feet, whereby they are enabled to stick on glass and other smooth bodies, and to walk on ceilings with their backs downward, by means of the pressure of the atmosphere on those flaps; the weight of which they easily overcome in warm weather, when they are brisk and alert. But, in the decline of the year, this resistance becomes too mighty for their diminished strength; and we see flies labouring along, and lugging their feet in windows, as if they stuck fast to the glass, and it is with the utmost difficulty they can draw one foot after another, and disengage their hollow caps from the slippery surface.

Upon the same principle that flies stick and support themselves, do boys, by way of play, carry heavy weights by only a piece of wet leather, at the end of a string, clapped close on the surface of a stone.

TIPULÆ, OR EMPEDES.—May.—Millions of *empedes*, or *tipulæ*, come forth at the close of day, and swarm to such a degree as to fill the air. At this juncture they sport and copulate; as it grows more dark they retire. All day they hide in the hedges. As they rise in a cloud they appear like smoke.

---

its eggs in the *larva* of the *tipula tritici*, an insect which, when it abounds greatly, is very prejudicial to the grains of wheat. This operation I have frequently seen it perform with wonder and delight.—MARKWICK.

* I have often seen this insect fly with great velocity, stop on a sudden, hang in the air in a stationary position for some time, and then fly off again; but do not recollect having ever seen it strike its tail against the ground, or any other substance.—MARKWICK.

I do not ever remember to have seen such swarms, except in the fens of the Isle of Ely. They appear most over grass grounds.

APHIDES. — On the first of August, about half an hour after three in the afternoon, the people of Selborne were surprised by a shower of *aphides* which fell in these parts. They who were walking the streets at that time found themselves covered with these insects, which settled also on the trees and gardens, and blackened all the vegetables where they alighted. These armies, no doubt, were then in a state of emigration, and shifting their quarters ; and might perhaps come from the great hop plantations of Kent or Sussex, the wind being that day at north. They were observed at the same time at Farnham, and all along the vale at Alton.

ANTS. — August 23. — Every ant-hill about this time is in a strange hurry and confusion ; and all the winged ants, agitated by some violent impulse, are leaving their homes, and, bent on emigration, swarm by myriads in the air, to the great emolument of the *hirundines*, which fare luxuriously. * Those that escape the swallows return no more to their nests, but, looking out for fresh settlements, lay a foundation for future colonies. All the females at this time are pregnant ; the males that escape being eaten, wander away and die.

October 2. — Flying ants, male and female, usually swarm and migrate on hot sunny days in August and September ; but this day a vast emigration took place in my garden, and myriads came forth, in appearance from the drain which goes under the fruit wall ; filling the air and the adjoining trees and shrubs with their numbers. The females were full of eggs. This late swarming is probably owing to the backward wet season. The day following, not one flying ant was to be seen.

Horse ants travel home to their nests laden with flies, which they have caught, and the *aureliæ* of smaller ants, which they seize by violence. †

---

* While the ants are a prey to swallows, they, in their turn, prey upon other insects ; that troublesome vermin, the *aphides*, are devoured in millions by ants, whose hills are near the bushes on which the *aphides* feed. Ants eat all kinds of animal food. — ED.

† In my *Naturalist's Calendar* for the year 1777, on September 6th, I find the following note to the article, Flying Ants : —

I saw a prodigious swarm of these ants flying about the top of some tall elm trees close by my house : some were continually dropping to the ground as if from the trees, and others rising up from the ground : many of them were joined together in copulation ; and I imagine their life is but short ; for as soon as produced from the egg by the heat of the sun, they propagate

GLOW-WORMS— By observing two glow-worms which were brought from the field to the bank in the garden, it appeared to us, that these little creatures put out their lamps between eleven and twelve, and shone no more for the rest of the night. *

Male glow-worms, attracted by the light of the candles, come into the parlour.

EARTH-WORMS. — Earth-worms make their casts most in mild weather, about March and April ; they do not lie torpid in winter, but come forth when there is no frost. They travel about in rainy nights, as appears from their sinuous tracks on the soft muddy soil, perhaps in search of food.

When earth-worms lie out a-nights on the turf, though they extend their bodies a great way, they do not quite leave their holes, but keep the ends of their tails fixed therein, so that, on the least alarm, they can retire with precipitation under the earth. Whatever food falls within their reach when thus extended, they seem to be content with, — such as, blades of grass, straws, fallen leaves, the ends of which they often draw into their holes ; even in copulation their hinder parts never quit their holes : so that no two, except they lie within reach of each other's bodies, can have any commerce of that kind ; but, as every individual is a hermaphrodite, there is no difficulty in meeting with a mate, as would be the case were they of different sexes.

SNAILS AND SLUGS. — The shelless snails called slugs are in motion all the winter, in mild weather, and commit great depredations on garden plants, and much injure the green wheat, the loss of which is imputed to earth-worms ; while the shelled snail, the φερεοικος, does not come forth at all till about April 10th, and not only lays itself up pretty early in

their species, and soon after perish. They were black, somewhat like the small black ant, and had four wings. I saw also, at another place, a large sort which were yellowish. On the 8th of September, 1785, I again observed the same circumstance of a vast number of these insects flying near the tops of the elms, and dropping to the ground.

On the 2d of March, 1777, I saw great numbers of ants come out of the ground. — MARKWICK.

* The male glow-worm yields light as well as the female, but much fainter. The eggs are also, in some degree, luminous. The light, which the worm has power to extinguish at pleasure, proceeds from brilliant spots on the three last rings of the body, and on the tail ; the luminous matter is a yellow substance contained in the vesicles; and when these vesicles are removed entire, they shine for some time afterwards ; but if lacerated, they are extinguished. — ED.

autumn, in places secure from frost, but also throws out round the mouth of its shell a thick *operculum* formed from its own saliva; so that it is perfectly secured, and corked up, as it were, from all inclemencies. The cause why the slugs are able to endure the cold so much better than shell-snails is, that their bodies are covered with slime, as whales are with blubber. *

Snails copulate about midsummer; and soon after deposit their eggs in the mould, by running their heads and bodies under ground. Hence, the way to be rid of them is, to kill as many as possible before they begin to breed.

Large, gray, shelless cellar snails, lay themselves up about the same time with those that live abroad: hence, it is plain, that a defect of warmth is not the only cause that influences their retreat.

SNAKE'S SLOUGH.

—— There the snake throws her enamel'd skin.
SHAKESPEARE'S *Mids. Night's Dream.*

About the middle of this month (September) we found, in a field near a hedge, the slough of a large snake, which seemed to have been newly cast. From circumstances, it appeared as if turned wrong side outward, and as drawn off backward, like a stocking, or woman's glove. Not only the whole skin, but scales from the very eyes, are peeled off, and appear in the head of the slough like a pair of spectacles. The reptile, at the time of changing his coat, had entangled himself intricately in the grass and weeds, so that the friction of the stalks and blades might promote this curious shifting of his *exuviæ*.

—— Lubrica serpens
Exuit in spinis vestem.—LUCRET.

It would be a most entertaining sight, could a person be an eye-witness to such a feat, and see the snake in the act of changing his garment. As the convexity of the scales of the eyes in the slough is now inward, that circumstance alone is a proof that the skin has been turned: not to mention that now the present inside is much darker than the outer. If you look through the scales of the snake's eyes from the concave side, viz. as the reptile used them, they lessen objects much. Thus it appears, from what has been said, that snakes crawl out of

---

* Slugs have the property of spinning a slimy thread, whereby they can let themselves down from a height in the manner of spiders. — ED.

the mouth of their own sloughs, and quit the tail part last, just as eels are skinned by a cook maid.   While the scales of the eyes are growing loose, and a new skin is forming, the creature, in appearance, must be blind, and feel itself in an awkward, uneasy situation. *

OBSERVATIONS ON VEGETABLES.

TREES, ORDER OF LOSING THEIR LEAVES.

ONE of the first trees that become naked is the walnut ; the mulberry, the ash, especially if it bears many keys, and the horse-chestnut come next. All lopped trees, while their heads are young, carry their leaves a long while.   Apple trees and peaches remain green very late, often till the end of November; young beeches never cast their leaves till spring, till the new leaves sprout and push them off : in the autumn, the beechen .eaves turn of a deep chestnut colour. Tall beeches cast their leaves about the end of October.

SIZE AND GROWTH. — Mr Marsham of Stratton, near Norwich, informs me by letter thus : — " I became a planter early ; so that an oak which I planted in 1720 is become now, at one foot from the earth, twelve feet six inches in circumference, and, at fourteen feet, (the half of the timber

---

* I have seen many sloughs, or skins of snakes, entire, after they have cast them off ; and, once in particular, I remember to have found one of these sloughs so intricately interwoven amongst some brakes, that it was with difficulty removed without being broken : this undoubtedly was done by the creature to assist in getting rid of its encumbrance.

I have great reason to suppose that the eft, or common lizard, also casts its skin, or slough, but not entire like the snake ; for, on the 30th of March, 1777, I saw one with something ragged hanging to it, which appeared to be part of its old skin.—MARKWICK.

It has been found by Pallas, that, after leeches have been used for medicinal purposes, they are most reproductive. He puts them into a box with argillaceous earth, six inches deep, at any time from the middle of August till the end of September. In five months, cocoons will be found, each containing twelve individuals. The cocoons are, on the outside, light, porous, and wooly, to keep out moisture and regulate the temperature. On the inside they are fibrous and dense, enclosing a thin multilocular pellicle, which contains germs. — ED.

length,) is eight feet two inches. So, if the bark were to be measured as timber, the tree gives one hundred and sixteen and a half feet, buyer's measure. Perhaps you never heard of a larger oak, while the planter was living. I flatter myself that I increased the growth by washing the stem, and digging a circle, as far as I supposed the roots to extend, and by spreading sawdust, &c. as related in the *Phil. Trans.* I wish I had begun with beeches, (my favourite trees, as well as yours ;) I might then have seen very large trees of my own raising. But I did not begin with beech till 1741, and then by seed ; so that my largest is now at five feet from the ground, six feet three inches in girth, and, with its head, spreads a circle of twenty yards diameter. This tree was also dug round, washed, &c. *Stratton,* 24*th July,* 1790."

The circumference of trees planted by myself, at one foot from the ground, (1790 :)

				Feet.	Inches.
Oak in	. . .	1730	. . . .	4	5
Ash	. . .	1730	. . . .	4	6½
Great fir	. . .	1751	. . . .	5	0
Greatest beech	.	1751	. . .	4	0
Elm	. . . .	1750	. . . .	5	3
Lime	. . .	1756	. . .	5	5

The great oak in the Holt, which is deemed by Mr Marsham to be the biggest in this island, at seven feet from the ground, measures, in circumference, thirty-four feet. It has, in old times, lost several of its boughs, and is tending to decay. Mr Marsham computes, that, at fourteen feet length, this oak contains one thousand feet of timber.

It has been the received opinion, that trees grow in height only by their annual upper shoot. But my neighbour, over the way, whose occupation confines him to one spot, assures me, that trees are expanded and raised in the lower parts also. The reason that he gives is this : the point of one of my firs began, for the first time, to peer over an opposite roof at the beginning of summer ; but, before the growing season was over, the whole shoot of the year, and three or four joints of the body beside, became visible to him, as he sits on his form in his shop. According to this supposition, a tree may advance in height considerably, though the summer shoot should be destroyed every year.

FLOWING OF SAP.— If the bough of a vine is cut late in the spring, just before the shoots push out, it will bleed considerably ; but, after the leaf is out, any part may be taken off without the least inconvenience. So oaks may be barked while the leaf is budding ; but, as soon as they are expanded, the bark will no longer part from the wood, because the sap that lubricates the bark, and makes it part, is evaporated off through the leaves.*

RENOVATION OF LEAVES.—When oaks are quite stripped of their leaves by chaffers, they are clothed again, soon after midsummer, with a beautiful foliage ; but beeches, horse-chestnuts, and maples, once defaced by those insects, never recover their beauty again for the whole season.

ASH TREES.—Many ash trees bear loads of keys every year ; others never seem to bear any at all. The prolific ones are naked of leaves, and unsightly ; those that are steril abound in foliage, and carry their verdure a long while, and are pleasing objects.†

BEECH.—Beeches love to grow in crowded situations, and will insinuate themselves through the thickest covert, so as to surmount it all : are therefore proper to mend thin places in tall hedges.

SYCAMORE.—May 12.—The sycamore, or great maple, is in bloom, and, at this season, makes a beautiful appearance, and affords much pabulum for bees, smelling strongly like honey. The foliage of this tree is very fine, and very ornamental to outlets. All the maples have saccharine juices.

GALLS OF LOMBARDY POPLAR.—The stalks and ribs of the leaves of the Lombardy poplar are embossed with large tumours of an oblong shape, which, by incurious observers, have been taken for the fruit of the tree. These galls are full of small insects, some of which are winged, and some not.

* A correspondent, in Loudon's *Magazine*, proposes a theory of the ascent of sap. " The theory which I wish to prove," says he, " is the following : — The sap, in its descent in the stem, becomes deprived of some of its constituents, more especially of its aqueous part : this deprivation is effected by the vital principle of the plant decomposing the aqueous parts, and assimilating the resulting gases to its own constituents. As the assimilation takes place, a partial vacuum is formed by the change of gas to a solid form; and this vacuum is immediately filled with sap rushing into it, according to the well-known law of the tendency of fluids to rush into any cavity deprived of the presence of air."—ED.

† Great irregularity exists in the fall of the leaf in ash trees. Many trees will already have cast their foliage, when others in the same hedge-row seem scarcely to have at all suffered from the chilling influence of autumnal winds. This cannot be attributed to difference of exposure, as we have observed them almost alternately with each other, in full leaf and denuded, for miles along a road side. — ED.

The parent insect is of the genus of *cynips*.   Some poplars in the garden are quite loaded with these excrescences.*

CHESTNUT TIMBER.—John Carpenter brings home some old chestnut trees, which are very long; in several places, the woodpeckers had begun to bore them.   The timber and bark of these trees are so very like oak, as might easily deceive an indifferent observer; but the wood is very shakey, and, towards the heart, *cup-shakey*, (that is to say, apt to separate in round pieces like cups,) so that the inward parts are of no use.   They are bought for the purpose of cooperage, but must make but ordinary barrels, buckets, &c.   Chestnut sells for half the price of oak; but has sometimes been sent into the king's dock, and passed off instead of oak.

LIME BLOSSOMS.—Dr Chandler tells, that, in the south of France, an infusion of the blossoms of the lime tree, (*tilia*,) is in much esteem as a remedy for coughs, hoarsenesses, fevers, &c.; and that, at Nismes, he saw an avenue of limes that was quite ravaged and torn in pieces by people greedily gathering the bloom, which they dried and kept for these purposes.

Upon the strength of this information, we made some tea of lime blossoms, and found it a very soft, well flavoured, pleasant, saccharine julep, in taste much resembling the juice of liquorice.

BLACKTHORN. — This tree usually blossoms while cold north-east winds blow; so that the harsh rugged weather obtaining at this season is called, by the country people, blackthorn winter.

IVY BERRIES.—Ivy berries afford a noble and providential supply for birds in winter and spring; for the first severe frost freezes and spoils all the haws, sometimes by the middle of November.   Ivy berries do not seem to freeze.

HOPS.—The culture of Virgil's vines corresponded very exactly with the modern management of hops.   I might instance in the perpetual diggings and hoeings, in the tying to the stakes and poles, in pruning the superfluous shoots, &c.; but lately, I have observed a new circumstance, which was, a neighbouring farmer's harrowing between the rows of hops

---

* Mr David Don, a botanist of distinguished talents, has discovered, that, on detaching the spiral vessels from vigorous young shoots of herbaceous plants, they frequently become violently agitated; the motion continues for some seconds, and may be somewhat similar to that of the heart of animals under similar circumstances.   These vessels abound in the stems of the *urtica nivea*, of *centaurea atro-purpurea*, and of the *malvaceæ*. —ED.

with a small triangular harrow, drawn by one horse, and guided by two handles.   This occurrence brought to my mind the following passage : —

—— ipsa
Flectere luctantes inter vineta juvencos.

Georgic II.

Hops are diécious plants : hence perhaps it might be proper, though not practised, to leave purposely some male plants in every garden, that their farina might impregnate the blossoms.   The female plants, without their male attendants, are not in their natural state : hence we may suppose the frequent failure of crop so incident to hop-grounds. *   No other growth, cultivated by man, has such frequent and general failures as hops.

Two hop gardens much injured by a hail storm, (June 5,) shew now (September 2) a prodigious crop, and larger and fairer hops than any in the parish.   The owners seem now to be convinced that the hail, by beating off the tops of the binds, has increased the side shoots, and improved the crop.   Query, Therefore, should not the tops of hops be pinched off when the binds are very gross and strong ?

---

* The various mechanical contrivances by which Nature has enabled plants to diffuse their seeds, are matters of common observation, and that of the violet is not the least remarkable.   The seeds of this natural order of plants are contained in a capsule of a single loculament, consisting, however, of three valves.   To the inner part of each of these three valves the seeds are attached, and remain so for some time after the valves, in the process of ripening, have separated and stood open.   The influence of the sun's heat, however, causes the sides of each valve to shrink and collapse; and, in this state, the edges press firmly upon the seed, which, from being before apparently irregular in its arrangement, comes into a straight line.   The seeds, it may be remarked, are not only extremely smooth, polished, and shining, but regularly egg-shaped; so that, when pressed upon by the collapsing edge of the valve, it slides gradually down the sloping part of the seed, and throws it, with a jerk, to a considerable distance.

There is another beautiful contrivance in the violets, (*violaceæ*,) well worthy our admiration.   Before the seed is ripe, the capsule hangs in a drooping position, with the persisting calyx spread over it, like an umbrella, to guard it from the rain and dews, which would retard the progress of ripening; but no sooner is the ripening completed, than the capsule becomes upright, with the calyx for a support.   This upright position appears to be intended by Nature to give more effect to the valvular mechanism for scattering the seeds, as it thus gains a higher elevation (in some cases more than an inch) from which to project them; and will give it, according to the laws of projectiles, a very considerable increase of horizontal extent. — ED.

SEED LYING DORMANT.—The naked part of the Hanger is now covered with thistles of various kinds. The seeds of these thistles may have lain probably under the thick shade of the beeches for many years, but could not vegetate till the sun and air were admitted. When old beech trees are cleared away, the naked ground in a year or two becomes covered with strawberry plants, the seeds of which must have lain in the ground for an age at least. One of the *slidders*, or trenches, down the middle of the Hanger, close covered over with lofty beeches near a century old, is still called *strawberry-slidder*, though no strawberries have grown there in the memory of man. That sort of fruit did once, no doubt, abound there, and will again, when the obstruction is removed. *

---

* Sir Thomas Dick Lauder, Bart. well known for his zeal for science, made some very curious and interesting experiments, in 1817, on the germination of seeds, which we shall give in his own words : — "A friend of mine possesses an estate in this county, a great part of which lying along the Moray Firth, was, at some period not very well ascertained, but certainly not less than sixty years ago, covered with sand, which had been blown from the westward, and overwhelmed the cultivated fields, so that the agriculturist was forced to abandon them altogether. My friend, soon after his purchase of the estate, began the arduous, but judicious operation of trenching down the sand, and bringing to the surface the original black mould. These operations of improvement were so productive, as to induce the very intelligent and enterprising proprietor to undertake, lately, a still more laborious task, viz. to trench down the superincumbent sand, on a part of the property where it was no less than eight feet deep.

"Conceiving this to be a favourable opportunity for trying some experiments relative to the length of time which seeds preserve their power of vegetation, even when immersed in the soil, I procured from my friend a quantity of the mould, taken fresh from under the sand, and carefully avoiding any mixture of the latter. This was instantly put into a jar, which was stopped up close, by means of a piece of bladder tied tightly over its mouth. Having prepared a couple of flower-pot flats, by drilling small holes in the bottom of them, so as to admit of the ascent of water, I filled the flats with some of the mould, and placing them in a very wide and shallow tub, made on purpose, I covered each of them with a large glass receiver. Each receiver, however, was provided with a brass rim, having little brass knobs on it, so as to raise its edge from the bottom of the tub, and leave a small opening for the admission of air. The whole apparatus was placed in my library, of which the door and windows were kept constantly shut.

"This was done on the 17th of February last. It is now the 6th of May; and, on examining the flats, I find about forty-six plants in them, apparently of four different kinds; but, as they are yet very young, I cannot determine their species with any degree of accuracy."

Sir Thomas has just informed us, that the seeds which germinated were all highly oleaginous ; and the plants produced were the mouse-ear,

BEANS SOWN BY BIRDS. — Many horse-beans sprang up in my field-walks in the autumn, and are now grown to a considerable height. As the Ewel was in beans last summer, it is most likely that these seeds came from thence; but then the distance is too considerable for them to have been conveyed by mice. It is most probable, therefore, that they were brought by birds, and, in particular, by jays and pies, who seem to have hid them among the grass and moss, and then to have forgotten where they had stowed them. Some peas are growing also in the same situation, and probably under the same circumstances.

CUCUMBERS SET BY BEES. — If bees, who are much the best setters of cucumbers, do not happen to take kindly to the frames, the best way is to tempt them by a little honey, put on the male and female bloom. When they are once induced to haunt the frames, they set all the fruit, and will hover with impatience round the lights in a morning, till the glasses are opened. *Probatum est.*

WHEAT. — A notion has always obtained, that, in England, hot summers are productive of fine crops of wheat; yet in the years 1780 and 1781, though the heat was intense, the wheat was much mildewed, and the crop light. Does not severe heat, while the straw is milky, occasion its juices to exude, which being extravasated, occasion spots, discolour the stems and blades, and injure the health of the plants?

TRUFFLES. — August. — A truffle-hunter called on us, having in his pocket several large truffles found in this neighbourhood. He says, these roots are not to be found in deep woods, but in narrow hedge-rows and the skirts of coppices. Some truffles, he informed us, lie two feet within the earth, and some quite on the surface; the latter, he added, have little or no smell, and are not so easily discovered by the dogs as those that lie deeper. Half-a-crown a pound was the price which he asked for this commodity.

Truffles never abound in wet winters and springs. They are in season, in different situations, at least nine months in the year. *

(*myosotis scorpiodes,*) scorpion grass, (*Lamium purpureum,*) red archangel, and (*spergula arvensis,*) corn spurrey. The earth thus experimented upon was taken from the lands of Inveragie. — ED.
* This singular vegetable belongs to the class of cryptogamic plants, and the *tuber cibarium* of Linnæus: it grows entirely under ground having neither root, stem, nor leaf, and of a black colour, strongly scented, of a globular shape, growing to the size of a large duck's egg,

TREMELLA NOSTOC.— Though the weather may have been ever so dry and burning, yet, after two or three wet days, this jelly-like substance abounds on the walks.

FAIRY RINGS.— The cause, occasion, call it what you will, of *fairy rings*, subsists in the turf, and is conveyable with it; for the turf of my garden-walks, brought from the down above, abounds with those appearances, which vary their shape, and shift situation continually, discovering themselves now in circles, now in segments, and sometimes in irregular patches, and spots. Wherever they obtain, puff-balls abound; the seeds of which were doubtless brought in the turf. *

METEOROLOGICAL OBSERVATIONS.

BAROMETER.— November 22, 1768.— A remarkable fall of the barometer all over the kingdom. At Selborne, we had no wind, and not much rain; only vast, swagging, rock-like clouds appeared at a distance.

PARTIAL FROST.— The country people, who are abroad in winter mornings long before sun-rise, talk much of hard frost in some spots, and none in others. The reason of these partial frosts is obvious, for there are at such times partial fogs about: where the fog obtains, little or no frost appears; but

with a rugged surface-like work. It is held in high estimation by epicures, being used in various dishes, stuffing of turkeys, and sometimes it is boiled in port wine and eaten with salt, and purchased, when scarce, at two guineas per pound weight. Truffles are produced in various parts of the Continent, where they are searched for with swine. In England, they are found in the southern counties growing in woods, chiefly in Sussex, Harts, and Berks, where they are discovered by dogs, the sagacity of these animals pointing out the places by the scent. The season for truffles commences in September.— ED.

* The true cause of this phenomenon is not yet properly understood. Mr Dovaston is of opinion that they are occasioned by electricity, and that the fungi which are seen on these rings are the effect rather than the cause, of these appearances. Mr Johnson, of Wetherby, in a paper in the fourth volume of the *Philosophical Journal*, attributes them to the droppings of starlings, which, when in large flights, frequently alight on the ground in circles, and sometimes are known to sit a considerable time in these annular congregations. — ED.

where the air is clear, there it freezes hard. So the frost takes place either on hill or in dale, wherever the air happens to be clearest and freest from vapour.

THAW.—Thaws are sometimes surprisingly quick, considering the small quantity of rain. Does not the warmth at such times come from below? The cold in still, severe seasons, seems to come down from above: for the coming over of a cloud in severe nights raises the thermometer abroad at once full ten degrees. The first notices of thaws often seem to appear in vaults, cellars, &c.

If a frost happens, even when the ground is considerably dry, as soon as a thaw takes place, the paths and fields are all in a batter. Country people say that the frost draws moisture. But the true philosophy is, that the steam and vapours continually ascending from the earth, are bound in by the frost, and not suffered to escape, till released by the thaw. No wonder, then, that the surface is all in a float; since the quantity of moisture by evaporation that arises daily from every acre of ground is astonishing.

FROZEN SLEET.—January 20. Mr H.'s man says, that he caught this day, in a lane near Hackwood-park, many rooks, which, attempting to fly, fell from the trees with their wings frozen together by the sleet, that froze as it fell. There were, he affirms, many dozen so disabled.

MIST, CALLED LONDON SMOKE.— This is a blue mist, which has somewhat the smell of coal smoke, and as it always comes to us with a north-east wind, is supposed to come from London. It has a strong smell, and is supposed to occasion blights. When such mists appear, they are usually followed by dry weather.*

* Fogs happen every where, caused by the upper regions of the atmosphere being colder than the lower, by which the ascent of aqueous vapour is checked, and kept arrested near the surface of the earth. But fogs are more dense about London, and probably all other great cities, than elsewhere: the reason is, because the vast quantity of fuliginous matter floating over such places mingles with the vapour, and renders the whole so thick, that darkness is sometimes produced at noonday, rendering candles and gas lights necessary for the transaction of ordinary business in the shops and public offices. Such circumstances happen frequently during winter; but on some occasions, (as about two o'clock P. M. on the 27th December, 1831,) this foggy darkness is truly awful. This extraordinary appearance is, however, caused by a very ordinary accident, namely, a change of wind. The west wind carries the smoke of the city to the westward in a long train, extending to the distance of twenty or thirty miles, as may be seen in a clear day by any person on an eminence five or six miles from the city. —ED.

REFLECTION ON FOG. — When people walk in a deep white fog by night with a lanthorn, if they will turn their backs to the light, they will see their shades impressed on the fog in rude gigantic proportions. This phenomenon seems not to have been attended to, but implies the great density of the meteor at that juncture.

HONEY DEW. — June 4, 1783. — Vast honey dews this week. The reason of these seems to be, that, in hot days, the effluvia of flowers are drawn up by a brisk evaporation, and then, in the night, fall down with the dews, with which they are entangled.

This clammy substance is very grateful to bees, who gather it with great assiduity; but it is injurious to the trees on which it happens to fall, by stopping the pores of the leaves. The greatest quantity falls in still, close weather; because winds disperse it, and copious dews dilute it, and prevent its ill effects. It falls mostly in hazy, warm weather. *

MORNING CLOUDS. — After a bright night and vast dews, the sky usually becomes cloudy by eleven or twelve o'clock in the forenoon, and clear again towards the decline of the day. The reason seems to be, that the dew drawn up by evaporation occasions the clouds; which, towards evening, being no longer rendered buoyant by the warmth of the sun, melt away, and fall down again in dews. If clouds are watched in a still, warm evening, they will be seen to melt away, and disappear.†

DRIPPING WEATHER AFTER DROUGHT. — No one that has not attended to such matters, and taken down remarks, can be aware how much ten days dripping weather will influence the growth of grass or corn after a severe dry season. This present summer, 1776, yielded a remarkable instance; for, till

---

* Mr William Curtis has discovered honey dew to be the excrement of the *aphides*; and justly remarks, that it is not to be found on any plant where these insects do not accompany it. These *aphides* bring forth ninety young, according to the observations of Reaumur, so that, in five generations, the produce from a single one would be five thousand nine hundred and four millions, nine hundred thousand. — ED.

† It may be useful to agriculturists to observe this small cloud, which is rapid in its formation and dispersion. It appears in the mild weather of spring, summer, and autumn. It is a small, delicately soft, thin, white, curved cloud, formed upon the summit of those fine, heaped clouds, termed *comuli*, which seem to tower up to a prodigious height. When this little "storm cap" is seen, it is closely over the rounded summit, like a white silken web. It disappears in a few seconds, and generally reappears, and again suddenly sinks. When this happens, foul weather is certain within twenty-four hours. — ED.

the thirtieth of May, the fields were burnt up and naked, and the barley not half out of the ground ; but now, June the tenth, there is an agreeable prospect of plenty. *

AURORA BOREALIS.—November 1, 1787.—The north aurora made a particular appearance, forming itself into a broad, red, fiery belt, which extended from east to west across the welkin ; but the moon rising at about ten o'clock, in unclouded majesty, in the east, put an end to this grand, but awful meteorous phenomenon. †

, BLACK SPRING, 1771.—Dr Johnson says, that, " in 1771, the season was so severe in the Island of Skye, that it is remembered by the name of the *black spring*. The snow, which seldom lies at all, covered the ground for eight weeks ; many cattle died, and those that survived were so emaciated, that they did not require the male at the usual season."   The case was just the same with us here in the south ; never was so many barren cows known as in the spring following that dreadful period. Whole dairies missed being in calf together.

At the end of March, the face of the earth was naked to a surprising degree : wheat hardly to be seen, and no signs of any grass ; turnips all gone, and sheep in a starving way ; all provisions rising in price. Farmers cannot sow for want of rain.

---

* The annual average quantity of dew deposited in this country is estimated at a depth of about five inches, being about one-seventh of the mean quantity of moisture supposed to be received from the atmosphere, over all Great Britain, during the year; or about 22,161,337,355 tons, taking the ton at two hundred and fifty-two imperial gallons. —ED.

† At what time this meteor was first observed, is not known ; none are recorded in the English annals till the remarkable one, which happened on the 30th January, 1560 ; another very brilliant one appeared in 1760.

M. Libos attributes the aurora to the decomposition of the two airs which compose the atmosphere, oxygen and nitrogen, in the polar regions, by an accumulation of the electric fluid there.   This explanation is supported by a very accurate attention to the chemical phenomena produced on the atmosphere by electricity, which decomposes it, and forms nitrous gas. —ED.

SUMMARY OF THE WEATHER.

Measure of Rain in Inches and Hundreds.

Year.	Jan.	Feb.	Mar.	Apr.	May	June	July	Aug.	Sep	Oct.	Nov.	Dec.	Total.
1782.	4.64	1.98	6.54	4.57	6.34	1.75	7.09	8.28	3.72	1.93	2.51	0.91	50.26
1783.	4.43	5.54	2.16	0.88	2.84	2.82	1.45	2.24	5.52	1.71	3.01	1.10	33.71
1784.	3.18	0.77	3.82	3.92	1.52	3.65	2.40	3.88	2.51	0.39	4.70	3.06	33.80
1785.	2.84	1.80	0.30	0.17	0.60	1.39	3.80	3.21	5.94	5.21	2.27	4. 2	31.55
1786.	6.91	1.42	1.62	1.81	2.40	1.20	1.99	4.34	4.79	5. 4	4.38		
1787.	0.88	3.67	4.26	0.74	2.60	1.50	6.53	0 83	1.56	5. 4	4. 9	5. 6	36.24
1788.	1.60	3.37	1.31	0.61	0.76	1.27	3.58	3.22	5.71	0. 0	0.86	0.23	22.50
1789.	4.48	4.11	2.47	1.81	4. 5	4.24	3.69	0.90	2.82	5. 4	3.67	4.62	42.—
1790.	1.99	0.49	0.45	3.64	4.38	0.13	3.24	2.30	0.66	2.10	6.95	5.94	32.27
1791.	6.73	4.64	1.59	1.13	1.33	0.91	5.56	1.73	1.73	6.49	8.16	4.93	44.93
1792.	6. 7	1.68	6.70	4.08	3.00	2.78	5.16	4.25	5.53	5.55	1.65	2.11	48.56
1793.	3.71	2.32	3.33	3.19	1.21								

1768. Begins with a fortnight's frost and snow ; rainy during February. Cold and wet spring ; wet season from the beginning of June to the end of harvest. Latter end of September, foggy, without rain. All October and the first part of November, rainy ; and thence to the end of the year alternate rains and frosts.

1769. January and February, frosty and rainy, with gleams of fine weather in the intervals. To the middle of March, wind and rain. To the end of March, dry and windy. To the middle of April, stormy, with rain. To the end of June, fine weather, with rain. To the beginning of August, warm, dry weather. To the end of September, rainy, with short intervals of fine weather. To the latter end of October, frosty mornings, with fine days. The next fortnight, rainy ; thence to the end of November, dry and frosty. December, windy, with rain and intervals of frost, and the first fortnight very foggy.

1770. Frost for the first fortnight ; during the 14th and 15th, all the snow melted. To the end of February, mild, hazy weather. The whole of March, frosty, with bright weather. April, cloudy, with rain and snow. May began with summer showers, and ended with dark cold rains. June, rainy, chequered with gleams of sunshine. The first fortnight in July, dark and sultry ; the latter part of the month, heavy rain. August, September, and the first fortnight in October, in general fine weather, though with frequent interruptions of rain ; from the middle of October to the end of the year, almost incessant rains.

1771. Severe frosts till the last week in January. To the first week in February, rain and snow ; to the end of February, spring weather. To the end of the third week in April, frosty weather. To the end of the first fortnight in May, spring weather, with copious showers. To the end of June, dry, warm weather. The first fortnight in July, warm, rainy weather. To the end of September, warm weather, but in general cloudy, with showers. October, rainy. November, frost, with intervals of fog and rain. December, in general bright, mild weather, with hoar frosts.

1772. To the end of the first week in February, frost and snow. To the end of the first fortnight in March, frost, sleet, rain, and snow. To the middle of April, cold rains. To the middle of May, dry weather, with cold piercing winds. To the end of the first week in June, cool showers. To the middle of August, hot, dry summer weather. To the end of September, rain, with storms and thunder. To December 22, rain, with mild weather. December 23, the first ice. To the end of the month, cold, foggy weather.

1773. The first week in January, frost ; thence to the end of the month, dark, rainy weather. The first fortnight in February, hard frost. To the end of the first week in March, misty, showery weather. Bright spring days to the close of the month. Frequent showers to the latter end of April. To the end of June, warm showers, with intervals of sunshine. To the end of August, dry weather, with a few days of rain. To the end of the first fortnight in November, rainy. The next four weeks, frost ; and thence to the end of the year, rainy.

1774. Frost and rain to the end of the first fortnight in March : thence to the end of the month, dry weather. To the 15th of April, showers: thence to the end of April, fine spring days. During May, showers and sunshine in about an equal proportion. Dark, rainy weather to the end of the third week in July : thence to the 24th of August, sultry, with thunder and occasional showers. To the end of the third week in November, rain, with frequent intervals of sunny weather. To the end of December, dark, dripping fogs.

1775. To the end of the first fortnight in March, rain almost every day. To the first week in April, cold winds, with showers of rain and snow. To the end of June, warm, bright weather, with frequent showers. The first fortnight in July, almost incessant rains. To the 26th August, sultry weather, with frequent showers. To the end of the third week in

September, rain, with a few intervals of fine weather. To the end of the year, rain, with intervals of hoar frost and sunshine.

1776. To January 24, dark, frosty weather, with much snow. March 24, to the end of the month, foggy, with hoar frost. To the 30th of May, dark, dry, harsh weather, with cold winds. To the end of the first fortnight in July, warm, with much rain. To the end of the first week in August, hot and dry, with intervals of thunder showers. To the end of October, in general fine seasonable weather, with a considerable proportion of rain. To the end of the year, dry, frosty weather, with some days of hard rain.

1777. To the 10th of January, hard frost. To the 20th of January, foggy, with frequent showers. To the 18th of February, hard, dry frost, with snow. To the end of May, heavy showers, with intervals of warm, dry spring days. To the 8th July, dark, with heavy rain. To the 18th July, dry, warm weather. To the end of July, very heavy rains. To the 12th October, remarkably fine, warm weather. To the end of the year, gray, mild weather, with but little rain, and still less frost.

1778. To the 13th of January, frost, with a little snow : to the 24th January, rain : to the 30th, hard frost. To the 23d February, dark, harsh, foggy weather, with rain. To the end of the month, hard frost, with snow. To the end of the first fortnight in March, dark, harsh weather. From the 1st, to the end of the first fortnight in April, spring weather. To the end of the month, snow and ice. To the 11th of June, cool, with heavy showers. To the 19th July, hot, sultry, parching weather. To the end of the month, heavy showers. To the end of September, dry, warm weather. To the end of the year, wet, with considerable intervals of sunshine.

1779. Frost and showers to the end of January. To 21st April, warm, dry weather. To 8th May, rainy. To the 7th June, dry and warm. To the 6th July, hot weather, with frequent rain. To the 18th July, dry, hot weather. To August 8, hot weather, with frequent rains. To the end of August, fine dry harvest weather. To the end of November, fine autumnal weather, with intervals of rain. To the end of the year, rain, with frost and snow.

1780. To the end of January, frost. To the end of February, dark, harsh weather, with frequent intervals of frost. To the end of March, warm, showery, spring weather. To the end of April, dark, harsh weather, with rain and frost.

To the end of the first fortnight in May, mild, with rain. To the end of August, rain and fair weather in pretty equal proportions. To the end of October, fine autumnal weather, with intervals of rain. To the 24th November, frost. To December 16th, mild, dry, foggy weather. To the end of the year, frost and snow.

1781. To January 25, frost and snow. To the end of February, harsh and windy, with rain and snow. To April 5th, cold, drying winds. To the end of May, mild spring weather, with a few light showers. June began with heavy rain, but thence to the end of October, dry weather, with a few flying showers. To the end of the year, open weather, with frequent rains.

1782. To February 4, open, mild weather. To February 22, hard frost. To the end of March, cold, blowing weather, with frost, and snow, and rain. To May 7, cold, dark rains. To the end of May, mild, with incessant rains. To the end of June, warm and dry. To the end of August, warm, with almost perpetual rains. The first fortnight in September, mild and dry ; thence to the end of the month, rain. To the end of October, mild, with frequent showers. November began with hard frost, and continued throughout, with alternate frost and thaw. The first part of December, frosty : the latter part, mild.

1783. To January 16, rainy, with heavy winds. To the 24th, hard frost. To the end of the first fortnight in February, blowing, with much rain. To the end of February, stormy, dripping weather. To the 9th of May, cold, harsh winds, (thick ice on the 5th of May.) To the end of August, hot weather, with frequent showers. To the 23d September, mild, with heavy driving rains. To November 12, dry, mild weather. To the 18th December, gray, soft weather, with a few showers. To the end of the year, hard frost.

1784. To February 19, hard frost, with two thaws : one the 14th January, the other 5th February. To February 28, mild, wet fogs. To the 3d March, frost, with ice. To March 10, sleet and snow. To April 2, snow and hard frost. To April 27, mild weather, with much rain. To May 12, cold, drying winds. To May 20, hot, cloudless weather. To June 27, warm, with frequent showers. To July 18, hot and dry. To the end of August, warm, with heavy rains. To November 6, clear, mild, autumnal weather, except a few days of rain at the latter end of September. To the end of the year, fog, rain, and hard frost, (on December 10, the thermometer one degree below 0.)

1785. A thaw began on the 2d January, and rainy weather, with wind, continued to January 28. To 15th March, very hard frost. To 21st March, mild, with sprinkling showers. To April 7, hard frost. To May 17, mild, windy weather, without a drop of rain. To the end of May, cold, with a few showers. To June 9, mild weather, with frequent soft showers. To July 13, hot, dry weather, with a few showery intervals. To July 22, heavy rain. To the end of September, warm, with frequent showers. To the end of October, frequent rain. To 18th of November, dry, mild weather. (Haymaking finished, November 9, and the wheat harvest, November 14.) To December 23, rain. To the end of the year, hard frost.

1786. To the 7th January, frost and snow. To January 13, mild, with much rain. To the 21st January, deep snow. To February 11, mild, with frequent rains. 21st February, dry, with high winds. To 10th March, hard frost. To 13th April, wet, with intervals of frost. To the end of April, dry, mild weather. On the 1st and 2d May, thick ice. To 10th May, heavy rain. To June 14, fine, warm, dry weather. From the 8th to the 11th July, heavy showers. To October 13, warm, with frequent showers. To October 19, ice. To October 24, mild, pleasant weather. To November 3, frost. To December 16, rain, with a few detached days of frost. To the end of the year, frost and snow.

1787. To January 24, dark, moist, mild weather. To January 28, frost and snow. To February 16, mild, showery weather. To February 28, dry, cool weather. To March 10, stormy, with driving rain. To March 24, bright, frosty weather. To the end of April, mild, with frequent rain. To May 22, fine, bright weather. To the end of June, mostly warm, with frequent showers, (on June 7, ice as thick as a crown-piece.) To the end of July, hot and sultry, with copious rain. To the end of September, hot, dry weather, with occasional showers. To November 23, mild, with light frosts and rain. To the end of November, hard frost. To December 21, still and mild, with rain. To the end of the year, frost.

1788. To January 13, mild and wet. To January 18, frost. To the end of the month, dry, windy weather. To the end of February, frosty, with frequent showers. To March 14, hard frost. To the end of March, dark, harsh weather, with frequent showers. To April 4, windy, with showers. To the end of May, bright, dry, warm weather, with a few occasional showers. From June 28 to July 17, heavy rains. To August 12, hot, dry weather. To the end of September, alternate showers and sunshine. To November 22, dry, cool weather. To the end of the year, hard frost.

1789. To January 13, hard frost. To the end of the month, mild, with showers. To the end of February, frequent rain, with snow showers, and heavy gales of wind. To 13th March, hard frost, with snow. To April 18, heavy rain with frost, and snow, and sleet. To the end of April, dark, cold weather, with frequent rains. To June 9, warm spring weather, with brisk winds, and frequent showers. From June 4, to the end of July, warm, with much rain. To August 29, hot, dry, sultry weather. To September 11, mild, with frequent showers. To the end of September, fine autumnal weather, with occasional showers. To November 17, heavy rain, with violent gales of wind. To December 18, mild, dry weather, with a few showers. To the end of the year, rain and wind.

1790. To January 16, mild, foggy weather, with occasional rains. To January 21, frost. To January 28, dark, with driving rains. To February 14, mild, dry weather. To February 22, hard frost. To April 5, bright, cold weather, with a few showers. To April 15, dark and harsh, with a deep snow. To April 21, cold, cloudy weather, with ice. To June 6, mild, spring weather, with much rain. From July 9 to July 14, cool, with heavy rain. To the end of July, warm, dry weather. To August 6, cold, with wind and rain. To August 24, fine harvest weather. To September 5, strong gales, with driving showers. To November 26, mild autumnal weather, with frequent showers. To December 1, hard frost and snow. To the end of the year, rain and snow, and a few days of frost.

1791. To the end of January, mild, with heavy rains. To the end of February, windy, with much rain and snow. From March to the end of June, mostly dry, especially June. March and April, rather cold and frosty. May and June, hot. July, rainy. Fine harvest weather, and pretty dry, to the end of September. Wet, October, and cold towards the end. Very wet and stormy in November. Much frost in December.

1792. Some hard frost in January, but mostly wet and mild. February, some hard frost, and a little snow. March, wet and cold. April, great storms on the 13th, then some very warm weather. May and June, cold and dry. July, wet and cold; indifferent harvest, rather late and wet. September, windy and wet. October, showery and mild. November, dry and fine. December, mild.

A COMPARATIVE VIEW

OF THE

NATURALIST'S CALENDAR,

AS KEPT AT SELBORNE, IN HAMPSHIRE, BY THE LATE
REV. GILBERT WHITE, M. A.

AND AT CATSFIELD, NEAR BATTLE, IN SUSSEX, BY
WILLIAM MARKWICK, ESQ. F. L. S.

FROM THE YEAR 1768, TO THE YEAR 1793.

N. B. — The dates in the following calendars, when more than one, express the *earliest* and the *latest* times in which the circumstance noted was observed.

Of the abbreviations used, fl. signifies *flowering* ; l. *leafing* ; and ap. the first *appearance*.

	WHITE.	MARKWICK.
Redbreast (sylvia rubecula) sings	Jan. 1 — 12	Jan. 3 — 31, and again Oct. 6
Larks (alauda arvensis) congregate	Jan. 1 — 18	Oct. 16, Feb. 9
Nuthatch (sitta europæa) heard	Jan. 1 — 14	March 3, April 10
Winter aconite (helleborus hiemalis) fl.	Jan. 1, Feb. 18	Feb. 28, April 17
Shelless snail or slug (limax) ap.	Jan. 2	Jan. 16, May 31
Gray & White wagtail (motacilla boarula) ap. (motacilla alba) ap.	Jan. 2 — 11	Jan. 24, March 26 Dec. 12, Feb. 23
Missel thrush (turdus viscivorus) sings	Jan. 2 — 14	Feb. 19, April 14
Bearsfoot (helleborus fœtidus) fl.	Jan. 2, Feb. 14	March 1, May 5
Polyanthus (primula polyantha) fl.	Jan. 2, April 12	Jan. 1, April 9
Double daisy (bellis perennis plena) fl.	Jan. 2, Feb. 1	Mar. 17, April 29
Mezereon (daphne mezereum) fl.	Jan. 3, Feb. 16	Jan. 2, April 4
Pansie (viola tricolor) fl.	Jan. 3	Jan. 1, May 10
Red dead-nettle (lamium purpureum) fl.	Jan. 3 — 21	Jan. 1, April 5
Groundsel (senecio vulgaris) fl.	Jan. 3 — 15	Jan. 1, April 9
Hazel (corylus avellana) fl.	Jan. 3, Feb. 28	Jan. 21, March 11
Hepatica (anemone hepatica) fl.	Jan. 4, Feb. 18	Jan. 17, April 9
Hedge sparrow (sylvia modularis) sings	Jan. 5 — 12	Jan. 16, March 13
Common flies (musca domestica) seen in numbers	Jan. 5, Feb. 3	May 15
Greater titmouse (parus major) sings	Jan. 6, Feb. 6	Feb. 17, March 17
Thrush (turdus musicus) sings	Jan. 6 — 22	Jan. 15, April 4
Insects swarm under sunny hedges	Jan. 6	
Primrose (primula vulgaris) fl.	Jan. 6, April 7	Jan. 3, March 22
Bees (apis mellifica) ap.	Jan. 6, Mar. 19	Jan. 31, April 11 ; last seen Dec. 30
Gnats play about	Jan. 6, Feb. 3	
Chaffinches, male and female, (fringilla cœlebs) seen in equal numbers	Jan. 6 — 11	Dec. 2, Feb. 3
Furze or gorse (ulex europæus) fl.	Jan. 8, Feb. 1	Jan. 1, March 27

	WHITE.	MARKWICK.
Wall-flower (cheiranthus cheiri ; seu fruticulosus of Smith) fl.	Jan. 8, April 1	Feb. 21, May 9
Stock (cheiranthus incanus) fl.	Jan. 8 — 12	Feb. 1, June 3
Emberiza alba (bunting) in great flocks	Jan. 9	
Linnets (fringilla linota) congregate	Jan. 9	Jan. 11
Lambs begin to fall	Jan. 9 — 11	Jan. 6, Feb. 21
Rooks (corvus frugilegus) resort to their nest trees	Jan. 10, Feb. 11	Jan. 23
Black hellebore (helleborus niger) fl.	Jan. 10	April 27
Snow-drop (galanthus nivalis) fl.	Jan. 10, Feb. 5	Jan. 18, March 1
White dead-nettle (lamium album) fl.	Jan. 13	March 23, May 10
Trumpet honey-suckle, fl.	Jan. 13	
Common creeping crow-foot (ranunculus repens) fl.	Jan. 13	April 10, May 12
House-sparrow (fringilla domestica) chirps	Jan. 14	Feb. 17, May 9
Dandelion (leontodon taraxacum) fl.	Jan. 16, Mar. 11	Feb. 1, April 17
Bat (vespertilio) ap.	Jan. 16, Mar. 24	Feb. 6, June 1, last seen Nov. 20
Spiders shoot their webs	Jan. 16	
Butterfly, ap.	Jan. 16	Feb. 21, May 8 ; last seen Dec. 22
Brambling (fringilla montifringilla) ap.	Jan. 16	Jan. 10 — 31
Blackbird (turdus merula) whistles	Jan. 17	Feb. 15, May 13
Wren (sylvia troglodytes) sings	Jan. 17	Feb. 7, June 12
Earth-worms lie out	Jan. 18, Feb. 8	
Crocus (crocus vernus) fl.	Jan. 18, Mar. 18	Jan. 20, March 19
Skylark (alauda arvensis) sings	Jan. 21	Jan. 12, Feb. 27 ; sings till Nov. 13
Ivy casts its leaves	Jan. 22	
Helleborus hiemalis, fl.	Jan. 22 — 24	Feb. 28, April 17
Common dor, or clock (scarabæus stercorarius)	Jan. 23	Feb. 12, April 19 ; last seen Nov. 24
Peziza acetabulum, ap.	Jan. 23	
Helleborus virid, fl.	Jan. 23, Mar. 5	
Hazel (corylus avellana) fl.	Jan. 23, Feb. 1	Jan. 27, March 11
Woodlark (alauda arborea) sings	Jan. 24, Feb. 21	Jan. 28, June 5
Chaffinch (fringilla cœlebs) sings	Jan. 24, Feb. 15	Jan. 21, Feb. 26
Jack-daws begin to come to churches	Jan. 25, Mar. 4	
Yellow wagtail (motacilla flava) ap.	Jan. 25, Apr. 14	April 13, July 3 ; last seen Sept. 8
Honeysuckle (lonicera periclymenum) l.	Jan. 25	Jan. 1, April 9
Field or procumbent speedwell (veronica agrestis) fl.	Jan. 27, Mar. 15	Feb. 12, March 29
Nettle butterfly (papilio urticæ) ap.	Jan. 27, April 2	Mar. 5, April 24 ; last seen June 6
White wagtail (motacilla alba) chirps	Jan. 28	March 16
Shell-snail (helix nemoralis) ap.	Jan. 28, Feb. 24	April 2, June 11
Earth-worms engender	Jan. 30	
Barren strawberry (fragaria sterilis) fl.	Feb. 1, Mar. 26	Jan. 13, March 26
Blue titmouse (parus cæruleus) chirps	Feb. 1	April 27
Brown wood-owls hoot	Feb. 2	
Hen (phasianus gallus) sits	Feb. 3	March 8, hatches
Marsh titmouse begins his two harsh sharp notes	Feb. 3	
Gossamer floats	Feb. 4, April 1	
Musca tenax, ap.	Feb 4, April 8	
Laroustine (viburnum tinis) fl.	Feb. 5	Jan. 1, April 5
Butcher's broom (ruscus aculeatus) fl.	Feb. 5	Jan. 1, May 10
Fox (canis vulpes) smells rank	Feb. 7	May 19, young brought forth
Turkey-cocks strut and gobble	Feb. 10	
Yellow-hammer (emberiza citrinella) sings	Feb. 12	Feb. 18, April 28
Brimstone butterfly (papilio rhamni) ap.	Feb. 13, April 2	Feb. 13, March 8 ; last seen Dec. 24

	WHITE.	MARKWICK.
Green woodpecker (picus viridis) makes a loud cry	Feb. 13, Mar. 23	Jan. 1, April 17
Raven (corvus corax) builds	Feb. 14—17	Ap. 1, has young ones June 1
Yew-tree (taxus baccata) fl.	Feb. 14, Mar. 27	Feb. 2, April 11
Coltsfoot (tussilago farfara) fl.	Feb. 15, Mar. 23	Feb. 18, April 13
Rooks (corvus frugilegus) build	Feb. 16, Mar. 6	Feb. 28, March 5
Partridges (perdix cinerea) pair	Feb. 17	Feb. 16, March 20
Peas (pisum sativum) sown	Feb. 17, Mar. 8	Feb. 8, March 31
House pigeon (columba domestica) has young ones	Feb. 18	Feb. 8
Field crickets open their holes	Feb. 20, Mar. 30	
Common flea (pulex irritans) ap.	Feb. 21—26	
Pilewort (ficaria verna) fl.	Feb. 21, April 13	Jan. 25, March 26
Goldfinch (fringilla carduelis) sings	Feb. 21, April 5	Feb. 28, May 5
Viper (coluber berus) ap.	Feb. 22, Mar. 26	Feb. 23, May 6; last seen Oct. 28
Wood-louse (oniscus asellus) ap.	Feb. 23, April 1	April 27, June 17
Missel thrushes pair	Feb. 24	
Daffodil (narcissus pseudonarcissus) fl.	Feb. 24, April 7	Feb. 26, April 18
Willow (salix alba) fl.	Feb. 24, April 2	Feb. 27, April 11
Frogs (rana temporaria) croak	Feb. 25	March 9, April 20
Sweet violet (viola odorata) fl.	Feb. 26, Mar. 31	Feb. 7, April 5
Phalæna tinea vestianella, ap.	Feb. 26	
Stone-curlew (otis oedicnemus) clamours	Feb. 27, Ap. 24	June 17
Filbert (corylus sativus) fl.	Feb. 27	Jan. 25, March 26
Ring-dove coos	Feb. 27, April 5	March 2, Aug. 10
Apricot-tree (prunus armeniaca) fl.	Feb.	Feb. 28, April 5
Toad (rana bufo) ap.	Feb. 28, Mar. 24	March 15, July 1
Frogs (rana temporaria) spawn	Feb. 28, Mar. 22	Feb. 9, April 10; tadpoles Mar. 19
Ivy-leaved speedwell (veronica hederifolia) fl.	Mar. 1, April 2	Feb. 16, April 10
Peach (amygdalus persica) fl.	Mar. 2, April 17	Mar. 4, April 29
Frog (rana temporaria) ap.	Mar. 2, April 6	March 9
Shepherd's purse (thlaspi bursa pastoris) fl.	March 3	Jan. 2, April 16
Pheasant (phasianus colchicus) crows	March 3—29	March 1, May 22
Land tortoise comes forth	March 4, May 8	
Lungwort (pulmonaria officinalis) fl.	Mar. 4, April 16	March 2, May 19
Podura fimetaria ap.	March 4	
Aranea scenica saliens, ap.	March 4	
Scolopendra forficata, ap.	March 5—16	
Wryneck (jynx torquilla) ap.	Mar. 5, April 25	Mar. 26, April 23; last seen Sept 14
Goose (anas anser) sits on its eggs	March 5	March 21
Duck (anas boschas) lays	March 5	March 28
Dog's violet (viola canina) fl.	Mar. 6, April 18	Feb. 28, April 22;
Peacock butterfly (papilio io) ap.	March 6	Feb. 13, April 20; last seen Dec. 25
Trouts begin to rise	March 7—14	
Field beans (vicia faba) planted	March 8	Apr. 29, emerge
Blood-worms appear in the water	March 8	
Crow (corvus corone) builds	March 10	July 1, has young ones
Oats (avena sativa) sown	March 10—18	Mar. 16, April 13
Golden crowned wren (sylvia regulus) sings	Mar. 12, April 30	April 15, May 27; seen Dec. 23, Jan. 26
Asp (populus tremula) fl.	March 12	Feb. 26, March 28
Common elder (sambucus nigra) l.	March 13—20	Jan. 24, April 22
Laurel (prunus laurocerasus) fl.	Mar. 15, May 21	April 2, May 27
Chrysomela Gotting, ap.	March 15	
Black ants (formica nigra) ap.	Mar. 15, April 22	March 2, May 18

	WHITE.	MARKWICK.
Ephemeræbisetæ ap.	March 16	
Gooseberry (ribes grossularia) l.	Mar. 17, Ap. 11	Feb. 26, April 9
Common stitchwort (stellaria holostea) fl.	Mar. 17, May 19	March 8, May 7
Wood anemone (anemone nemorosa) fl.	Mar. 17, Ap. 22	Feb. 27, April 10
Blackbird (turdus merula) lays	March 17	April 14, young ones May 19
Raven (corvus corax) sits	March 17	April 1, builds
Wheatear (sylvia oenanthe) ap.	March 18—30	Mar. 13, May 23; last seen Oct. 26
Musk wood crowfoot (adoxa moschatel-lina) fl.	Mar. 18, Ap. 13	Feb. 23, April 28
Willow wren (sylvia trochilus) ap.	Mar. 19, Ap. 13	Mar. 30, May 16; sits May 27; last seen Oct. 23
Fumaria bulbosa, fl.	March 19	
Elm (ulmus campestris) fl.	Mar. 19, April 4	Feb. 17, April 25
Turkey (meleagris gallopavo) lays	Mar. 19, April 7	Mar. 18—25, sits April 4, young ones April 30
House pigeons (columba domestica) sit	March 20	March 20, young hatched
Marsh marigold (caltha palustris) fl.	Mar. 20, Ap. 14	March 22, May 8
Buzz-fly (bombylius medius) ap.	Mar. 21, Ap. 28	March 15, Ap. 30
Sand marten (hirundo riparia) ap.	Mar. 21, Ap. 12	April 8, May 16; last seen Sept. 8
Snake (coluber natrix) ap.	Mar. 22—30	Mar. 3, April 29; last seen Oct. 2
Horse ant (formica herculeana) ap.	Mar. 22, Ap. 18	Feb. 4, March 26; last seen Nov. 12
Greenfinch (loxia chloris) sings	Mar. 22, Ap. 22	March 6, April 26
Ivy (hedera helix) berries ripe	Mar. 23, Ap. 14	Feb. 16, May 19
Periwinkle (vinca minor) fl.	March 25	Feb. 6, May 7
Spurge laurel (daphne laureola) fl.	Mar. 25, April 1	April 12—22
Swallow (hirundo rustica) ap.	Mar. 26, Ap. 20	April 7—27; last seen Nov. 16
Black-cap (sylvia atricapilla) heard	Mar. 26, May 4	April 14, May 18; seen April 14, May 20; last seen Sept. 19
Young ducks hatched	March 27	April 6, May 16
Golden saxifrage (chrysosplenium opposi-tifolium) fl.	Mar. 27, Ap. 9	Feb. 7, March 27
Marten (hirundo urbica) ap.	Mar. 28, May 1	April 14 May 8; last seen Dec. 8
Double hyacinth (hyacinthus orientalis) fl.	Mar. 29, Ap. 22	Mar. 13, April 24
Young geese (anas anser)	March 29	Mar. 29, April 19
Wood sorrel (oxalis acetosella) fl.	Mar. 30, Ap. 22	Feb. 26, April 26
Ringousel (turdus torquatus) seen	Mar. 30, Ap. 17	October 11
Barley (hordeum sativum) sown	Mar. 31, Ap. 30	April 12, May 20
Nightingale (sylvia luscinia) sings	April 1, May 1	April 5, July 4; last seen Aug. 29
Ash (fraxinus excelsior) fl.	April 1, May 4	March 16, May 8
Spiders' webs on the surface of the ground	April 1	
Chequered daffodil (fritillaria meleagris) fl.	April 2—24	April 15, May 1
Julus terrestris, ap.	April 2	
Cowslip (primula veris) fl.	April 3—24	March 3, May 17
Ground-ivy (glecoma hederacea) fl.	April 3—15	Mar. 2, April 16
Snipe pipes	April 3	
Box-tree (buxus sempervirens) fl.	April 3	March 27, May 8
Elm (ulmus campestris) l.	April 3	April 2, May 19
Gooseberry (ribes grossularia) fl.	April 3—14	March 21, May 1
Currant (ribes hortense) fl.	April 3—5	Mar. 24, April 28
Pear-tree (pyrus communis) fl.	April 3, May 29	Mar. 30, April 30
Lacerta vulgaris (newt, or eft) ap.	April 4	Feb. 17, April 15; last seen Oct. 9

	WHITE.	MARKWICK.
Dog's mercury (mercurialis perennis) fl.	April 5—19	Jan 20, April 16
Wych elm (ulmus glabra seu montana of Smith) fl.	April 5	April 19, May 10
Ladysmock (cardamine pratensis) fl.	April 6—20	Feb. 21, April 26
Cuckoo (cuculus canorus) heard	April 7—26	April 15, May 3; last heard June 28
Black-thorn (prunus spinosa) fl.	April 7, May 10	March 16, May 8
Death-watch (termes pulsatorius) beats	April 7	March 28, May 28
Gudgeon spawns	April 7	
Red-start (sylvia phænicurus) ap.	April 8—28	April 5, sings Apr. 25 ; last seen Sept. 30
Crown imperial (fritillaria imperialis) fl.	April 8—24	April 1, May 13
Tit-lark (alauda pratensis) sings	April 9—19	April 14—29, sits June 16, 17
Beech (fagus sylvatica) l.	April 10, May 8	April 24, May 25
Shell-snail (helix nemoralis) comes out in troops	April 11, May 9	May 17, June 11 ap.
Middle yellow wren, ap.	April 11	
Swift (hirundo apus) ap.	April 13, May 7	April 28, May 19
Stinging-fly (conops calcitrans) ap.	April 14, May 17	
Whitlow grass (draba verna) fl.	April 14	Jan. 15, March 24
Larch-tree (pinus larix rubra) l.	April 14	April 1, May 9
Whitethroat (sylvia cinerea) ap.	April 14, May 14	April 14, May 5, sings May 3—10, last seen Sept. 23
Red ant (formica rubra) ap.	April 14	April 9, June 26
Mole cricket (gryllus gryllotalpa) churs	April 14	
Second willow, or laughing wren ap.	Ap. 14—19—23	
Red rattle (pedicularis sylvatica) fl.	April 15—19	April 10, June 4
Common flesh-fly (musca carnaria) ap.	April 15	
Lady cow (coccinella bipunctata) ap.	April 16	
Grasshopper-lark (alauda locustæ voce) ap.	April 16—30	
Willow wren, its shivering note heard	April 17, May 7	April 28, May 14
Middle willow wren (regulus non cristatus medius) ap.	April 17—27	
Wild cherry (prunus cerasus) fl.	Ap. 18, May 12	March 30, May 10
Garden cherry (prunus cerasus) fl.	Ap. 18, May 11	March 25, May 6
Plum (prunus domestica) fl.	April 18, May 5	March 24, May 6
Hare-bell (hyacinthus non scriptus seu scilla nutans of Smith) fl.	April 19—25	March 27, May 8
Turtle (columba turtur) coos	April 20—27	May 14, Aug. 10, seen
Hawthorn (cratægus seu mespilus oxycantha of Smith) fl.	Ap. 20, June 11	April 19, May 26
Male fool's orchis (orchis mascula) fl.	April 21	March 29, May 13
Blue flesh fly (musca vomitoria) ap.	Ap. 21, May 23	
Black snail, or slug (limax ater) abounds	April 22	Feb. 1, Oct. 24, ap.
Apple-tree (pyrus malus sativus) fl.	Ap. 22, May 25	April 11, May 26
Large bat, ap.	Ap. 22, June 11	
Strawberry, wild wood (fragaria vesca sylvia) fl.	April 23—29	April 8, 9
Sauce alone (erysimum alliaria) fl.	April 23	March 31, May 8
Wild or bird cherry (prunus avium) fl.	April 24	March 30, May 10
Apis hypnorum, ap.	April 24	
Musca meridiana, ap.	Ap. 24, May 28	
Wolf-fly (asilus) ap.	April 25	
Cabbage butterfly (papilio brassicæ) ap.	Ap. 29, May 20	April 29, June 15
Dragon-fly (libellula) ap.	Ap. 30, May 21	April 18, May 13, last seen Nov. 10
Sycamore (acer pseudoplatanus) fl.	Ap. 30, June 6	April 20, June 4
Bombylius minor, ap.	May 1	
Glow-worm (lampyris noctiluca) shines	May 1, June 11	June 19, Sept. 28
Fern-owl, or goatsucker (caprimulgus europæus) ap.	May 1—26	May 16, Sept. 14

	WHITE.	MARKWICK.
Common bugle (ajuga reptans) fl.	May 1	March 27, May 10
Field crickets (gryllus campestris) crink	May 2—24	
Chaffer, or May-bug (scarabæus melolontha) ap.	May 2—26	May 2, July 7
Honeysuckle (lonicera periclymenum) fl.	May 3—30	April 24, June 21
Toothwort (lathræa squamaria) fl.	May 4—12	
Shell-snails copulate	May 4, June 17	
Sedge warbler (sylvia salicaria) sings	May 4	June 2—30
Mealy tree (viburnum lantana) fl.	May 5—17	April 25, May 22
Fly-catcher (stoparola, muscicapa gris.) ap.	May 10—30	April 29, May 21
Apis longicornis, ap.	May 10, June 9	
Sedge warbler (sylvia salicaria) ap.	May 11—13	Aug. 2
Oak (quercus robur) fl.	May 13—15	April 29, June 4
Admiral butterfly (papilio atalanta) ap.	May 13	
Orange-tip (papilio cardamines) ap.	May 14	March 30, May 19
Beech (fagus sylvatica) fl.	May 15—26	April 23, May 28
Common maple (acer campestre) fl.	May 16	April 24, May 27
Barberry-tree (berberis vulgaris) fl.	May 17—26	April 28, June 4
Wood argus butterfly (papilio ægeria) ap.	May 17	
Orange lily (lilium bulbiferum) fl.	May 18, June 11	June 14, July 22
Burnet moth (sphinx filipendulæ) ap.	May 18, June 13	May 24, June 26
Walnut (juglans regia) l.	May 18	April 10, June 1
Laburnum (cytisus laburnum) fl.	May 18, June 5	May 1, June 23
Forest fly (hippobosca equina) ap.	May 18, June 9	
Saintfoin (hedysarum onobrychis) fl.	May 19, June 8	May 21, July 28
Peony (pæonia officinalis) fl.	May 20, June 15	April 18, May 26
Horse chestnut (æsculus hippocastanum) fl.	May 21, June 9	April 19, June 7
Lilac (syringa vulgaris) fl.	May 21	April 15, May 30
Columbine (aquilegia vulgaris) fl.	May 21—27	May 6, June 13
Medlar (mespilus germanica) fl.	May 21, June 20	April 8, June 19
Tormentil (tormentilla erecta seu officinalis of Smith) fl.	May 21	April 17, June 11
Lily of the valley (convallaria majalis) fl.	May 22	April 27, June 13
Bees (apis mellifica) swarm	May 22, July 22	May 12, June 23
Woodroof (asperula odorata) fl.	May 22—25	April 14, June 4
Wasp, female (vespa vulgaris) ap.	May 23	April 2, June 4; last seen Nov. 2
Mountain ash (sorbus seu pyrus aucuparia of Smith) fl.	May 23, June 8	April 20, June 8
Birds-nest orchis (ophrys nidus avis) fl.	May 24, June 11	May 18, June 12
White-beam tree (cratægus seu pyrus aria of Smith) L	May 24, June 4	May 3
Milkwort (polygala vulgaris) fl.	May 24, June 7	April 13, June 2
Dwarf cistus (cistus helianthemum) fl.	May 25	May 4, Aug. 8
Gelder rose (viburnum opulus) fl.	May 26	May 10, June 8
Common elder (sambucus nigra) fl.	May 26, June 25	May 6, June 17
Cantharis noctiluca, ap.	May 26	
Apis longicornis bores holes in walks	May 27, June 9	
Mulberry-tree (morus nigra) l.	May 27, June 13	May 20, June 11
Wild service tree (cratægus seu pyrus torminalis of Smith) fl.	May 27	May 13, June 19
Sanicle (sanicula europæa) fl.	May 27, June 13	April 23, June 4
Avens (geum urbanum) fl.	May 28	May 9, June 11
Female fool's orchis (orchis morio) fl.	May 28	April 17, May 20
Ragged Robin (lychnis flos cuculi) fl.	May 29, June 1	May 12, June 8
Burnet (poterium sanguisorba) fl.	May 29	April 30, Aug. 7
Foxglove (digitalis purpurea) fl.	May 30, June 22	May 23, June 15
Corn-flag (gladiolus communis) fl.	May 30, June 20	June 9, July 8
Serapias longifolium fl.	May 30, June 13	
Raspberry (rubus idæus) fl.	May 30, June 21	May 10, June 16
Herb Robert (geranium Robertianum) fl.	May 30	March 7, May 16
Figwort (scrophularia nodoso) fl.	May 31	May 12, June 20
Gromwell (lithospermum officinale) fl.	May 31	May 10—24
Wood spurge (euphorbia amygdaloides) fl.	June 1	March 23, May 13
Ramsons (allium ursinum) fl.	June 1	April 21, June 4

	WHITE.	MARKWICK.
Mouse-ear scorpion grass (myosotis scorpioides) fl.	June 1	April 11, June 1
Grasshopper (gryllus grossus) ap.	June 1—14	March 25, July 6, last seen Nov. 3
Rose (rosa hortensis) fl.	June 1—21	June 7, July 1
Mouse-ear hawkweed (hieracium pilosella) fl.	June 1, July 16	April 19, June 12
Buckbean (menyanthes trifoliata) fl.	June 1	April 20, June 8
Rose chaffer (scarabæus auratus) ap.	June 2—8	April 18, Aug. 4
Sheep (ovis aries) shorn	June 2—23	May 23, June 17
Water-flag (iris pseudo-acorus) fl.	June 2	May 8, June 9
Cultivated rye (secale cereale) fl.	June 2	May 27
Hounds tongue (cynoglossum officinale) fl.	June 2	May 11, June 7
Helleborine (serapias latifolia) fl.	June 2, Aug. 6	July 22, Sept. 6
Green-gold fly (musca cæsar) ap.	June 2	
Argus butterfly (papilio moera) ap.	June 2	
Spearwort (ranunculus flammula) fl.	June 3	April 25, June 13
Birdsfoot trefoil (lotus corniculatus) fl.	June 3	April 10, June 3
Fraxinella or white ditany (dictamnus albus) fl.	June 3—11	June 9, July 24
Phryganea nigra, ap.	June 3	
Angler's May-fly (ephemera vulgaris) ap.	June 3—14	
Ladies' finger (anthyllis vulneraria) fl.	June 4	June 1, Aug. 16
Bee-orchis (ophrys apifera) fl.	June 4, July 4	
Pink (dianthus deltoides) fl.	June 5—19	May 26, July 6
Mock orange (philadelphus coronarius) fl.	June 5	May 16, June 23
Libellula virgo, ap.	June 5—20	
Vine (vitis vinifera) fl.	June 7, July 30	June 18, July 29
Portugal laurel (prunus lusitanicus) fl.	June 8, July 1	June 3, July 16
Purple-spotted martagon (lilium martagon) fl.	June 8—25	June 18, July 19
Meadow cranes-bill (geranium pratense) fl.	June 8, Aug. 1	
Black bryony (tamus communis) fl.	June 8	May 15, June 21
Field pea (pisum sativum arvense) fl.	June 9	May 15, June 21
Bladder campion (cucubalus behen seu silene inflata of Smith) fl.	June 9	May 4, July 13
Bryony (bryonia alba) fl.	June 9	May 13, Aug. 17
Hedge-nettle (stachys sylvatica) fl.	June 10	May 28, June 24
Bittersweet (solanum dulcamara) fl.	June 11	May 15, June 20
Walnut (juglans regia) fl.	June 12	April 18, June 1
Phallus impudicus, ap.	June 12, July 23	
Rosebay willow-herb (epilobium angustifolium) fl.	June 12	June 4, July 28
Wheat (triticum hybernum) fl.	June 13, July 22	June 4—30
Camfrey (symphytum officinale) fl.	June 13	May 4, June 23
Yellow pimpernel (lysimachian emorum) fl.	June 13—30	April 10, June 12
Tremella nostoc, ap.	June 15, Aug. 24	
Buckthorn (rhamnus catharticus) l.	June 16	May 25
Cuckow-spit insect (cicada spumaria) ap.	June 16	June 2—21
Dog-rose (rosa canina) fl.	June 17, 18	May 24, June 21
Puff-ball (lycoperdon bovista) ap.	June 17, Sept. 3	May 6, Aug. 19
Mullein (verbascum thapsus) fl.	June 18	June 10, July 22
Viper's bugloss (echium anglicum seu vulgare of Smith) fl.	June 19	May 27, July 3
Meadow hay cut	June 19, July 20	June 13, July 7
Stag beetle (lucanus cervus) ap.	June 19	June 14—21
Borage (borago officinalis) fl.	June 20	April 22, July 26
Spindle-tree (evonymus europæus) fl.	June 20	May 11, June 25
Musk thistle (carduus nutans) fl.	June 20, July 4	June 4, July 25
Dogwood (cornus sanguinea) fl.	June 21	May 28, June 27
Field scabious (scabiosa arvensis) fl.	June 21	June 16, Aug. 14
Marsh thistle (carduus palustris) fl.	June 21—27	May 15, June 19
Dropwort (spiræ filipendula) fl.	June 22, July 9	May 8, Sept. 3
Great wild valerian (valeriana officinalis) fl.	June 22, July 7	May 22, July 21
Quail (perdix coturnix) calls	June 22, July 4	July 23, seen Sept. 1—18

	WHITE.	MARKWICK.
Mountain willow-herb (epilobium montanum) fl.	June 22	June 5—21
Thistle upon thistle (carduus crispus) fl.	June 23—29	May 22, July 22
Cow-parsnep (heracleum sphondylium) fl.	June 23	May 27, July 12
Earth-nut (bunium bulbocastanum seu flexuosum of Smith) fl.	June 23	May 4—31
Young frogs migrate	June 23, Aug. 2	
Oestrus curvicauda ap.	June 24	
Vervain (verbena officinalis) fl.	June 24	June 10, July 17
Corn poppy (papaver rhoeas) fl.	June 24	April 30, July 15
Self-heal (prunella vulgaris) fl.	June 24	June 7—23
Agrimony (agrimonia eupatoria) fl.	June 24—29	June 7, July 9
Great horse-fly (tabanus bovinus) ap.	June 24, Aug. 2	
Greater knapweed (centaurea scabiosa) fl.	June 25	June 7, Aug. 14
Mushroom (agaricus campestris) ap.	June 26, Aug. 30	April 16, Aug. 16
Common mallow (malva sylvestris) fl.	June 26	May 27, July 13
Dwarf mallow (malva rotundifolia) fl.	June 26	May 12, July 30
St John's wort (hypericum perforatum) fl.	June 26	June 15, July 12
Broom-rape (orobanche major) fl.	June 27, July 4	May 9, July 25
Henbane (hyoscyamus niger) fl.	June 27	May 13, June 19
Goats-beard (tragopogon pratense) fl.	June 27	June 5—14
Deadly nightshade (atropa belladonna) fl.	June 27	May 22, Aug. 14
Truffles begin to be found	June 28, July 29	
Young partridges fly	June 28, July 31	July 8—28
Lime-tree (tilia europea) fl.	June 28, July 31	June 12, July 30
Spear thistle (carduus lanceolatus) fl.	June 28, July 12	June 27, July 18
Meadow sweet (spiræa ulmaria) fl.	June 28	June 16, July 24
Greenweed (genista tinctoria) fl.	June 28	June 4, July 24
Wild thyme (thymus serpyllum) fl.	June 28	June 6, July 19
Stachys germanic, fl.	June 29, July 20	
Day-lily (hemerocallis flava) fl.	June 29, July 4	May 29, June 9
Jasmine (jasminum officinale) fl.	June 29, July 30	June 27, July 21
Holly-oak (alcea rosea) fl.	June 29, Aug. 4	July 4, Sept. 7
Monotropa hypopithys, fl.	June 29, July 23	
Ladies' bedstraw (galium verum) fl.	June 29	June 22, Aug. 3
Galium palustre, fl.	June 29	
Nipplewort (lapsana communis) fl.	June 29	May 30, July 24
Welted thistle (carduus acanthoides) fl.	June 29	
Sneezewort (achillea ptarmica) fl.	June 30	June 22, Aug. 3
Musk mallow (malva moschata) fl	June 30	June 9, July 14
Pimpernel (anagallis arvensis) fl.	June 30	May 4, June 22
Hoary beetle (scarabæus solsit) ap.	June 30, July 17	
Corn saw-wort (serratula arvensis seu carduus arvensis of Smith) fl.	July 1	June 15, July 15
Pheasant's eye (adonis annua seu autumnalis of Smith) fl.	July 1	April 11, July 15
Red eyebright (euphrasia seu bartsia odontites of Smith) fl.	July 2	June 20, Aug. 10
Thorough wax (bupleurum rotundifol.) fl.	July 2	
Cockle (agrostemma githago) fl.	July 2	May 14, July 25
Ivy-leaved wild lettuce (prenanthes muralis) fl.	July 2	June 2, July 25
Feverfew (matricaria seu pyrethrum parthenium of Smith) fl.	July 2	June 19, July 24
Wall pepper (sedum acre) fl.	July 3	June 8, July 12
Privet (ligustrum vulgare) fl.	July 3	June 3, July 13
Common toadflax (antirrhinum linaria) fl.	July 3	June 21, Aug. 2
Perennial wild flax (linum perenne) fl.	July 4	April 21, July 6
Whortleberries ripe (vaccinium ulig.)	July 4—24	
Yellow base rocket (reseda lutea) fl.	July 5	July 19
Blue-bottle (centaurea cyanus) fl.	July 5	May 15, Oct. 14
Dwarf carline thistle (carduus acaulis) fl.	July 5—12	June 30, Aug. 4
Bull-rush, or cats-tail (typha latifolia) fl.	July 6	June 29, July 21
Spiked willow-herb (lythrum salicaria) fl.	July 6	June 24, Aug. 17
Black mullein (verbascum niger) fl.	July 6	

	WHITE.	MARKWICK.
Chrysanthemum coronarium, fl.	July 6	May 28, July 28
Marigolds (calendula officinalis) fl.	July 6—9	April 20, July 16
Little field madder (sherardia arvensis) fl.	July 7	Jan. 11, June 6
Calamint (melissa seu thymus calamintha of Smith) fl.	July 7	July 21
Black horehound (ballota nigra) fl.	July 7	June 16, Sept. 12
Wood betony (betonica officinalis) fl.	July 8—19	June 10, July 15
Round-leaved bell-flower (campanula rotundifolia) fl.	July 8	June 12, July 29
All-good (chenopodium bonus henricus) fl.	July 8	April 21, June 15
Wild-carrot (daucus carota) fl.	July 8	June 7, July 14
Indian cress (epopæolum majus) fl.	July 8—20	June 11, July 25
Cat-mint (nepeta cataria) fl.	July 9	
Cow-wheat (melampyrum sylvaticum seu pratense of Smith) fl.	July 9	May 2, June 22
Crosswort (valantia cruciata seu galium cruciatum of Smith) fl.	July 9	April 10, May 28
Cranberries ripe	July 9—27	
Tufted vetch (vicia cracca) fl.	July 10	May 31, July 8
Wood vetch (vicia sylvatica) fl.	July 10	
Little throat-wort (campanula glomerata) fl.	July 11	July 28, Aug. 18
Sheep's scabious (jasione montana) fl.	July 11	June 10, July 25
Pastinaca sylvatica, fl.	July 12	
White lily (lilium candidum) fl.	July 12	June 21, July 22
Hemlock (conium maculatum) fl.	July 13	June 4, July 20
Caucalis anthriscus, fl.	July 13	
Flying ants, ap.	July 13—Aug. 11	Aug. 20, Sept. 19
Moneywort (lysimachia nummularia) fl.	July 13	June 14, Aug. 16
Scarlet martagon (lilium chalcedonicum) fl.	July 14—Aug. 4	June 21, Aug. 6
Lesser stitchwort (stellaria graminea) fl.	July 14	May 8, June 23
Fool's parsley (æthusa cynapium) fl.	July 14	June 9, Aug. 9
Dwarf elder (sambucus ebulus) fl.	July 14—29	
Swallows and martens congregate	July 14, Aug. 29	Aug. 12, Sept. 8
Potato (solanum tuberosum) fl.	July 14	June 3, July 12
Angelica sylvestris, fl.	July 15	
Digitalis ferruginosus, fl.	July 15—25	
Ragwort (senecio jacobæa) fl.	July 15	June 22, July 13
Golden rod (solidago virgaurea) fl.	July 15	July 7, Aug. 29
Star thistle (centaurea calcitrapa) fl.	July 16	July 16, Aug. 16
Tree primrose (oenothera biennis) fl.	July 16	June 12, July 18
Peas (pisum sativum) cut	July 17, Aug. 14	July 13, Aug. 15
Galega officinalis, fl.	July 17	
Apricots (prunus armeniaca) ripe	July 17, Aug. 21	July 5, Aug. 16
Clown's allheal (stachys palustris) fl.	July 17	June 12, July 14
Branching willow-herb (epilobium ramosum) fl.	July 17	
Rye harvest begins	July 17, Aug. 7	
Yellow centaury (chlora perfoliata) fl.	July 18, Aug. 15	June 15, Aug. 13
Yellow vetchling (lathyrus aphaca) fl.	July 18	
Enchanter's nightshade (circæa lutetiana) fl.	July 18	June 20, July 27
Water hemp agrimony (eupatorium cannabinum) fl.	July 18	July 4, Aug. 6
Giant throatwort (campanula trachelium) fl.	July 19	July 13, Aug. 14
Eyebright (euphrasia officinalis) fl.	July 19	May 28, July 19
Hops (humulus lupulus) fl.	July 19, Aug. 10	July 20, Aug. 17
Poultry moult	July 19	
Dodder (cuscuta europæa seu epithymum of Smith) fl.	July 20	July 9, Aug. 7
Lesser centaury (gentiana seu chironia centarium of Smith) fl.	July 20	June 3, July 19
Creeping water parsnep (sium nodiflorum) fl.	July 20	July 10, Sept. 11
Common spurrey (spergula arvensis) fl.	July 21	April 10, July 16

	WHITE.	MARKWICK.
Wild clover (trifolium pratense) fl.	July 21	May 2, June 7
Buckwheat (polygonum fagopyrum) fl.	July 21	June 27, July 10
Wheat harvest begins	July 21, Aug. 23	July 11, Aug. 26
Great bur-reed (sparganium erectum) fl.	July 22	June 10, July 23
Marsh St John's-wort (hypericum elodes) fl.	July 22—31	June 16, Aug 10
Sun-dew (drosera rotundifolia) fl.	July 22	Aug. 1
Marsh cinquefoil (comarum palustre) fl.	July 22	May 27, July 12
Wild cherries ripe	July 22	
Lancashire asphodel (anthericum ossifragum) fl.	July 22	June 21, July 29
Hooded willow-herb (scutellaria galericulata) fl.	July 23	June 2, July 31
Water dropwort (œnanthe fistulosa) fl.	July 23	
Horehound (marrubium vulgare) fl.	July 23	
Seseli carnifolia, fl	July 24	
Water plantain (alisma plantago) fl.	July 24	May 31, July 21
Alopecurus myosuroides, fl.	July 25	
Virgin's bower (clematis vitalba) fl.	July 25, Aug. 9	July 13, Aug. 14
Bees kill the drones	July 25	
Teasel (dipsacus sylvestris) fl.	July 26	July 16, Aug. 3
Wild marjoram (origanum vulgare) fl.	July 26	July 17, Aug. 29
Swifts (hirundo apus) begin to depart	July 27—29	Aug. 5
Small wild teasel (dipsacus pilosus) fl.	July 28, 29	
Wood sage (teucrium scorodonia) fl.	July 28	June 17, July 24
Everlasting pea (lathyrus latifolius) fl.	July 28	June 20, July 30
Trailing St John's-wort (hypericum humifusum) fl.	July 29	May 20, June 22
White hellebore (veratrum album) fl.	July 30	July 18—22
Camomile (anthemis nobilis) fl.	July 30	June 21, Aug. 20
Lesser field scabious (scabiosa columbaria) fl.	July 30	July 13, Aug. 9
Sun-flower (helianthus multiflorus) fl.	July 31, Aug. 6	July 4, Aug. 22
Yellow loosestrife (lysimachia vulgaris) fl.	July 31	July 2, Aug. 7
Swift (hirundo apus) last seen	July 31, Aug. 27	Aug. 11
Oats (avena sativa) cut	Aug. 1—16	July 26, Aug. 19
Barley (hordeum sativum) cut	Aug. 1—26	July 27, Sept. 4
Lesser hooded willow-herb (scutellaria minor) fl.	Aug. 1	Aug. 8, Sept. 7
Middle fleabane (inula dysenterica) fl.	Aug. 2	July 7, Aug. 3
Apis manicata ap.	Aug. 2	
Swallow-tailed butterfly (papilio machaon) ap.	Aug. 2	April 20, June 7, last seen Aug. 28
Whame or burrel-fly (oestrus bovis) lays eggs on horses	Aug. 3—19	
Sow thistle (sonchus arvensis) fl.	Aug. 3	June 17, July 21
Plantain fritillary (papilio cinxia) ap.	Aug. 3	
Yellow succory (picris hieracioides) fl.	Aug. 4	June 6—25
Musca mystacea, ap.		
Canterbury bells (campanula medium) fl.	Aug. 5	June 5, Aug. 11
Mentha longifolia, fl.	Aug. 5	
Carline thistle (carlina vulgaris) fl.	Aug. 7	July 21, Aug. 18
Venetian sumach (rhus cotinus) fl.	Aug. 7	June 5, July 20
Ptinus pectinicornis, ap.	Aug. 7	
Burdock (arctium lappa) fl.	Aug. 8	June 17, Aug. 4
Fell-wort (gentiana amarella) fl.	Aug. 8, Sept. 3	
Wormwood (artemisi absinthium) fl.	Aug. 8	July 22, Aug. 21
Mugwort (artemisia vulgaris) fl.	Aug. 8	July 9, Aug. 10
St Barnaby's thistle (centaurea solstitialis) fl.	Aug. 10	
Meadow saffron (colchicum autumnale) fl.	Aug. 10, Sept. 13	Aug. 15, Sept. 29
Michaelmas daisy (aster tradescanti) fl.	Aug. 12, Sept. 27	Aug. 11, Oct. 8
Meadow rue (thalictrum flavum) fl.	Aug. 14	
Sea holly (eryngium maritimum) fl.	Aug. 14	
China aster (aster chinensis) fl.	Aug. 14, Sept. 28	Aug. 6. Oct. 2
Boletus albus, ap.	Aug. 14	May 10

	WHITE	MARKWICK.
Less Venus looking-glass (campanula hybrida) fl.	Aug. 15	May 14
Carthamus tinctor, fl.	Aug. 15	
Goldfinch (fringilla carduelis) young broods ap.	Aug. 15	June 15
Lapwings (tringa vanellus) congregate	Aug. 15, Sept. 12	Sept 25, Feb. 4
Black-eyed marble butterfly (papilio semele) ap.	Aug. 15	
Birds reasume their spring notes	Aug. 16	
Devil's bit (scabiosa succisa) fl.	Aug. 17	June 22, Aug. 23
Thistle down floats	Aug. 17, Sept. 10	
Ploughman's spikenard (conyza squarrosa) fl.	• Aug. 18	
Autumnal dandelion (leontodon autumnale) fl.	Aug. 18	July 25
Flies abound in windows	Aug. 18	
Linnets (fringilla linota) congregate	Aug. 18, Nov. 1	Aug. 22, Nov. 8
Bulls make their shrill autumnal noise	Aug. 20	
Aster amellus, fl.	Aug. 22	
Balsam (impatiens balsamina) fl.	Aug. 23	May 22, July 26
Milk thistle (carduus marianus) fl.	Aug. 24	April 21, July 18
Hop-picking begins	Aug. 24, Sept. 17	Sept. 1 — 15
Beech (fagus sylvatica) turns yellow	Aug. 24, Sept. 22	Sept. 5 — 29
Soapwort (saponaria officinalis) fl.	Aug. 25	July 19, Aug. 23
Ladies' traces (ophrys spiralis) fl.	Aug. 27, Sept. 12	Aug. 18, Sept. 18
Small golden black-spotted butterfly (papilio phlæas) ap.	Aug. 29	
Swallow (hirundo rustica) sings	Aug. 29	April 11, Aug. 20
Althæa frutex (hibiscus syriacus) fl.	Aug. 30, Sept. 2	July 20, Sept. 28
Great fritillary (papilio paphia) ap.	Aug. 30	
Willow red under-wing moth (phalæna pacta) ap.	Aug. 31	
Stone curlew (otis oedicnemus) clamours	Sept. 1, Nov. 7	June 17
Phalæna russula, ap.	Sept. 1	
Grapes ripen	Sept. 4, Oct. 24	Aug. 31, Nov. 4
Wood owls hoot	Sept. 4, Nov. 9	
Saffron butterfly (papilio hyale) ap.	Sept. 4	Aug. 5, Sept. 26
Ringousel appears on its autumnal visit	Sept. 4 — 30	
Flycatcher (muscicapa grisola) last seen	Sept. 6 — 29	Sept. 4 — 30
Beans (vicia faba) cut	Sept. 11	Aug. 9, Oct. 14
Ivy (hedera helix) fl.	Sept. 12, Oct. 2	Sept. 18, Oct. 28
Stares congregate	Sept. 12, Nov. 1	June 4, March 21
Wild honeysuckles fl. a second time	Sept. 25	
Woodlark sings	Sept. 28, Oct. 24	
Woodcock (scolopax rusticola) returns	Sept. 29, Nov. 11	Oct. 1, Nov. 1; young ones Ap.28; last seen Ap. 11
Strawberry-tree (arbutus unedo) fl.	Oct. 1	May 21, Dec. 10
Wheat sown	Oct. 3, Nov. 9	Sept. 23, Oct. 19
Swallows last seen. (N.B. The house marten the latest)	Oct. 4, Nov. 5	Nov. 16
Redwing (turdus iliacus) comes	Oct. 10, Nov. 10	Oct. 1, Dec. 18; sings Feb. 10, March 21; last seen April 13
Fieldfare (turdus pilaris) returns	Oct. 12, Nov. 23	Oct. 13, Nov. 18; last seen May 1
Gossamer fills the air	Oct. 15 — 27	
Chinese holly-oak (alcea rosea) fl.	Oct. 19	July 7, Aug. 21
Hen chaffinches congregate	Oct. 20, Dec. 31	
Wood pigeons come	Oct. 23, Dec. 27	
Royston crow (corvus cornix) returns	Oct. 23, Nov. 29	Oct. 13, Nov. 17, last seen April 16
Snipe (scolopax gallinago) returns	Oct. 25, Nov. 20	Sept. 29, Nov. 11; last seen April 14

	WHITE.	MARKWICK.
Tortoise begins to bury himself	Oct. 27, Nov. 26	
Rooks (corvus frugilegus) return to their nest trees	Oct. 31, Dec. 25	June 29, Oct. 20
Bucks grunt	Nov. 1	
Primrose (primula vulgaris) fl.	Nov. 10	Oct. 7, Dec. 30
Green whistling plover, ap.	Nov. 13, 14	
Helvella mitra, ap.	Nov. 16	
Greenfinches flock	Nov. 27	
Hepatica, fl.	Nov. 30, Dec. 29	Feb. 19
Furze (ulex europæus) fl.	Dec. 4—21	Dec. 16—31
Polyanthus (primula ponyantha) fl.	Dec. 7—16	Dec. 31
Young lambs dropped	Dec. 11—27	Dec. 12, Feb. 21
Moles work in throwing up hillocks	Dec. 12—23	
Helleborus fœtidus, fl.	Dec. 14—30	
Daisy (bellis perennis) fl.	Dec. 15	Dec. 26—31
Wall-flower (cheiranthus cheiri seu fruti-culosus of Smith) fl.	Dec. 15	Nov. 5
Mezereon, fl.	Dec. 15	
Snowdrop, fl.	Dec. 29	

IN SESE VERTITUR ANNUS.

INDEX.

THE END.

EDINBURGH:

Printed by Andrew Shortrede, Thistle Lane.

Lightning Source UK Ltd.
Milton Keynes UK
UKHW020658200421
382299UK00005B/439